"The photographer documents a New York City borough defined by its many contradictions." —***Publishers Weekly***

"From shops, street markets, and festivals to single-family homes and high-rise apartments, the many dozens of photographs in *Global Queens* give a wonderful sense of how Asian, Caribbean, and Latin American immigration has transformed the landscape of what is now the most diverse county in the nation." —**Nancy Foner**, author of *One Quarter of the Nation: Immigration and the Transformation of America*

"With kaleidoscopic views into the raw and eclectic urban landscapes of Queens, *Global Queens* takes us on a journey through the making of the most ethnically diverse place in the nation. As an immigrant and a former resident of the borough, I realized from the visual journey that each of us, past and present, has played a part in its becoming, including its unique sense of multiplicity and belonging." —**Jeff Hou**, University of Washington, Seattle

"*Global Queens* gives us a close and intimate look at a world built by immigrant communities over multiple generations. Heathcott's gift is to provide a panoramic view of this dizzyingly expansive and profoundly complex place, showing how diverse landscapes and social relations don't just happen; they are the result of hard work by millions of people adapting the city to suit their lives." — **Hitomi Iwasaki**, Head of Exhibitions and Curator, Queens Museum

"*Global Queens* challenges us to think about the personal and economic ties that connect places near and far, crossing national borders on all parts of the globe, and about how we define a city and its people." —**Steven T. Moga**, Smith College

"*Global Queens* is a quotidian elegy to the vast and intricate composition of movement, textures, and vocabulary that vitalizes New York. Joseph Heathcott's poignant images of everyday life capture the fragile and persistent way we make meaning together. This lively document of Queens neighborhoods offers a nuanced and necessary view of a spirited social mosaic, formed amidst the pervasive politics of racial violence and reactionary nationalism." —**Suzanne Hall**, Professor in Sociology, London School of Economics & Political Science, UK

"With vision and hard political work, Queens could become a template for what many cities might be, in its fortunate confluence of almost everyone and everything, creating a spaciousness for and from practices of all kinds, a rough-and-tumble world worth living, whose images Heathcott offers as a gift." —**AbdouMaliq Simone**, author of *The Surrounds: Urban Life Within and Beyond Capture*

"It's easy to overlook Queens. Lacking Manhattan's glamour or Brownstone Brooklyn's charm, it can appear to the casual observer as a jumble of unremarkable working- and middle-class neighborhoods glimpsed through a taxi window on the way to the airport. Yet this is a mistake. In recent decades Queens has emerged as one of most diverse and fascinating places on the planet. Joseph Heathcott's remarkable photographs and rich, evocative descriptions capture the borough's dense urbanism in all of its vibrance and layered complexity. For anyone interested in the future of superdiverse cities, this is a must-read." —**Philip Kasinitz**, Presidential Professor of Sociology, Graduate Center of the City University of New York

"Heathcott's treatment of the 'World's Borough,' with all its shapes, faces, and overlapping presents and pasts—there are so many!—is impressively researched and dynamically photographed. As a transplant moving through his adopted hometown with camera, informed curiosity, and a clear, deep respect for its residents, Heathcott has created a super-informed walking tour–style prismatic portrait of an ever-changing Queens as it stands today—or yesterday in some cases! On each page, another fascinating fact and/or image leads to more and more questions about the center-less borough of neighborhoods that has organically become the most diverse city on Earth. Even in the most banal-seeming of streetscapes, Heathcott's love of Queens is charismatically catching." —**John Wang and Storm Garner**, co-authors of *The World Eats Here: Amazing Food and the Inspiring People Who Make It at New York's Queens Night Market*

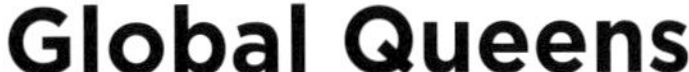
Global Queens

GLOBAL QUEENS

An Urban Mosaic

Joseph Heathcott

Empire State Editions

An imprint of Fordham University Press

New York 2023

The project received a grant from the Zolberg Insitute on Migration and Mobility at The New School.

Funding for this book was provided by a David R. Coffin publication grant administered through the UVA Center for Cultural Landscapes' Landscape Studies Initiative.

Fordham University Press also publishes its books in a variety of electronic formats. Some content that appears in print may not be available in electronic books.

Visit us online at www.fordhampress.com/empire-state-editions.

Library of Congress Cataloging-in-Publication Data available online at https://catalog.loc.gov.

Printed in Canada

25 24 23   5 4 3 2 1

First edition

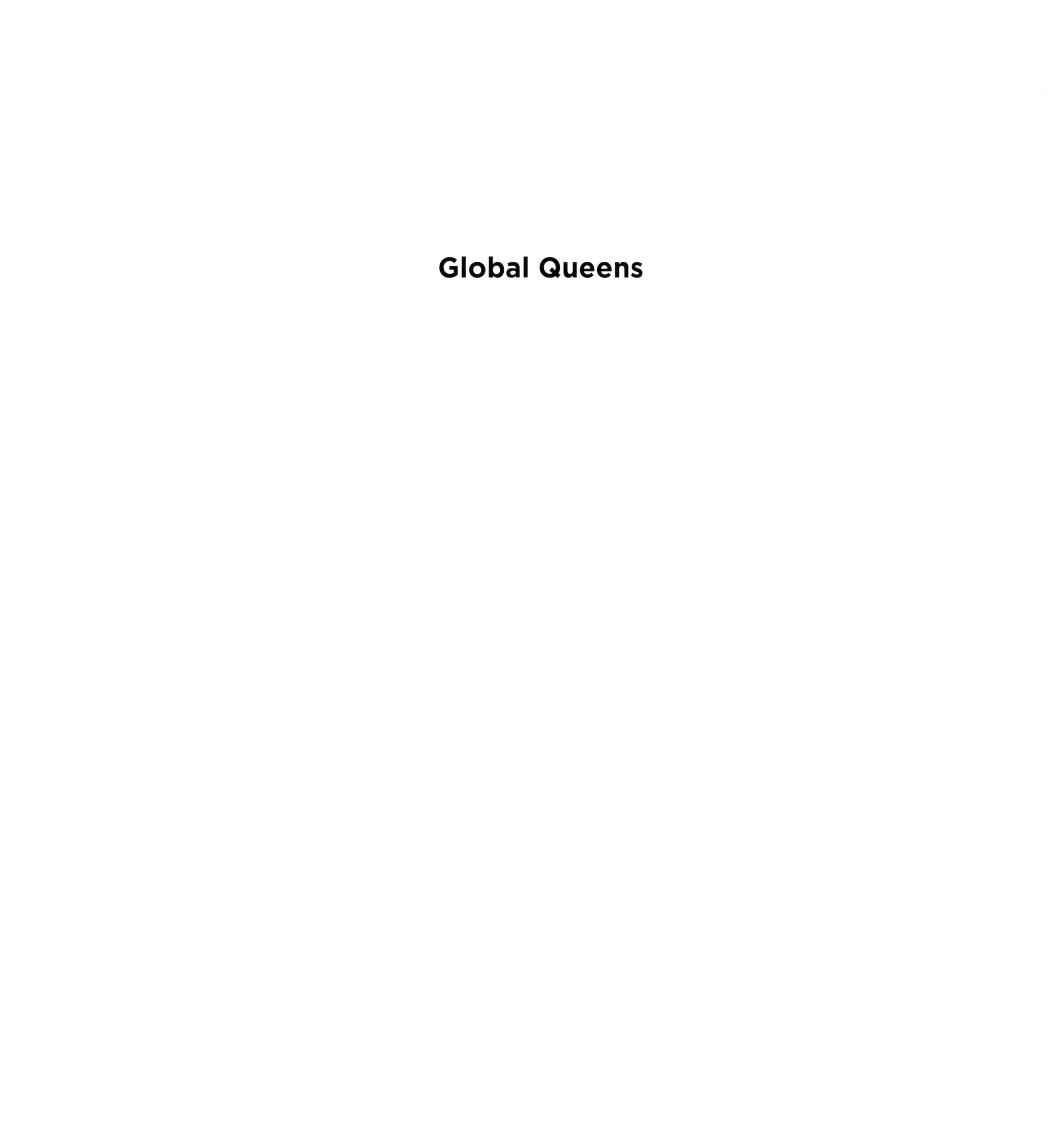

Global Queens

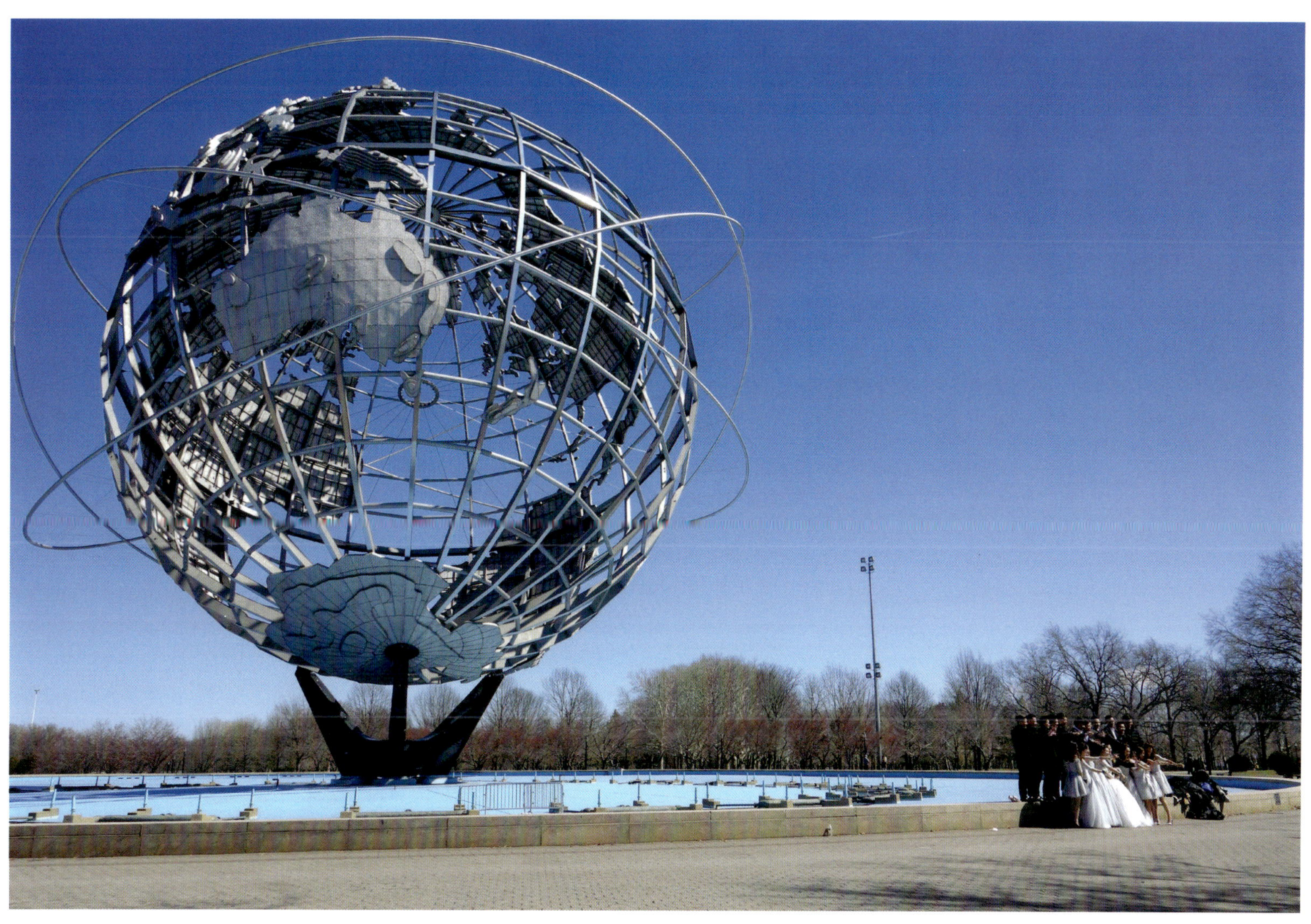

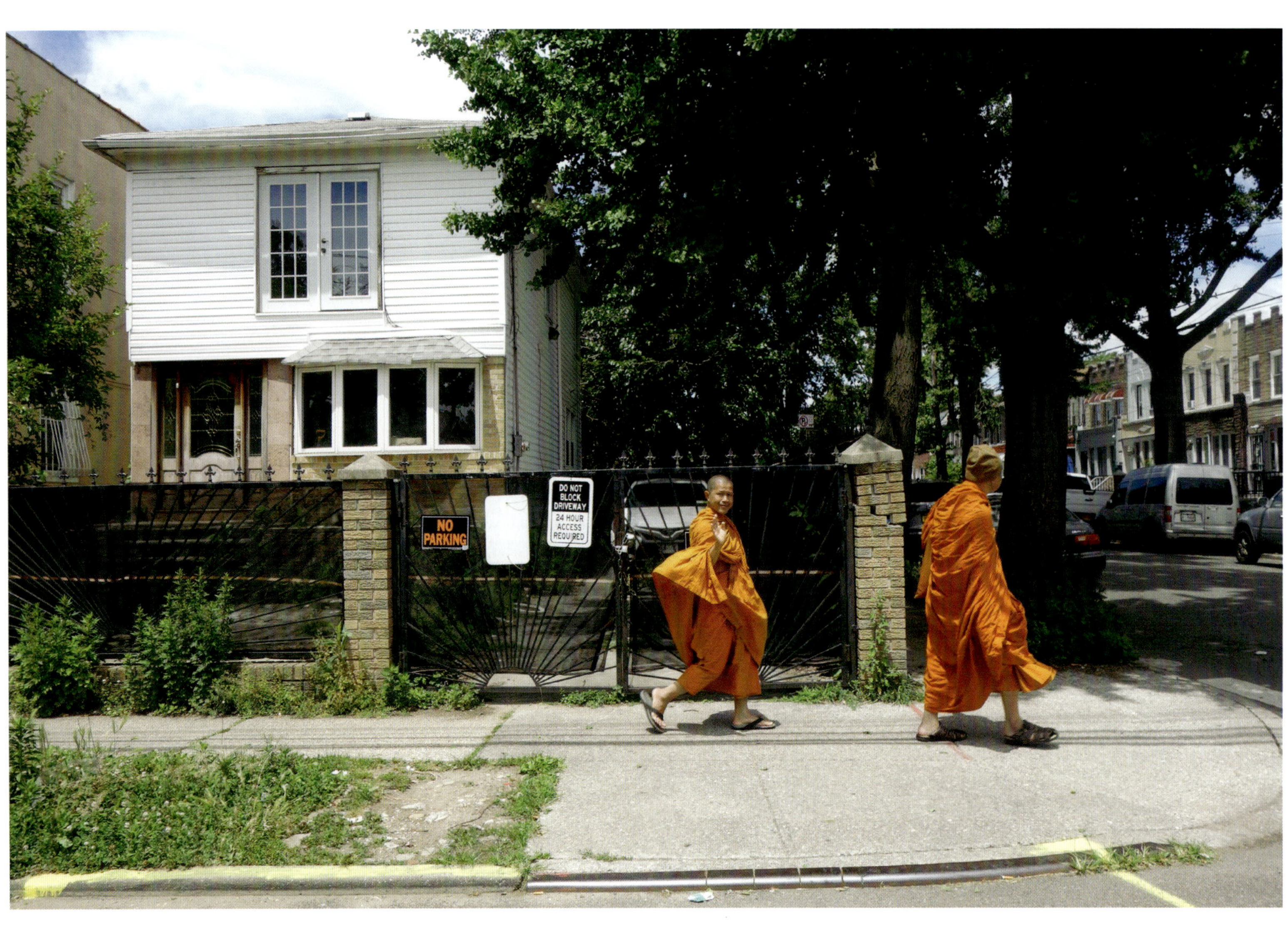
NO PARKING
DO NOT BLOCK DRIVEWAY
24 HOUR ACCESS REQUIRED

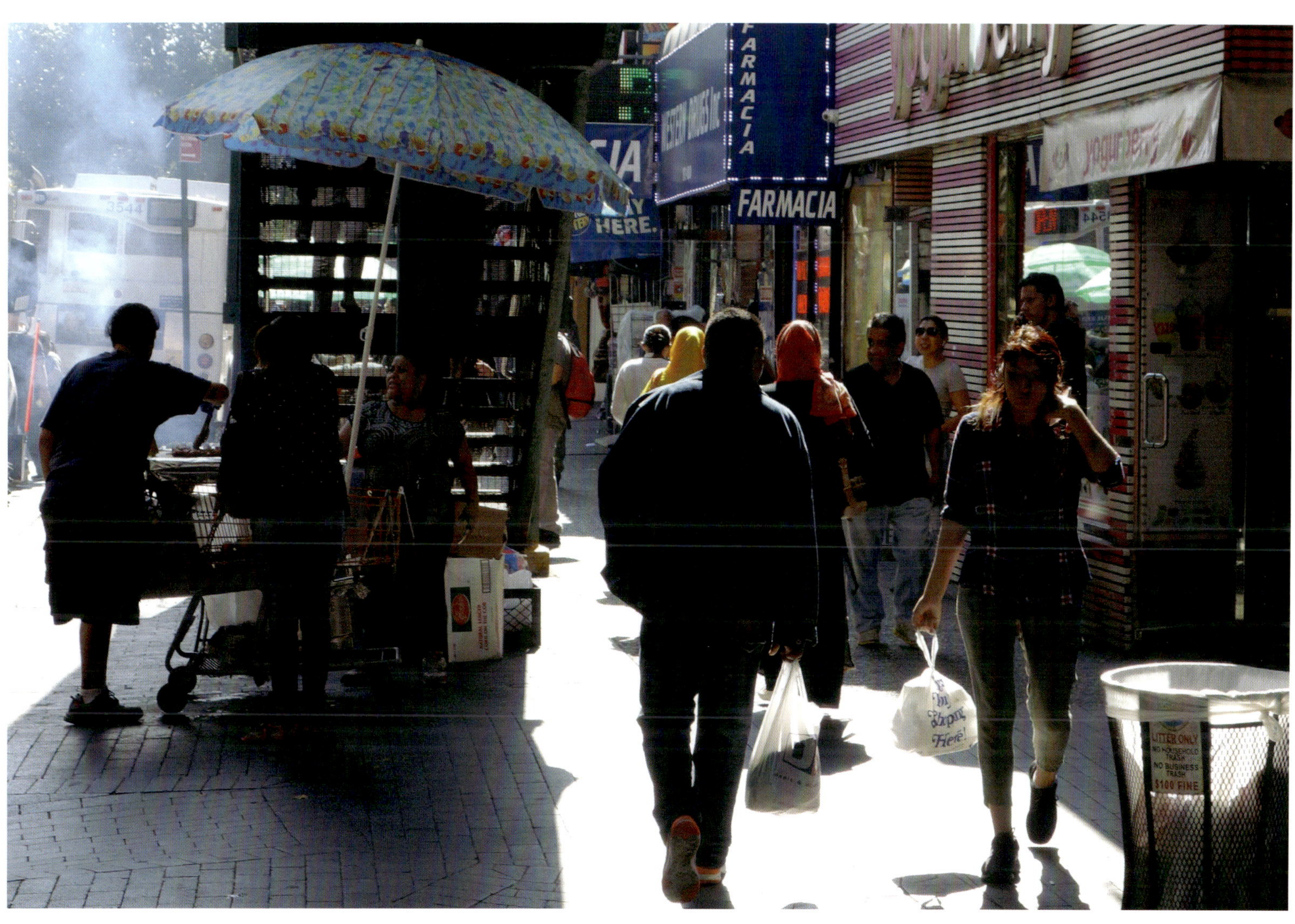
3544
FARMACIA
FARMACIA
HERE.

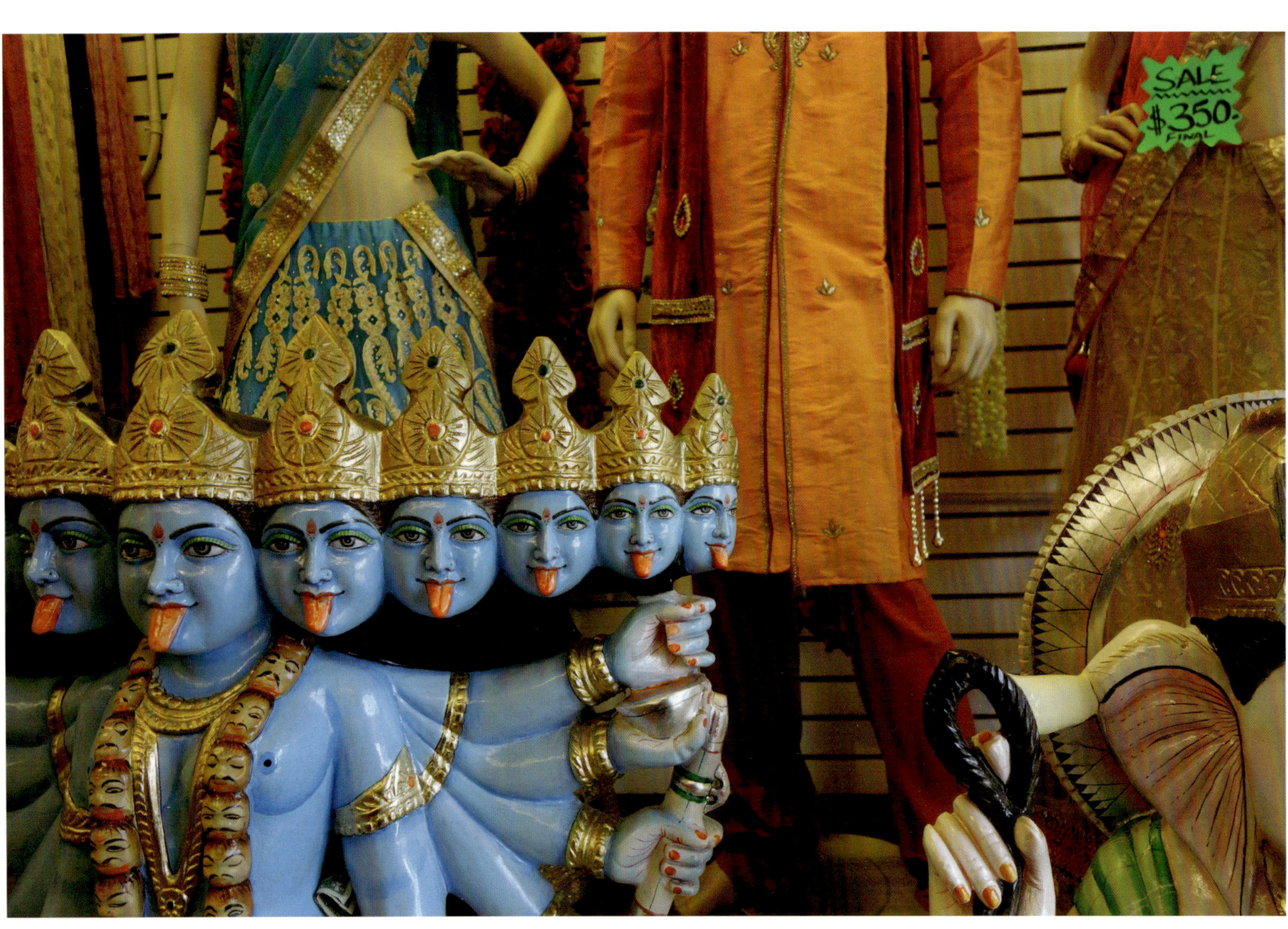
SALE
$350.
FINAL

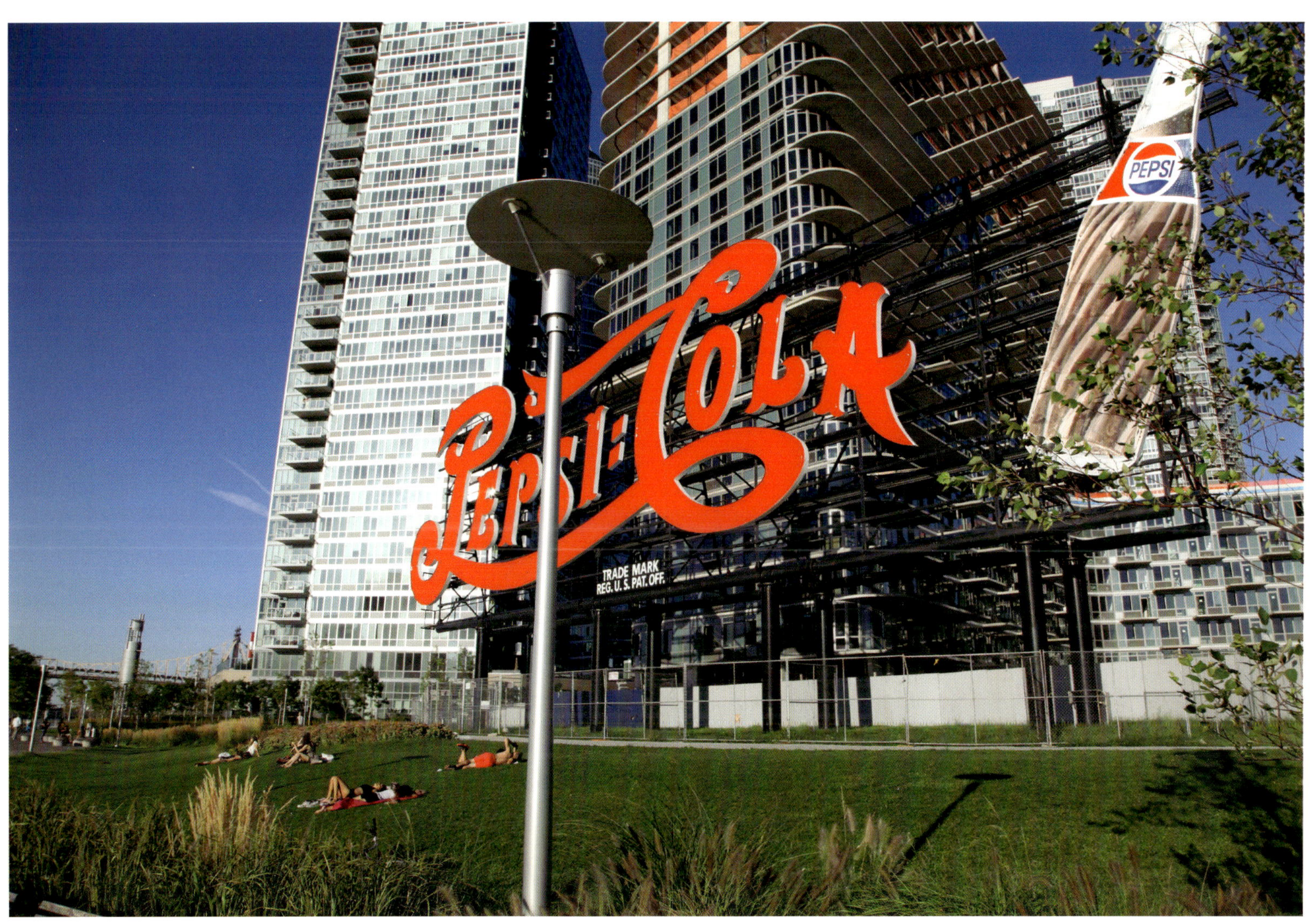
Pepsi-Cola
TRADE MARK
REG. U. S. PAT. OFF.
PEPSI

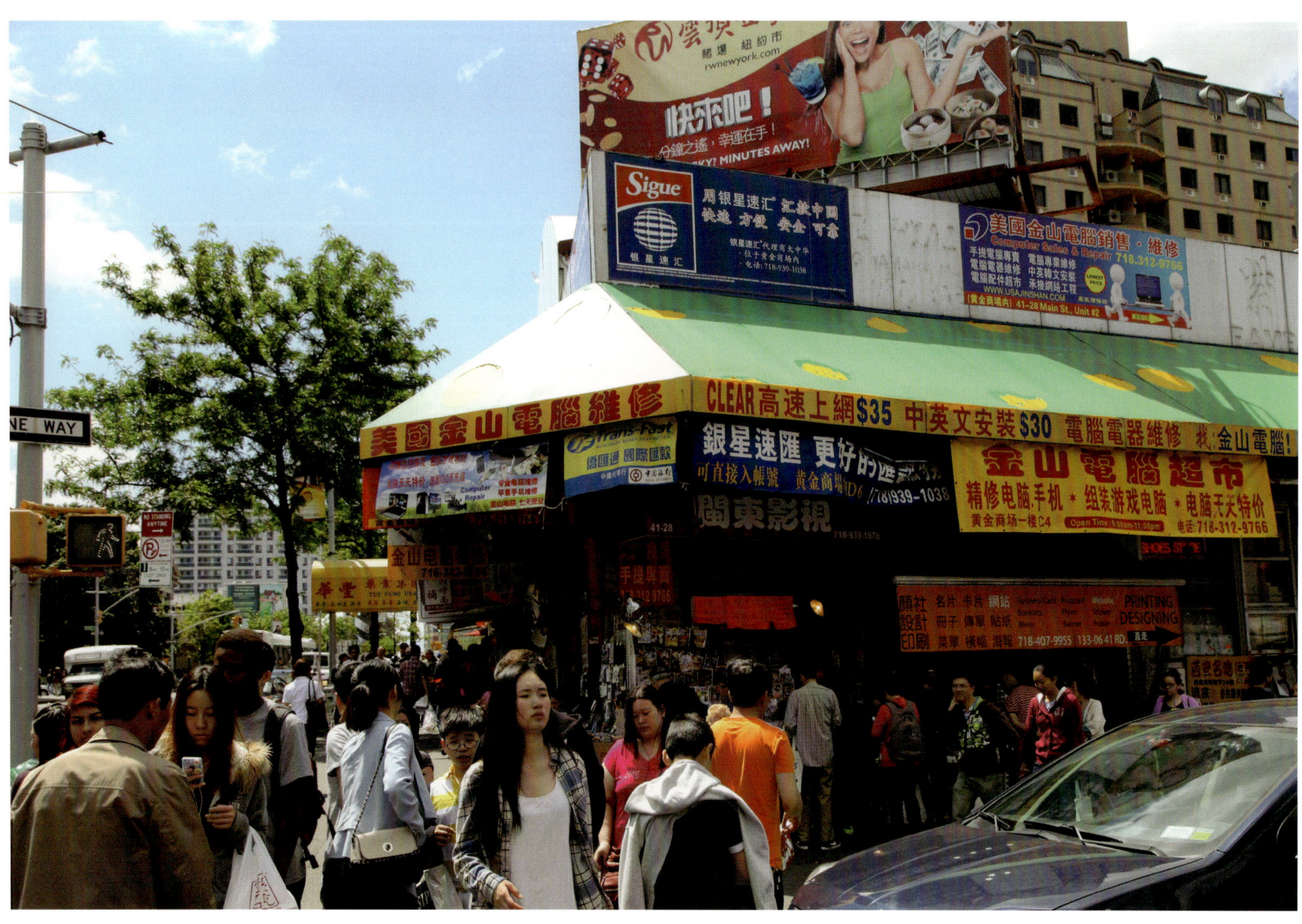

rwnewyork.com
快來吧!
Sigue
美國金山電腦銷售·維修
美國金山電腦維修
CLEAR高速上網$35 中英文安裝$30 電腦電器維修
金山電腦超市
精修电脑.手机 * 组装游戏电脑 * 电脑天天特价
閩東影視
PRINTING
DESIGNING

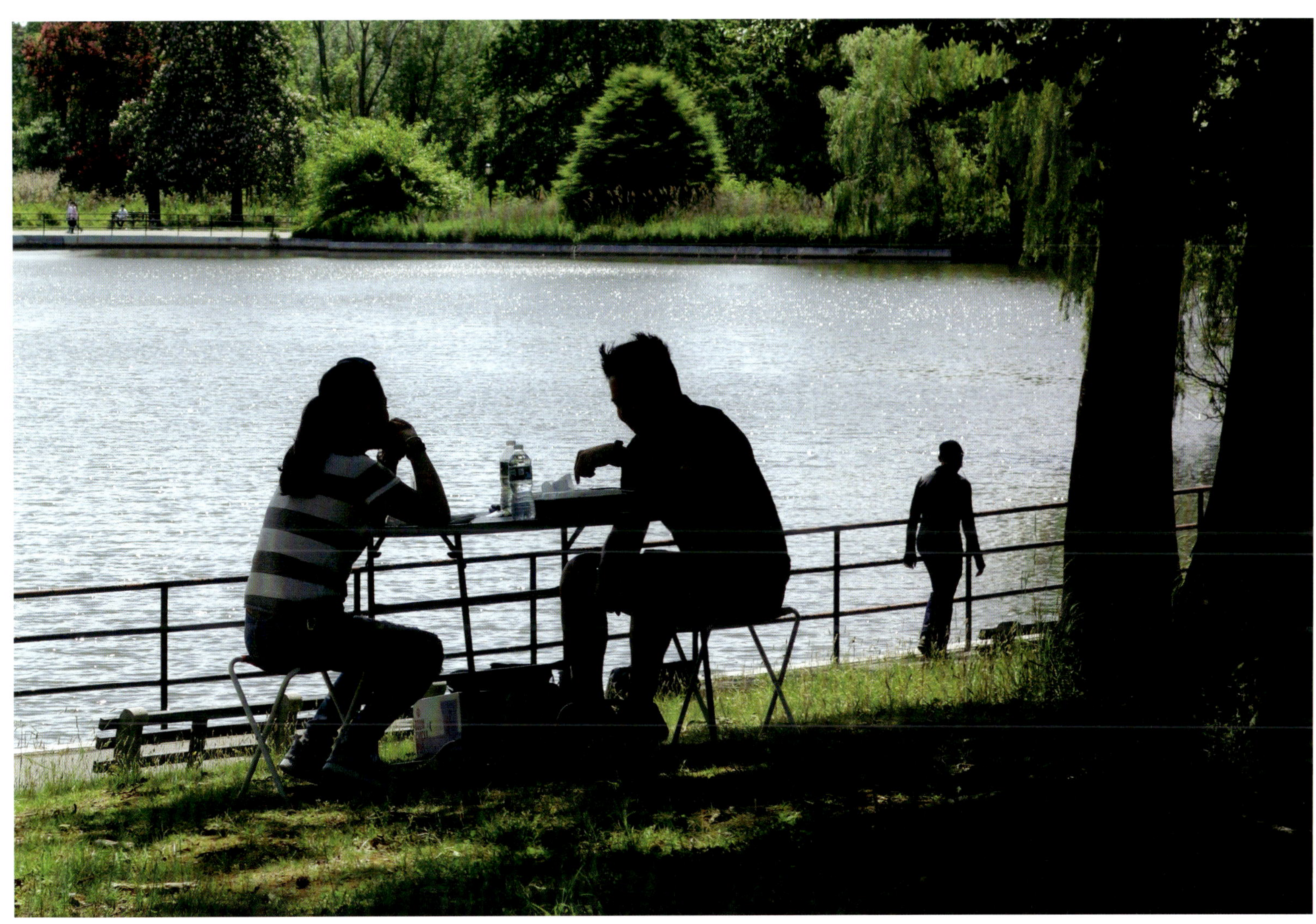

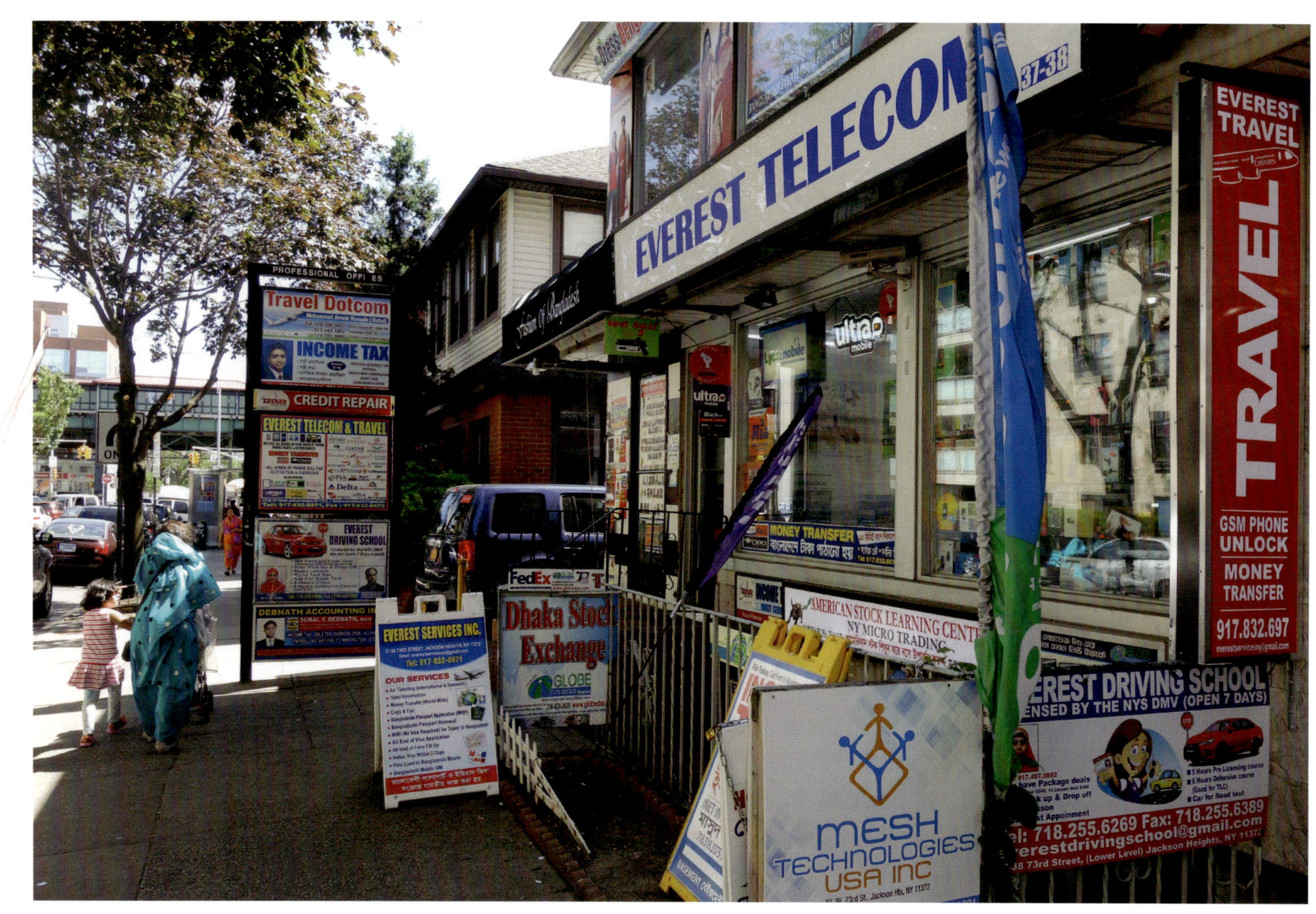
EVEREST TELECOM
37-38
EVEREST TRAVEL
TRAVEL
GSM PHONE UNLOCK
MONEY TRANSFER
917.832.697
Travel Dotcom
INCOME TAX
CREDIT REPAIR
EVEREST TELECOM & TRAVEL
EVEREST DRIVING SCHOOL
EVEREST SERVICES INC.
OUR SERVICES
Dhaka Stock Exchange
GLOBE
MONEY TRANSFER
AMERICAN STOCK LEARNING CENT
NY MICRO TRADING
EREST DRIVING SCHOOL
ENSED BY THE NYS DMV (OPEN 7 DAYS)
el: 718.255.6269 Fax: 718.255.6389
verestdrivingschool@gmail.com
MESH
TECHNOLOGIES
USA INC

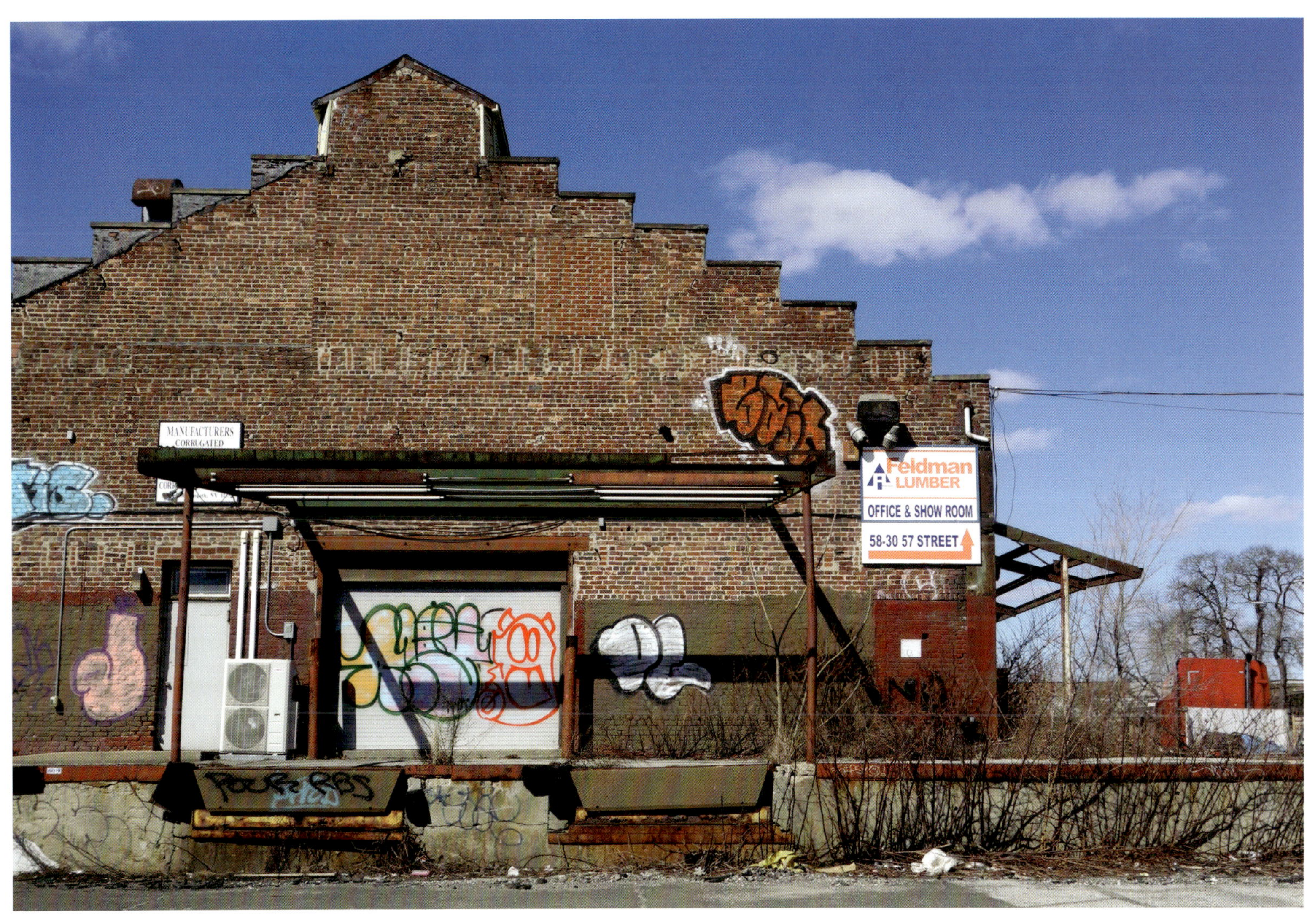
MANUFACTURERS
CORRUGATED
Feldman
LUMBER
OFFICE & SHOW ROOM
58-30 57 STREET

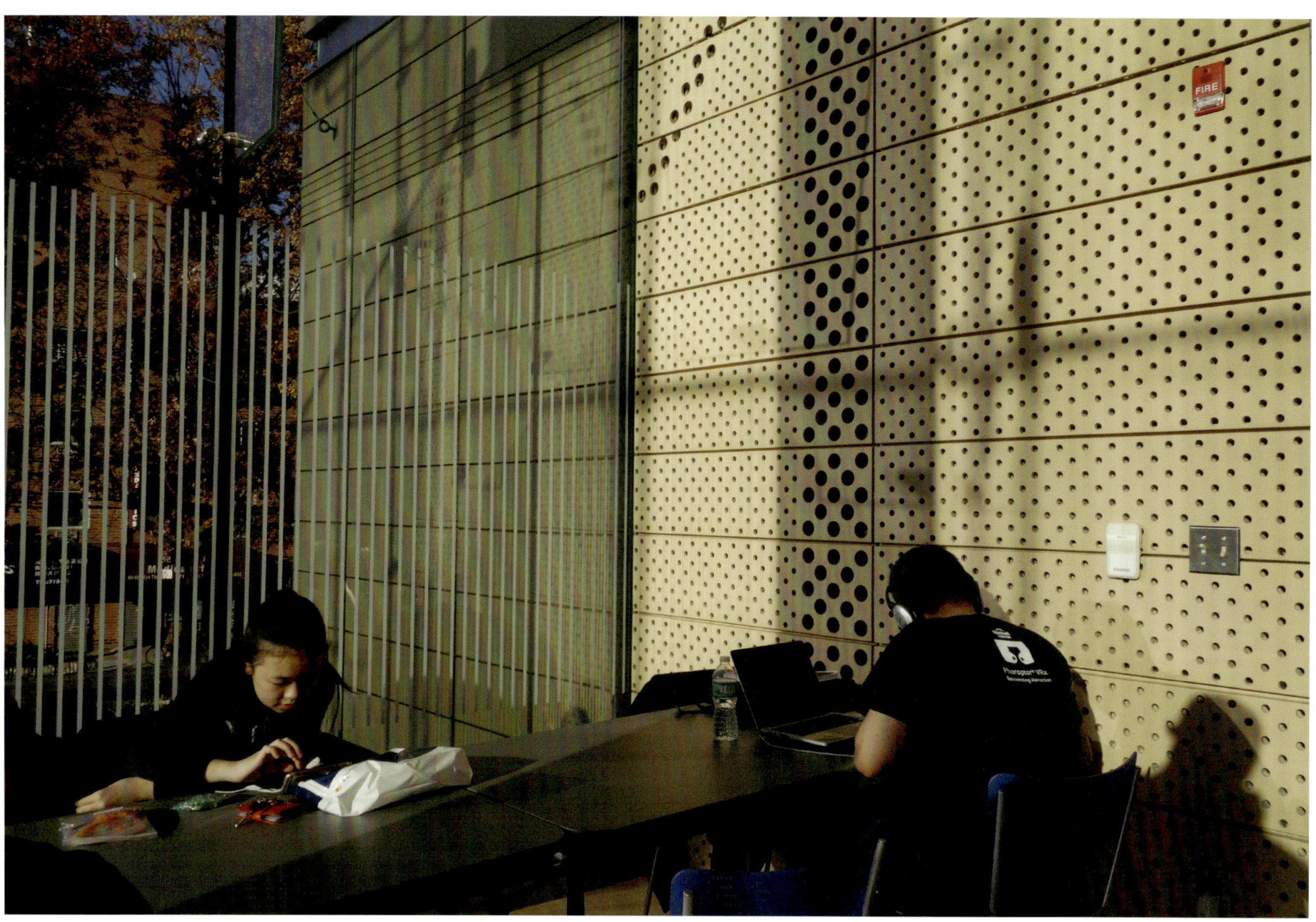
FIRE

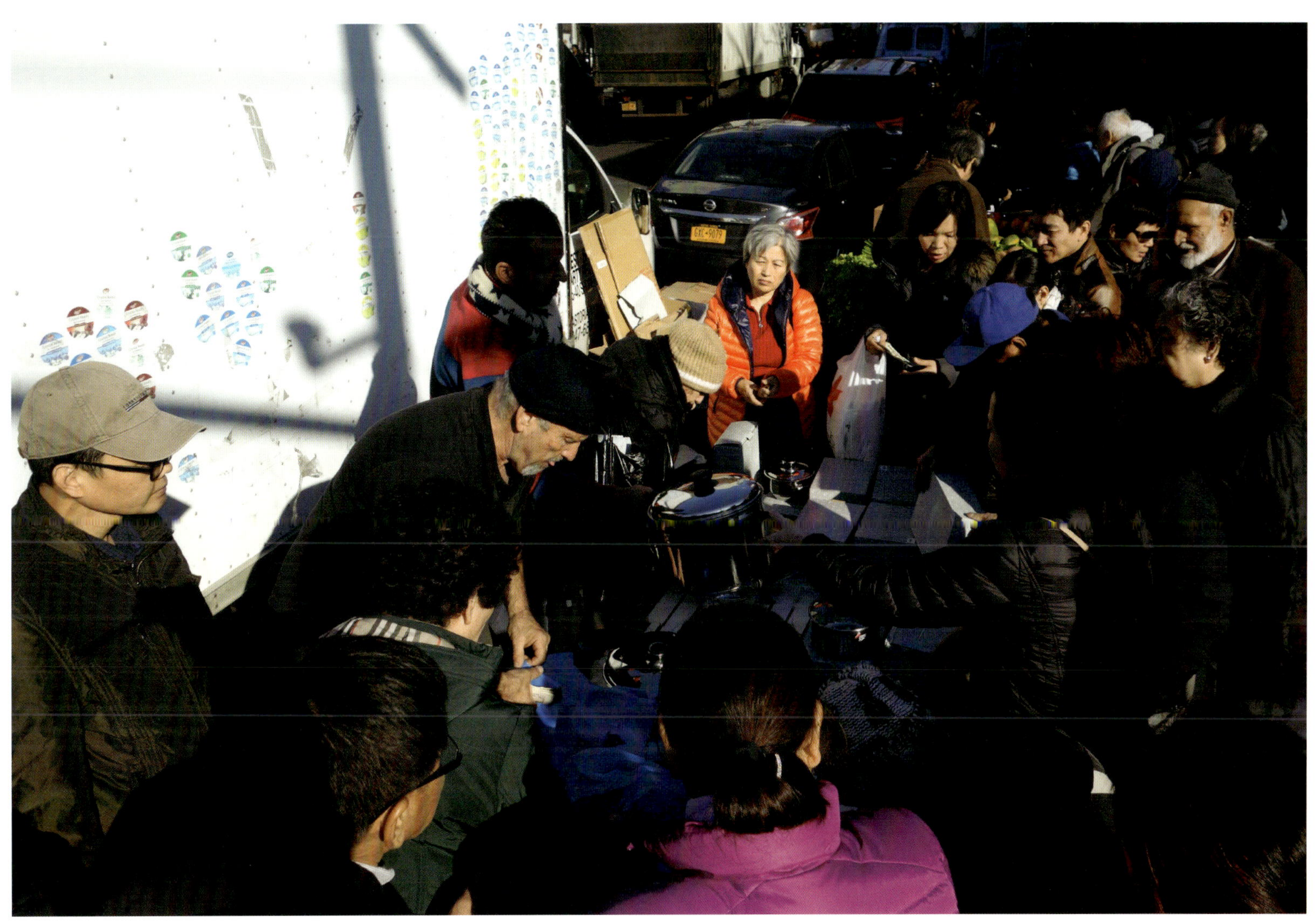

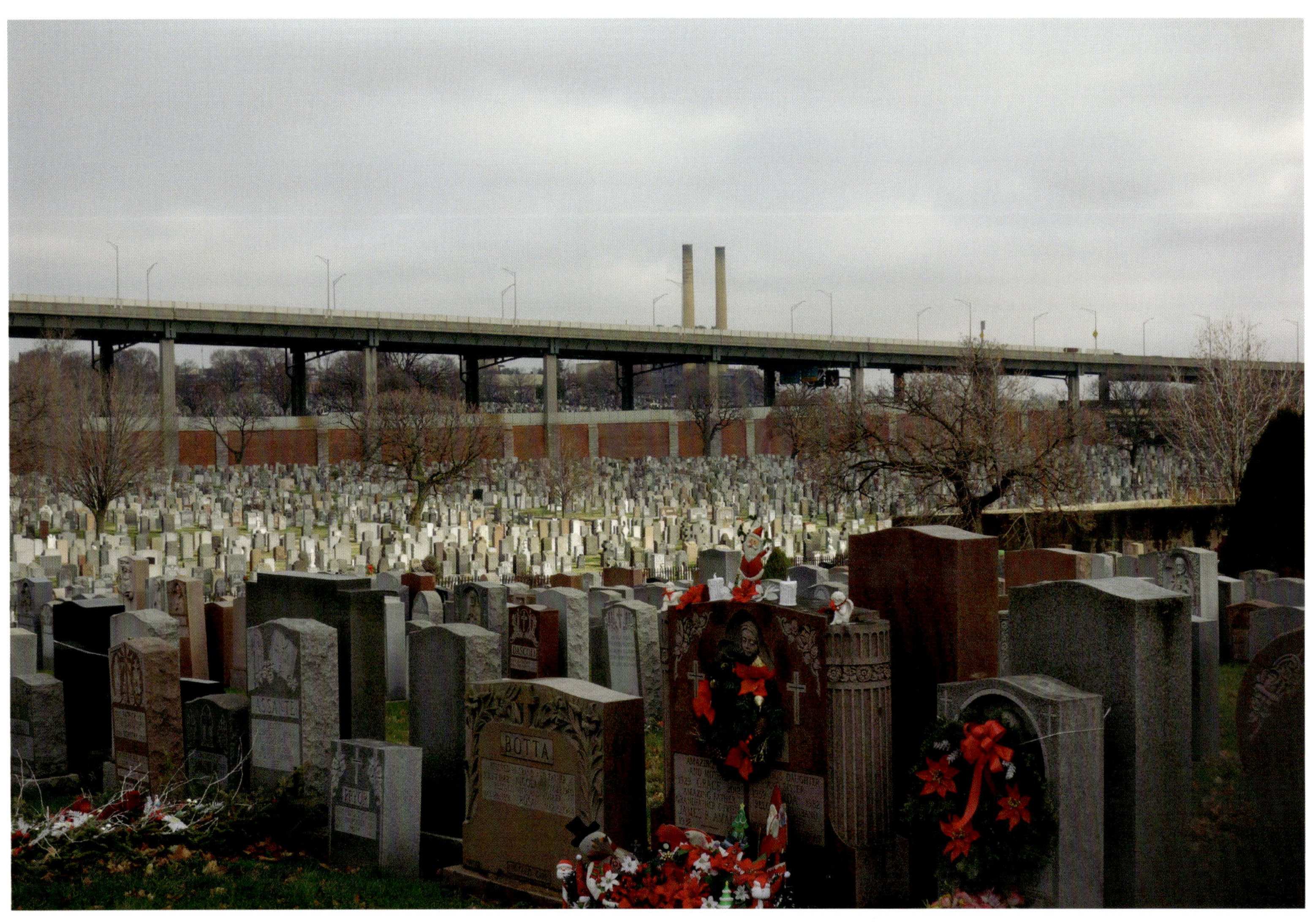
BOTTA

Introduction

On a cool spring morning a few years ago, I found myself walking around St. Albans, a quiet residential neighborhood in Southeastern Queens. Trim white Cape Cod houses and Tudor cottages lined the street, their small yards laden with rosebushes, box hedges, ornamental grasses, and the occasional statue of the Virgin Mary or St. Francis. Birds bustled and chirped about the blooming cherry and dogwood trees, and the sun shone brightly, though slate grey storm clouds lay on the horizon. Taking careful position with my camera, I framed the scene, focused the lens, and captured an image.

"What are you doing?" came a voice from a porch just behind me. Turning around, I saw an elderly woman with a shock of white hair wearing a flowing flower-print housedress coming down from her porch. Clearly, she played an important role in the community, watching the coming and going of people, making sure her neighbors stayed safe. So I knew I had to account for my presence on her block with the utmost respect. "I'm taking pictures of your beautiful street, ma'am," I replied. "Is that OK?" She supposed it was, but then asked, "Why would you want to do that?" I explained that I was trying to learn as much as I could about Queens neighborhoods and that one of the ways that I do this is to take pictures. She nodded a tentative approval; I don't think she was wary so much as dubious that anyone could make a living running around taking pictures.

Nevertheless, over the next half hour, she related her experience growing up in St. Albans, an incredible gift of time and memory. Her father had emigrated from Barbados and very soon married her mother, who had come up from North Carolina as a teenager to find work. They started their family in Harlem, then moved to Brooklyn, where she was born, and then in 1952, bought the house in which she now lives. Her father was the first Black man to own a home on the block. Now, she said proudly, her neighbors are all prosperous Black families with ties to the American South and to Jamaica, Barbados, Haiti, St. Vincent, and other islands. More recently, she added, families of Indian descent from Trinidad and Suriname have purchased homes in the neighborhood. "How has that gone down?" I asked. "Oh, fine," she replied, "everyone is welcome here. Just keep your yard clean."

Within these ordinary houses in St. Albans, an extraordinary array of people has put down roots.[1] They come from many places, speak many languages, and bring many traditions of food, dress, and worship. It is this juxtaposition of the ordinary and extraordinary, the mundane and the surprising, that best characterizes Queens. The photographs collected here explore this juxtaposition through a close look at the staggering social diversity that has taken hold within a relatively unremarkable urban landscape. This is a story about the multiplicity, creativity, adaptations, and variations on themes that have made Queens what it is today. More than any other place, Queens is a testament to how a diverse population can fit itself into an already-built environment and, in the process, reshape the urban landscape to suit new needs and purposes. It is a landscape whose ordinariness and lack of pretension have left it remarkably open to wave after wave of newcomers.

As a writer, photographer, and resident of Queens for fifteen years, I am interested in what diverse neighborhoods and communities can tell us about the world in which we live. These places play an important role in reshaping ideas of citizenship and belonging in a globalizing age. The world is crisscrossed with millions of refugees from political violence and upheaval, while many more millions of people continue to pull up stakes and leave their homes for opportunities in new lands. Nations on the receiving end of large-scale migration grow increasingly fractured over questions of pluralism and diversity, giving rise to reactionary politics and racial violence. Amid this hostility, cities from Istanbul and Berlin to London, Kuala Lumpur, Paris, Hong Kong, Toronto, Sydney, and Los Angeles have had to step in to provide newcomers with a semblance of sanctuary in a political culture where the nation is no longer the stable guarantor of citizenship.[2]

This book explores Queens as a lifeworld forged through unprecedented social diversity. At the heart of the story are two separate but entwined histories: the rapid expansion of the borough's built environment through the twentieth century and the millions of people who have traveled from near and far to call Queens home. Here, they have established a multiracial, multiethnic polity where people must experiment continuously with encounters across lines of difference just as the price of getting along and making do in a bustling, hectic metropolis. It has not been easy, by any measure: Newcomers have had to confront discrimination, White racial hostility, legal challenges, and language barriers. They have struggled to find adequate housing, places to worship, and jobs that pay enough to survive. And they have done all this in the jumbled collection of neighborhoods, housing types, civic and religious institutions, factories and warehouses, commercial streets, and strip malls that characterize Queens as a place.

Thus, the book is not about social diversity *per se*. Nor is it about the particular character of the built environment. Rather, it is about how these phenomena work together to shape everyday life in Queens.[3] It is about spaces of encounter and the people who create and inhabit them. It is about the many ways people have settled into a landscape they did not build but must make viable for their lives. They have done so through an intricate process of incremental adaptation, drawing on and recombining vernacular forms of cuisine, adornment, architecture, gardening, street life, public culture, worship, and other practices. To capture these varied practices as they intersect with the ordinary landscape of Queens, I draw on demographic data, archival sources, planning documents, news stories, and reports. However, I make primary use of documentary photography to bring these social and spatial realities of everyday life into relief.

The Urbanity of Queens

For many New Yorkers, Queens is a puzzle: sprawling, expansive, tangled, multiform, low-slung, and centerless. Unlike Manhattan, it is not known for its nightlife, grand skylines, iconic architecture, or great historic sites. It offers little of the dignity and aged charm of Brooklyn, the separatist fervor of Staten Island, or the edginess and renown of the Bronx. It is not "beautiful" in a way that conjures images of Central Park, the Grand Concourse, or Brownstone Brooklyn. There is no Guggenheim or Radio City Music Hall or Lincoln Center. Nobody wrote their *Rockaway Beach Memoirs*, tried to sell the 59th Street Bridge, or declared that "Ladies and Gentlemen, Queens Is Burning." It is, quite simply, New York City's most enigmatic borough.

And yet, Queens has quietly emerged as one of the most socially diverse places on earth. Not only is there no majority culture, but nearly half of all residents are foreign-born, and more than 55 percent speak a language other than English in the home. As Rebecca Solnit and Joshua Jelly-Schapiro note, "The capital of linguistic diversity, not just for the five boroughs, but for the human species, is Queens."[4] This goes far beyond the languages you would expect to hear in any pluralistic U.S. city, such as Spanish, Mandarin Chinese, Hindi, and Arabic, with a few pockets of Italian, Portuguese, Bengali, Korean, Greek, Urdu, or Tagalog. Queens has these in abundance. But there are also rare, even disappearing languages spoken in the streets and homes of the borough, such as Seke from Nepal, Quechua from Ecuador and Peru, Waray from the Philippines, Hakka from China, and Minangkabu and Bahasa from Indonesia.[5] Some of these ancient languages may be living their last days, and could soon pass into extinction, in Queens.

This astonishing linguistic and social diversity is spread across 117 square miles. Queens is the largest borough in the city, with one-third of the total landmass of New York City, and it has the longest coastline. You could fit seven Manhattans into Queens with room to spare. It is the second most populous borough after Brooklyn, and as a stand-alone city of 2.4 million people, it would rank fourth in the nation. Unlike Manhattan, the Bronx, and Brooklyn, Queens never lost population, and it experienced the highest decennial growth rate of any borough in the twentieth century—a staggering 130-percent increase between 1920 and 1930. Queens also has the largest, busiest, and most multilingual public library system in the United States, with a network of sixty-three branches dispersed in such a way that very few residents live more than one mile from a library.[6] The Port Authority of New York operates two of the country's busiest airports, JFK and La Guardia, from locations on the East River to the north and the Atlantic Ocean to the south, leading Queens to be oft disparaged as "the airport borough." Queensbridge Houses, the nation's largest public housing project, is located near the East River in Long Island City. Along with Chicago, Queens is the only place in the United States to have hosted two world's fairs.

But these varied superlatives reveal very little about Queens as a place. Despite its sheer size and diversity, Queens is probably the least coherent of the boroughs. It offers an urbanity distinct from its sister boroughs, but you would be at a loss to describe it. Indeed, it is precisely this nondescript character that has made Queens an ideal setting for television shows and movies that take place in New York City but require the signature features of a workaday world. Archie Bunker groused about the changing world around him from his armchair in Glendale. Betty Suarez schlepped to her Manhattan job from a modest town house in Jackson Heights, as did "Meet Millie" Bronson some fifty years before her. Doug Heffernan, the King of Queens, lived with his brash wife, Carrie, in Rego Park, and when he wasn't slinging webs around Manhattan as Spiderman, humble Peter Parker lived with his aunt and uncle in Forest Hills. When the Prince of Zamunda (Eddie Murphy) tells a cab driver to take him to "the most common part" of Queens, the cabbie replies, "That's easy—if there's one thing Queens has got a lot of, it's common parts."[7]

In this way, the humdrum borough has served as tableaux for the projection of a range of urban imaginaries. Queens is inchoate, a landscape betwixt and between. Stretched by the gravitational forces of high-rise Manhattan to the west and low-slung Long Island to the east, it never resolves itself into a discernable whole. An administrative subset of New York City, it presents no center of its own and endures a historically weak identity as a unit. Unlike Manhattan and Staten Island, Queens is not a self-contained geologic entity; it is one of the four arbitrarily drawn political boundaries that segment Long Island, along with the counties of Suffolk, Nassau, and Kings (Brooklyn). While Manhattan marched relatively unimpeded northward through the Bronx, the connection between "The City" and Queens was never a foregone conclusion. And unlike highly urbanized Brooklyn, Queens was never a city in its own right, but rather a county composed of a patchwork of small towns, marshes, trade roads, bottomlands, forests, and farms.

One notable legacy of this centerless quality is that even today, residents tend to identify intensely with their neighborhoods. Such loyalties are reflected in customary geocoding: Queens is the only borough of New York City that hyphenates its street addresses and uses neighborhood names for U.S. Mail delivery. Queens residents had been hyphenating their addresses since the advent of regular postal service in the nineteenth century. In 1911, the city imposed a grid system onto the roiling and confusing spaghetti-like street network of Queens, which erased the dozen Main Streets and Washington Avenues in favor of numbered thoroughfares. This grid eventually led to 271 numbered north-south streets, places, and lanes and 161 numbered east-west avenues, roads, and drives. Oh, and some boulevards, crescents, and terraces were thrown in for good measure.[8]

The hyphenated addresses were adapted to the new locational system to indicate the north-south coordinate (the first number increasing southward) and the west-east coordinate (the second number increasing eastward). Eventually, the U.S. Post Office proposed the elimination of hyphenated street numbers and the neighborhood names for the address, but Queens residents resisted these further impositions. Today, for residents of any neighborhood in Brooklyn, the address convention is Brooklyn, NY—whereas for residents of Rosedale in Queens, to take one example, the address convention is Rosedale, NY. I proudly receive my mail at Jackson Heights, NY. The U.S. Postal Service has tried numerous times to squelch these obscure and pointless practices. In 1995, postal officials tried to impose four multi-district zones called Flushing, Jamaica, Long Island City, and Rockaway, provoking an intense three-year revolt. ''I live in Woodside,'' Dorothea Osbourne declared in a letter to the *Tribune* in 1998, ''and I do not wish to be a Flushingite.''[9] Ultimately the U.S. Post Office relented, and the neighborhood addresses endure thanks to the stubbornness of Queens residents and their fierce attachment to locality.

Meanwhile, the immense volume of ink spilled on the history, culture, and politics of New York City is primarily devoted to events that unfold in Manhattan and, to a lesser extent, Brooklyn. The Bronx erupted into American consciousness during the urban crisis of the 1970s and 1980s as an exemplar of physical decay. The perennial agitation of Staten Island residents for secession from New York City, grounded in a strong place identity and affinity with New Jersey, has thrust the self-contained island borough into the limelight.[10] But Queens has gone about its business, quietly making do, even though it has rapidly become the most diverse place in the nation. Somehow the borough's beaches, trains, airports, expressways, bridges, neighborhoods, shopping malls, and homes have not historically added up to a coherent sense of "Queens" as a place, and today it remains little understood.

The photographs you will see in this book embrace the inchoate nature of Queens. My purpose in taking and selecting images is not to "explain" or "clarify" Queens; in many ways, it has become even less comprehensible to me the more I study it. What the photographs do accomplish, I hope, is a richer, more nuanced sense of the borough as an assemblage of places connected by time and circumstance. What emerges from the images is a story of Queens as a sprawling, multinucleated, highly varied urban place into which generations of diverse families and communities have folded their lives, adapting the world around them to suit their needs and aspirations.

Layered Landscapes

It is impossible to understand the people and landscapes of Queens without considering the borough's complicated history and layered landscapes. Before the arrival of European colonists in 1609, a network of Native communities dotted the landmass of Long Island, including the Lenape, Shinnecock, and other Algonquian-speaking groups. They maintained settlements, roadways, hunting grounds, and fish camps, laying down place names such as Canarsie, Rockaway, Manhasset, and Montauk.[11] After initial forays into the region, the Dutch West India Company launched a campaign of land seizure and removal of indigenous people that persisted through the seventeenth century. The company then awarded these lands to Dutch and English colonists in what would become Queens County. While Brooklyn would eventually dominate Kings County, Queens grew more haphazardly as settlement radiated outward from five principal towns: Flushing, Hempstead, Jamaica, Newtown, and Oyster Bay.[12]

During the eighteenth and nineteenth centuries, Queens was home primarily to Dutch and English farmers, a dwindling and dislocated population of Native people, and residents of African descent, including enslaved, manumitted, and freeborn.[13] The first decennial census in 1790 reported the county's population at 5,393, including more than one thousand enslaved people. Dutch and English farms were typically smallholdings organized for self-sufficiency, although wealthy Dutch colonists held the largest tracts of land and comprised the predominant users of enslaved labor.[14] The Flushing Remonstrance of 1657 laid down the tradition of religious liberty in the county, which attracted Quakers, Catholics, and eventually Eastern Orthodox and Jewish settlers. Free African men and women established congregations that would endure in various forms across the centuries.[15] And while the Dutch maintained their language, customs, and political prominence well into the eighteenth century, English rapidly became the lingua franca of trade and negotiation across Long Island.

In 1664, the British took control of New Netherland, imposed the county system, and established Kings and Queens counties through royal decree in 1683. While the official border would not be firmly fixed until 1931, Queens achieved its general shape in stages: first in 1768 with the addition of Rockaway, then in 1899 through the partition from what would become Nassau County to the east, and subsequently through numerous adjustments to accommodate the expansion of settlements. Queens began the twentieth century as a borough of the City of New York and a county of the State of New York.

Settler colonists brought with them to Queens their varied architectural "pattern languages"—mental maps of how a home should look. Farmers might have initially built distinctly "Dutch" or "English" houses but, throughout the eighteenth century, borrowed ideas, technical know-how, and architectural fashions from one another and from African laborers who undertook much of the carpentry and stonework. Home builders also responded to successive waves of style and construction from abroad, mixing frames, roof shape, window sizes, door placements, and other elements.[16] As a result, older rural English and Dutch influences faded over the eighteenth and nineteenth centuries as residents began experimenting with new forms like row houses, duplexes, apartments, and tightly packed residential blocks suitable to a burgeoning urban landscape.

Still, by the end of the nineteenth century, as Queens merged with four other counties into the Greater City of New York, the borough largely remained a rural landscape of farms, forests, and meadows punctuated by villages and crossings. Indeed, the population had grown slowly, from 45,000 after the Civil War to 150,000 in 1900; Kings County, by comparison, had reached over one million residents by the turn of the century. The five principal towns had become bustling, active nodes of marketing and trade but remained small. Newtown village, for example, was still a cluster of thirty to forty households in 1873, with a few gravel streets, a Long Island Railroad station, and a post office. That same year, Flushing, the largest of the towns, boasted a railroad crossing, a steamboat landing, numerous churches, and a grand town hall where Frederick Douglass delivered a major speech in 1865. Flushing was divided into some four hundred platted properties, though only half contained buildings; many remained marshland or open fields.[17]

Throughout the nineteenth century, an ever-growing network of roads connected residents into an intricate mosaic patchwork of towns, villages, and farmsteads. Railroad stops served as key attractors, with each station surrounded by clusters of houses, stores, and workshops. By the late nineteenth century, some of these clusters grew into larger communities that remain as neighborhoods today, from Maspeth and Astoria to Woodside, St. Albans, Edgemere, and Bayside. These nodes and connections would form the underlying blueprint for the borough's explosive growth in the twentieth century.

The Expanding Metropolis

If you took a carriage ride from Corona to Woodside along Roosevelt Avenue in 1916, you might have thought it a strange scene. The road had only recently been completed, still a dusty gravel ribbon through Western Queens. Stretching out in all directions from the road, sparsely settled farmsteads grew potatoes and cabbages, interspersed with a copse or creek here, an old cemetery there. However, in the distance, you catch sight of row houses and apartment buildings set among the fields, as if they had been plopped down from nowhere, newly finished and waiting. Continuing westward, you come across a work crew erecting great steel stanchions along either side of the road, topped with a lattice of girders and timbers. The play of sunbeams through this industrial tracery creates a dazzling alternation of light and shadow as you drive on. It is a train track set over a gravel road among farm fields. It brings the future.

The Queens we know today arose from the ferocious energies of twentieth-century urban development. During the first three decades, the population swelled from 150,000 in 1900 to 1 million in 1930, with the highest growth rate (130 percent) in the boom years of the roaring twenties. Most new residents came from the crowded precincts of Manhattan, eager for the light, air, and space promised by real estate promoters. Newly platted residential grids appeared almost overnight to accommodate this rapid growth. "Where potatoes were hoed until a year or two ago," the Queens Chamber of Commerce effused in their 1920 report, "are now located streets of attractive homes. On every block throughout the borough, the noise of the hammer and the music of the saw is heard, and yet, with all this building activity, the demand for homes is unprecedented."[18]

These new bits of urban fabric spread outward from the five principal towns, or found purchase on isolated rural farmsteads and marshlands. The expansion was haphazard and uneven: sometimes developers would sell off parcels, and homebuilding would commence even before streets were laid; other times, paved roads and sewers awaited property buyers. In the first decade of the twentieth century, the most rapid growth occurred in Western Queens, particularly Long Island City and Astoria. Over the next two decades, this growth shifted to the vast tracts of land in the "Second Ward," including neighborhoods like Elmhurst, Corona, Forest Hills, Maspeth, Middle Village, Woodside, and Glendale. All the while, some seven to ten miles eastward, towns and villages such as Flushing and Jamaica spread rapidly into their hinterlands. Eventually, this patchwork mosaic of subdivisions and settlements collided into a tangled mess of grids as the gaps filled in over time. It is this "crazy quilt" quality that most distinguishes the urban landscape and built environment of Queens.

This rapid, multinuclear expansion was made possible by a succession of large-scale infrastructure projects that tightened the connection of Queens to Manhattan. The completion of the 59th Street Bridge in 1909 set the stage for the borough's inexorable growth, replacing the sluggish ferries and allowing for automobile and trolley traffic. The trolley system, already threaded through several neighborhoods, expanded to nearly all parts of the borough by the 1920s. Following closely on the heels of the new bridge, the opening of the East River tunnels in 1910 connected the trains of Long Island to Manhattan, creating a major new commuter network. This network was further extended in fits and starts, from the construction of the overhead IRT Flushing Line between 1915 and 1928 to the cut-and-cover extension of the IND subway line below a newly widened Queens Boulevard between 1936 and 1956.

Despite the increased availability of train connections, it was the automobile that provided the motive force for Queens's growth, catalyzed by the emergence of Robert Moses's bridge and expressway system linking Queens to Manhattan, Bronx, New Jersey, and Upstate New York.[19] Throughout the 1930s and 1940s, Moses invested public funds in massive automobile-oriented infrastructure projects in Queens, opening the Triborough and Throgs Neck Bridges in 1936, the Whitestone Bridge in 1939, and the Midtown Tunnel in 1940. Meanwhile, under the New Deal and later the Interstate Highway Act, transportation officials dramatically transformed Queens by creating major roads, expressways, and parkways, many of which were grade separated for rapid flow. These included Interstate-linked projects such as the Brooklyn-Queens Expressway (BQE) and the Long Island Expressway (LIE) and major connector roads such as the Jackie Robinson and Cross-Island Parkways. In 1940, the city's Board of Transportation took over the privately owned Brooklyn and Queens Transit Corporation, leading to the gradual replacement of some thirty-two streetcar lines with buses in Queens. Eventually, all buses and trains would consolidate under the jurisdiction of the New York City Transit Authority.

By the closing of the World's Fair in 1940, Queens had grown to a population of 1.3 million spread unevenly across the borough's 117 square miles, connected by a growing network of roads and highways. Over the next few decades, its growth rate would slow appreciably even while the absolute numbers increased from 1.5 million in 1950 to nearly 2 million in 1970. Many new residential developments filled in the borough's gaps in the postwar decades of the 1950s and 1960s—most of which connected to the rest of the city only by the automobile. Large-scale projects also continued to reshape the borough, including Flushing-Meadows Park, La Guardia and Idlewild (John F. Kennedy) Airports, Shea Stadium, Astoria and Ravenswood power plants, a scattering of public housing projects, and the massive middle-class towers of Rochdale Village and LeFrak City. If nothing else, Queens embodies all the furious energies of twentieth-century urban development, exhausted through the streets, blocks, light industries, shops, parks, cemeteries, stadiums, roads, and highways of the expanding metropolitan landscape.

The Borough of Homes

With these infrastructure developments taking shape in stages through the first half of the twentieth century, the borough's highly varied housing stock exploded across the landscape in fits and starts, following the boom and bust cycles of the speculative real estate market.[20] What that housing would look like was an open question in 1900, but by 1920 the Chamber of Commerce promoted Queens as "the borough of homes."[21] Of course, this was a highly charged description, reflecting the common American notion that only privately owned, detached single family dwellings made for a proper home; everything else was just housing, apartments, or shelter. Still, it was a notion that powered the frenetic energies of development in Queens. Indeed, 70 percent of all housing built in Queens by 1930 came in single-family form, compared to 18.5 percent in the Bronx, which was dominated by rental apartments.

The openness of Queens to development and its growing connection to Manhattan made it attractive for housing reformers interested in experimenting with new living arrangements. Heavily influenced by Ebenezer Howard and the Garden City movement, reform-minded architects, housing experts, and real estate investors formed corporations to purchase land for planned residential development. In some cases, they pooled their capital into limited equity arrangements, while other developments received backing from philanthropic institutions such as those associated with the Phipps family, Metropolitan Life, and the Russell Sage Foundation.[22] Between 1910 and 1940, these corporations developed a range of new communities, including the curvilinear landscape of Forest Hills Gardens (1908–1917); the garden apartments of Jackson Heights (1915–1940); Metropolitan Houses (1924), and other model tenements; the low-rise courtyard houses of Sunnyside Gardens (1924–1928); and middle-class tower blocks such as Boulevard Gardens (1935) and Rochdale Village (1939–1960).[23] The New York City Housing Authority (NYCHA) added to this stock with the opening of Queensbridge Houses in 1939, the first in what would become a series of public housing complexes scattered across the borough, from Astoria and Woodside to Flushing and Rockaway.

Of course, while reformers racked up an array of experiments, these were episodic and limited compared to the rapid expansion of single-family houses across the borough. To accommodate swelling demand, much of the borough's build-out came at increasing economies of scale. During the first three decades of the twentieth century, the small parcel improvement pattern once common to Queens gave way to larger companies backed by pooled capital developing multiple parcels with great rapidity.[24] These larger building firms exploited the increasing availability of standardized products, such as dimensional lumber, precut roof trusses, and interchangeable windows and doors. Catalog houses, such as those available from Sears and other firms, also appeared throughout the borough. Today, streets containing rows of similar houses comprise the classic signature of rapid urban development by large building firms.

To maximize profits, developers delivered many of the single-family houses in the form of attached dwellings, either as duplexes or row houses. "In Woodside, Elmhurst, and Corona," the Chamber of Commerce noted in 1920, "hundreds of houses of the two family type, tenements and small cottages, suitable for the thrifty industrial workers are under construction." Further east, however, in neighborhoods such as Murray Hill, Bowne Park, and Auburndale, detached houses were the rule. "At Broadway-Flushing," for example, "225 detached dwellings are now being erected on the property of the Rickert-Brown Company."[25] Most newly constructed homes in this period adopted and modified successive waves of architectural revival styles. In the 1910s and 1920s, this resulted in block after block of Tudor and Queen Anne confections, with their half-timbering, gothic gables and diamond-paned windows, and gambrel-roofed Dutch colonials. This congeries of styles expanded with Federal row houses, bungalows, and Cape Cods built in profusion from the 1920s through the 1960s.[26]

After World War II, the pattern of "fast and cheap" housing persisted as new subdivisions and in-fill areas cropped up across the borough. As the cost of land increased, developers added more and more row houses and apartment buildings to neighborhoods that had comprised single-family dwellings, especially on the eastern and southern periphery and on hitherto open lands near airports and expressways. Many of the new developments of the 1950s and 1960s took extra measures to accommodate the automobile, now the overwhelmingly dominant mode of transportation in Queens. Blocks of older detached frame cottages fell to brick row house complexes, which replaced the front yards with underground parking or attached multilevel garages. New row house complexes converted postage-stamp front yards into driveways at grade or sloping down toward a basement garage.[27] Gas stations, strip malls, and parking lots proliferated throughout the borough. By the 1960s, residents bore witness to the unfolding of a version of the American Dream: an abundance of single-family houses with driveways and garages for private vehicles, all circulating along commodious streets, expressways, and interstates.

Still, Queens offers a diverse mix of housing. New waves of real estate investment since the 1980s have tended toward higher-density construction, such as skyscrapers in Long Island City and tower block apartments in Flushing. Developers even demolish lower-scale land uses where zoning allows for high-density construction. But the predominance of the single-family house remains a defining feature of the borough's residential landscape and aspirational urban culture.

The Social Mosaic

In many ways, the availability of relatively cheap land and low-cost housing in various forms has been a crucial factor in the tremendous social diversity of Queens. In the eighteenth and nineteenth centuries, Dutch and English farm families had already begun subdividing their lands and selling them off into smaller and smaller farmsteads, which were purchased by people of more modest means from varied and divergent backgrounds. Throughout the second half of the nineteenth century, the old Dutch and English settler culture gave way to second- and third-generation German and Irish families and a trickle of upstart transplants from Manhattan. After the Civil War, a small but growing African American community established churches and homes in areas that would become Jamaica, Elmhurst, and Corona. They would be joined in the late nineteenth and twentieth centuries by Black migrants from the Caribbean and the rural South and, in the second half of the twentieth century, by families from Harlem and Brooklyn seeking greener pastures.[28]

The borough opened up in the 1910s and 1920s just when large numbers of "cliff dwellers" were looking for an escape from the crowding and congestion of Manhattan. Some of these newcomers were middle-class WASP families eager to dissociate from the "alien" languages, customs, and religious practices of immigrant New York and able to afford large houses in exclusive white enclaves. However, with rapid homebuilding and burgeoning neighborhoods, Italian, Greek, Polish, and Jewish families began moving into Queens, particularly in the 1930s when the Great Depression made homebuilders desperate to sell to whoever could put cash on the table. While these groups scattered across the borough, they did form concentrations: Greeks in Astoria and Whitestone, Italians in Corona and Howard Beach, Poles in Ridgewood and Maspeth, and Jewish people in Forest Hills and Flushing.[29]

Meanwhile, racial segregation remained a powerful organizing force in the settlement of Queens throughout much of the twentieth century. Larger building firms tended to use racially restrictive covenants more often so that, as construction shifted away from small builders, nearly half of all new subdivisions built in Queens in the 1920s and 1930s contained racial covenants.[30] Neighborhoods such as Jackson Heights initially maintained covenants that prohibited sales of apartments to Jews, Catholics, and Blacks, although the onset of the Great Depression effectively mooted such selectivity.[31] Still, throughout the post–World War II decades, Whites continued to oppose racial integration. If they could no longer rely on racial covenants or Federal Housing Administration (FHA) loan restrictions, they frequently resorted to outright hostility and violence. In the 1960s, 1970s, and 1980s, highly publicized White attacks on Black people occurred in Rosedale and Howard Beach, while White residents of Forest Hills, Whitestone, Flushing, and Jackson Heights vehemently opposed school integration and the expansion of public housing into their neighborhoods.[32] As a result, Black residential enclaves grew throughout the twentieth century: Louis and Lucille Armstrong moved to Corona in 1943; Malcolm X and Betty Shabazz settled in East Elmhurst in 1957; and Ella Fitzgerald, Jackie Robinson, and W. E. B. Du Bois all lived in Addisleigh Park.

Thanks to sustained resistance from Black civil rights groups and fair housing activists, segregation has lessened across New York City over the last fifty years. Even as neighborhoods such as Hollis and Jamaica transitioned from white to African American and Afro-Caribbean, high levels of middle-class home ownership enabled Black residents to escape much of the decline that rocked analogous neighborhoods in the Bronx and Brooklyn during the city's infamous fiscal crisis.[33] Throughout the 1990s and 2000s, Queens was one of only a handful of counties in the United States where the median Black family income exceeds that of Whites.[34] Still, despite becoming the most diverse county in the United States, large pockets of Queens remain highly resistant to Black residential expansion.[35]

Above all, it was the passage of the 1965 Immigration Reform Act that led to the greatest social transformation in the borough's history. While newcomers found their way into all parts of New York City, Queens received the lion's share. Even before the Act's passage, Puerto Rican and Dominican families had begun relocating from Manhattan to Queens in the 1940s and 1950s, searching for home ownership and job opportunities. Throughout the 1960s and 1970s, immigrant families from Mainland China and Korea settled in Flushing and Auburndale in ever-increasing numbers, opening many new businesses in the flagging downtown.[36] Families from India and Bangladesh concentrated in Jackson Heights: between 1970 and 1980, its South Asian population shot up from virtually nil to more than 6,000, more than doubling again to 13,000 by 1990.[37] Migrants from Taiwan, Hong Kong, Vietnam, Thailand, and the Philippines revitalized waning neighborhoods such as Elmhurst and Woodside. A wave of Afro-Caribbean and Indo-Caribbean immigrants—especially from Jamaica, Haiti, Trinidad, and Guyana—purchased homes and built lives in Jamaica, Hollis, Richmond Hills, and Ozone Park.[38]

In the 1970s and 1980s, new diasporic trajectories brought increasing numbers of families from Colombia, Ecuador, Honduras, Peru, and Argentina. Many fled wars, insurgencies, autocratic governments, and other political perils. These newcomers found homes in many parts of the borough but concentrated in Woodside, Jackson Heights, and Corona.[39] Additionally, Bukharan Jews, Tajiks, and other refugees from the Soviet Union established a vibrant community in the streets and shops of Rego Park, while Mexican and Mexican-American families carved out a place for themselves in Corona.[40]

Most recently, in the 1990s and 2000s, new waves of immigration brought Lebanese, Yemeni, and Egyptian people to Astoria, Fujian and Hong Kong Chinese to Flushing, and Nepalese and Tibetans to the streets of Jackson Heights and Elmhurst. By the time of the 1990 U.S. Census, Queens had already become the most ethnically diverse county in the country, and its diversity only increased.[41]

This diversity is by no means without friction. After all, the presence of people from many countries often reflects multiple trajectories of suffering and trauma. It can be devastating to uproot oneself, especially when forced to do so because of war, political violence, or economic precarity. To an outsider, diverse urban neighborhoods might appear like the pleasurable symphony of human social multiplicity playing out in the daily ballet of the street, to paraphrase Jane Jacobs. But to an immigrant, diversity might feel like an incidental outcome of a heart-breaking flight from a homeland, the sudden shock of new laws and customs, the painful barriers of language, the competition for cheap housing, and the endless struggle to find work in a highly segmented labor market.[42]

Moreover, diverse urban communities are often divided over factors such as religion, place of origin, class, and citizenship. Among Spanish-speaking communities, for example, median incomes diverge considerably based on national origin, with higher and increasing incomes among Puerto Rican and Dominican families and lower and decreasing incomes among Colombians, Mexicans, and Ecuadoreans. Asian immigrants, a large and sweeping category, have highly divergent incomes and status, often related to how long they have been in the United States. In Community District 3, which includes Jackson Heights, East Elmhurst, and North Corona, families from South, Southeast, and East Asia had a higher median income than Whites and Blacks in 1990. By the mid-2000s, however, that situation reversed, primarily because of the influx of poorer immigrants from Fujian Province in China, Nepali and Tibetan families, and Indo-Caribbeans from poorer countries such as Surinam and Guyana. These groups tended to have lower earnings and less disposable income than older established populations of African Americans, Afro-Caribbeans, Chinese, Koreans, and Bengalis.[43]

Religion and ideology frequently divide communities, often without incident but occasionally giving rise to tensions. On the streets of Flushing, for example, devotees of Falun Gong can be found on many days protesting the treatment of their counterparts in Mainland China. Thai residents in Elmhurst and Woodside are divided among Buddhists, Catholics, and Muslims, while in the same neighborhood, churches and mosques open their doors to multiethnic congregations.[44] Charismatic Protestant denominations have made significant inroads among once stalwart Catholic Mexican and Central American communities of Corona. In Jackson Heights, Hindus, Jains, Muslims, Buddhists, Jews, and Christians all live cheek by jowl in the neighborhood's row houses and co-ops, while immigrants from India, Bangladesh, Nepal, Pakistan, and Afghanistan have knitted together pan-South Asian community organizations to advance their common interests.[45] Meanwhile, Bengali immigrants in the same area are divided by religion—Hindu and

Muslim—as well as by nationality: some come from Bangladesh, while others arrived from West Bengal State in India.[46]

These various divisions and abrasions, however, emerge and submerge over time within a borough of kaleidoscopic, ever-changing social diversity. Conflicts erupt continually both within and between ethnic groups over politics, resources, language, immigration policy, law enforcement, and space. Meanwhile, what happens on the streets of Port-au-Prince, Seoul, and Manila reverberates in Cambria Heights, Auburndale, and Woodside. Such conflicts are never straightforward or easy, but they are part of the fabric of everyday life in Queens. Sometimes together, sometimes apart, residents have come to understand their borough as a diverse urban place where people encounter each other across various lines of difference and, in so doing, at least have the possibility of finding common ground. It is this tension between difference and commonality, as much as between the extraordinary (social diversity) and ordinary (urban landscape), that emerges most palpably from the pages in this book.

Photographing the Borough

I did not set out to make a book about Queens. I began photographing the borough for much the same reason I photograph any place: to learn about it, to try to find patterns in its streets, shops, and houses, and to deepen my understanding of its intricately textured spaces. The difference between Queens and other locations, however, is that I have lived here for fifteen years and have had a lot of time to visit and revisit its many neighborhoods, make repeated exposures, and build up a large collection. But for the most part, I approach making images of Queens as I do anywhere.

My work as a photographer is oriented toward the exploration of cities and city life.[47] The key challenge for this work is to study the very thing in which I am embedded, the very thing that surrounds me. Like fish, it can be difficult to see the water in which we swim. To grapple with this conundrum, I begin with the premise that any city is greater than the sum of its parts but that the greater sum is ultimately unknowable. Since no one person can know the whole of a city, I am compelled to search through its traces—those signals, noises, edges, ghosts, and dreams that reveal something about the urban condition. I am interested in how we construct and inhabit our urban world, constantly contesting and reshaping the landscapes that surround us. I am particularly interested in how photography can pry open the urban moment—the tiny increments of experience that spark into existence within the everyday spaces and places of the city. The photographs in this book are full of such moments.

Since my visual practice is geared toward the city as both object and muse, it is necessarily part social research and part creative endeavor. While I work within the traditions of architectural and documentary photography, my upbringing in the industrial Midwest has profoundly shaped how I approach this work, disposing me toward the ordinary, the quotidian, and the banal. For example, I take many pictures of buildings, but I am not an architectural photographer in the classic sense, where I use images to lionize elite or iconic buildings. Rather, I use photography to explore the mundane spaces and landscapes that surround us. And unlike most documentarians, I use photography not to construct fixed narratives of individuals or groups or places but to explore contingent relationships between people and the cities they inhabit.

In my work, then, I am interested in photography not merely as illustration, but as method. The images that I make collude with, and sometimes contradict, other forms of social evidence, such as migration and resettlement patterns, shifting gender and class relations, civic and political formation, architectural program, urban spatial patterns, commerce and exchange, and the narrated experiences of people in motion. In documenting social phenomena through photography, I am engaging in a conversation with people and places. And while the images included in this book necessarily emerge from one point of view, it is (hopefully) an informed point of view—one that weaves together visual, textual, and experiential forms of evidence to produce a new understanding of the urban world, however tentative.

As I said earlier, my guiding priority as a photographer is to make images that help me understand a place in a new or different way. I am not a completist aiming for saturation of a geographic area. Nor am I an artist chasing the perfect exposure. If I admire great photographers of cities, such as Berenice Abbott, Gordon Parks, Ara Güler, Teenie Harris, Alexander Rodchenko, Vivian Maier, Weegee, Robert Doisneau, Brassaï, and Garry Winogrand, I am not compelled by the aesthetic considerations that drove them. Nor am I a portrait photographer striving to capture depth of meaning in human visage and bodily expression. Of course, people do show up in my photographs, and technically there are no restrictions on including any person, house, or object in a public setting. However, there are moral and ethical dimensions to consider. People are vulnerable, and photography can feel intrusive. Thus, you will find very few photographs in this book where people are the primary focus, and in those cases where they do feature prominently, I made sure to obtain their verbal consent.

As a White male taking pictures in immigrant neighborhoods and communities of color, it is of paramount importance that I remain vigilantly attuned to power dynamics and that I proceed with the utmost caution and respect.[48] It is not only about how I deploy my lens, frame settings, and make exposures; it is also about how I comport my embodied privilege in public life. Drawing on long experience living in and engaging diverse communities, I have learned that it is important to make myself as conspicuous as possible: I always wave at people while I am working, and I make sure that my camera can be seen. This encourages people to query me if they so desire. If anyone asks what I am doing, I give as full an explanation as they care to hear. More often than not, this sparks interesting and useful conversations about a street, a neighborhood, a church, or a temple. Over the years, I have found that people are almost always curious, friendly, and accommodating—the very opposite of the stereotype of New Yorkers. They want to share their knowledge and be heard. Only once have I ever been asked to delete a photograph by a person who happened to be caught in the frame, and I did so without hesitation.

For me, then, photography is primarily fieldwork, a method for carefully and ethically gathering social information. Any given exposure that I make is not an end in itself, but a means to an end. I am interested in the knowledge one can gain from the field, which the photograph partially captures. Of course, the process varies. Sometimes I will select a neighborhood, travel there, and walk around, taking photos. Other times, I may happen to be passing through an area and would stop off for a few shots. On several occasions, I have waited an hour or more for shadows to clock away from a scene I was trying to capture. By contrast, there have been a few times when I barely slowed down the car to grab a quick shot of a building—slow down too much in Queens, and you will get an earful of honking from behind! In all cases, I organize photographs into folders by location and date and make notes about the people, buildings, and neighborhoods that I encounter. Thus, the photographs are not so much instrumental, where a given image serves a predetermined outcome. Nor are they illustrative, where this image indexes that specific phenomenon. Rather, they are archival, sitting in a relationship to each other, suggesting juxtapositions and contradictions, idiosyncracies and patterns.

Every image included in the book was born digital. The transition to digital was not easy for me. I learned photography at an early age from my father using his U.S. Army–issued Mamiya Sekor TL500, an excellent but no-frills manual single-lens reflex camera. In college, I pursued the study of photography, including black and white, color, and large format, and through much of graduate school I had access to a darkroom. However, when I moved to New York City in 2007, getting regular access to a darkroom proved difficult, so I made the shift to digital. The photographs for this book were taken either with a Canon 5D Mark II shooting in RAW format or a Sony DSC RX 100 with Zeiss lens shooting 20-megapixel JPEGs, converted into lossless files. Occasionally, I have cropped a photograph to draw focus, reduce visual noise or static, or straighten the horizon. Here and there I have used Photoshop to improve the white balance, dodge or burn a segment, or change contrast. However, most photographs included in the book are reproduced as they were taken. Whatever my own reservations may be about digital photography, the shift to digital has allowed me to build up a sizable visual archive at low cost and with relative ease.

Organizing the Book

The photographs that follow have been selected from an archive of some 7,500 taken throughout Queens. The most recent photograph is from 2022, and the oldest is from 2010. About a quarter of these are the result of chance moments and encounters while traversing the borough, while the rest come from determined "shoots" of specific neighborhoods, corridors, or building types. Nearly all the photographs depict scenes outdoors, from vantages accessible to anyone in the public realm. There are very few interior scenes or portraitures; those could furnish material for entirely separate books.

Even with these imposed limits, selecting a couple hundred photographs to include in this book was a difficult, at times painful, process. The first criterion for inclusion was not the aesthetic quality of the photograph—though that certainly entered into the decision at times. Rather, the most important criterion was whether or not a given photograph contributes to a larger story, whether or not it captures something about Queens that I hope to convey. Many lovely and technically strong photographs did not make the cut. Likewise, more than a few images included here fall well short of representing my best work. Another key criterion was the location: Some areas of Queens, such as Flushing and Jackson Heights (where I live), are overrepresented in the archive. If I have ten photographs taken along Roosevelt Avenue, it doesn't matter how good that eleventh one is, it has to be dropped to make way for something less well-represented. In the end, it is the ensemble of images, how they work together in a mosaic, and how they contribute to a sense of Queens as a place that comprises the overriding consideration.

The next task in organizing the book was to develop a roster of themes for two-page spreads that could incorporate multiple images. This approach would not only allow me to include more photographs in the book, but it would also capture the serial nature of bridges, libraries, waterfronts, building façades, and other featured phenomena. In many cases, one photograph on one page will suffice to develop a theme or at least gain a small purchase on a particular idea, location, or experience. In other cases, such information is more compelling when conveyed through multiple images. For example, the built landscape of Queens features an abundance of vernacular styles; one or even two photographs could hardly cover the sheer number and diversity of architectural expressions, but with a dozen or more images, one can at least suggest some sense of multiplicity. Thus, throughout the book, you will encounter sixteen two-page spreads that explore, in addition to vernacular architecture, such phenomena as industrial landscapes, ecology, infrastructure, and religious devotion.

Perhaps the most difficult decision was how to arrange and sequence the photographs for the book. Using Lightroom and Flickr as databases, I tried a variety of organizational scenarios, including grouping the photographs by neighborhood location, building type, and even by when taken. None of them felt right: They either created imbalances in representation or did not support the story I wanted to tell. Finally, one day, feeling frustrated with the process, I just clicked on "random sort" on Flickr, and there was the mosaic I had been seeking! Of course, it needed some adjustment, for which I applied a simple algorithm: 1) distribute the sixteen two-page spreads evenly throughout the book; 2) each two-page spread should be followed by eight single-page images; 3) within each single-image run, no neighborhood can be represented more than twice. Following these rules, it only took a few rearrangements of images to get it right. As a result, you will encounter the photographs much as you would Queens itself as a place: jumbled, mundane, expansive, dreary, weird, contradictory, curious, and inchoate.

Conclusion: Queens Unfinished

So this is the story that I hope to tell with this book. Queens is a staggeringly diverse, richly textured place that, like a mosaic, only becomes a little clearer as you step away for a broader look. But as soon as you step back, you are drawn again to the parts and begin to lose the picture. After all, there is no grand ensemble of buildings, no unifying civic landscape, and no downtown or central place to focus attention. You must continually shift registers in order to see the borough's patchy fabric, spread over 178 square miles of land and water, crisscrossed by multiple roads, train lines, street grids, bridges, viaducts, bottomlands, ridges, creeks, harbors, and bays. You must zoom in and out to grasp the incredibly varied ways people have adapted and reshaped this landscape to accommodate their needs and desires over time. And just when you think you have a handle on it all, just when you feel like there is little more to learn, you encounter something altogether new, surprising, strange, or inexplicable. In this way, you begin to clock the ever-shifting array of people, networks, boundaries, and flows of a landscape constantly in the making.

The photographs gathered here work as an ensemble, like tiles in a mosaic. They provide cumulative evidence of a world in formation. Over the last century, an increasingly diverse range of people have found their way into the ordinary homes, shops, factories, warehouses, parks, and playgrounds of Queens. As one immigrant community after another flows into the borough, they begin the hard work of establishing roots and building networks of mutual aid and solidarity. As they do so, they struggle to define their needs, resist discrimination, and build resonant institutions to advance their interests. Long-term residents and newcomers encounter one another in the spaces of everyday life and begin devising ways of getting along, of living together in a shared urban landscape. The process is not simple or smooth, and it is not without abrasions and setbacks and heartache. But it is necessary for building lives in a socially heterogeneous world.

Ultimately, the goal of this book is to illuminate these processes, exploring the tensions between globalization and locality, urban neighborhoods and diasporic flows, difference and belonging. And out of this churning condition, perhaps the borough of Queens emerges as a space of possibility for working out an urban future.

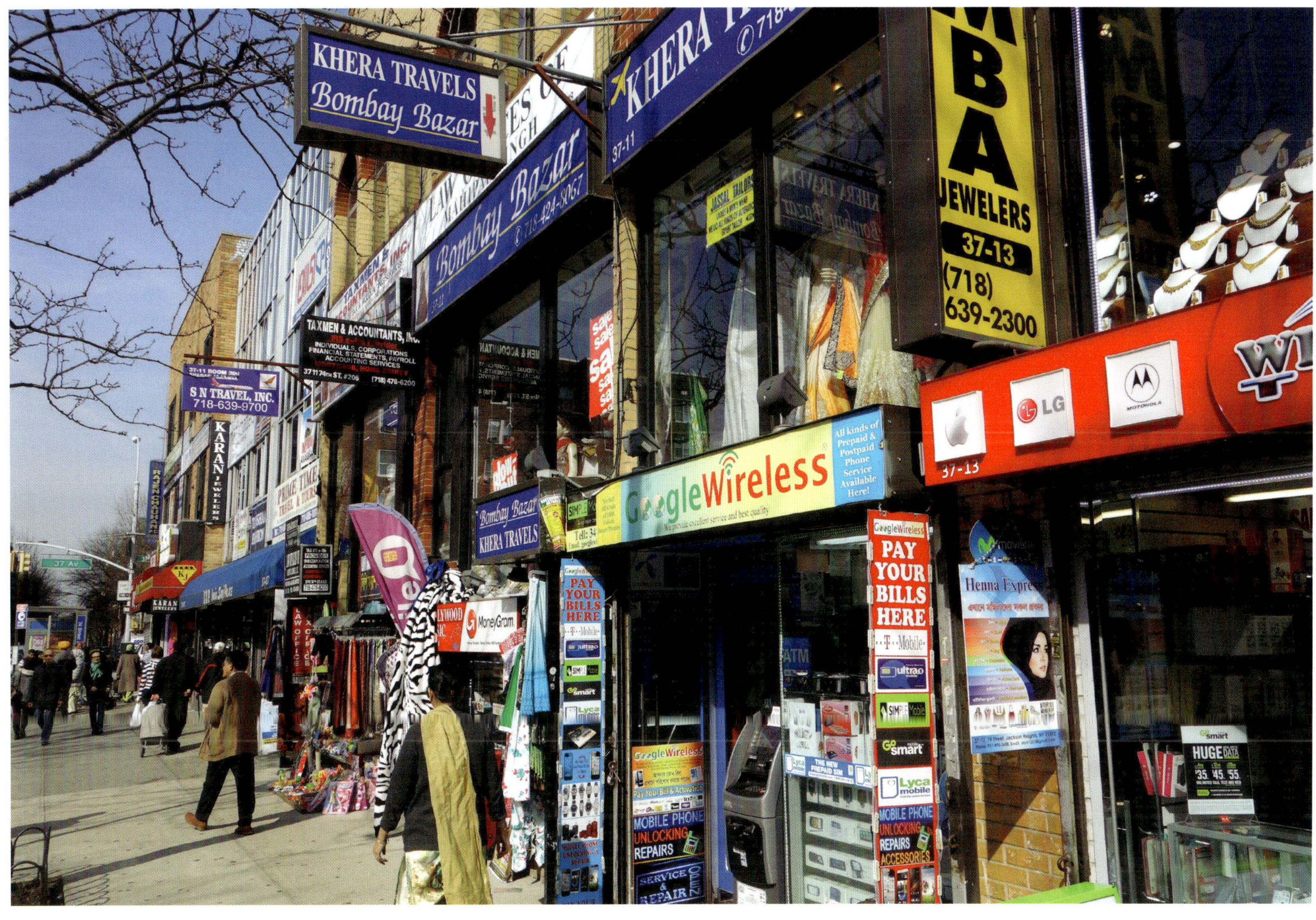

Shops on 74th Street, Jackson Heights

Jackson Heights features many businesses that cater to the needs of South Asian immigrant families, such as phone card shops, tax accountants, travel agencies, wire transfer stalls, groceries, clothiers, and restaurants. There is also an active gold trade with global connections to Mumbai, Calcutta, and Dhaka. Most of the merchants are Bengali, either from Bangladesh or Indian West Bengal. Other merchants come from Punjab and Gujarat as well as Pakistan, Afghanistan, and Nepal. Events in South Asia, such as political unrest, labor conflicts, natural disasters, and economic downturns, can reverberate in Jackson Heights. Likewise, the decline in the value of the dollar can affect remittances sent from Jackson Heights to South Asia.

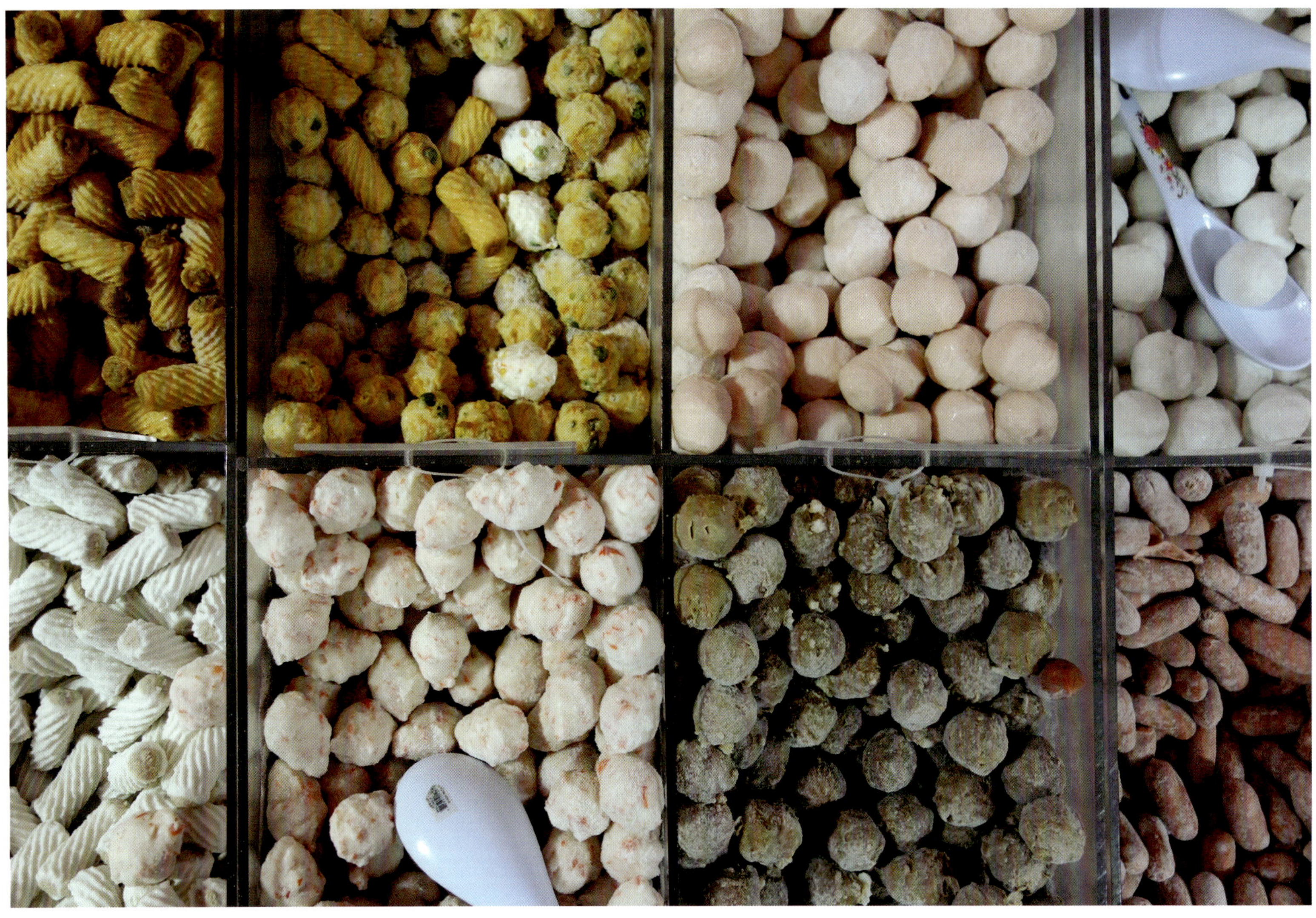

Snack bins, Elmhurst

Savory sesame bites and other snacks are on offer at a Chinese grocery in Elmhurst. The East and Southeast Asian communities of Elmhurst are very diverse. As an older Korean community moved out to Flushing in the 1960s and 1970s, they gave way to Chinese Americans, immigrants from Hong Kong and Taiwan, and ethnic Chinese from Singapore, Malaysia, and Vietnam. Since the 1990s, there has been a growing cluster of northern and southern Thai families, a new wave of immigrants from post-Communist Vietnam, and a rapidly growing Indonesian population. Several Buddhist temples have cropped up around the neighborhood over the last decade to serve a growing population of devotees.

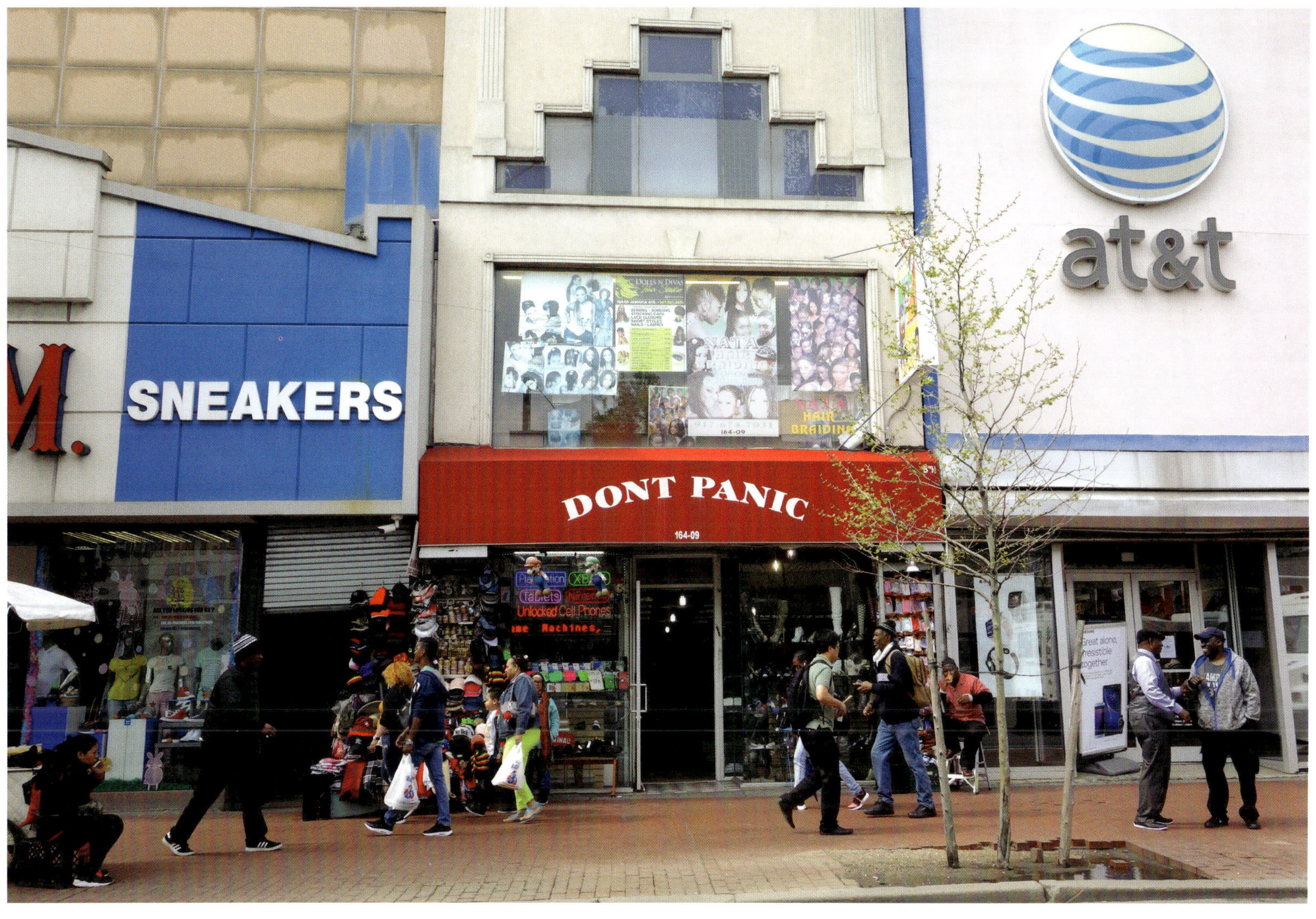

Downtown Jamaica

One of the largest and most vibrant neighborhoods of Queens, Jamaica, spreads over nearly three square miles in the eastern portion of the borough. Like Flushing, it was one of the original "five towns" of Queens County, and the old village streets still function as a downtown commercial hub. The neighborhood's name comes from the Lenape word "yamecha," meaning "beaver." Today it is home to a large Black middle-class community comprising African American families and immigrants from Jamaica, Haiti, and Barbados, among other countries. Queens is one of a handful of counties in the United States where Black median income surpasses that of Whites.

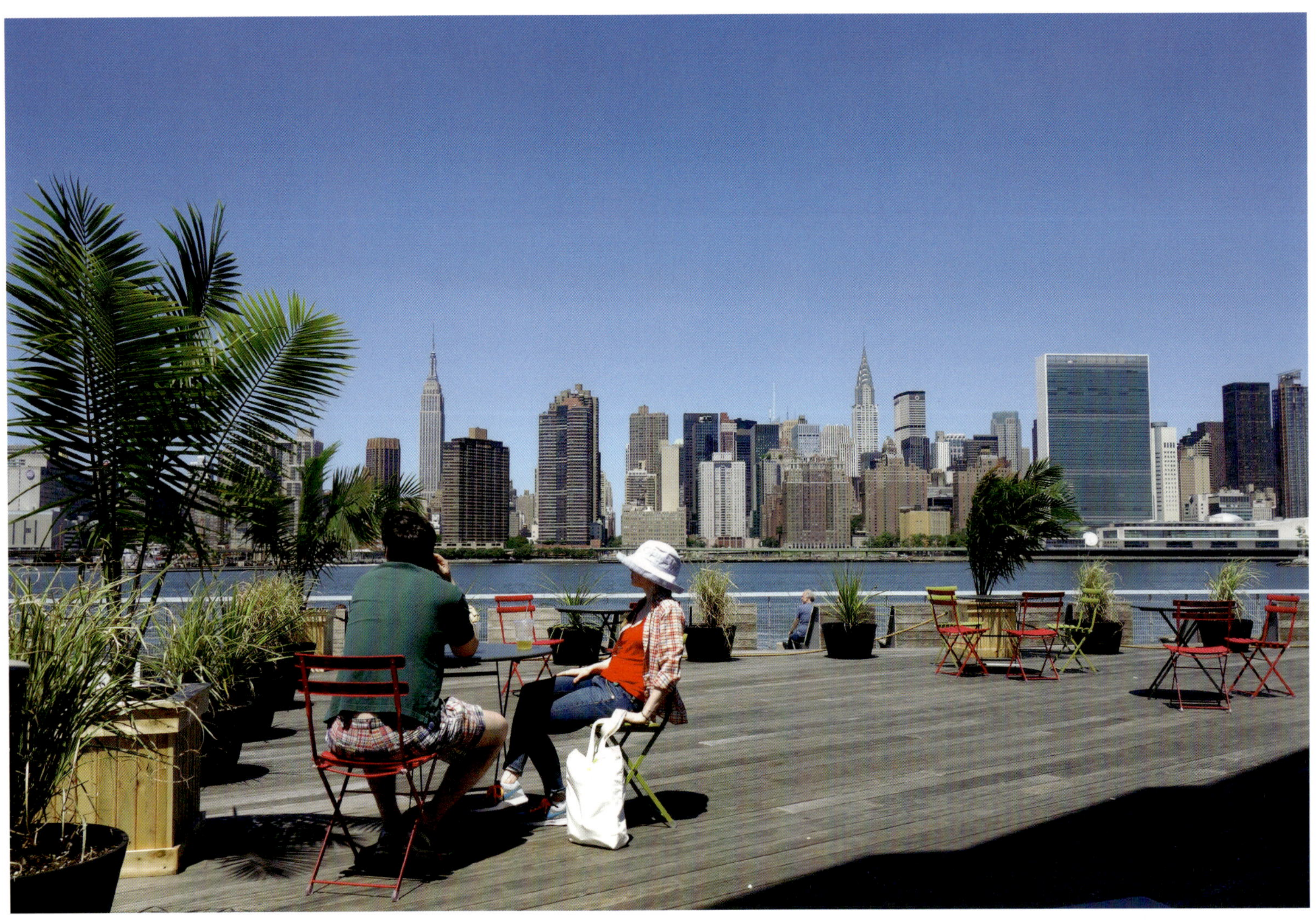

View of Manhattan from Long Island City

The Waterfront Promenade at Hunters Point South Park in Long Island City offers one of the grandest vistas of the Manhattan skyline. At left, the Empire State Building marks 34th Street in Manhattan, while the iconic spire of the Chrysler Building rises at 42nd Street, and the United Nations compound stretches from 42nd to 47th Street facing the East River. For much of the twentieth century, this waterfront area just north of Newtown Creek included docks, gantries, and staging grounds for industrial operations. City officials transformed the area into a park between 2008 and 2018, working with designs by Thomas Balsley Associates and Weiss/Manfredi.

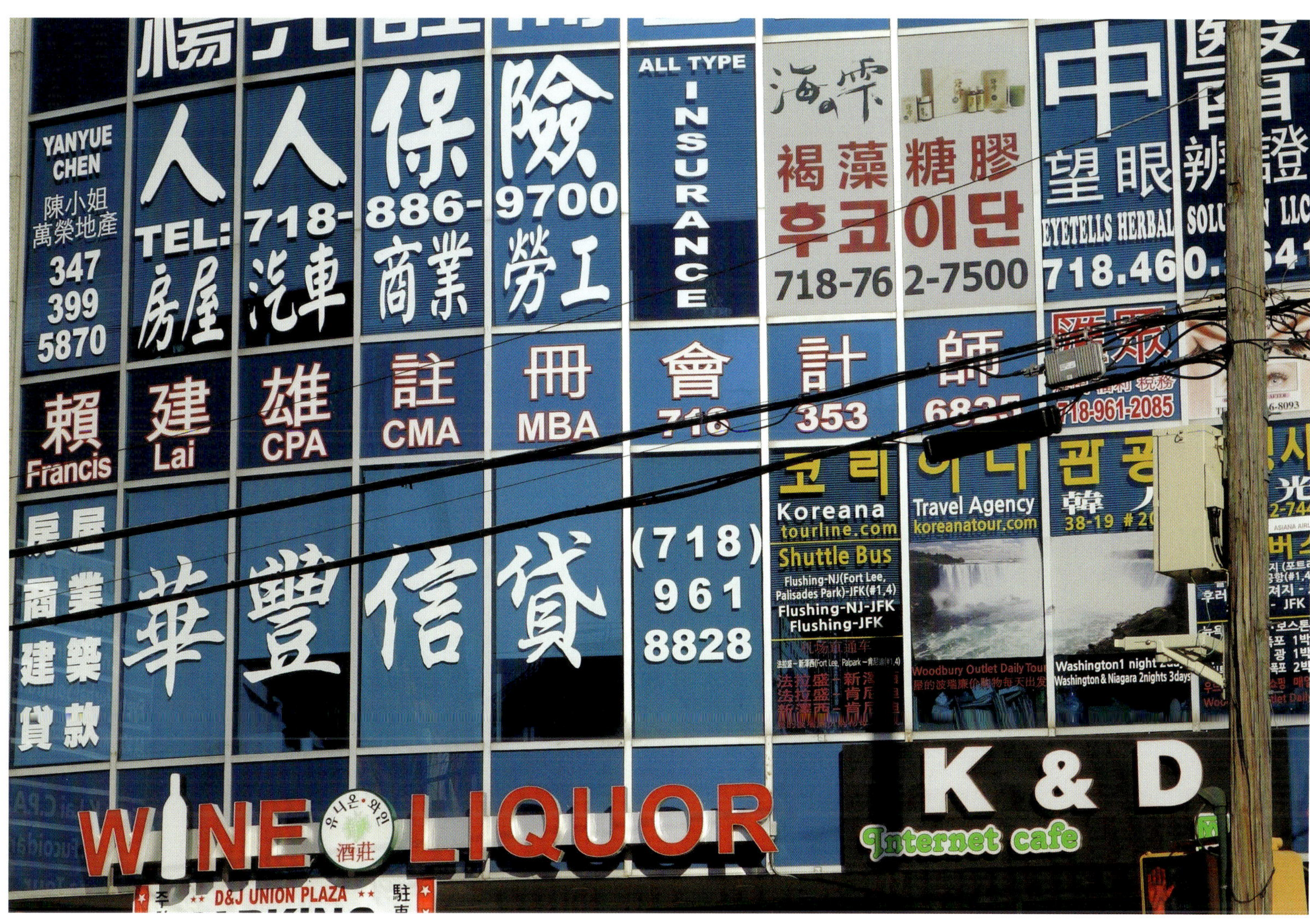

Office building in Flushing

Chinese and Korean businesses advertise their services on the glass façade of this office building at Union Street and 39th Avenue in Flushing. Flushing's downtown Asian community was predominantly Mainland Chinese and Korean in the 1960s and 1970s. In the 1980s, immigrants from Taiwan, Hong Kong, and Fujian province began moving to New York City, many settling in Flushing. Meanwhile, Korean families started their long trek eastward in the 1990s and 2000s, moving to Auburndale, Murray Hill, and Bayside, along with more affluent Chinese families. Today, the reach of their companies is both local and global, enhanced by strong connections to East Asian financial markets.

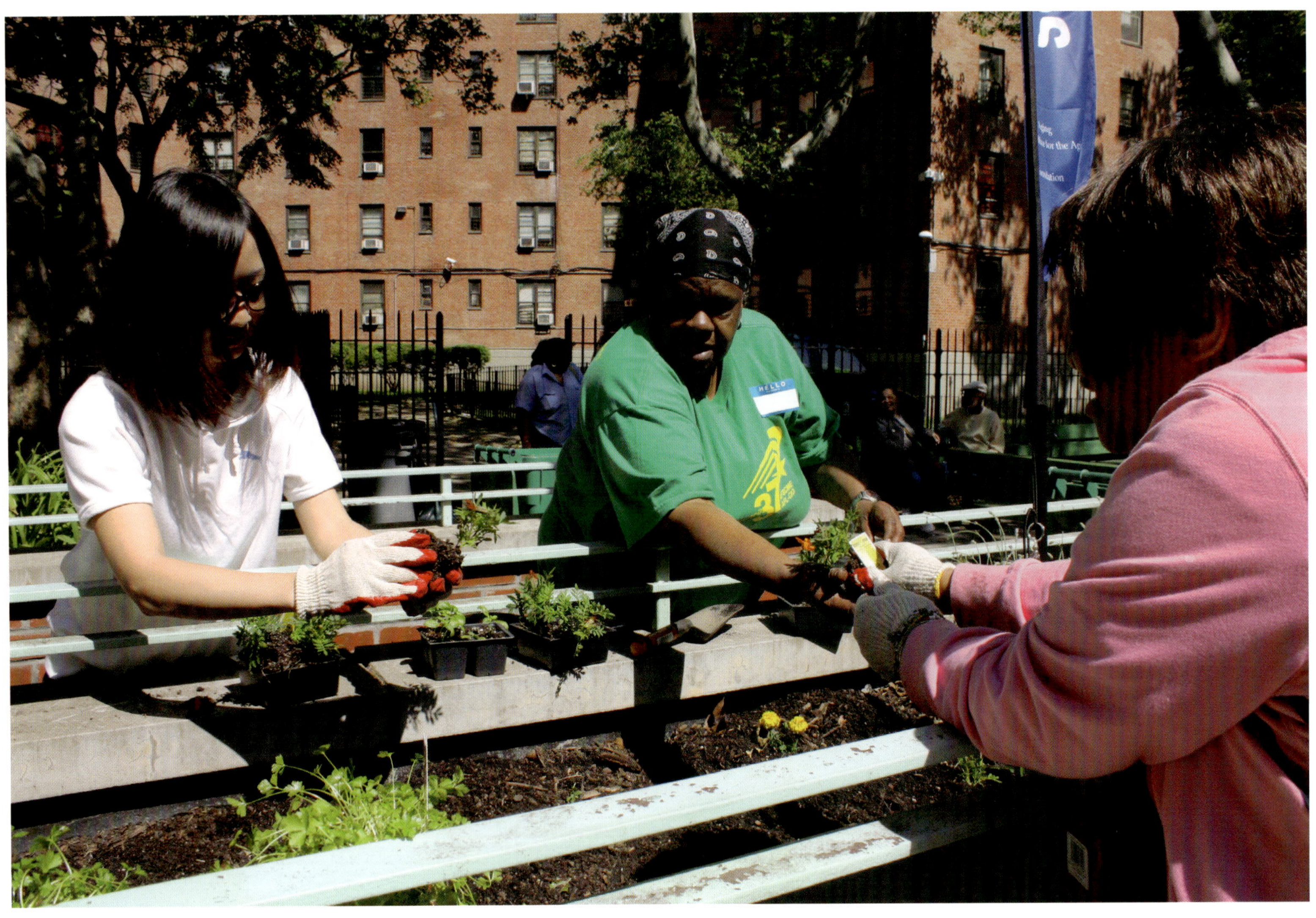

Gardening at Queensbridge Houses

Residents of Queensbridge Houses lay out herbs in a planter at the Jacob Riis Community Center. The center runs various programs for children, teens, and elderly residents. Opened in 1939, Queensbridge is the largest public housing complex in the nation, with 3,142 units spread through 96 buildings. Though the population of Queensbridge is diverse, it is home to a large population of African American families, many of whom migrated from the Southern United States after World War II. They brought language, foodways, and horticultural knowledge from rural areas of Georgia, Florida, Virginia, and the Carolinas, remaking the culture of the borough in the process.

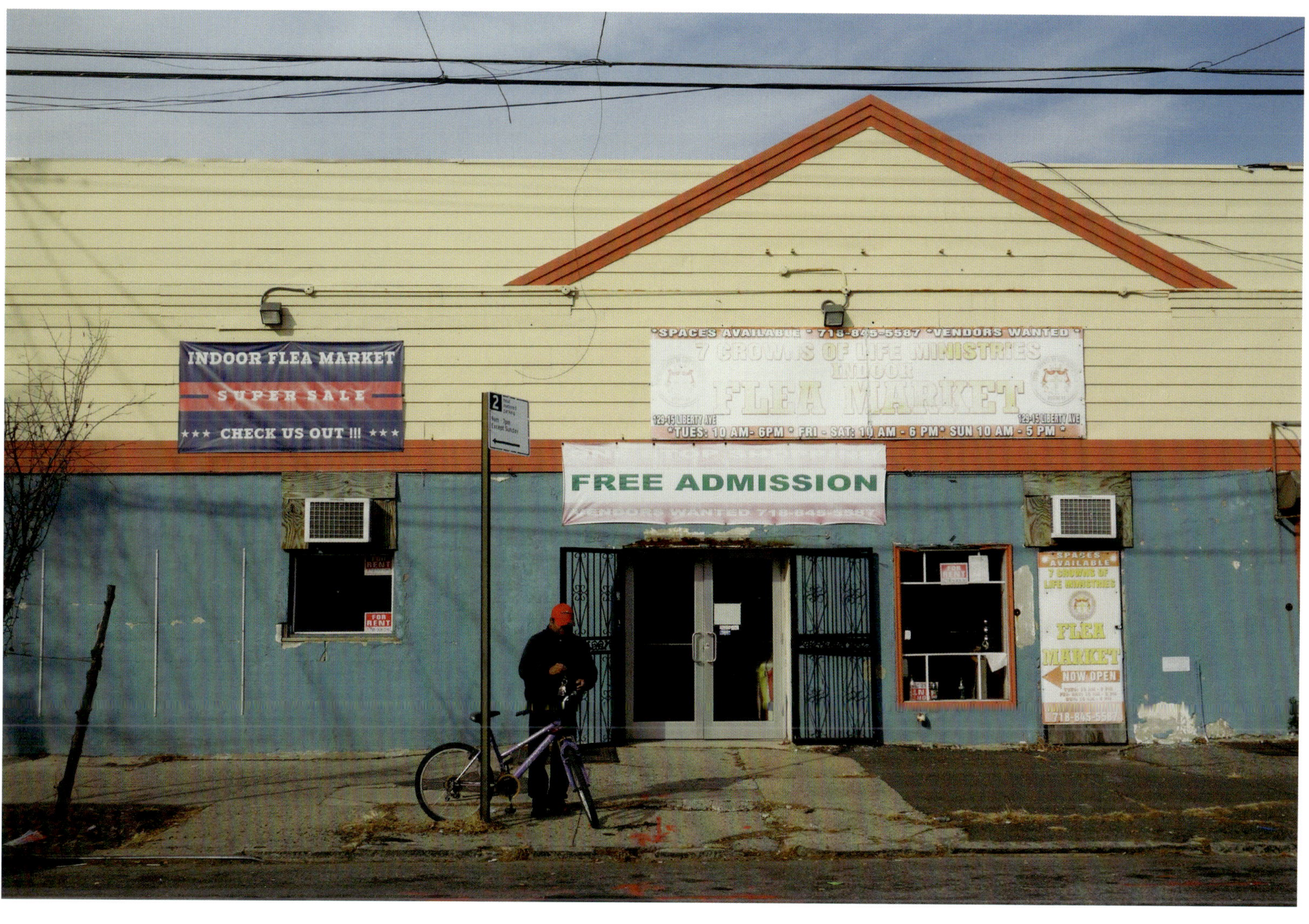

Flea market, Richmond Hill

Flea markets can be found in most immigrant and working-class communities, selling a mix of new and used items on the cheap. Some operate privately on a for-profit basis, while others support churches and nonprofit groups. Most are organized on a concessionary basis, where separate vendors pay a fee for using the space. Many flea markets set up as annual or monthly events in outdoor spaces, such as churchyards and parking lots. Others set up in adapted buildings; the flea market shown here, for example, operates out of a former grocery store that also served for many years as an Evangelical church.

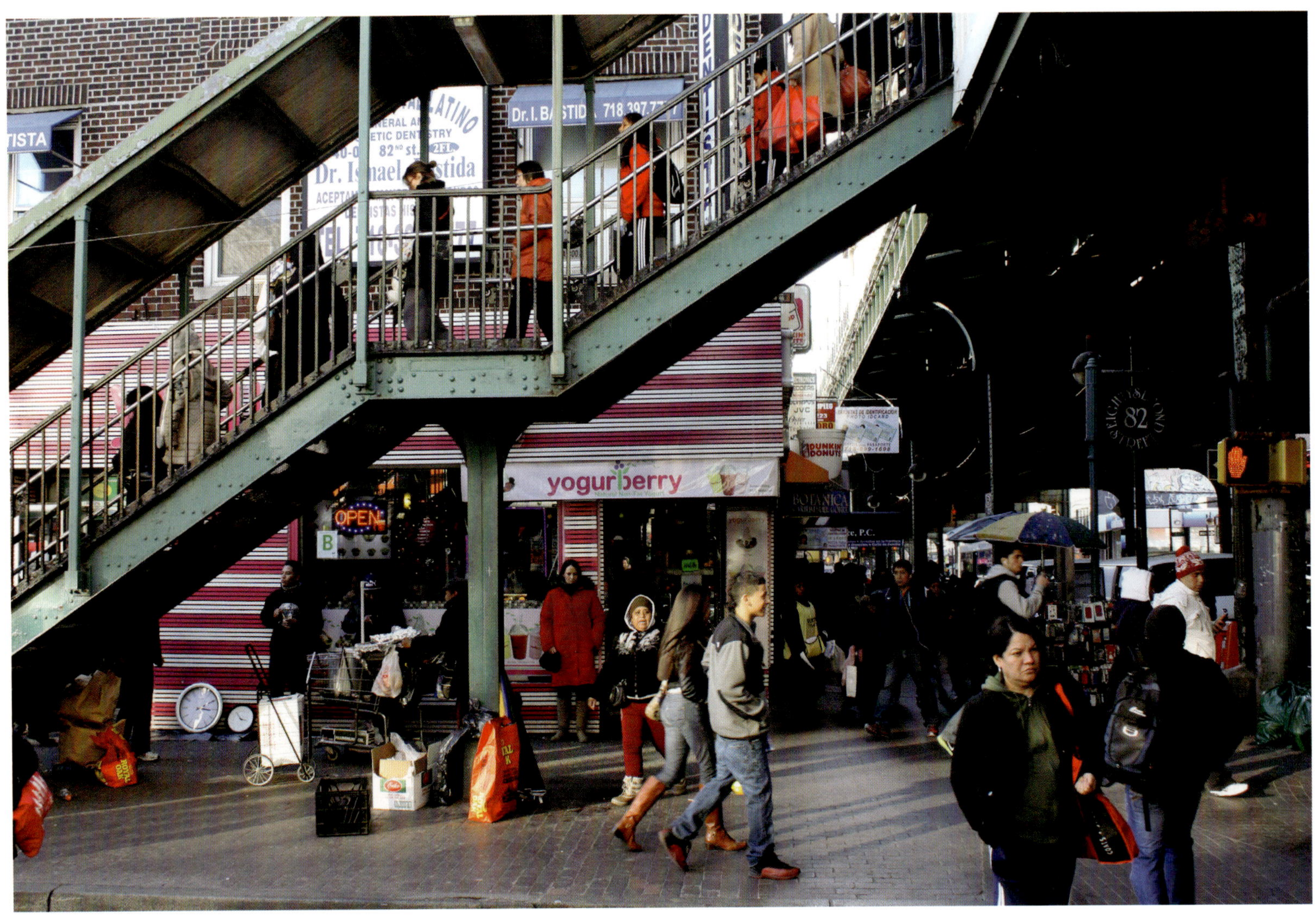

MTA infrastructure in Queens

The Metropolitan Transportation Authority (MTA) operates eleven train lines that pass through Queens, both elevated and underground, with local and express services stopping at a total of eighty-one stations. The oldest line is the M train extension from Brooklyn, which reached Middle Village, Queens, in 1906. However, it was the 7 train that opened up large areas of the borough for rapid development in the 1910s and 1920s, and that has long served as the lifeline of immigrant communities. With so much wear and tear as the system ages and funding remains scarce, the infrastructure of both elevated and underground trains is worn down. The system is in a state of constant repair as the MTA upgrades signals and switches, replaces tracks, and scrapes away decades of corrosion.

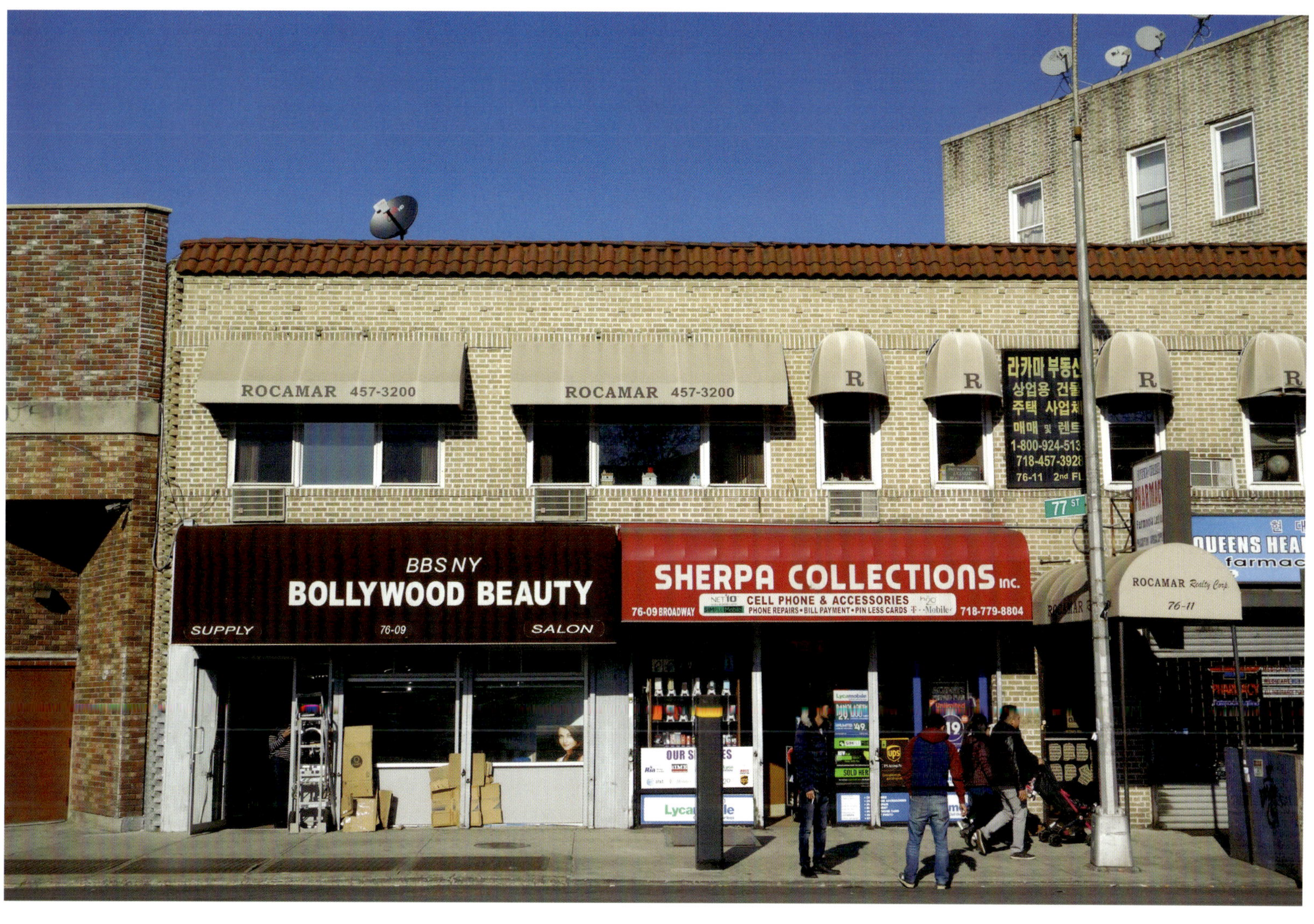

Bollywood beauty, Elmhurst

Indian, Nepalese, and Korean businesses cluster on Broadway at 77th Street. With seven out of ten people hailing from outside the United States, Elmhurst has the highest proportion of foreign-born residents of any neighborhood in New York City. Tibetan and Nepalese immigrants constitute the latest group of newcomers, bringing their languages, cultures, foodways, and religious institutions to the community. Some Tibetans migrated directly from Tibet, and others from Nepal, India, and China. Many Nepalese came from areas devastated by the 2015 earthquake. Over the last decade, they have established numerous restaurants, groceries, and service organizations.

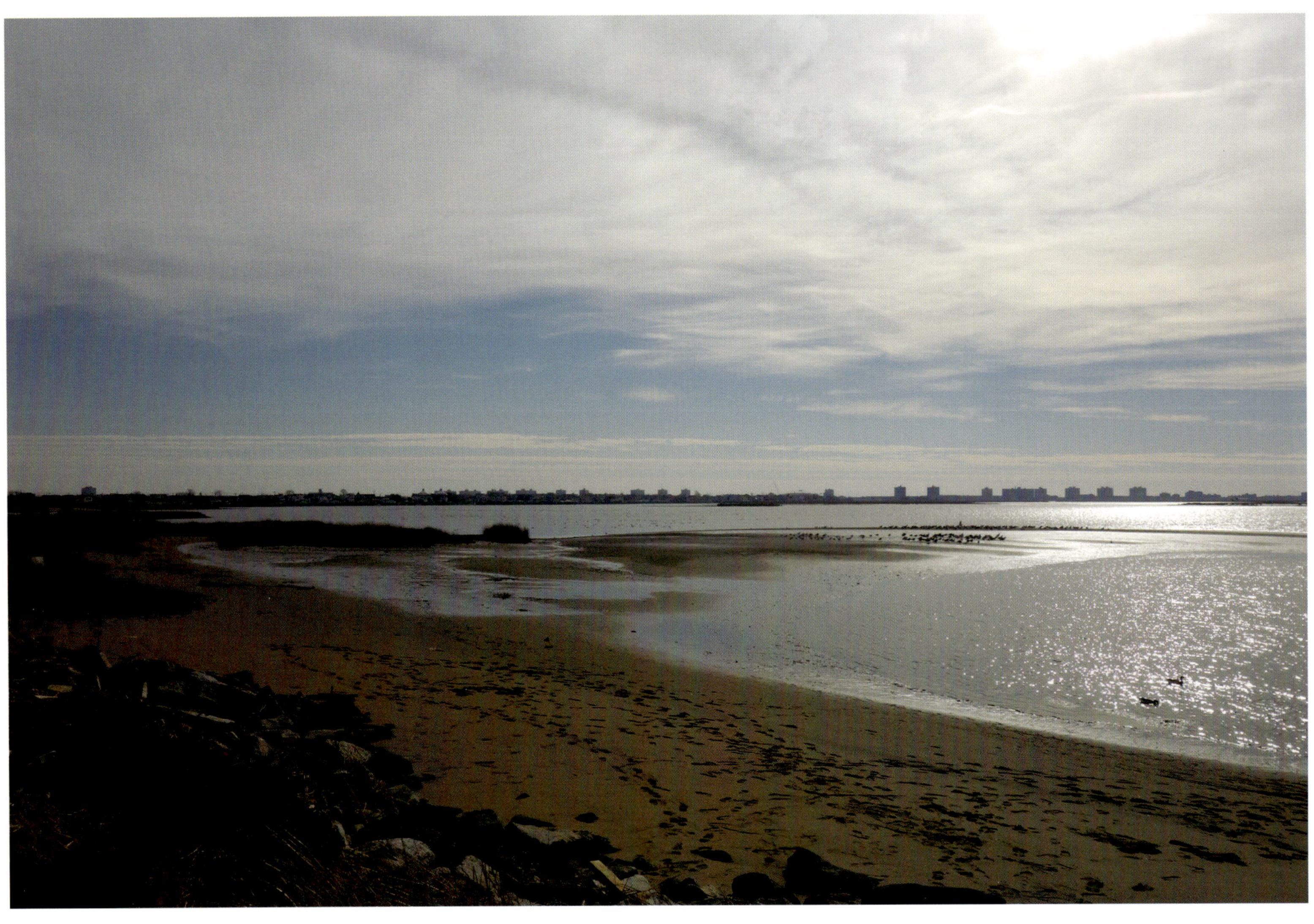

Vistas of a liquid city

New York City sits in a tidal estuary where the Hudson River brings fresh water into the swirling currents of the Atlantic Ocean. As the waters move around Manhattan, Staten Island, Rockaway Peninsula, Long Island, and other land masses in the estuary, it forms bodies of water that interact in complex ways with the 520-mile coastline. Out of all the boroughs, Queens has the longest coastline, defined by numerous watercourses, bays, and inlets. To the west lies the East River and Newtown Creek. Flushing Bay, Long Island Sound, and Kissena River shaped the north of the borough. And along the south coast, creeks and rivulets empty into Jamaica Bay and the Atlantic Ocean.

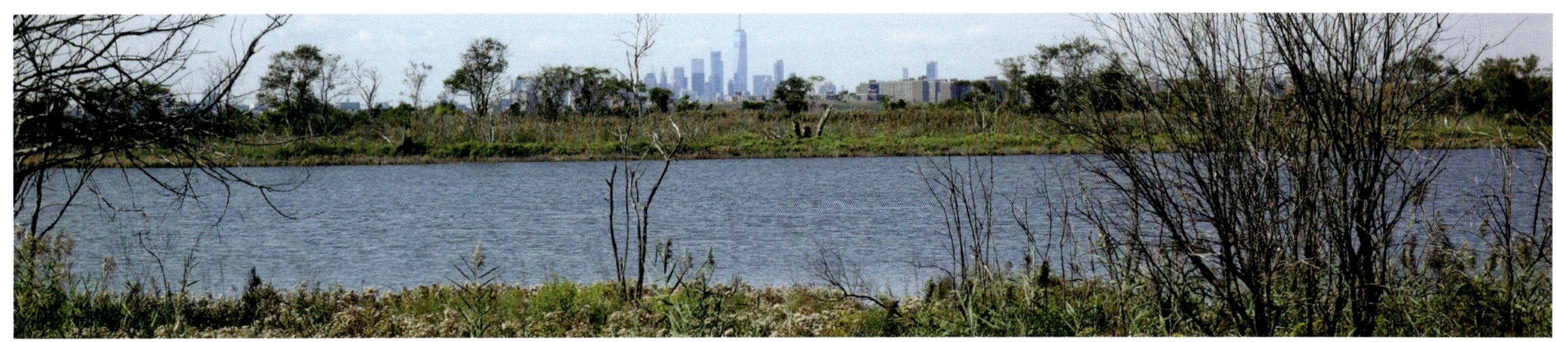

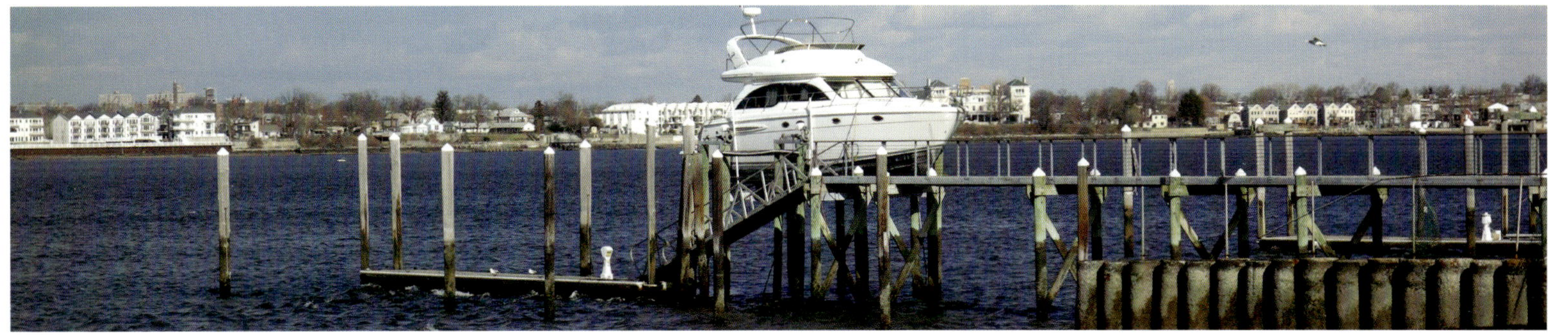

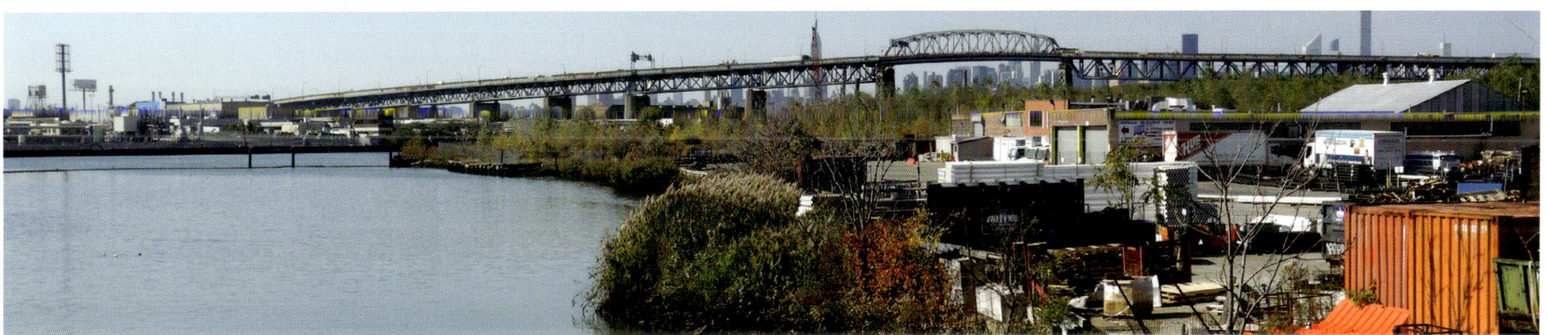

Opposite page: Beach in Jamaica Bay. The bay is a large bowl formed behind Rockaway Peninsula, with a brackish marshland ecology. It is home to many keystone species of the area, such as the diamondback terrapin, horseshoe crab, heron, and osprey. Today it is part of the Jamaica Bay Wildlife Refuge, established by the National Park Service in 1972. This page, top: Marshland shore in Jamaica Bay, with the towers of Manhattan rising in the distance. Middle: A lone boat sits at a marina in Whitestone Cove at the northern tip of Queens, looking north across the East River Sound toward the Bronx. Bottom: Edge of Newtown Creek looking east from Grant Street in Maspeth toward the old Kosciuszko Bridge, which was replaced in 2017.

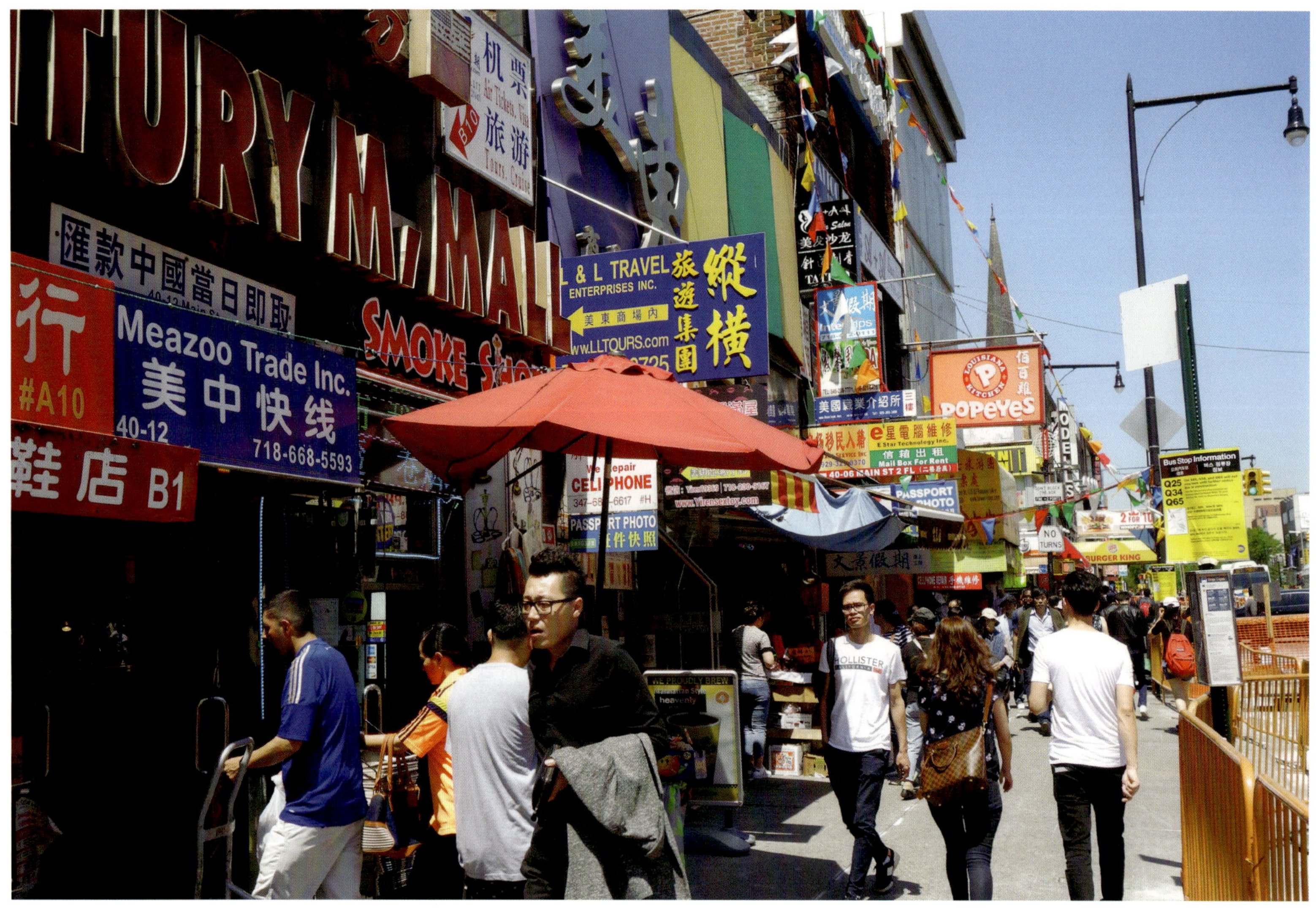

The texture of Flushing Main Street

Main Street in Flushing is a bustling commercial thoroughfare of restaurants, groceries, dry goods stores, bakeries, travel and tax services, apothecaries, and electronics shops. Vendors set up tables to sell clothes, snacks, trinkets, Chinese language books, and other goods up and down the street. As a result, the sidewalks are frequently very crowded, especially during rush hour. While Manhattan has the oldest Chinatown in the city, Flushing is the largest with more than 30,000 Chinese and Chinese Americans. Queens as a whole is home to 235,000 people from Mainland China, Hong Kong, and Taiwan, giving it the highest population of Chinese people in the Western Hemisphere.

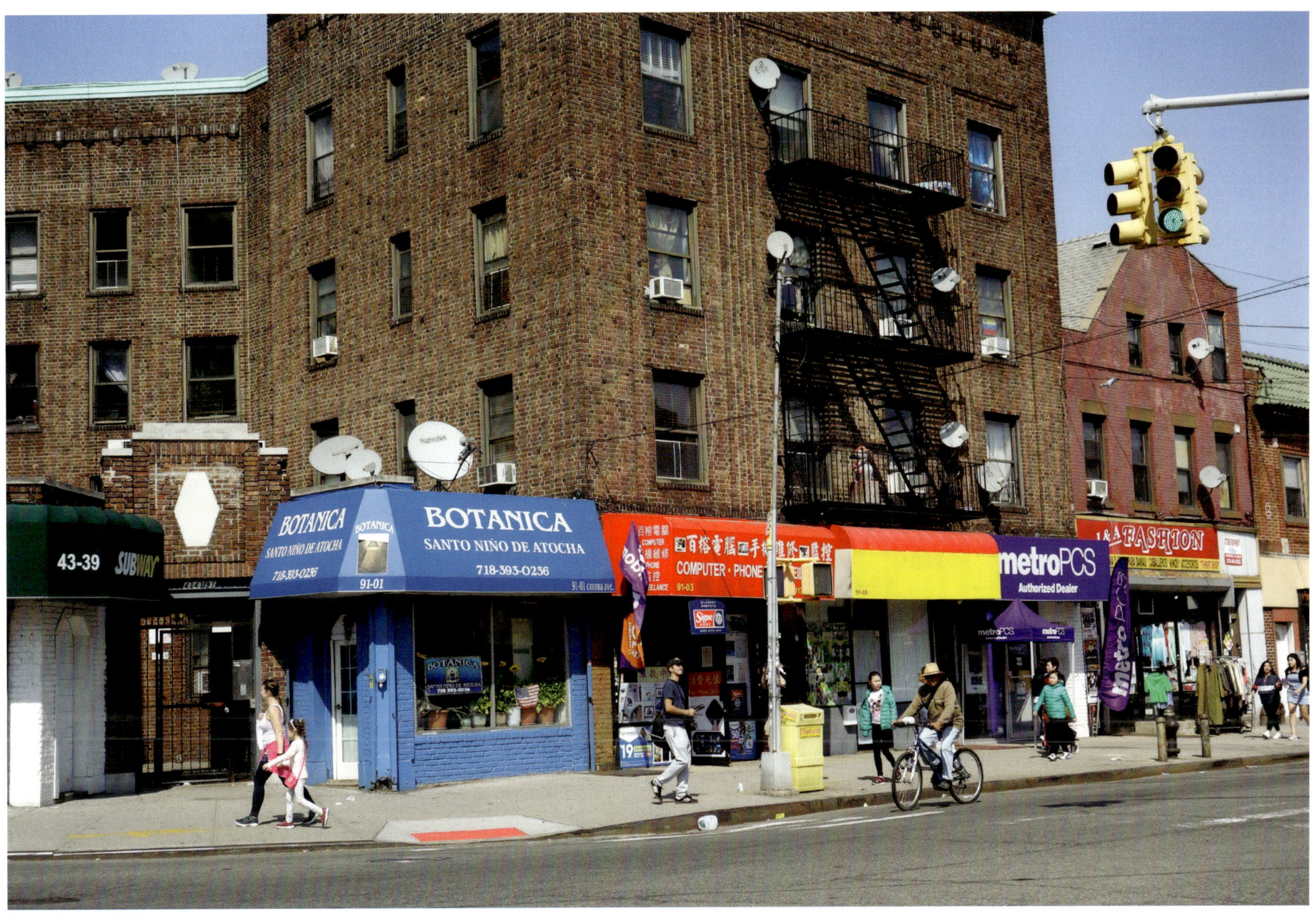

Apartment block and shops in Elmhurst

The large apartment block at 91st Place and Corona Avenue is typical of the housing stock in Elmhurst. The buildings range from four to six stories, with small units of two or three bedrooms and ground-floor shops on the commercial streets. Botanica Santo Niño de Atocha is one of many serving the Mexican, Central, and South American communities in the area. Unlike Jackson Heights just to the north, Elmhurst never developed many cooperatives. Consequently, more than three-quarters of the residents are renters. With rents rising, tenants have formed stronger associations to hold landlords accountable and protect rent-stabilized buildings.

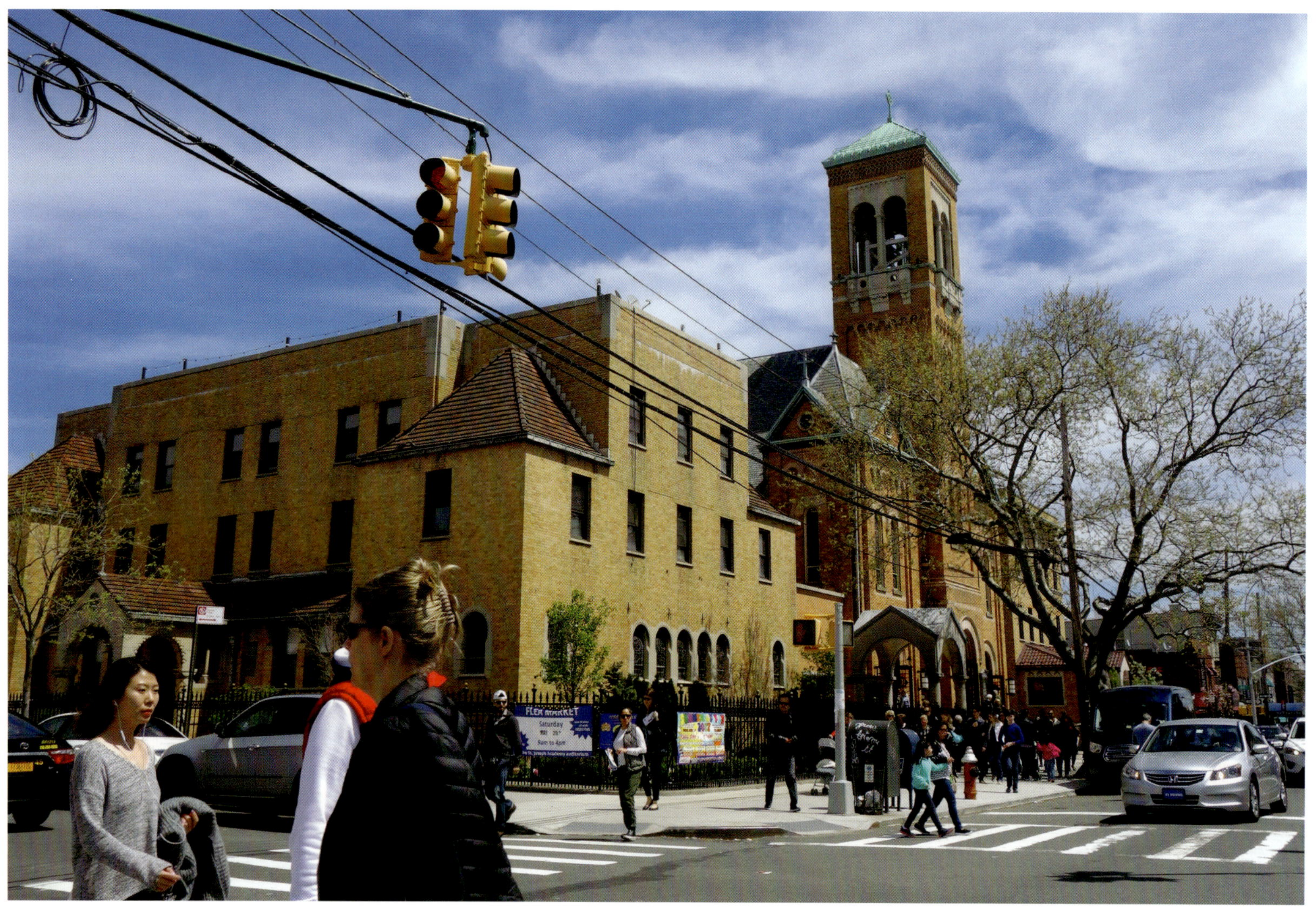

Sunday afternoon in Astoria

On a calm spring afternoon in Astoria, the Italianate spire of St. Joseph Roman Catholic Church rises along 30th Avenue between 43rd and 44th Streets, and people walk about in light jackets. The London Plane tree on the right is just starting to bud. Worshippers gather in front of the church after mass before going about their day. Astoria's large Greek population is predominantly Orthodox, but several Roman Catholic parishes in the neighborhood serve a mixed population of Greek, East Asian, and Latino Catholics. There is also a small population of Byzantine Catholics, though their only churches are located in Manhattan, Yonkers, and New Jersey.

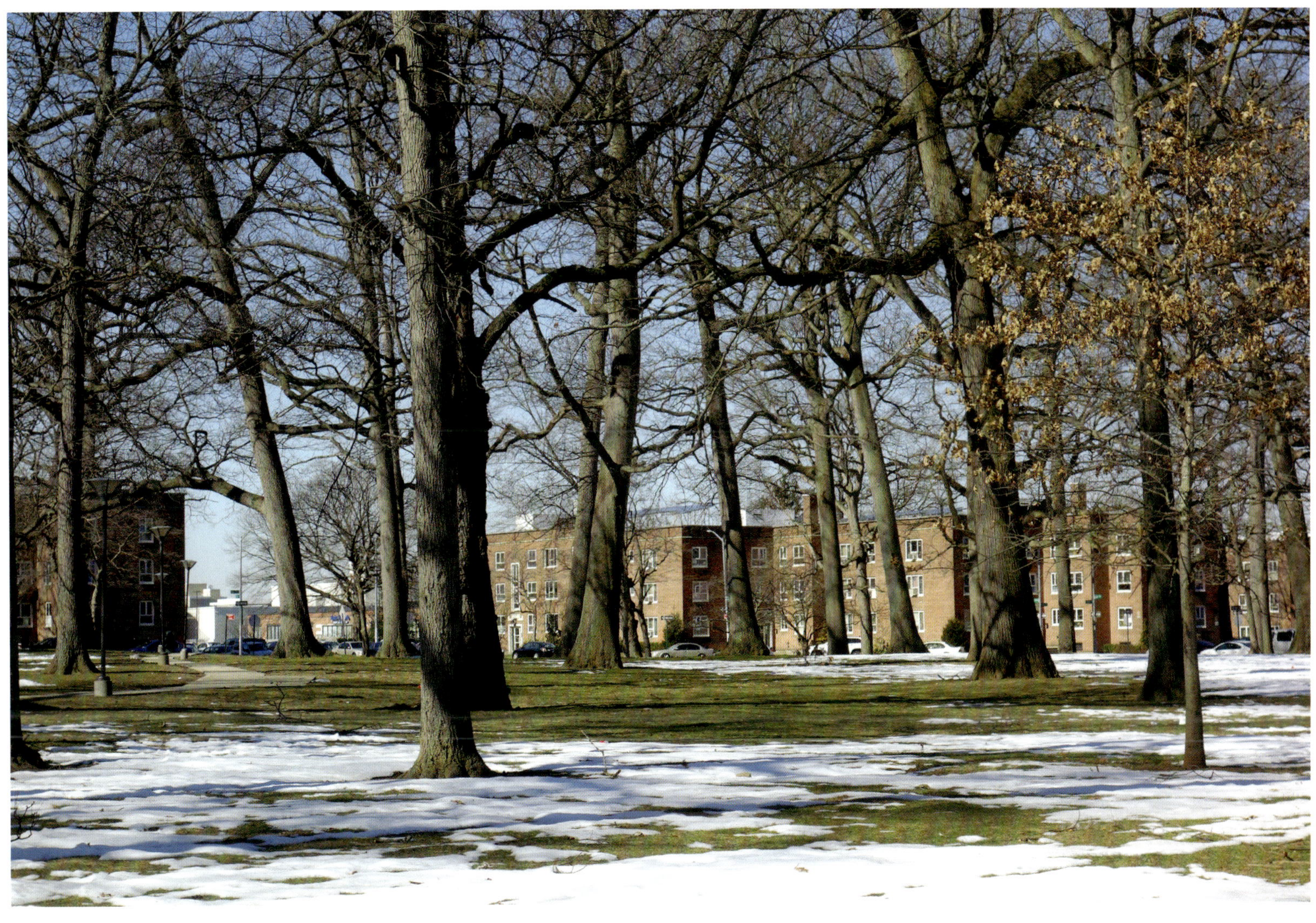

Oak Grove Park, Fresh Meadows

Oak Grove is a six-acre park in Fresh Meadows with an impressive stand of old oak trees. The area was forest and farmland until the twentieth century when a group of Brooklyn investors established the Fresh Meadows Country Club. In 1946, the New York Life Insurance Company purchased the club's land, and in the next twenty years, they built a planned community of row houses, mid-rise apartment buildings, and high-rise towers surrounded by green spaces and a nearby shopping center. As with many postwar developments, it carried racial covenants restricting occupancy to White families, which civil rights organizations fought for decades. Today, Whites make up less than a third of the population that is predominantly South and East Asian.

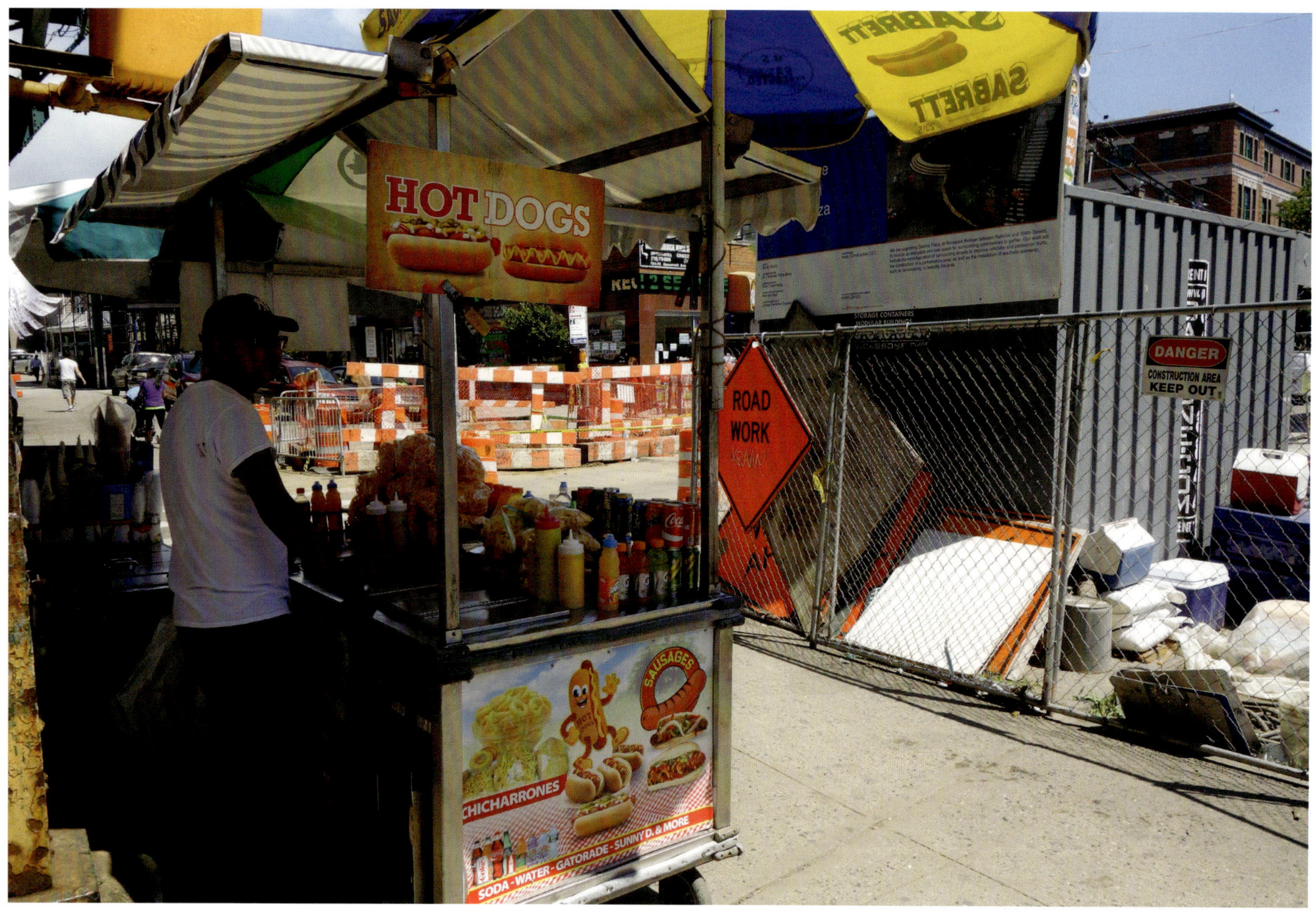

Street vendor in Corona

On a hot summer day in Corona, this vendor sells hot dogs, chicharrones, ice cream, and paletas under the shade of the 7 train. He must deal with noise and dust from the construction of the new pedestrian plaza between 103rd and 104th Streets. Thousands of residents in Queens work in the mobile food industry, including food trucks, carts, and deliverers. It is one of the most common entry-level positions available to new immigrants in the borough, whether the vendor owns or rents the cart or works for someone who owns or rents it. The city regulates such operations through both the Health and Transportation Departments, and vendors are required to have licenses, though many operate informally.

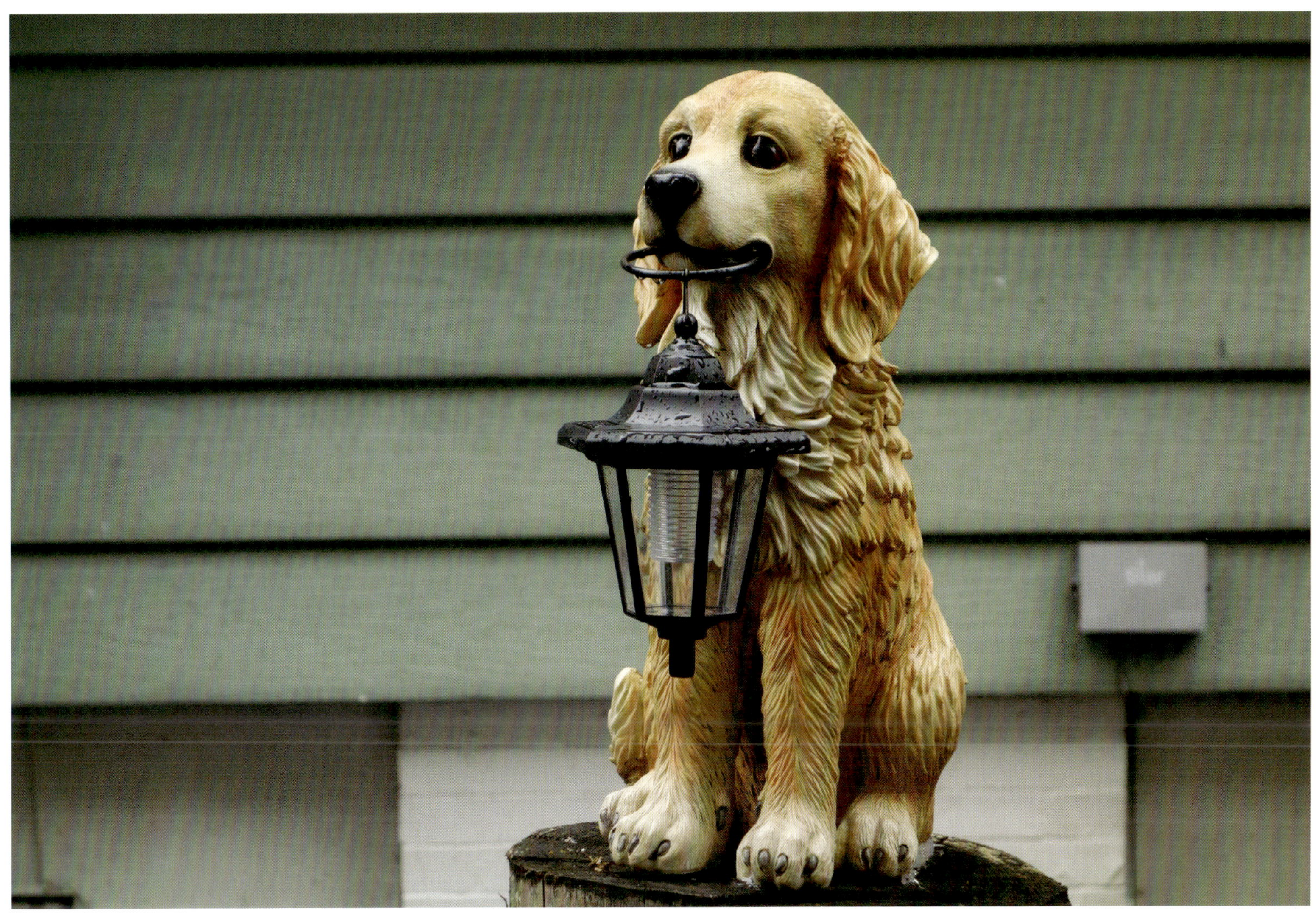

Keeping watch, Ridgewood

Working-class German and Polish families dominated Ridgewood for much of the twentieth century. Since the 1960s, newcomers from Puerto Rico, Dominican Republic, and the former Yugoslavia moved in. Meanwhile, just across Cypress Avenue, the Bushwick neighborhood remained predominantly African American and Afro-Caribbean. After the infamous blackout of 1977, Ridgewood residents appealed for a separate zip code to dissociate themselves from Bushwick, bringing to a head the long-standing White racial animosity. Even today, only 2 percent of the residents identify as Black, while 40 percent identify as White, though Spanish-speaking households now outnumber all others.

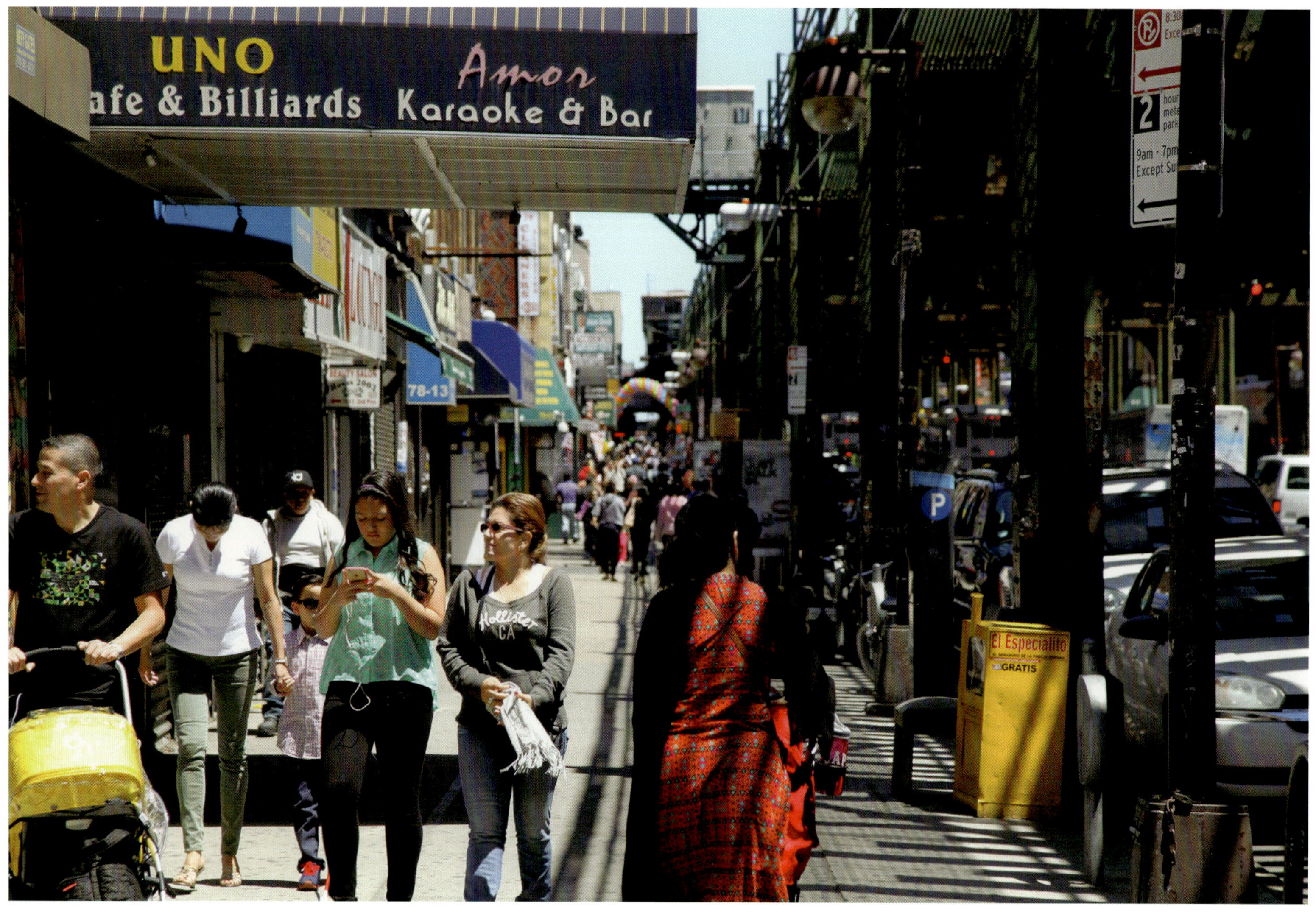

Sidewalk along Roosevelt Avenue

Roosevelt Avenue is a very different street by day and night. During the day, its broad sidewalks provide space for people strolling along or hustling to and from trains, buses, cabs, and delivery trucks. Shop owners hand out fliers while street vendors call out their wares, and delivery workers thread the crowds with their scooters and handcarts. At night, Latin dance clubs like Amor draw large crowds of gay, straight, trade, and transgender patrons. An entirely different group of food vendors set up at night, selling arepas and other snacks. As the clubs wind down in the small hours of the night, the sidewalks fill with revelers, prostitutes, johns, and cab drivers waiting for fares.

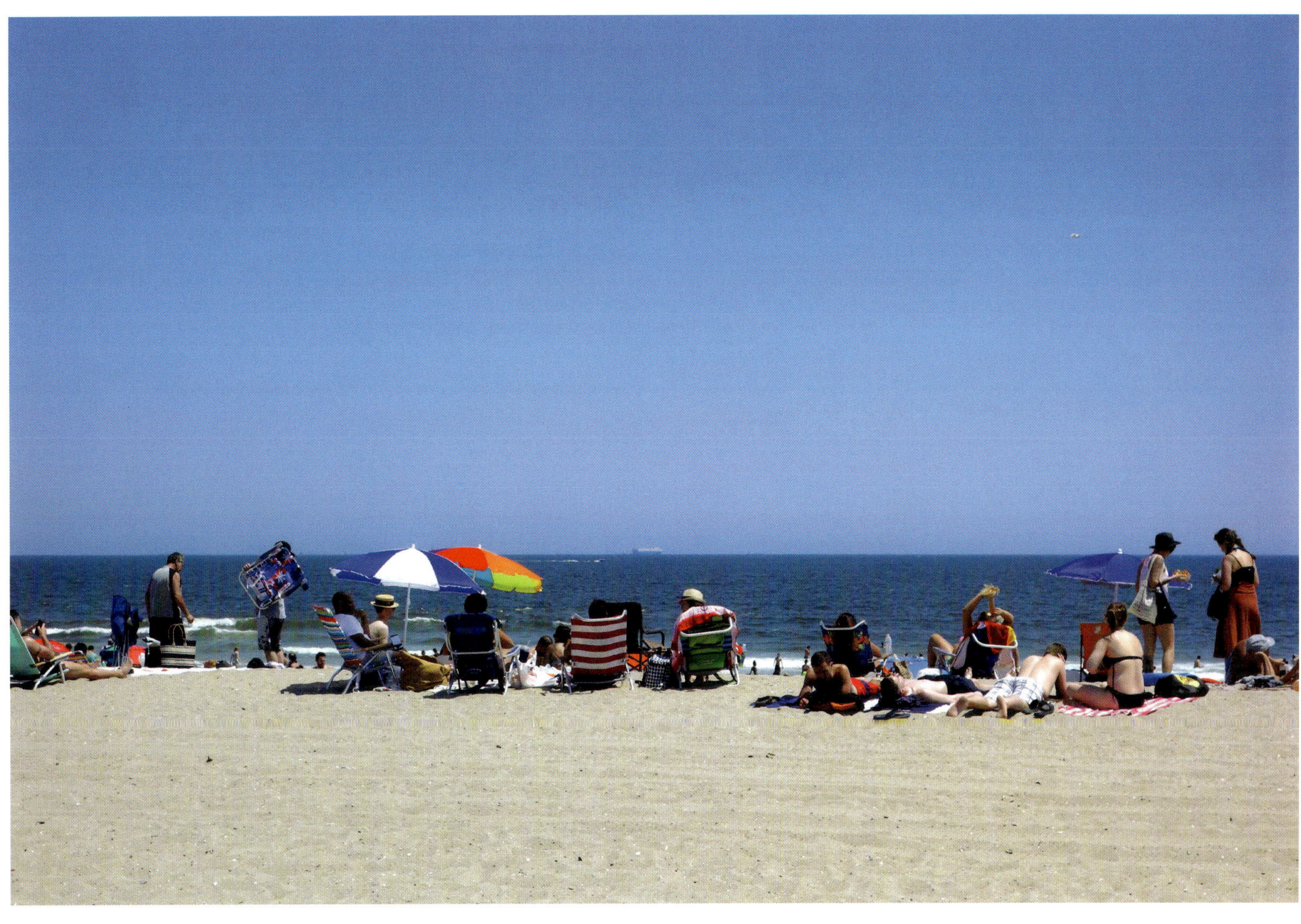

Rockaway Beach

Made famous in song by the Ramones, Rockaway Beach has been a destination for overheated residents of Queens since the early twentieth century. The coastline was a main resource for the Lenape people, who taught Dutch and English colonists the fine arts of fishing and oyster harvesting. Small villages and resorts cropped up in the nineteenth century, but it was not until the twentieth century that Rockaway began to take its current form. The Parks Department completed the beach and boardwalk in stages between the 1920s and the 1960s, replacing the wooden boardwalk with concrete after Hurricane Sandy. Today the beach stretches for seven miles along the peninsular coast and the open waters of the Atlantic Ocean.

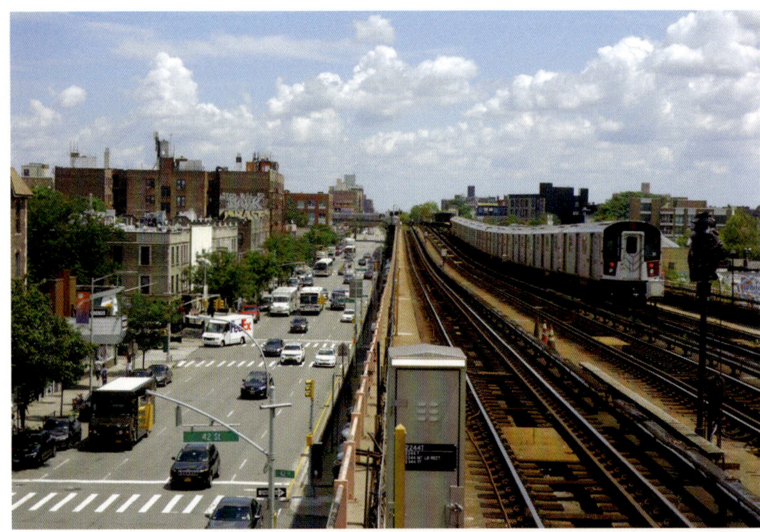

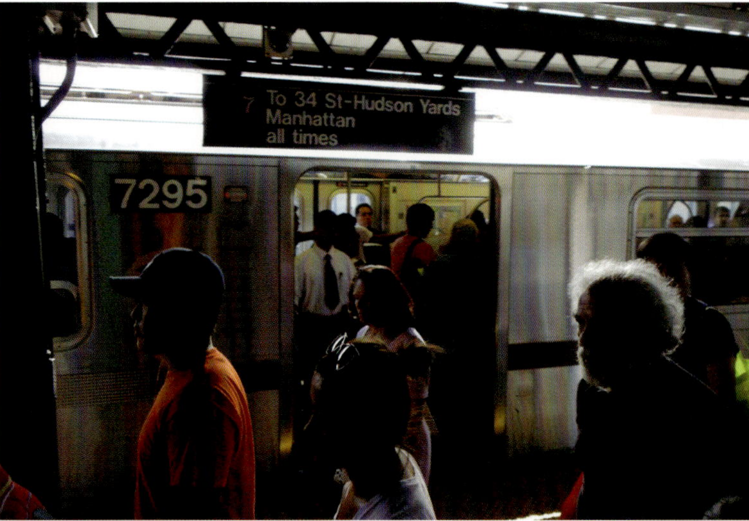

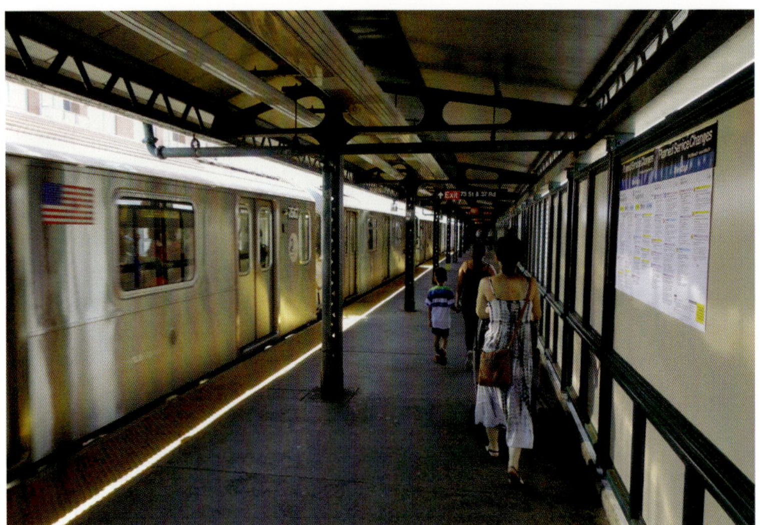

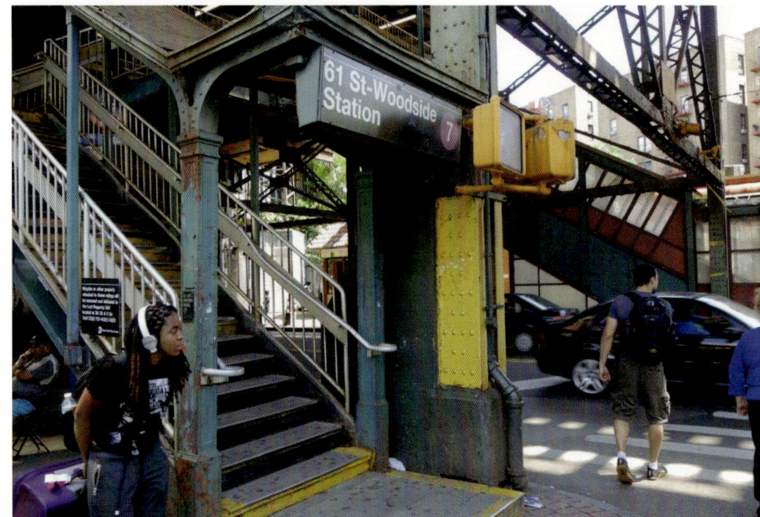

The 7 train

Figures 19a–19h. Often called "the international express," the Interborough Rapid Transit (IRT) Flushing Line—today's 7 train—has served generations of immigrants from around the world and remains the lifeblood of Western Queens. Built between 1912 and 1928, it was the first train to connect Queens directly to Manhattan via the East River tunnel. The IRT was consolidated with all other lines in 1940 under the city's Board of Transportation and then under the MTA in 1953. It runs local and express lines above Queens Boulevard and Roosevelt Avenue, with eighteen stations between Long Island City and Flushing. In 1999, the Clinton Administration designated the 7 train a "National Millennial Trail."

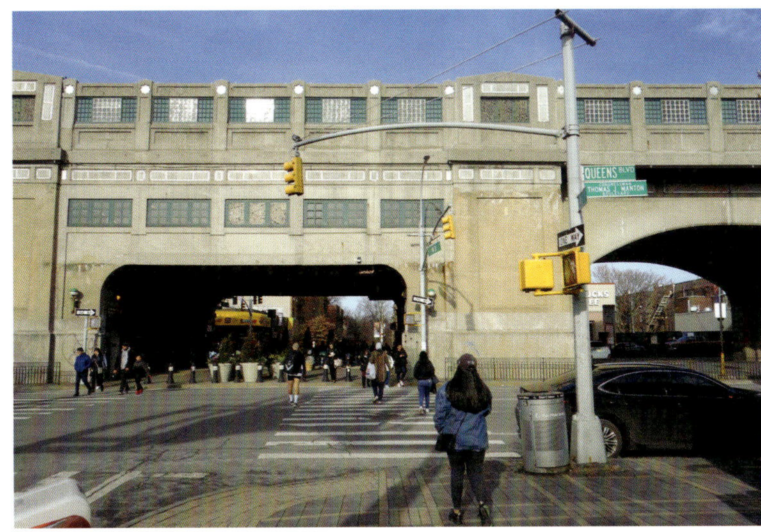

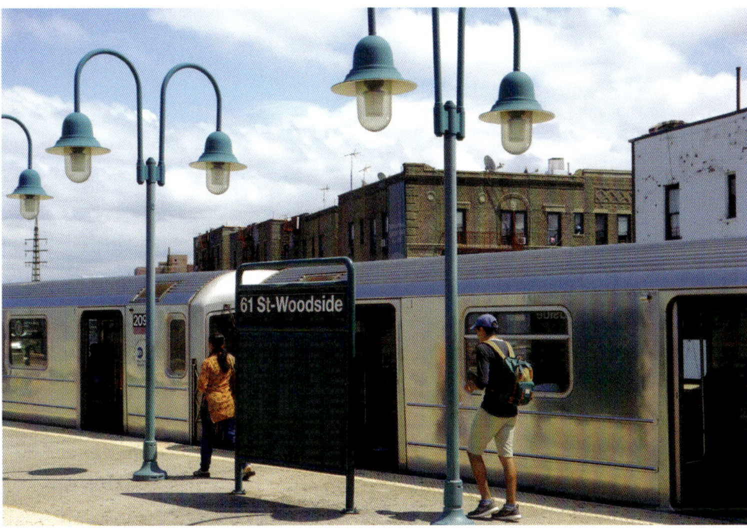

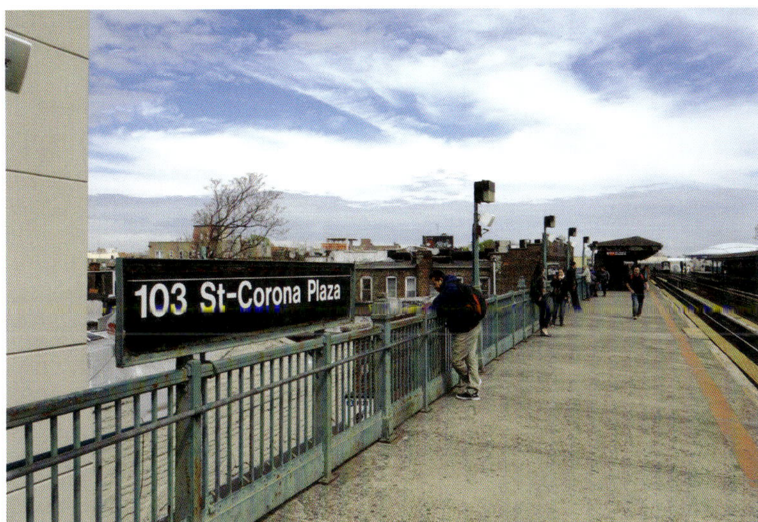

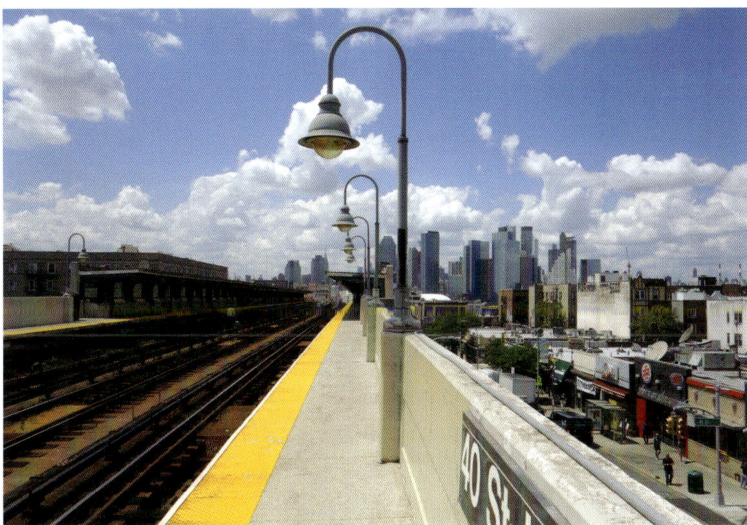

Opposite page, top left: View of an eastbound train leaving the 40th Street–Lowery Street station. Top right: Passengers at 74th Street–Roosevelt Avenue station in Jackson Heights. Bottom left: Exiting the 74th Street–Roosevelt Avenue station via 73rd Street. The dreaded "planned service changes" poster is on the right. Bottom right: Staircase to the station at 61st Street–Woodside. This page, top left: The massive concrete viaduct carries the 7 train along Queens Boulevard, seen here at the 46th Street–Bliss Street station in Sunnyside. Top right: Train waiting in the station at 61st Street–Woodside. Bottom left: Platform at 103rd Street–Corona Plaza. Bottom right: Platform at 40th Street–Lowery Street looking west toward Manhattan.

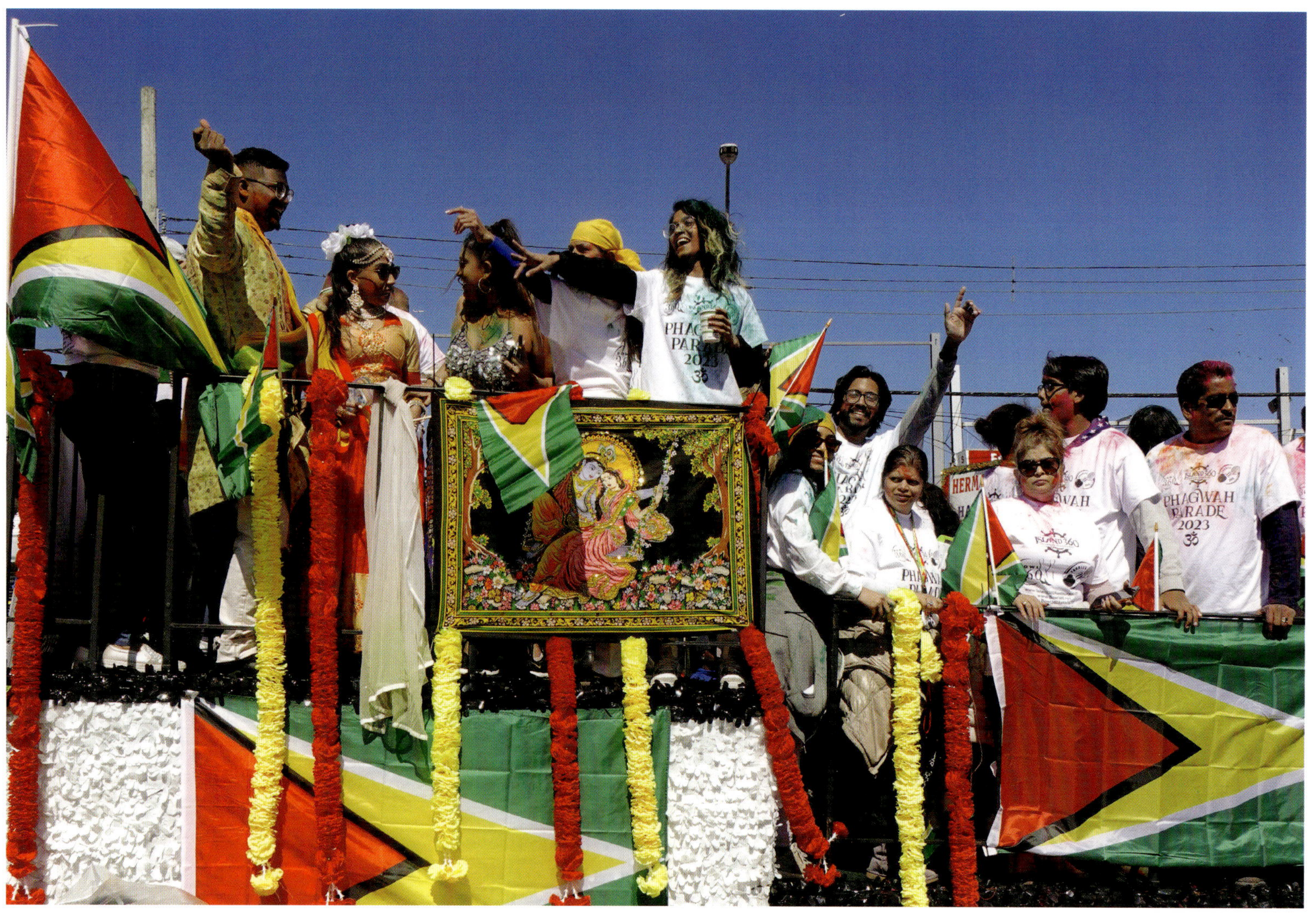

Phagwah Parade, Richmond Hill

For more than three decades, Richmond Hill has hosted the annual Phagwah Parade to celebrate Holi, the festival of color, love, and spring. The parade begins at Liberty Avenue and 133rd Street and proceeds west along Liberty until reaching 125th Street, at which point it turns north and ends at Phil Rizzuto Park. A succession of artfully adorned floats represents local religious, political, and commercial organizations. Throughout the day, revelers throw dyed powders and water on each other in celebration, saturating everyone in a rainbow of colors. For the Indo-Caribbean community, comprising families predominantly from Guyana and Trinidad, the parade has become an important moment to celebrate their diasporic identity.

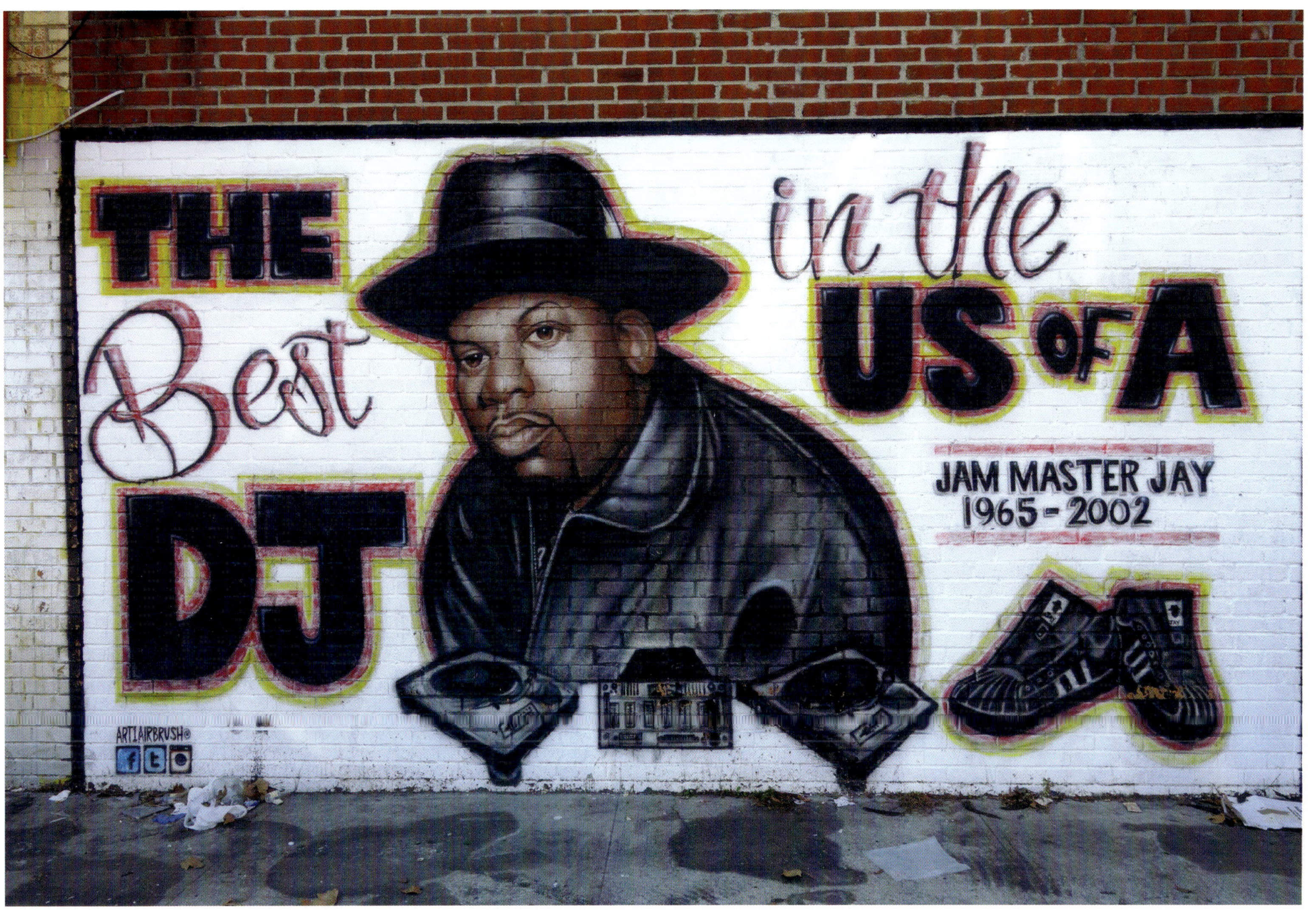

Jam Master Jay mural in Hollis

Hip-hop may have been born in the Bronx, but Queens contributed immensely to its global rise. Jason Mizell, aka Jam Master Jay, was among the great DJs of the age, part of the legendary Run-DMC crew. He was born in Brooklyn, but, like many African American families, his parents sought greener pastures in middle-class Queens. Mizell grew up in Hollis, attended high school in Cambria Heights, and lived in Queens for most of his life. The mural at 205th Street and Hollis Avenue commemorates his life and tragic end when he was shot to death in his recording studio. Run-DMC inspired generations of Queens hip-hop artists such as Roxanne Shanté, Marley Marl, LL Cool J, Nas, Mobb Deep, and 50 Cent.

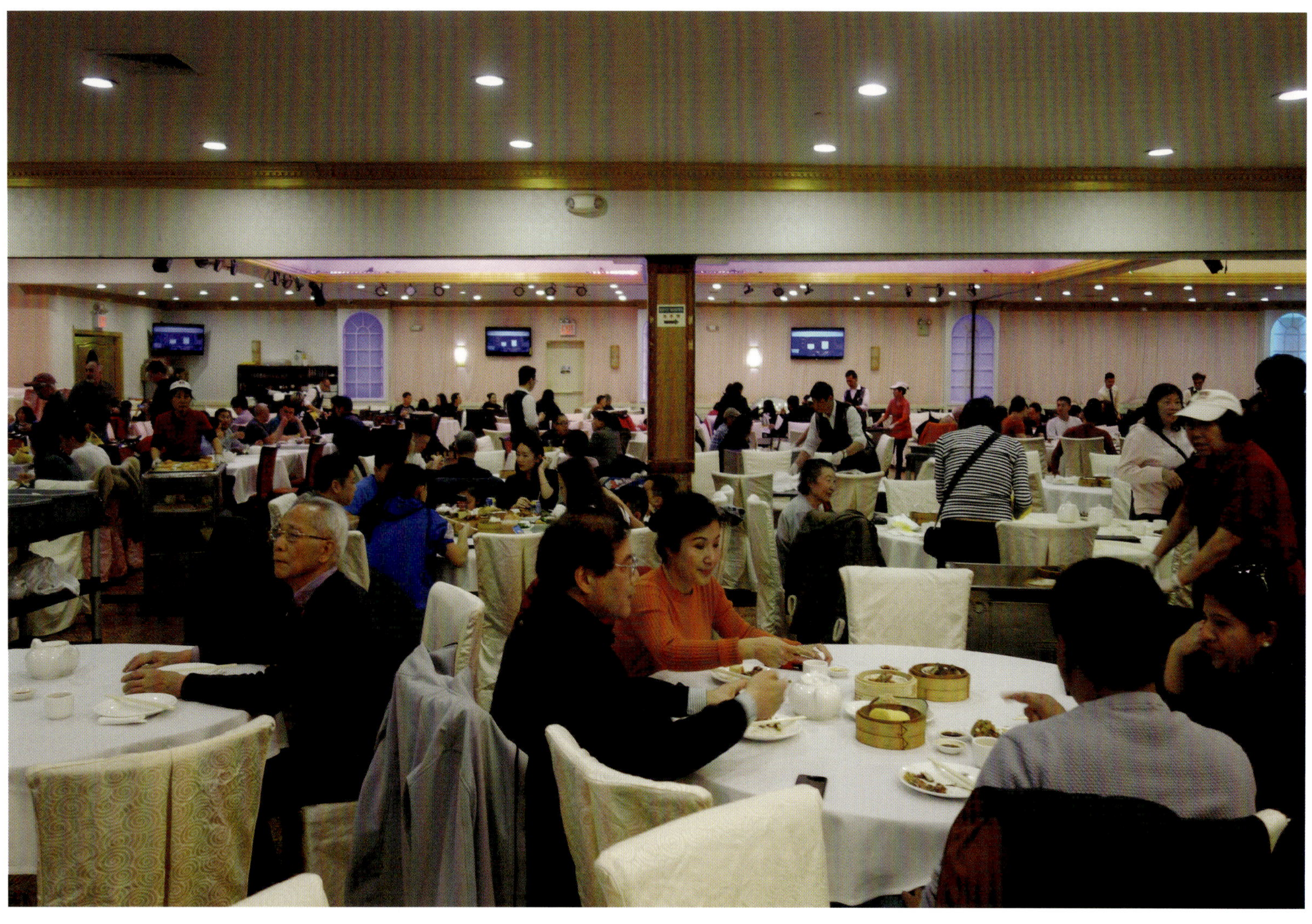

Banquet hall, Flushing

Chinese banquet halls are one of the great institutions of everyday life in New York City and a repository of culinary knowledge and practice. They typically feature a large central dining hall as well as rooms for midsize parties and small, intimate business lunches. Chinese families often hold important celebration meals at banquet halls—especially weddings, birthdays, and graduations. At Good Fortune in Flushing, shown here, patrons enjoy Saturday brunch while servers wheel around carts loaded with dozens of Dim Sum options such as pig's feet, taro dumplings, sticky rice wrapped in lotus leaf, barbecue pork buns, siu mai, scallion pancakes, and short ribs in black bean sauce.

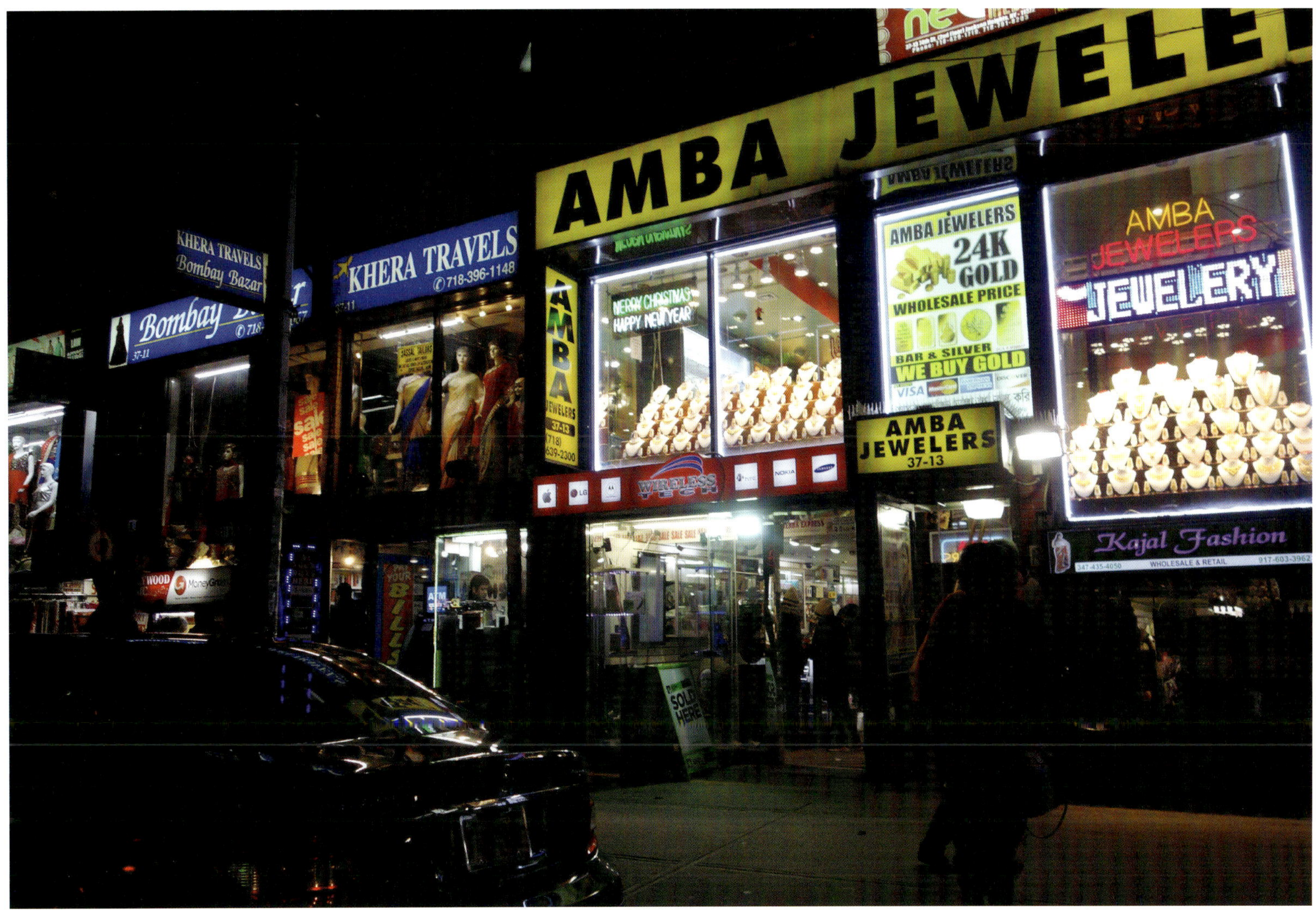

Nighttime Queens

Queens is not a 24-hour borough like Manhattan. Apart from a few club zones and hot spots, much of Queens shuts down soon after dark. Of course, there are the odd bodegas and pizza joints that stay open late into the night, but they are the exception to the rule. On prominent commercial streets like 74th Street in Jackson Heights, merchants might keep their shops open a bit later, up to nine or ten o'clock in the evening. In the winter scene here, brightly illuminated storefronts entertain the last trickle of customers before closing. Soon they will pull down the metal gates, and the street will become darker and quieter. Most shops will not open until nine or ten o'clock the following morning.

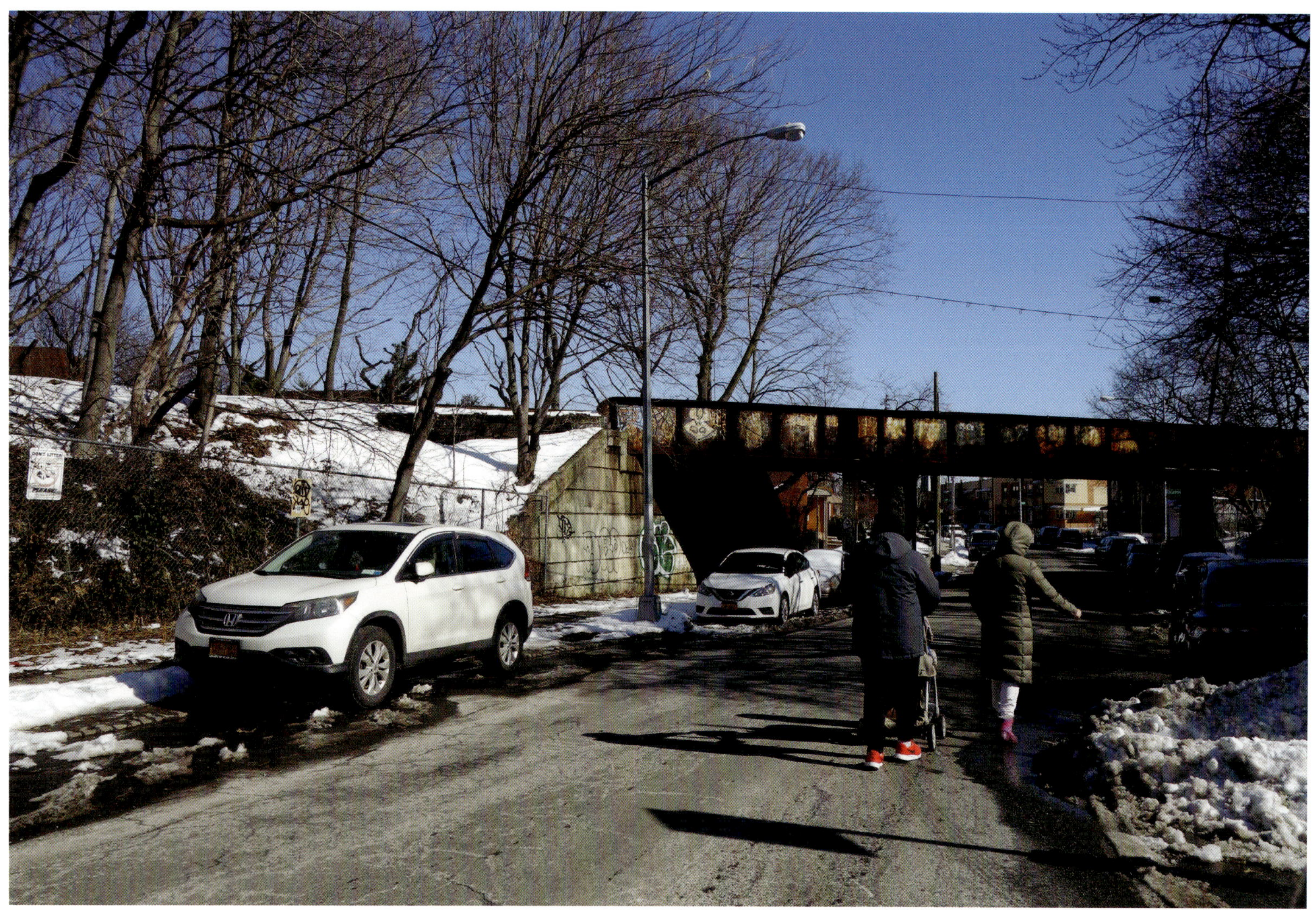

Winter walk in Maspeth

A family strolls along Calamus Avenue as the sun melts the last of the snow laid down the previous week. The low rusting viaduct carries the Bay Ridge Branch train line from Hell Gate through the neighborhood and into Brooklyn. The branch line, operated by the Long Island Railroad (LIRR), served passengers until 1968 when it was converted to freight-only. However, deindustrialization has led to significantly reduced freight traffic since the 1980s. Recently, the MTA unveiled plans to transform the line back to passenger service as the Interborough Express. This change would provide a much-needed rapid transit connection between Queens and Brooklyn since more people now commute in that direction than into Manhattan.

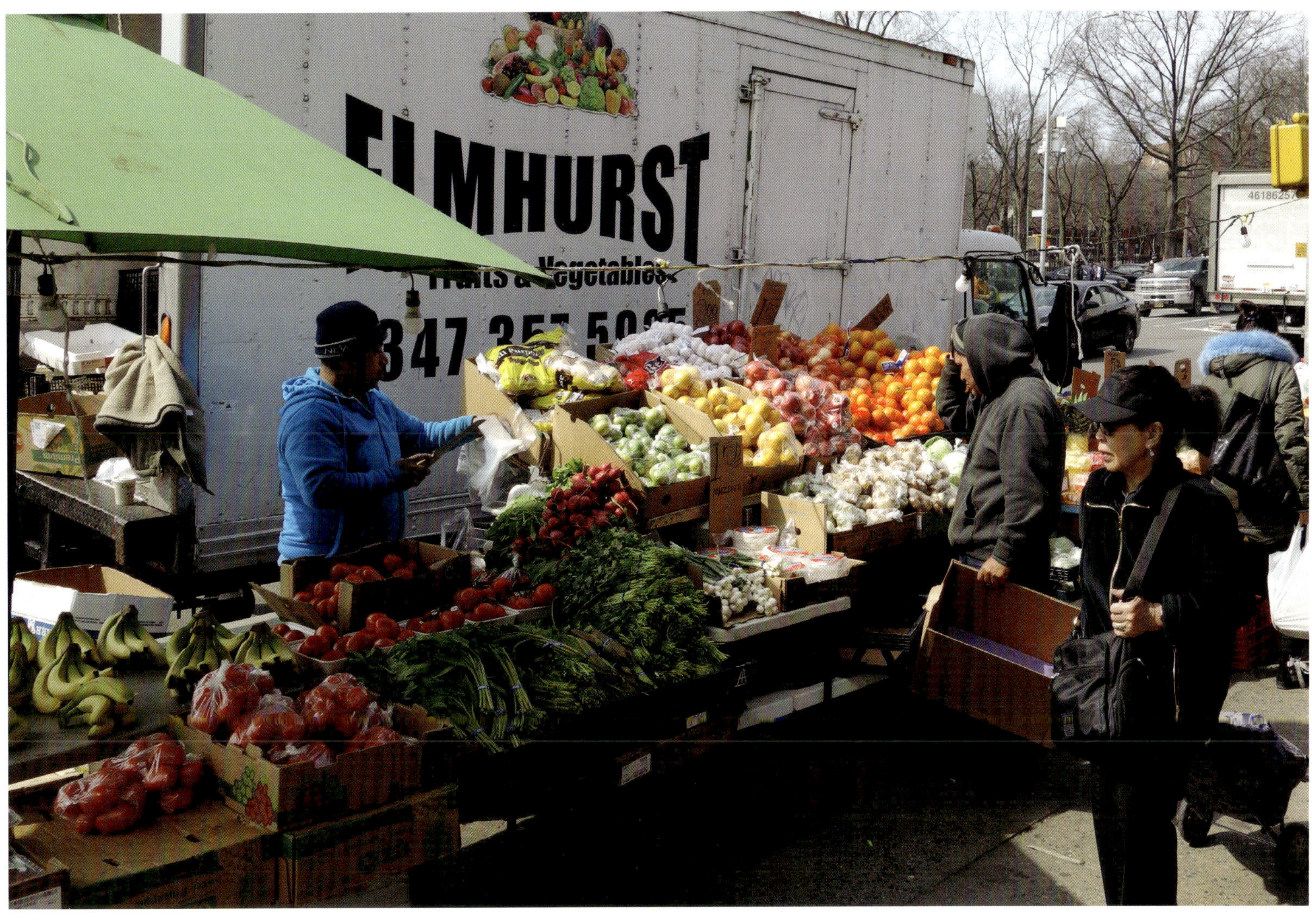

Selling produce on Broadway in Elmhurst

On a cold early spring morning, a street vendor sells fruits and vegetables at Broadway and 45th Avenue in Elmhurst. He has rigged a cordon rope to hang bags, supplies, and light bulbs for night sales. Since it is only March, most of the produce is imported, though he will incorporate more locally grown food as the season kicks in. Far from a food desert, Western Queens is abundant in grocery stores, greengrocers, farmer markets, and street vendors. Thus, while Elmhurst has a poverty rate that is 7 percent higher than that of New York City, a lack of food options is not an issue, particularly given the high demand among Chinese and Southeast Asian families for fresh produce.

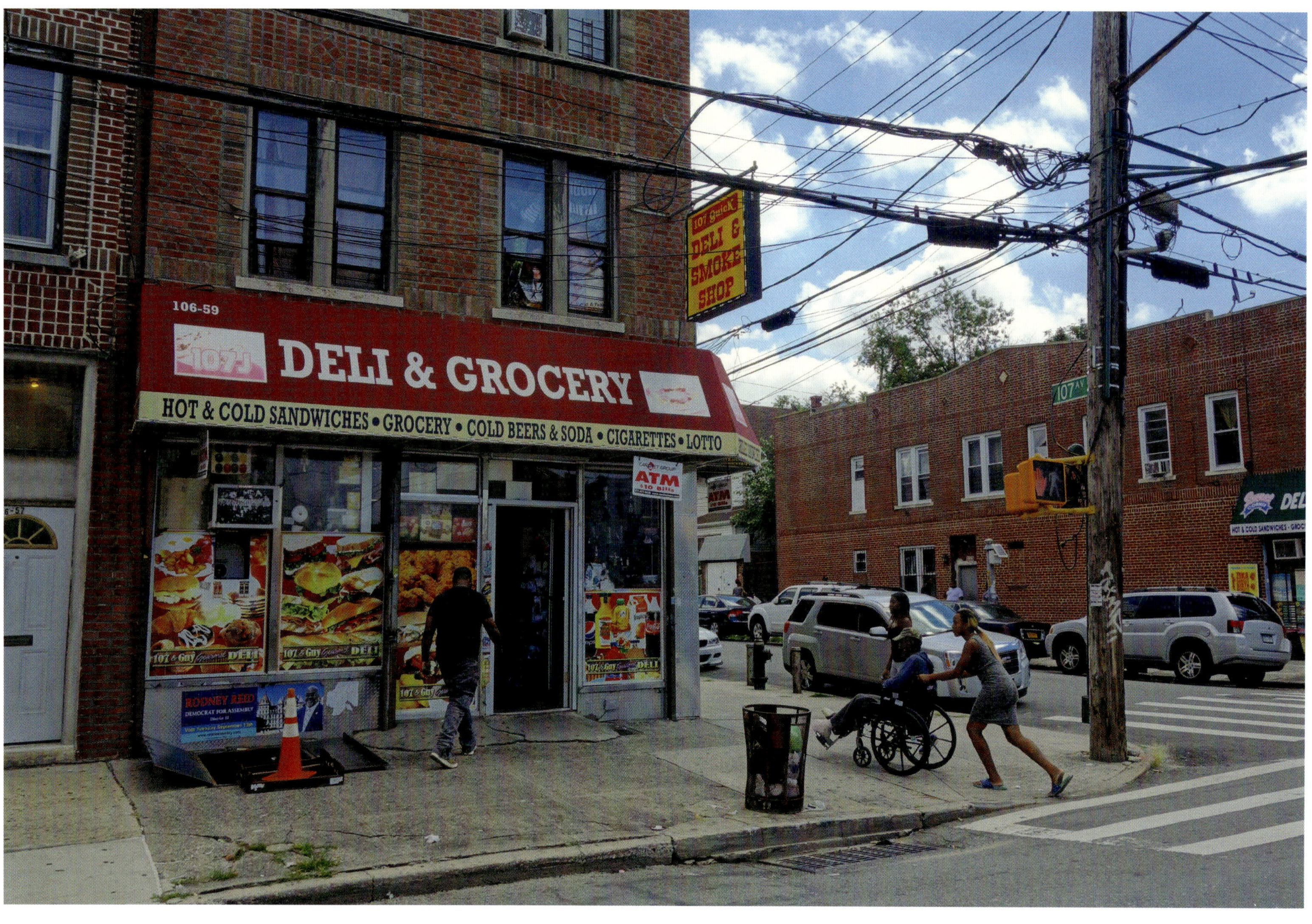

Bodega at 107th Avenue and Guy Brewer Boulevard, Jamaica

One of the most ubiquitous features of everyday life in Queens and New York is the bodega. Alternatively known as the "corner deli" or "convenience store," the bodega sells basic goods such as milk, beer, cigarettes, canned goods, snacks, and items that reflect the specific needs of the surrounding community. They often serve as neighborhood hubs, like this bodega in Jamaica. Established by Puerto Rican migrants in the 1920s, bodegas now offer entry-level business and employment opportunities for many newcomers. Since the 1980s, a growing number of South Asian, Caribbean, and Middle Eastern families have opened bodegas on the Puerto Rican model.

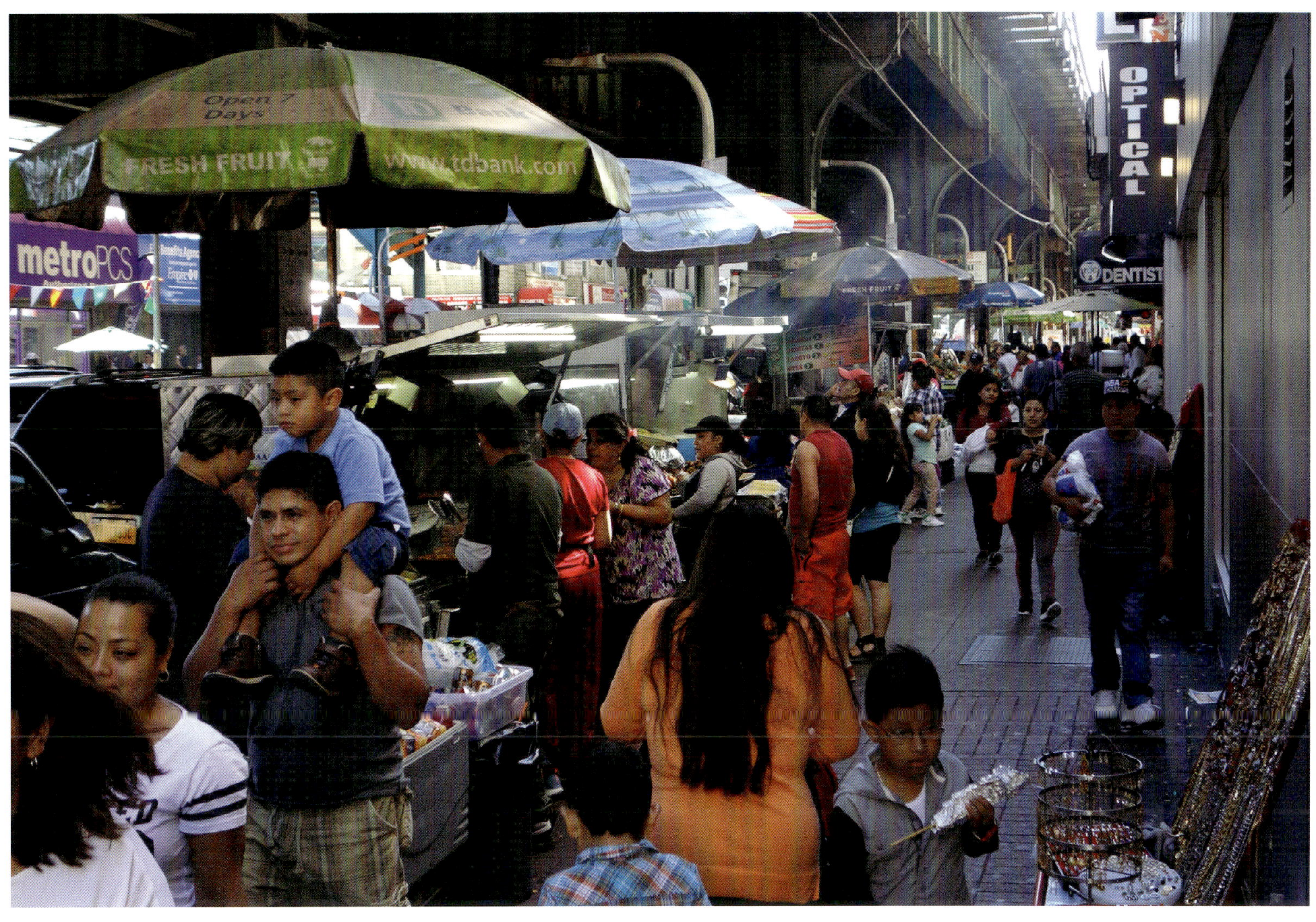

Street food, Roosevelt Avenue at Junction Boulevard

Junction Boulevard serves as the boundary line between Jackson Heights and Corona. One of the busiest intersections in Western Queens, Junction Boulevard at Roosevelt Avenue attracts dozens of street food vendors who set up daily below the 7 train tracks. They serve customers from late morning through the wee hours of the night, when the clubs close and patrons flood the sidewalks. Most food trucks and carts in this section of Roosevelt Avenue are operated by families from Colombia, Mexico, Honduras, and El Salvador. The photograph here shows vendors and customers on a warm autumn day, enveloped in smoke from roasting corn and grilling meats and vegetables.

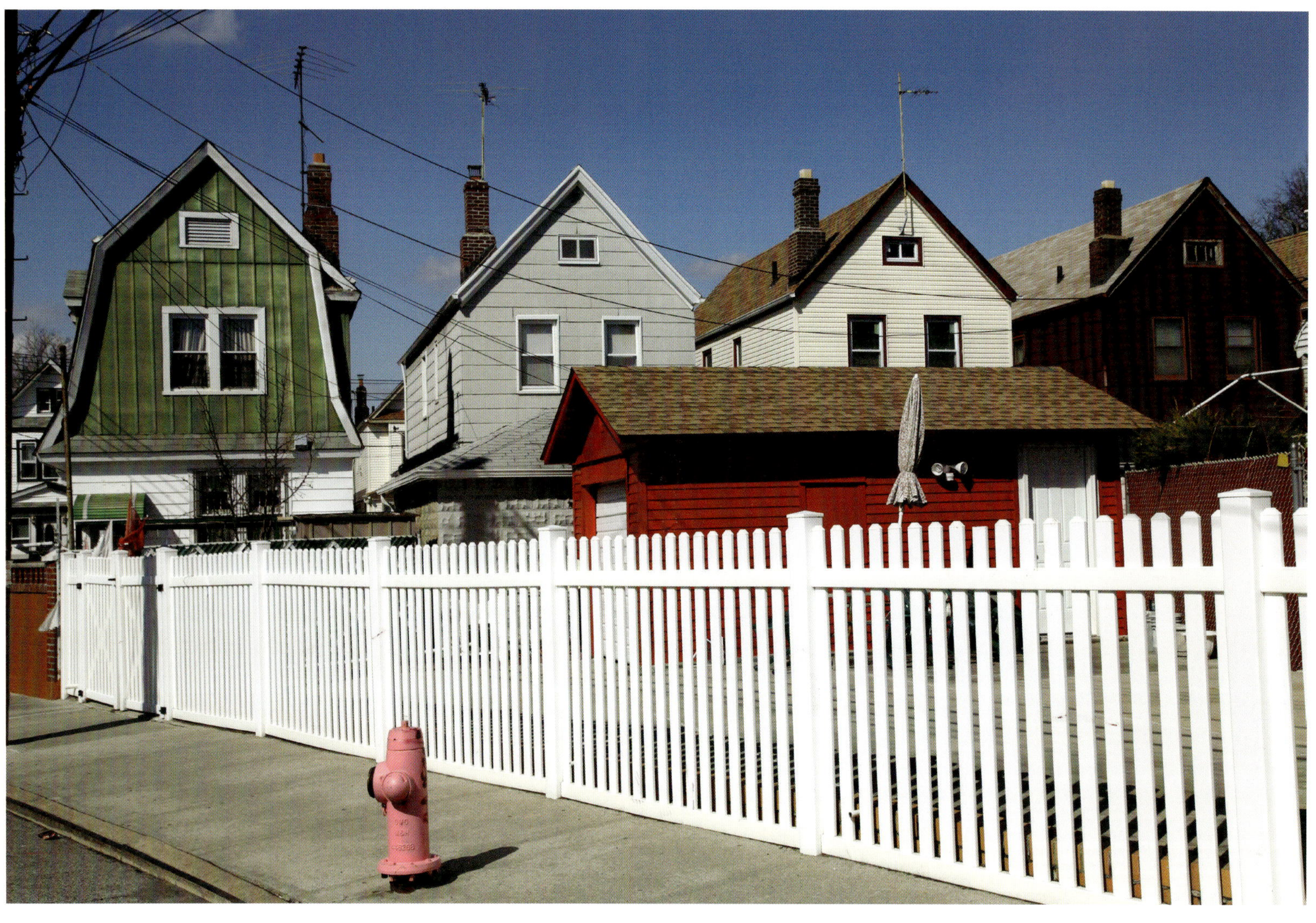

Spectacular vernacular

Figures 28a–28q. Queens has a staggering variety of forms and styles of residential architecture, from the narrow cottages shown here to sprawling suburban split-level houses and from duplexes and row houses to mid-rise apartments and high-rise tower blocks. This variety stems from three key factors. First, the borough grew rapidly in the twentieth century because of the availability of cheap land. Second, development shifted from small firms building a few houses at a time to large firms creating whole new subdivisions. Third, all this occurred during a period of experimentation with housing forms and a rapid succession of architectural tastes. Finally, a "fast and cheap" ethos prevailed as aspiring middle-class families sought homes in the crowded metropolis.

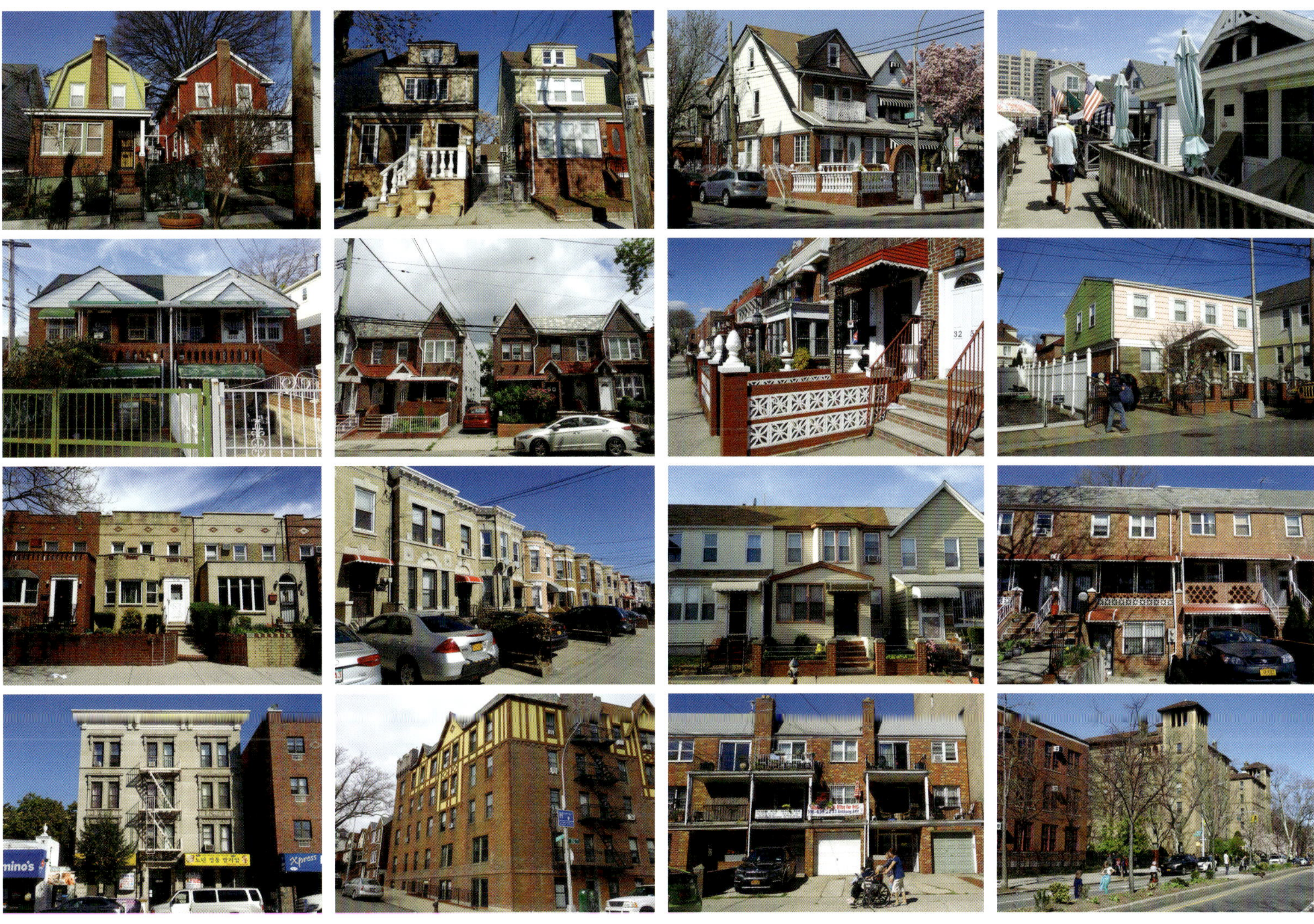

Top row, detached single-family houses (l to r): Murray Hill houses with gambrel and gable roofs; houses with enclosed porches and third-story dormers, Ozone Park; narrow bungalow in Corona; craftsman beach cottages, Rockaway. Second row, multiplexes (l. to r.): attached bungalows with converted basement flats, East Elmhurst; four-plexes with Gothic gables, Jackson Heights; duplexes, Jackson Heights; center-entry duplex in Flushing. Third row, row houses (l to r): with projecting ground floors, Astoria; Italianate row with front yards converted to driveways, Elmhurst; variable façades, Flushing; post–World War II, Jackson Heights. Bottom row, apartment buildings (l to r): Italianate tenement, Murray Hill; Tudor co-op, Flushing; postwar flats, Corona; Tuscan revival garden apartments, Jackson Heights.

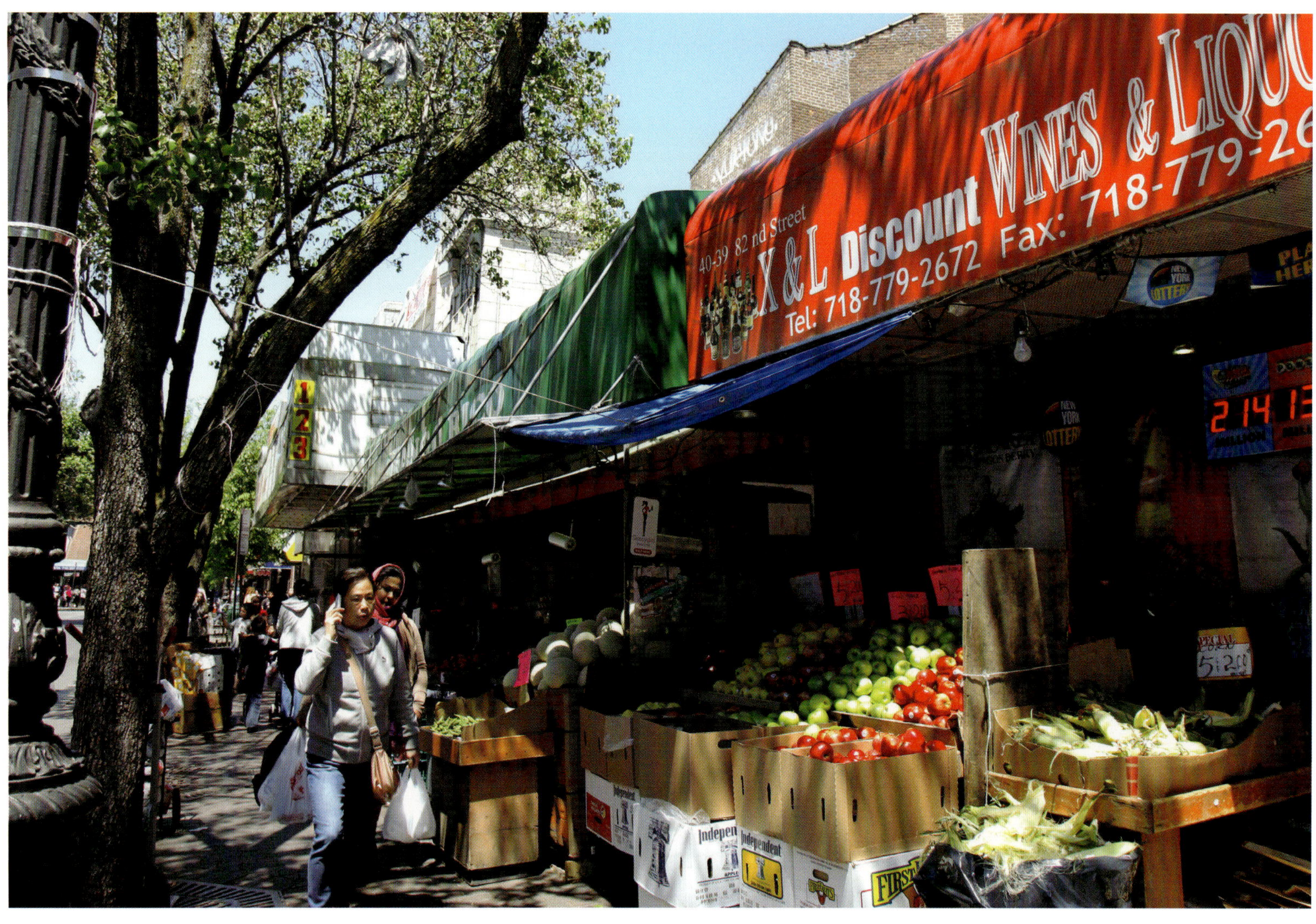

82nd Street, Elmhurst

This commercial block in Elmhurst extends just south of the 7 train on Roosevelt Avenue. At the time of the photograph, the block featured numerous small businesses, including a cinema, greengrocers, Colombian bakeries, optometrists, nail and hair salons, a tax prep office, a jeweler, and a liquor store. The cinema screened new-release and second-run feature films, often dubbed into Spanish, and broadcasted World Cup matches, Cricket tests, and other sporting events relevant to the surrounding communities. In 2018, everything shown in this photograph was demolished and replaced with a Target store and a Chipotle restaurant.

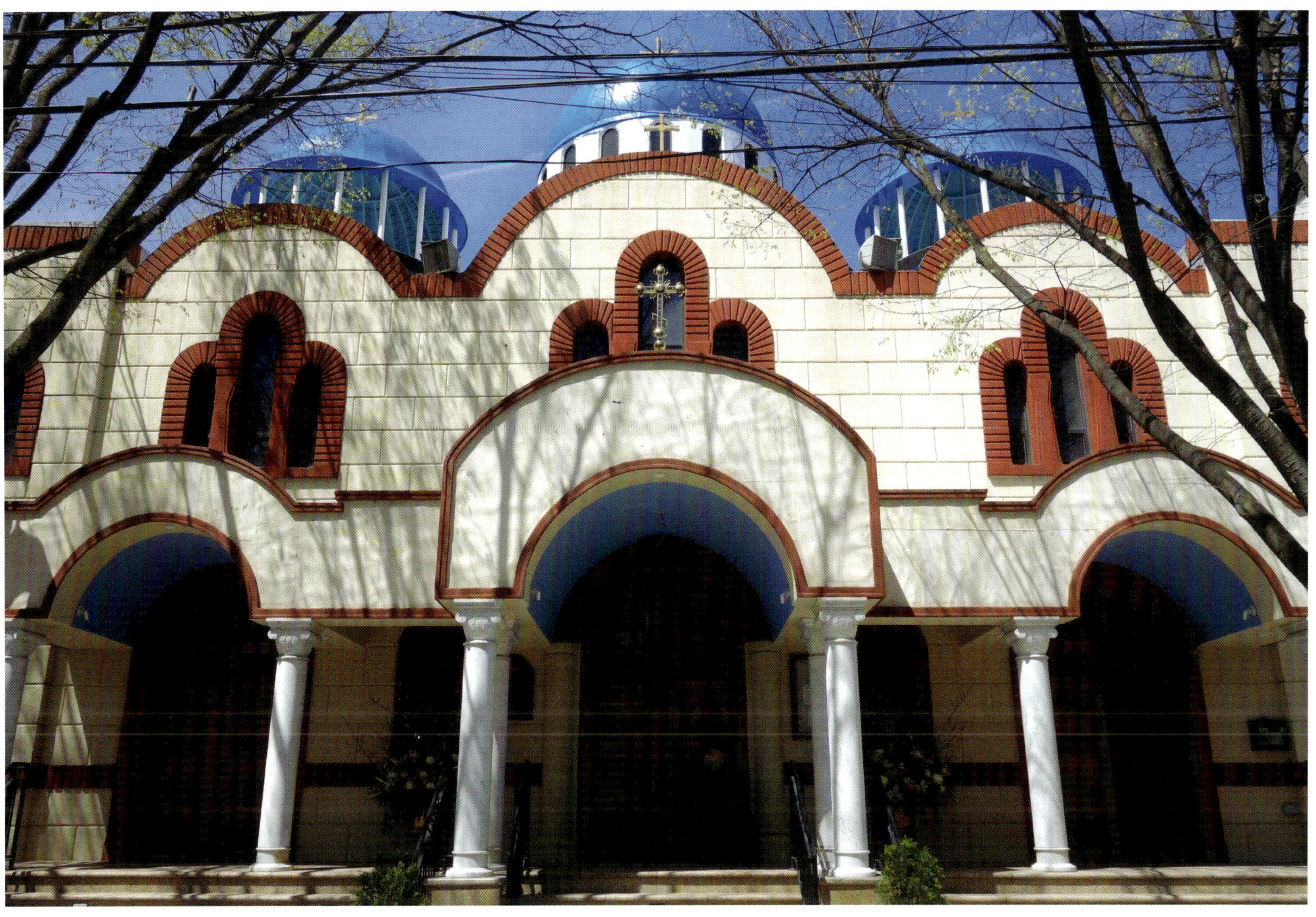

Priest on the porch, Astoria

A priest enjoys a cool spring day on the porch of St. Markella Greek Orthodox Cathedral in Astoria. St. Markella was built in 1954 to serve as the seat of the Metropolitan Bishop of the Old Calendar order, which broke away from the mainstream church after a dispute over how to determine the celebration of feast days. Similar splits have occurred in the Romanian and Bulgarian Orthodoxies, though, in all cases, the breakaway churches represent a small fraction of the devoted. In the end, such plural beliefs show that even within one ethnic group, Greeks, religious conflicts can spread from countries of origin to reverberate in the homes and streets of Queens.

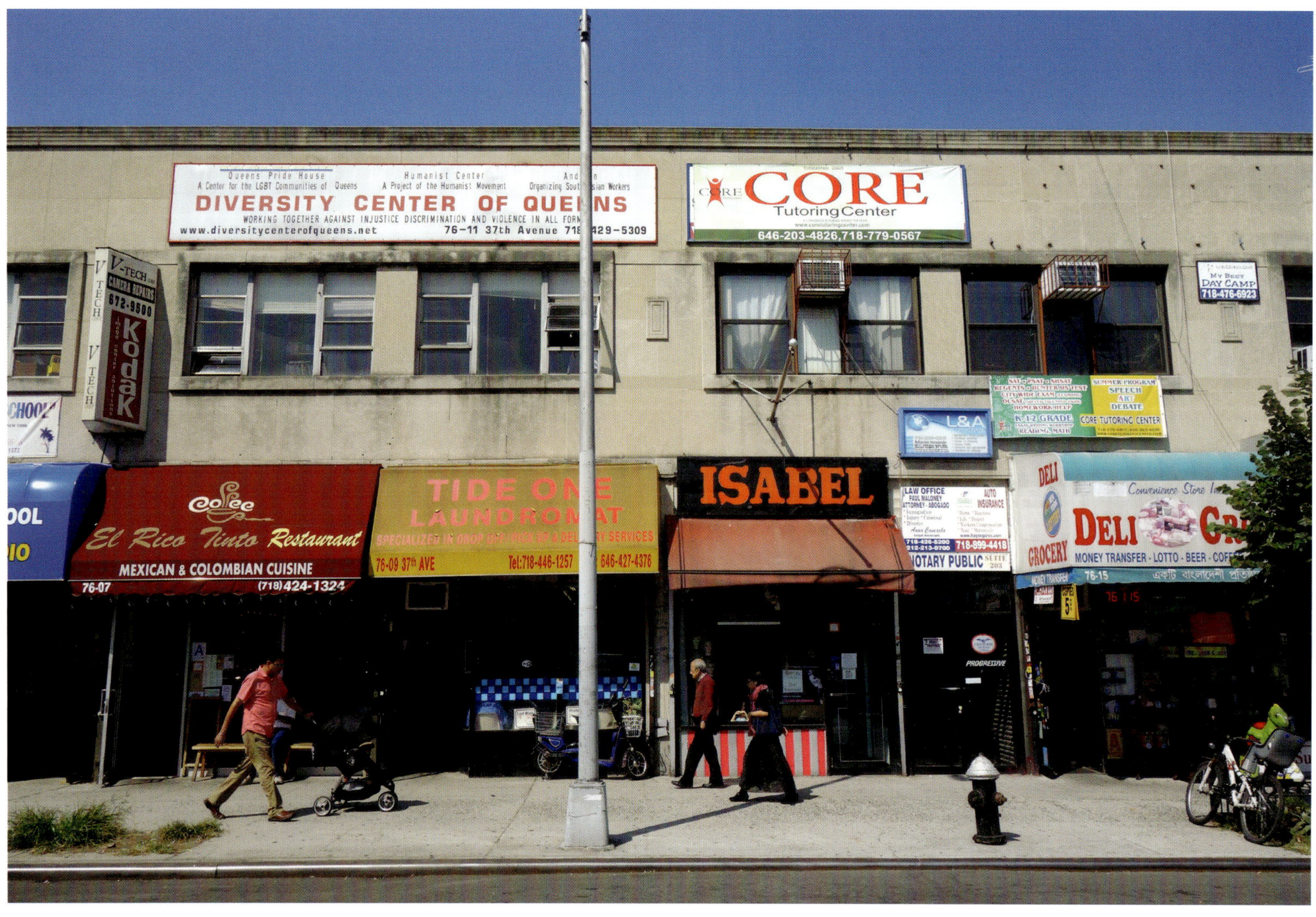

Diversity Center of Queens, Jackson Heights

The Diversity Center of Queens is a hub of organizations serving multiple communities of Jackson Heights and surrounding neighborhoods. Queens Pride House, founded in the 1990s, is an organization of central importance to the large LGBTQ community, and the Humanist Center has a long history of fighting prejudice and bigotry. South Asian women founded Andolan in 1998 to advocate for workers' rights; they have been instrumental in exposing sweatshop labor practices and workplace sexual violence in Queens. The organizations share the second floor of this otherwise nondescript commercial building on 37th Avenue with Core, an English language tutoring service.

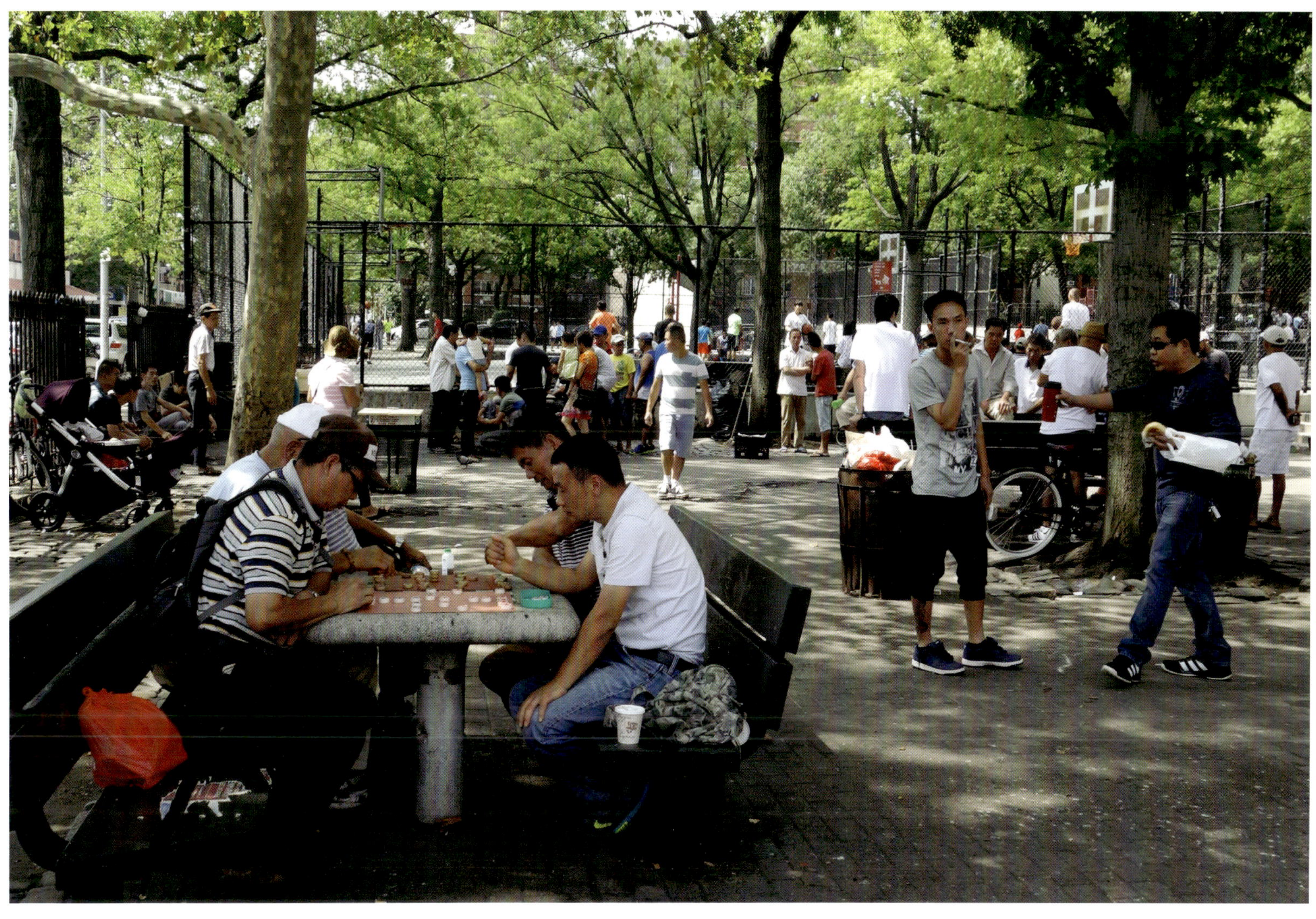

Moore Homestead Playground, Elmhurst

There is a lot going on in this lively scene of the Moore Homestead Playground, where Elmhurst residents go to escape the heat in the summer. Typical of New York's small city parks, it offers benches under large, mature shade trees, basketball and handball courts, playground equipment, bathrooms, and a water feature for kids. It is a favored spot for Chinese men and women to meet for Mahjong, cards, checkers, and other games. The men in the photograph are playing Xiàngqí, a Chinese game similar to chess. The park is also a popular spot for outdoor dining, with families bringing meals from home or from one of the many nearby Chinese, Thai, and Malaysian restaurants.

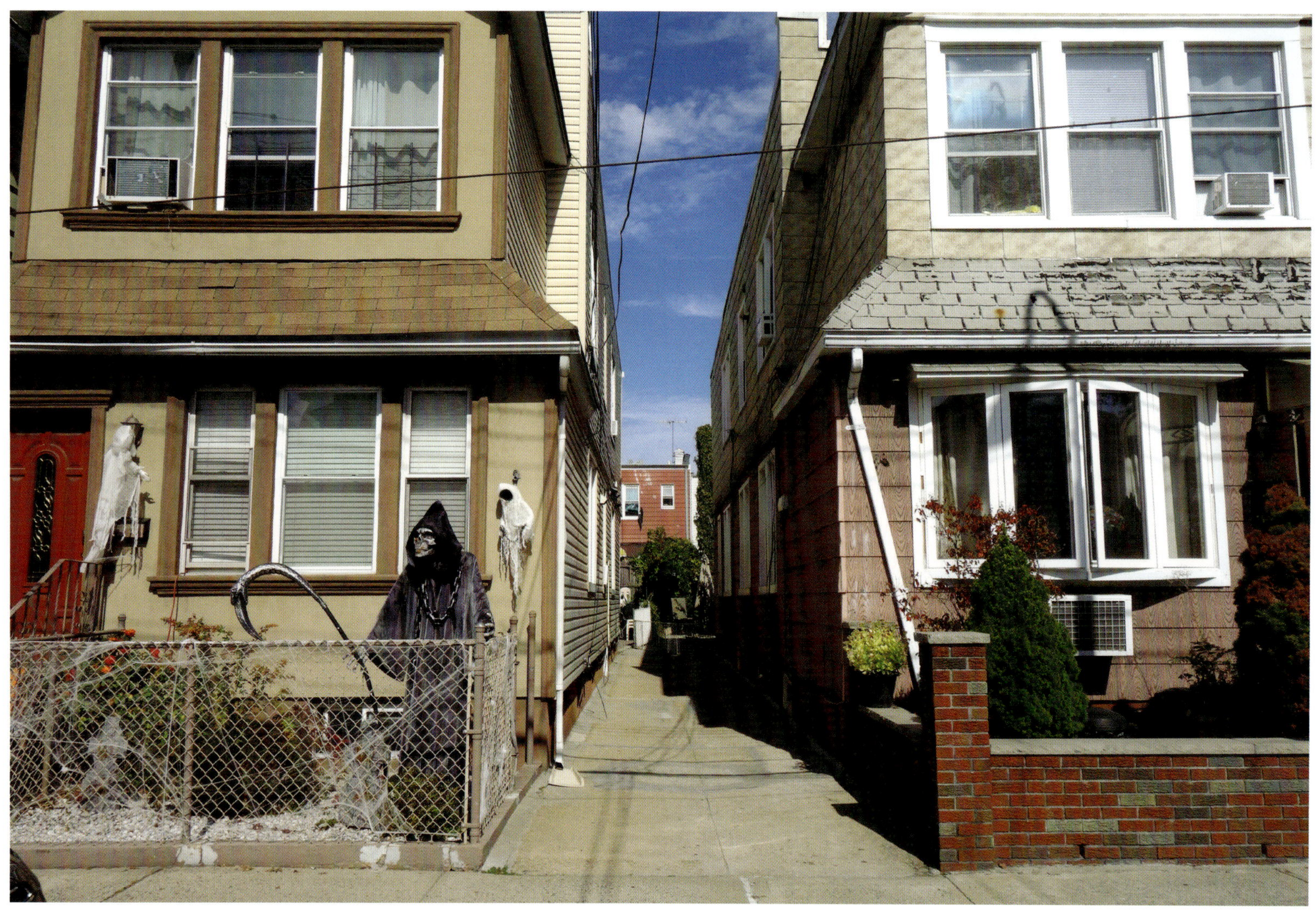

Halloween in Maspeth

Originally home to the Mespeatches Indians, Dutch and English colonial settlers farmed this part of Queens from the 1640s, establishing Maspeth village in 1652. The area industrialized with mill operations along Newtown and Maspeth Creeks in the eighteenth and nineteenth centuries. By the 1910s and 1920s, the area attracted real estate developers, who rapidly built up the neighborhood with single-family houses and small commercial streets. A mix of Irish, Italian, and Polish families moved in, as did new factories. The residential pockets were surrounded by cemeteries and low-lying industrial zones, creating an insular, village-like feel that persists today.

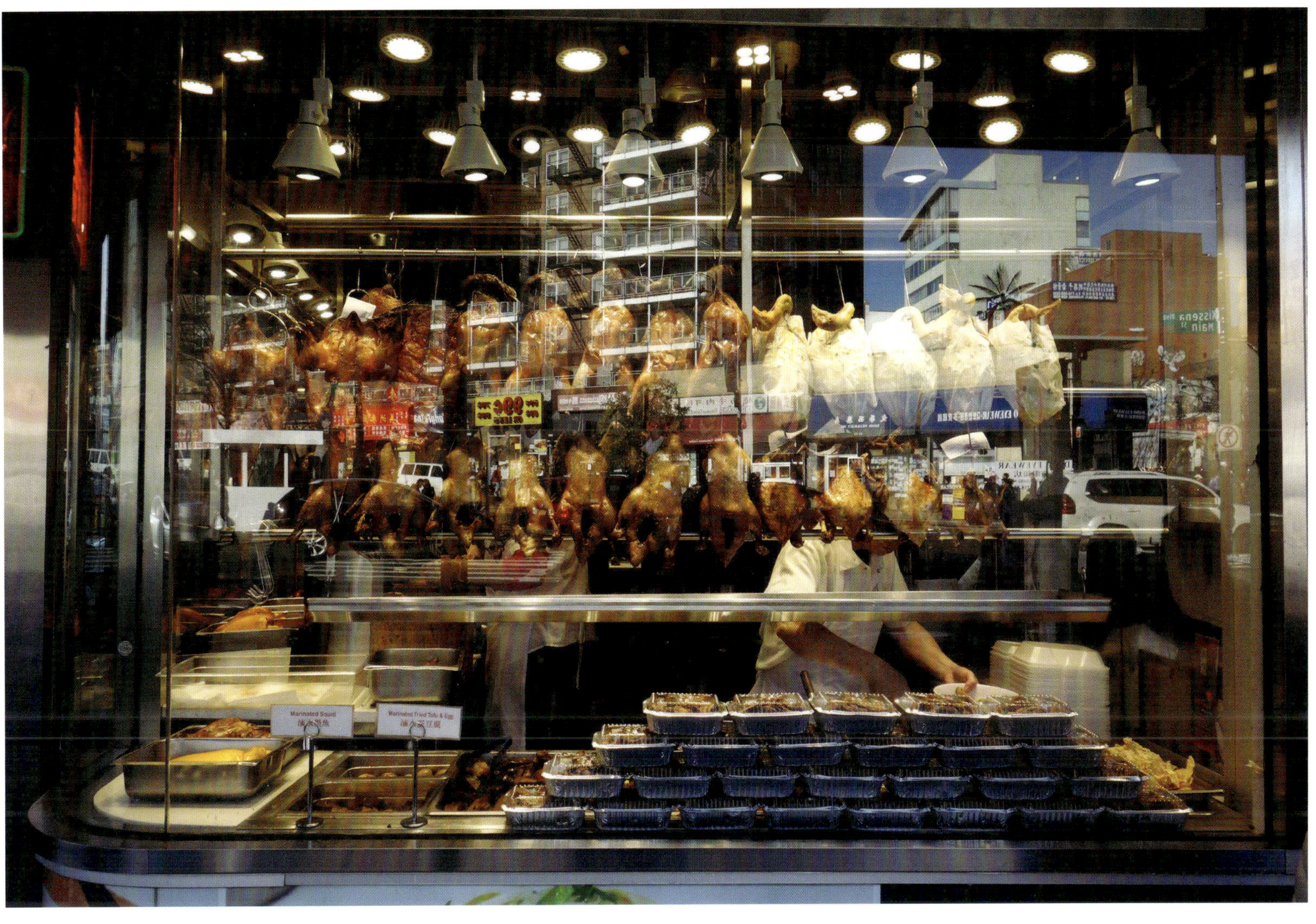

Hanging fowl, Flushing Main Street

Restaurants and banquet halls in Flushing process thousands of ducks and chickens daily for hungry patrons. Food businesses comprise 12 percent of the neighborhood's 5,500 commercial establishments, making it a renowned destination for Chinese and Korean fare. Still, the neighborhood has a bifurcated service industry, with high earners working in finance and tech and low-wage workers toiling in non-union kitchens, supermarkets, and warehouses. New Chinese immigrants continue to make up the majority of labor in Chinese restaurants, but in Korean establishments, there is an increasing presence of Latinos in the kitchens and busing tables.

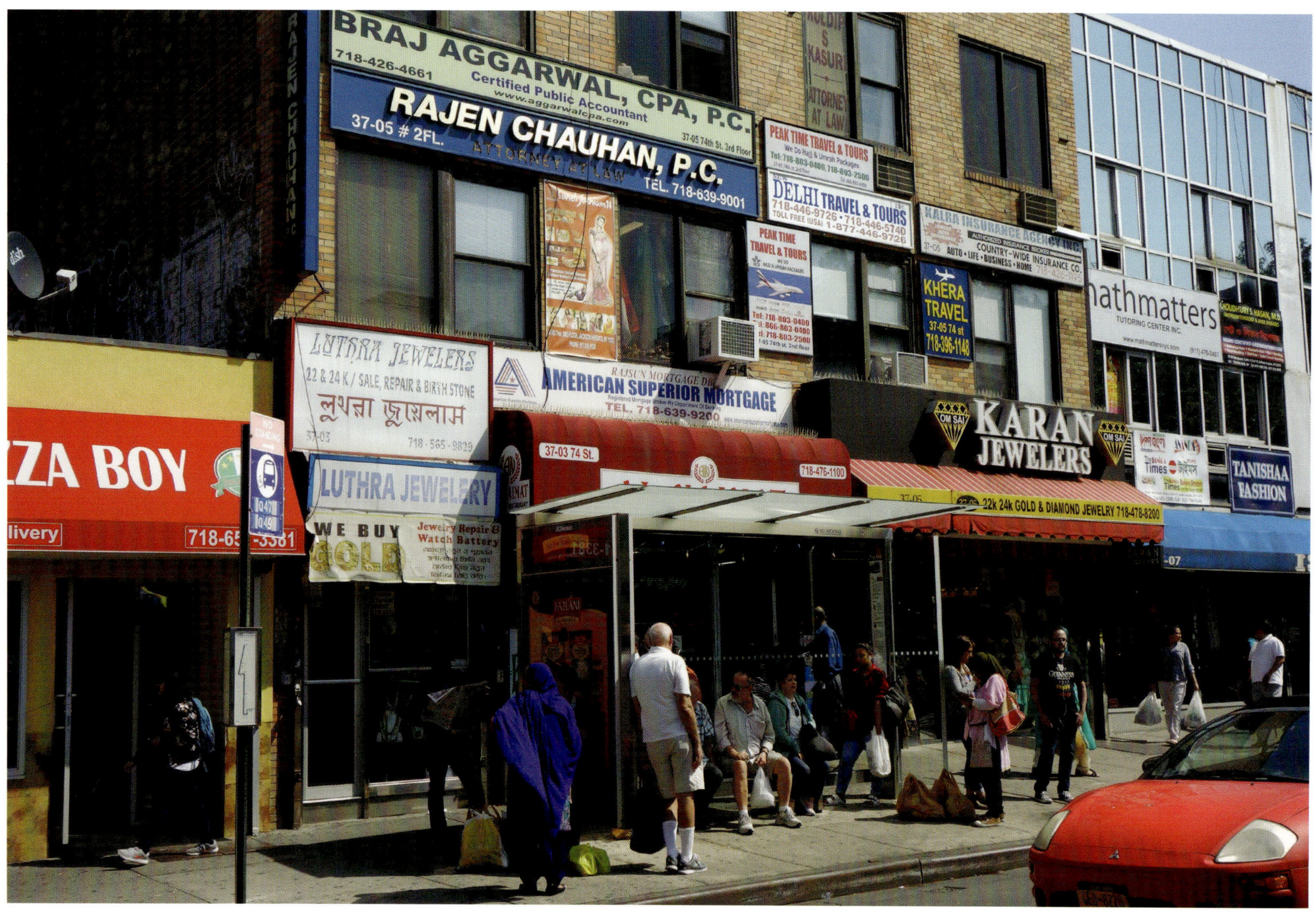

Bus stop, Jackson Heights

Residents brave the July heat wave to wait for the Q47 and Q49 buses in Jackson Heights. A few of them take advantage of the shade thrown by the kiosk. While Northwestern Queens is relatively well served by public transportation, much of this sprawling borough has no connection to trains and only minimal bus routes. Of all the city's boroughs, it is the one most associated with the automobile and its accompanying landscape of expressways, strip malls, and low-slung neighborhoods. This scene in Jackson Heights is a reminder of the uneven experiences residents have of mobility in their highly varied and fragmentary borough.

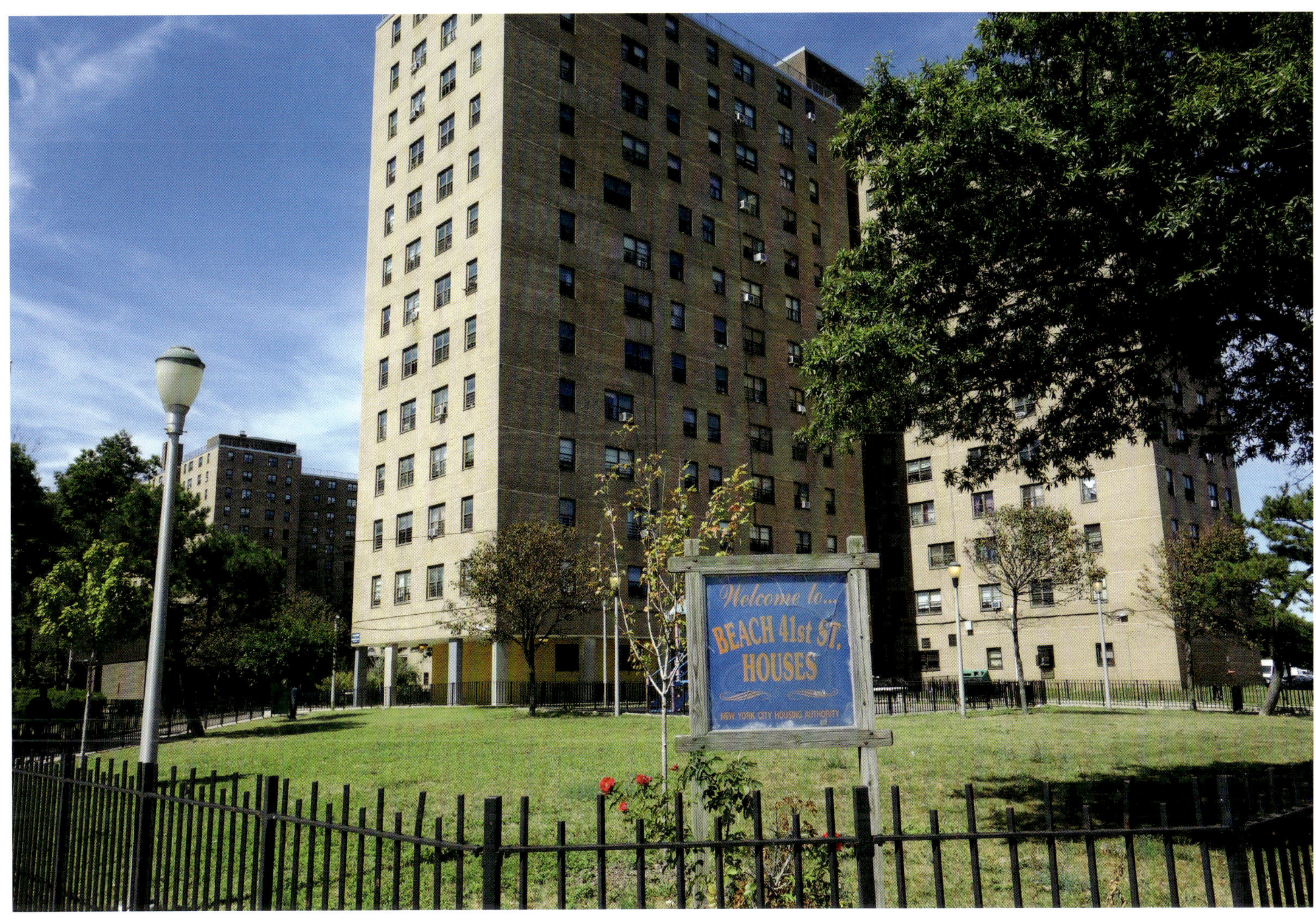

Beach 41st Street Houses, Edgemere

In the postwar decades, the New York City Housing Authority constructed a series of large housing projects on the Rockaway Peninsula, including Beach 41st Street Houses, completed in 1965. These had the effect of deepening racial segregation and isolation of Black working-class New Yorkers. Tenant associations have pressed hard for changes over the past decade, led by women of color who have struggled to create a safer place to raise children. This has resulted in some improvements, such as lead and mold abatement, new playgrounds and gardens, and the reopening of community centers. Residents have also insisted on having a voice in coastal resilience planning in the wake of Hurricane Sandy.

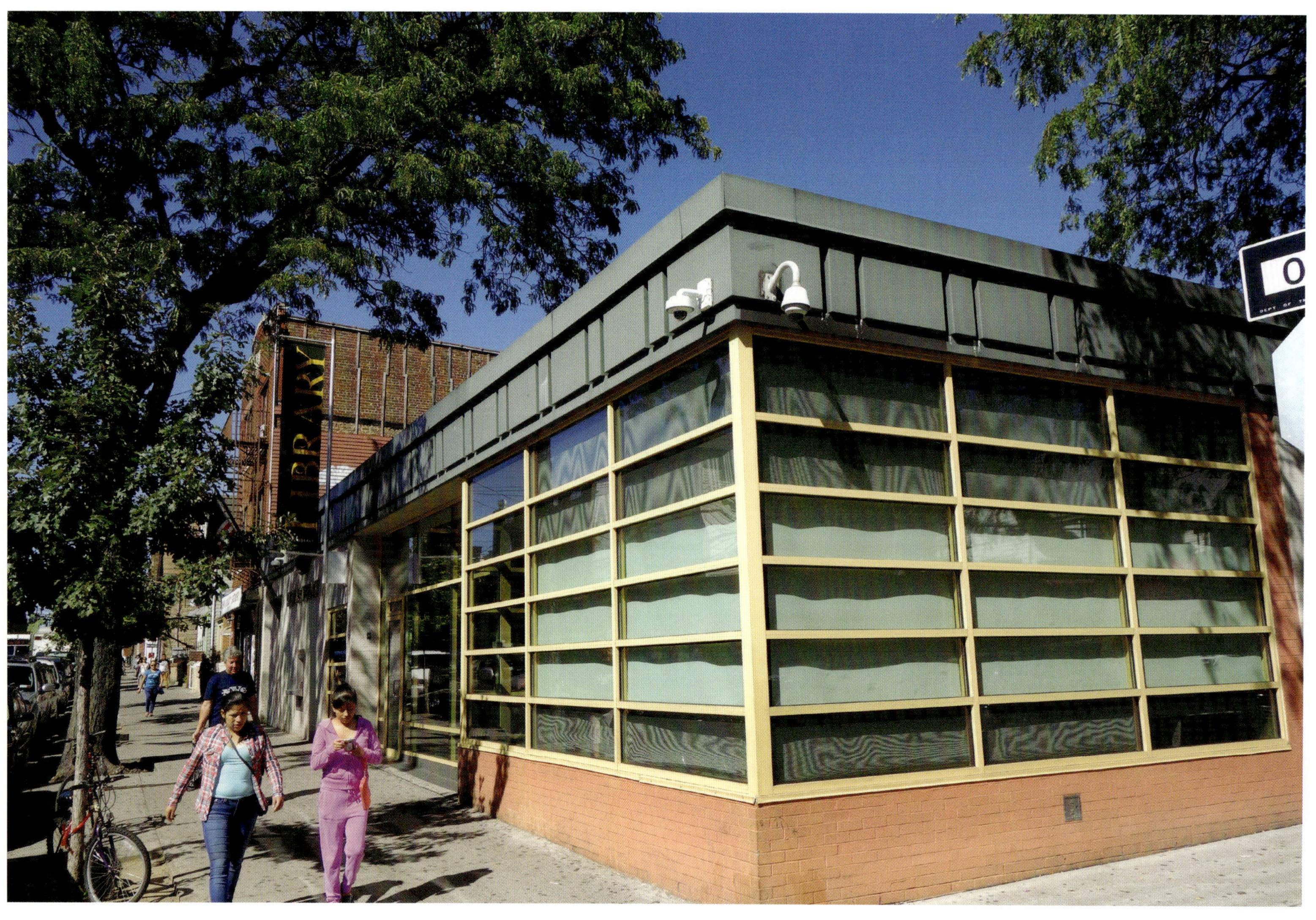

The Queens Public Library

Figures 37a–37e. The Queens Public Library system is one of the busiest and most multilingual in the United States. With sixty-two branches, few residents of the borough live beyond walking distance from a library. The Corona branch, shown here, serves a diverse Latino community from its new building along 104th Street at 39th Avenue. The library also provides language and citizenship classes, as well as information for job seekers. Where once libraries encouraged assimilation into a dominant Anglo-American society, today's librarians are active promoters of linguistic and cultural diversity. Some branches have even organized oral history projects to record dialects whose few remaining speakers live in Queens.

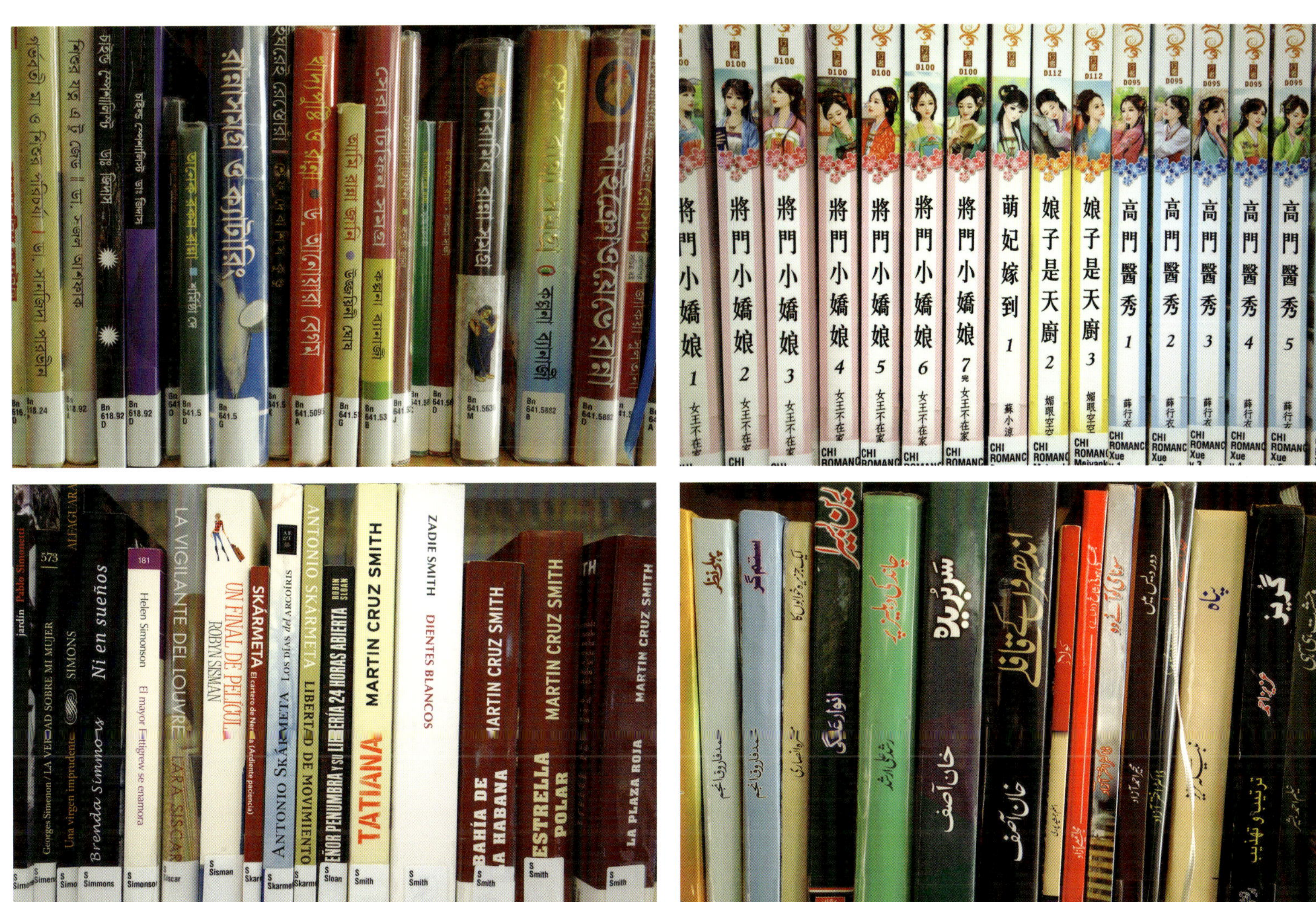

Above: Materials line the shelves at Elmhurst Library. Queens library branches stock books, magazines, DVDs, CDs, and newspapers in a staggering variety of languages. English, Spanish, and Chinese predominate, but one can also readily find materials in Hindi, Bengali, Urdu, Arabic, Thai, and Vietnamese. Neighborhood branches often specialize: Astoria for Greek and Arabic materials, Woodside for Tagalog and Thai, Forest Hills for Hebrew, and Rego Park for Uzbek. Many of the branches subscribe to daily and weekly newspapers as well as magazines from the home countries of immigrant families who reside in the service area. The Queens Library is one of the borough's most popular institutions.

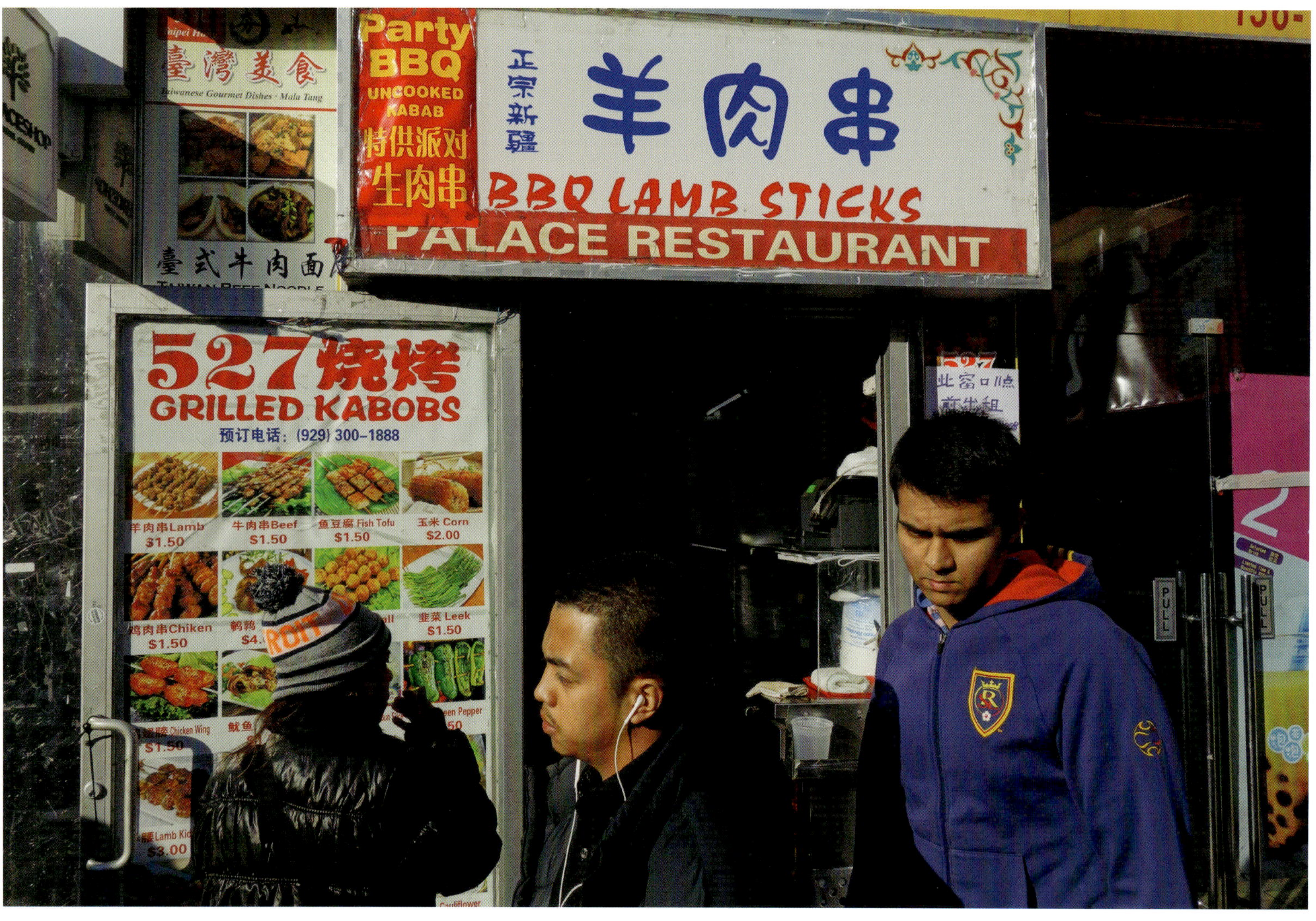

Palace Restaurant, Flushing

Like many small eateries in Queens, Palace is optimized for the highest volume of sales from the smallest possible footprint. It features a grill and steam table just inside the entrance, and a small shelf on the opposite wall for people to eat standing up. However, Palace is primarily a takeout affair, even serving patrons on the go from the open door on the sidewalk. Palace is one of several businesses run by Uighur migrants—Chinese Muslims from Xinjiang province as well as from Kazakhstan and Kyrgyzstan—who have begun migrating to New York over the last decade. Their foodways have much more in common with Central Asia and Afghanistan than with Eastern China, adding to the incredible culinary diversity of Flushing.

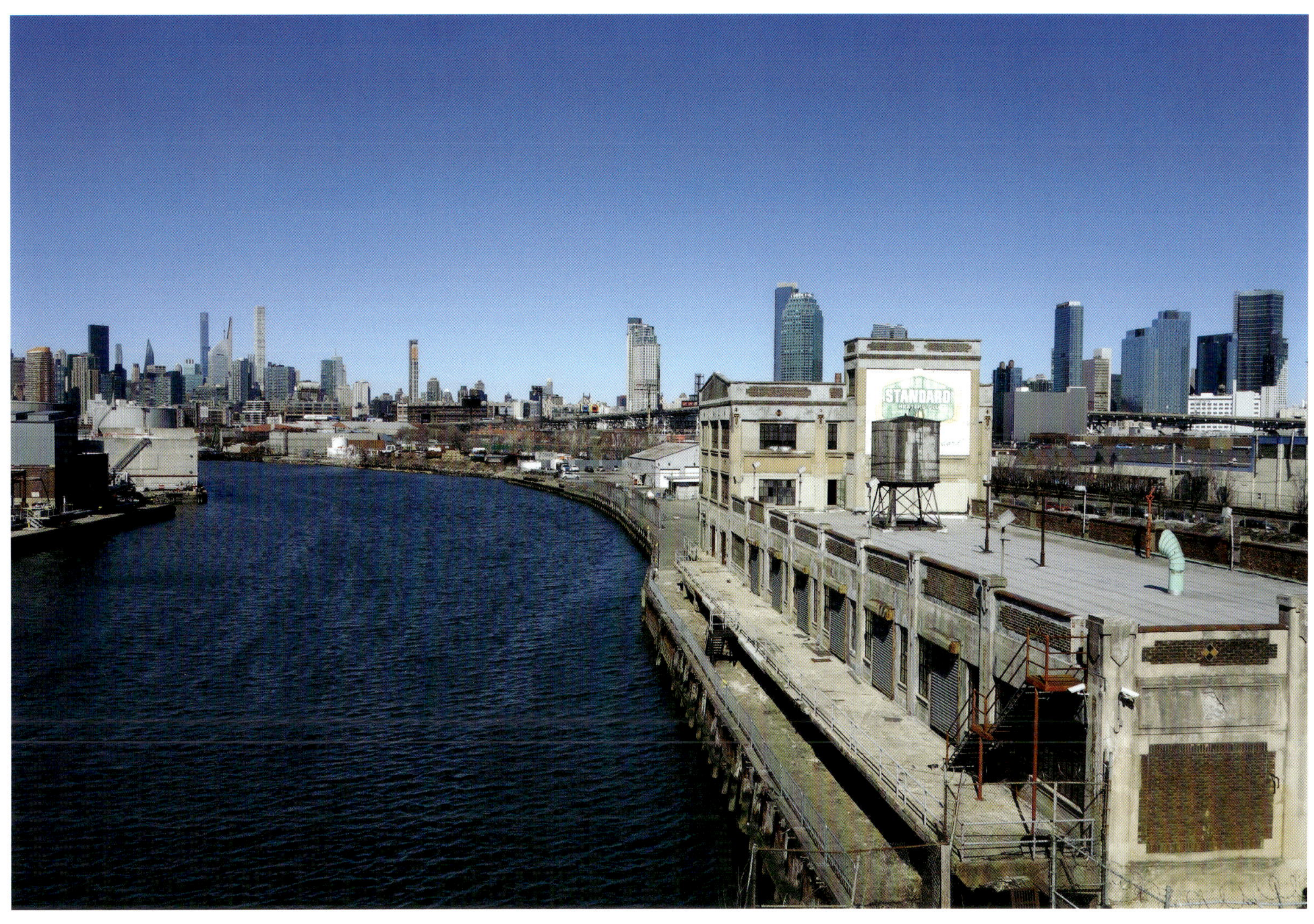

Newtown Creek, Hunters Point

Newtown Creek separates Greenpoint, Brooklyn (left), from Hunters Point, Queens (right). During the twentieth century, the waterway accumulated an armature of industrial operations. Factories, animal rendering plants, and fuel storage facilities dumped effluent directly into the creek so that it would drain away via the East River into the ocean. However, significant amounts of this discharge settled into the murky creek bed and accumulated over many decades. Consequently, it is heavily laden with toxins such as PCBs, pesticides, mercury, arsenic, and lead. The EPA declared the creek a Superfund site in 2010, and some progress has been made in cleaning it up.

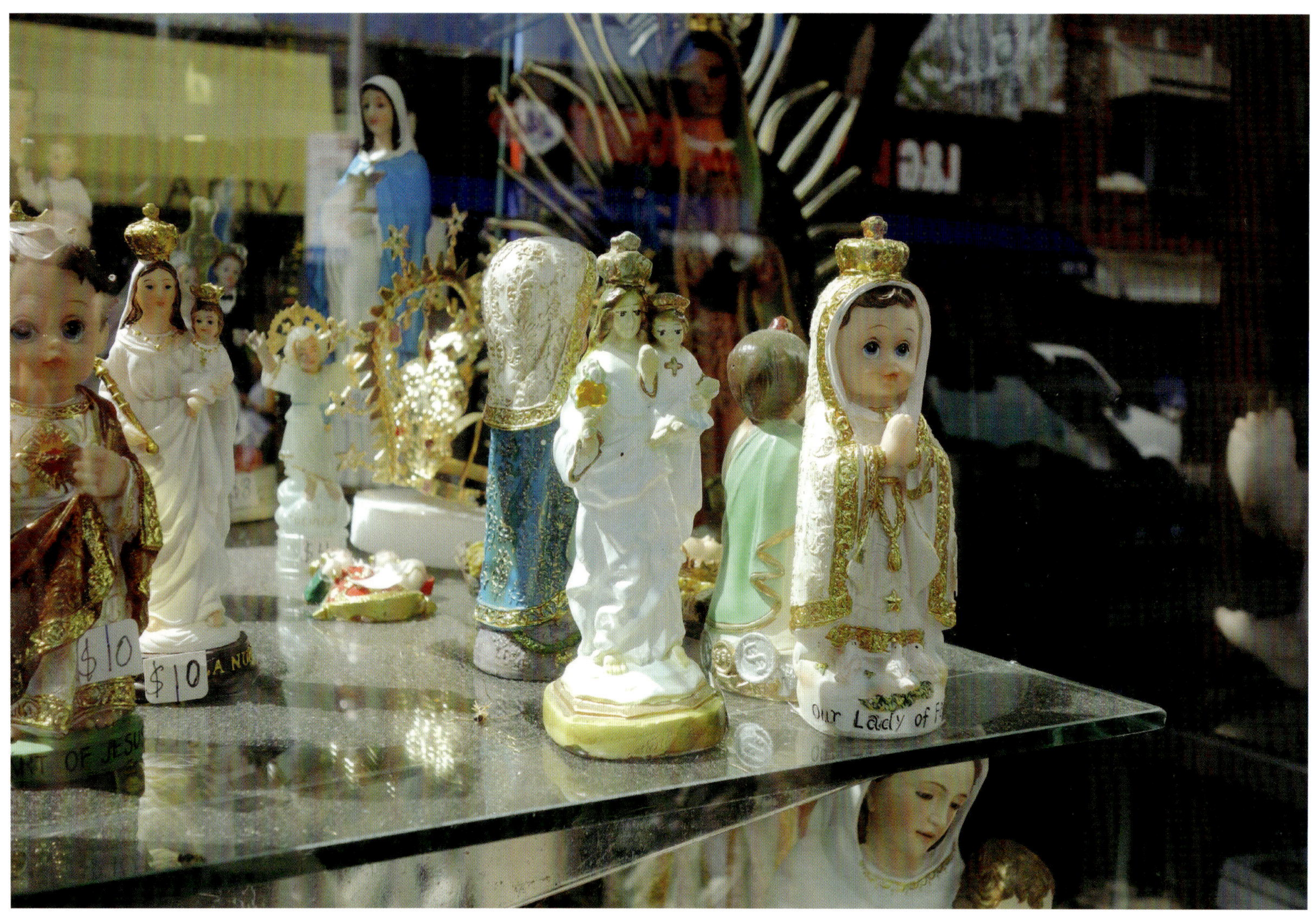

Botanica shop window, Corona

A collection of religious figurines adorns the front window of this Botanica on 104th Street in Corona. Botanicas are an important feature of Mexican, Puerto Rican, Haitian, and Central American neighborhoods. They sell a mix of items, including statuettes, medallions, herbs, oils, devotional candles, bibles, crosses, and "milagros," tiny metal pieces fashioned into arms, hearts, feet, and other body parts where people may be afflicted. Some even sell over-the-counter medicines that patrons use in combination with more traditional approaches. The shop owners themselves are often healing practitioners or part of families that have practiced healing arts for generations.

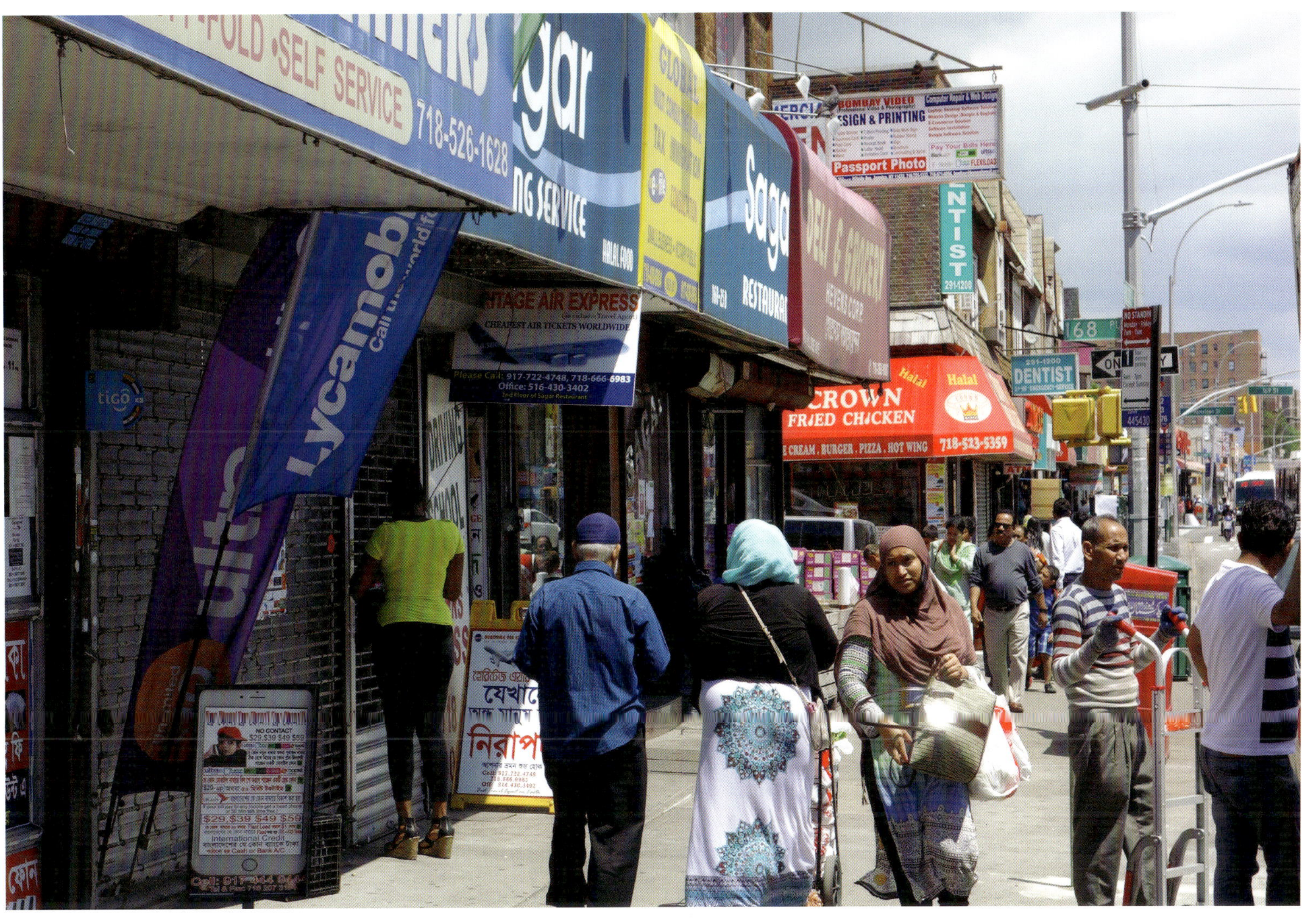

Summer scene in Jamaica Hills

The various "hills" in Jamaica Hills, Hillcrest, and Hollis Hills all take their name from the terminal moraine, a ridge of land pushed up by a glacier during the last ice age. Hillside Avenue, shown here, runs along the base of the terminal moraine's southern slope. It serves as the commercial high street for Jamaica Hills, a relatively quiet, middle-class neighborhood of single-family homes inhabited by a diverse mix of immigrants from Bangladesh, Guyana, Haiti, and Trinidad, as well as an older population of African American families. It features the usual mix of restaurants, grocers, travel agencies, driving schools, wire transfer stations, phone card shops, household goods and clothing stores, and legal and tax preparation services.

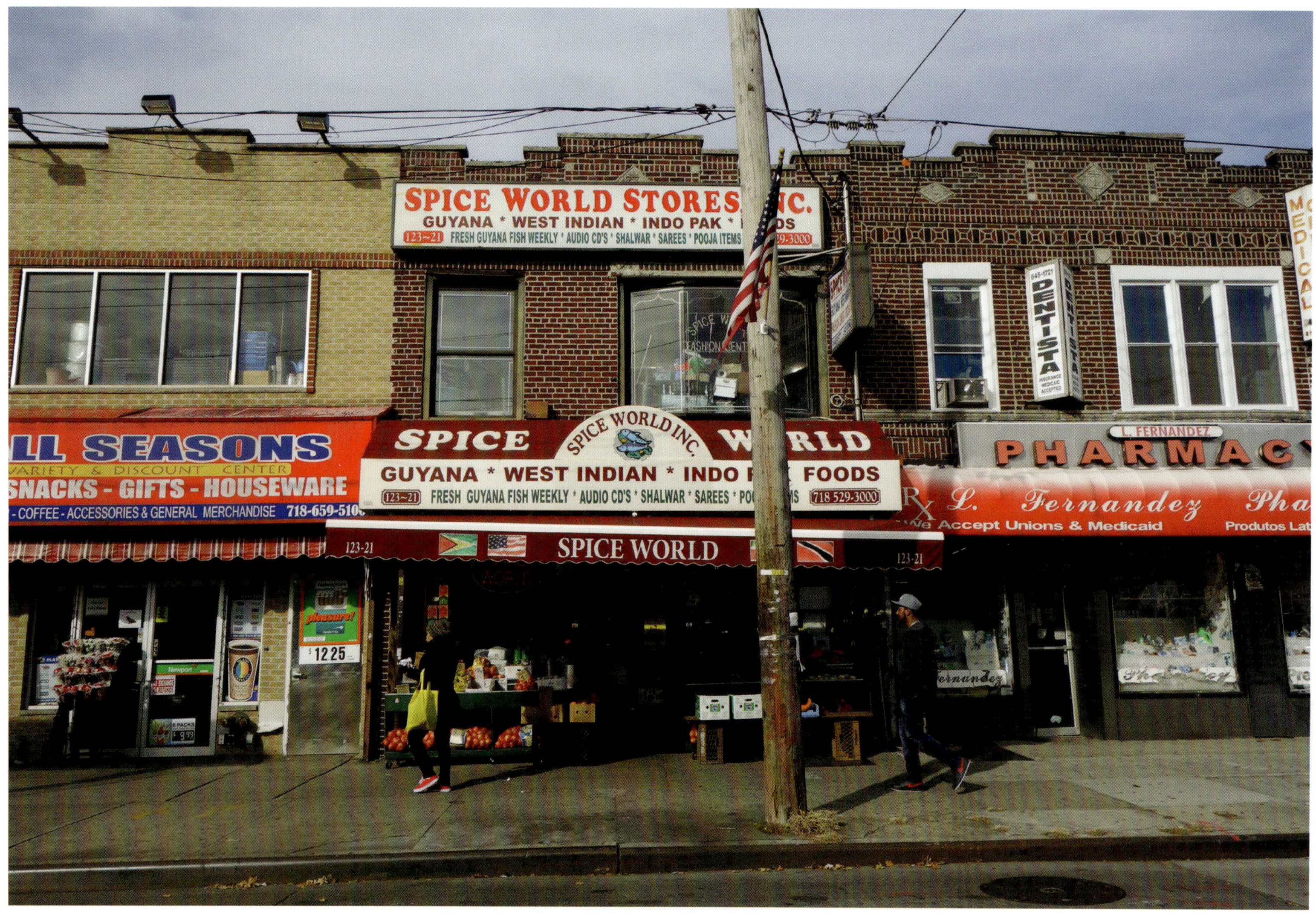

Storefronts in Richmond Hill

This block of shops along Liberty Avenue is typical of the low-slung commercial architecture present throughout areas of Queens developed in the 1920s. The restrained brick structures were built to serve a rapidly growing population and feature shops on the first floor and apartments on the second, though in many cases the upper story has been converted to commercial use. The modest scale suggests that this was primarily a local high street, unlike downtown Jamaica just two miles east. The types of businesses operating from these buildings shift over time to reflect the cultural mix of the neighborhood, as with this Indo-Caribbean Spice shop and Latino pharmacy and dentist in polyglot Richmond Hill.

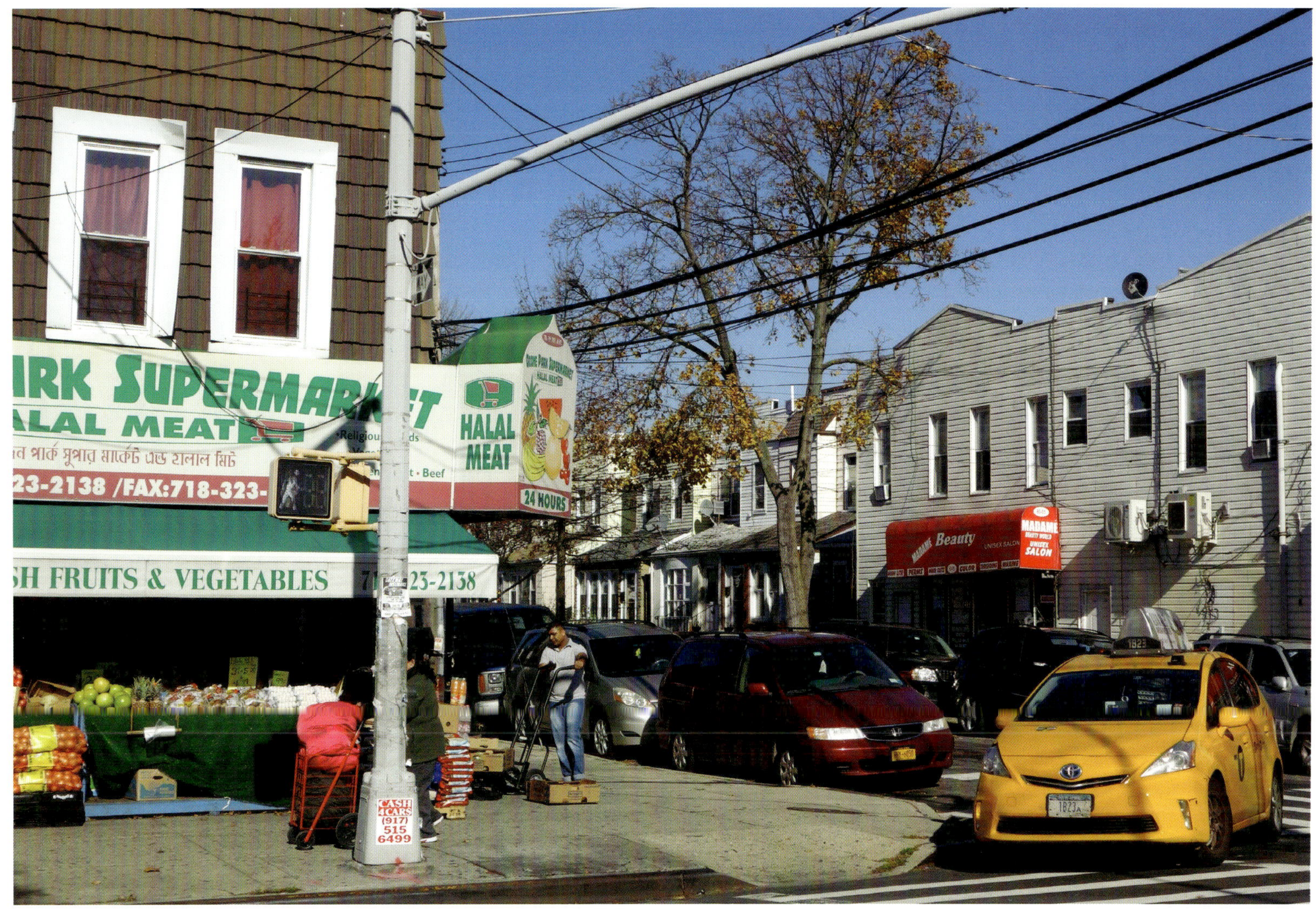

Ozone Park Supermarket

This corner market at 80th Street and 101st Avenue specializes in halal meat. Halal and kosher markets are important elements of the alimentary landscape of Queens, responding to religious dietary laws and restrictions. Businesses serving halal and kosher foods must be certified by the New York State Department of Agriculture and Markets. The Bengali-owned Ozone Park Supermarket serves a South Asian population comprising immigrant families from Bangladesh, India, and Pakistan, as well as from Trinidad, Guyana, and Suriname. In addition to meat and produce, they sell bulk lentils, chickpeas, rice, spices, masalas, and snacks.

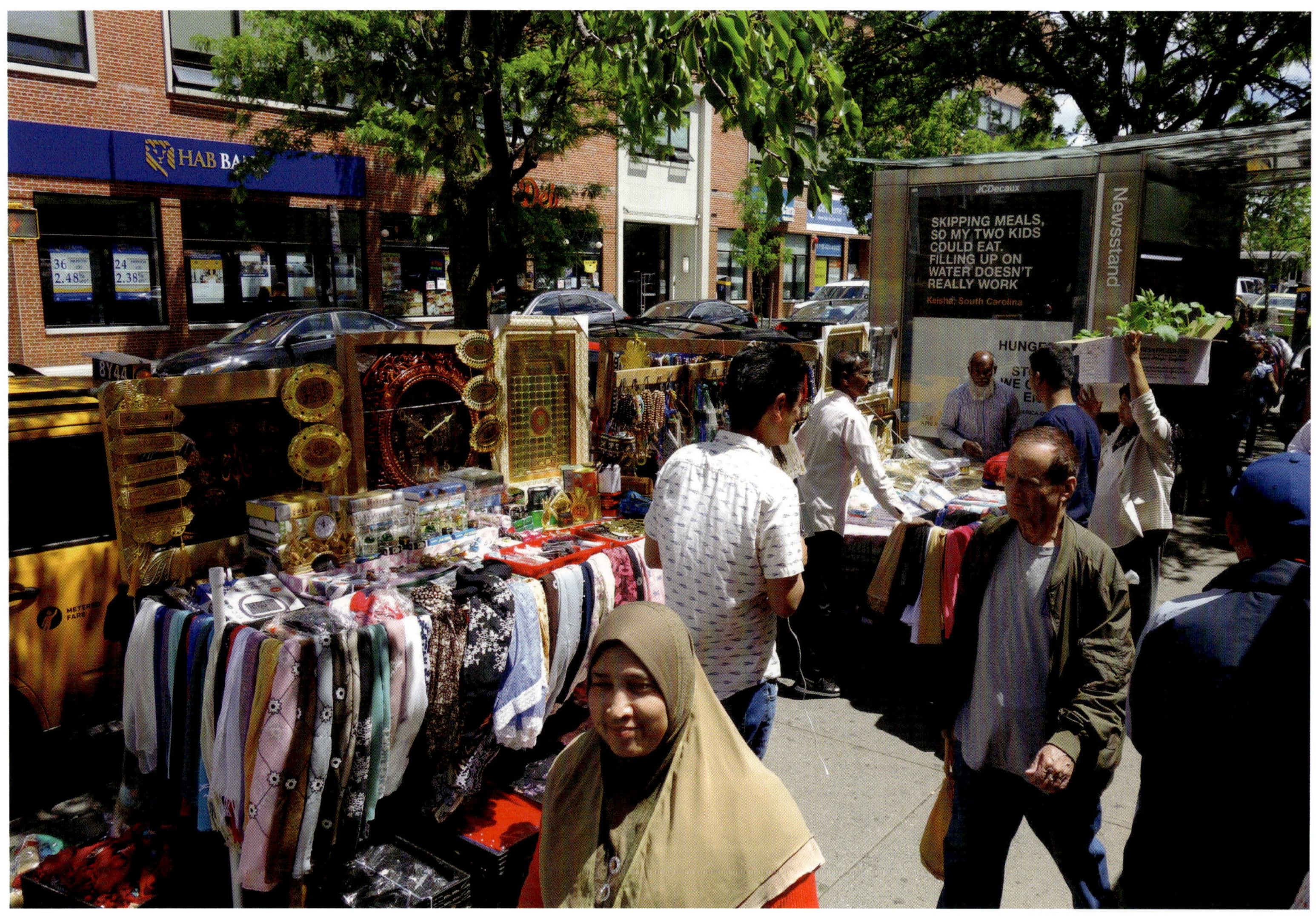

Bengali street merchants, Jackson Heights

Here at 74th Street and 37th Avenue, Bengali street merchants sell scarves, hijabs, kofias, Korans, prayer beads, rugs, peacock feathers, and other items for a largely Muslim clientele. South Asians began moving to Jackson Heights in the 1960s, predominantly from Gujarat and Punjab, and by the 1980s, the area was called “Little India.” Bengali immigrants constituted a second wave in the 1990s, coming from both Bangladesh and West Bengal state in India. While they worked primarily as day laborers and cab drivers in the early stages of migration, many have become merchants, doctors, and lawyers, growing politically and economically influential. They have also built strong advocacy organizations.

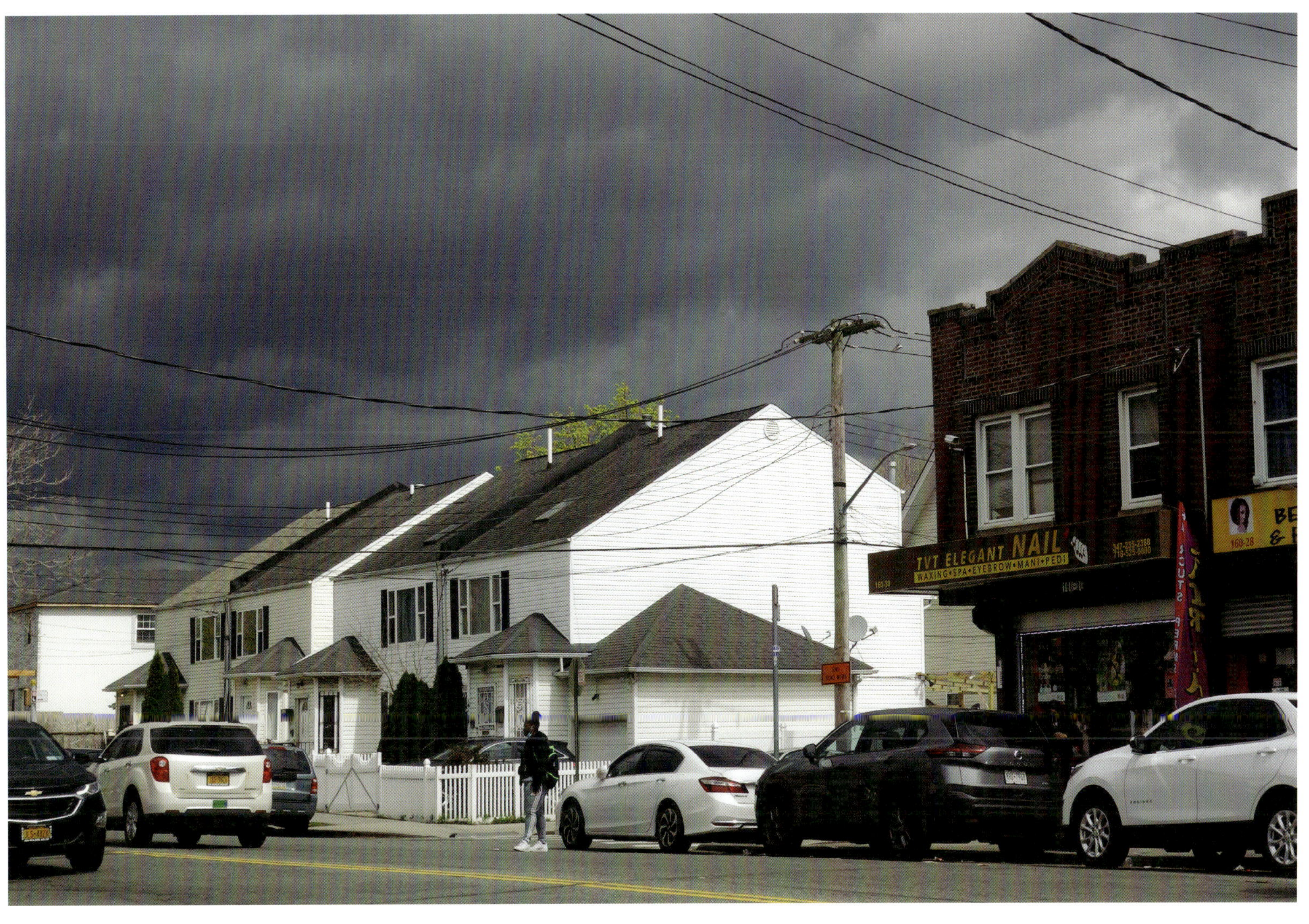

Storm clouds gathering over South Jamaica

Southeastern Queens presents a landscape of low-slung single-family homes and duplexes stretching from Jamaica down through Hollis, St. Albans, Laurelton, South Ozone Park, and Cambria Heights. Middle-class African American families began moving into South Jamaica as early as the 1920s to take advantage of new housing largely free of racial covenants. From the 1960s through the 1980s, the city concentrated a series of large housing projects and the campus of York College on the old Jamaica Race Course. The neighborhood suffered increased crime and violence during the crack epidemic of the 1980s and 1990s, but active community organizations have helped the area recover.

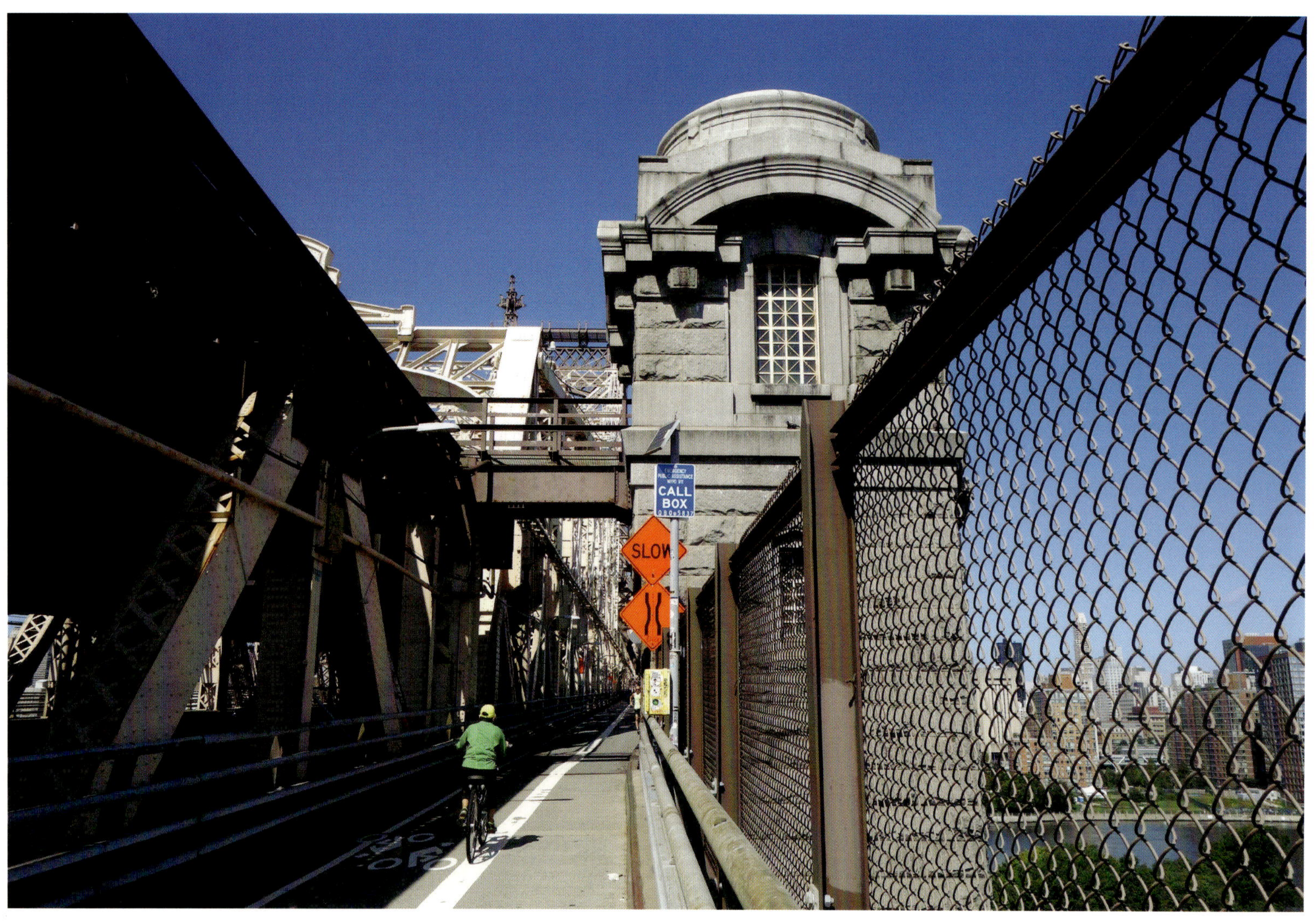

Bridging the borough

Figures 46a–46d. In 1909, the Queensboro Bridge opened, setting the stage for the borough's rapid development. The historical convergence of train and automobile connection to Manhattan, the availability of vast tracts of farm and woodland in Queens, and a nationwide building boom in the 1910s and 1920s led to the explosive growth of affordable housing for working-class and middle-class New Yorkers. The completion of the Hell Gate railway bridge and viaduct in 1916 finally connected Queens to the continental mainland via Randall's Island. Today, the five boroughs are knitted together by some two dozen bridges, viaducts, and tunnels.

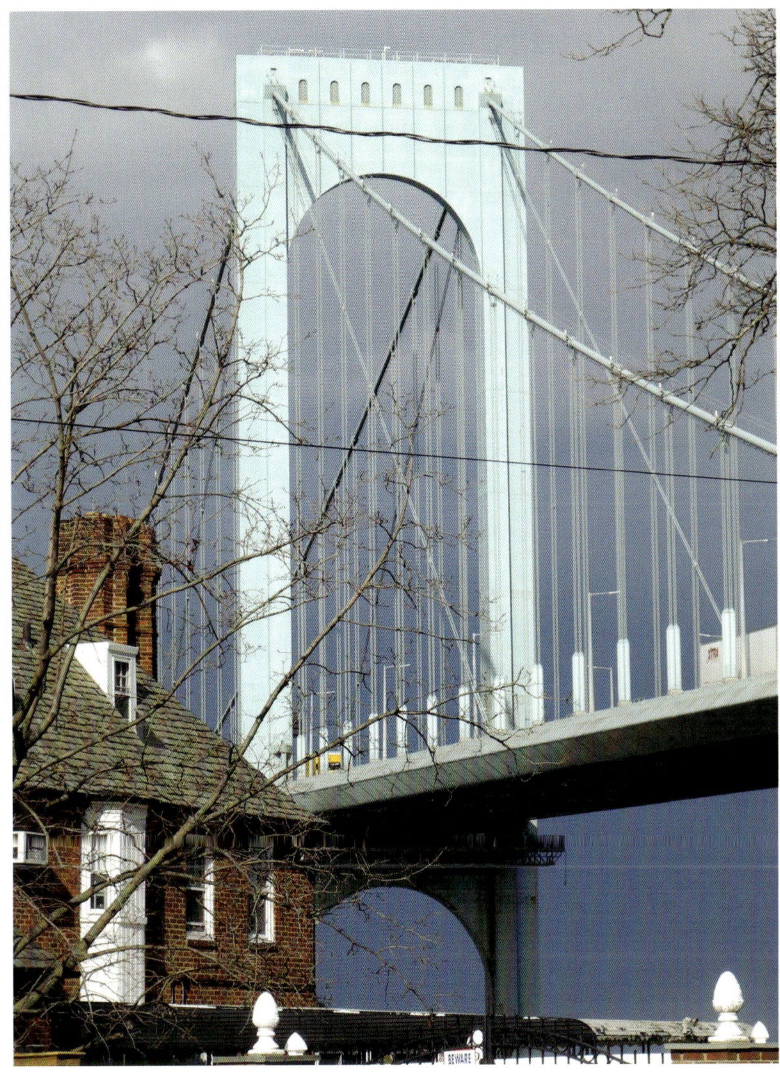

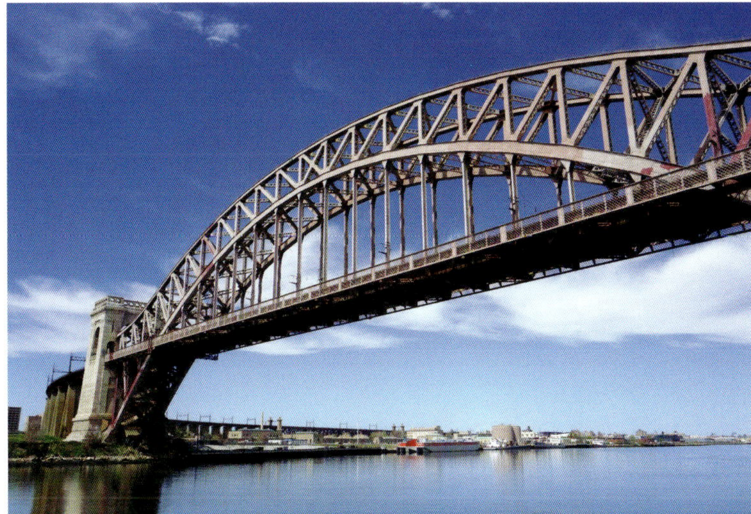

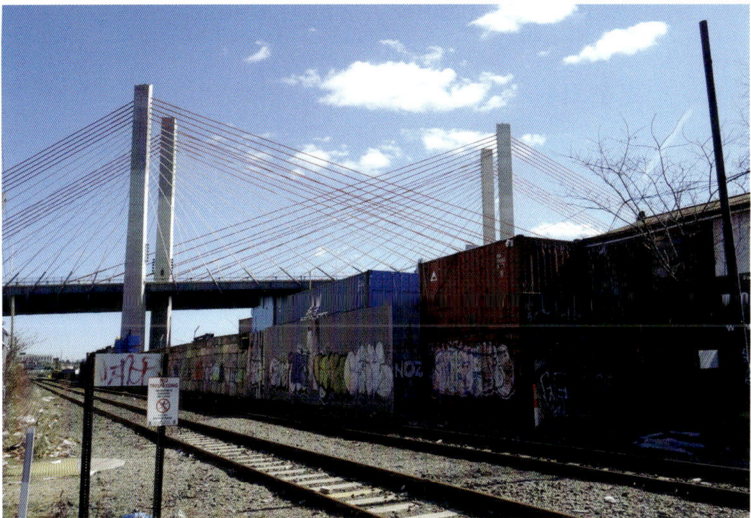

Opposite page: Cycling and pedestrian approach to the easternmost granite pier of the Queensboro Bridge. This page, left: The south pier of the Whitestone Bridge rises over the neighborhood that gave it its name. Completed in 1939, it is the second of three bridges connecting Queens with the Bronx across the East River. Top right: The Hell Gate Bridge, designed by Gustav Lindenthal. The inverted bowstring truss carries freight and passenger trains between Astoria, Queens, and Randall's Island, from where it heads north. Bottom right: Piers and cable stays of the recently rebuilt Kosciuszko Bridge, connecting Greenpoint, Brooklyn, to Maspeth, Queens, over Newtown Creek.

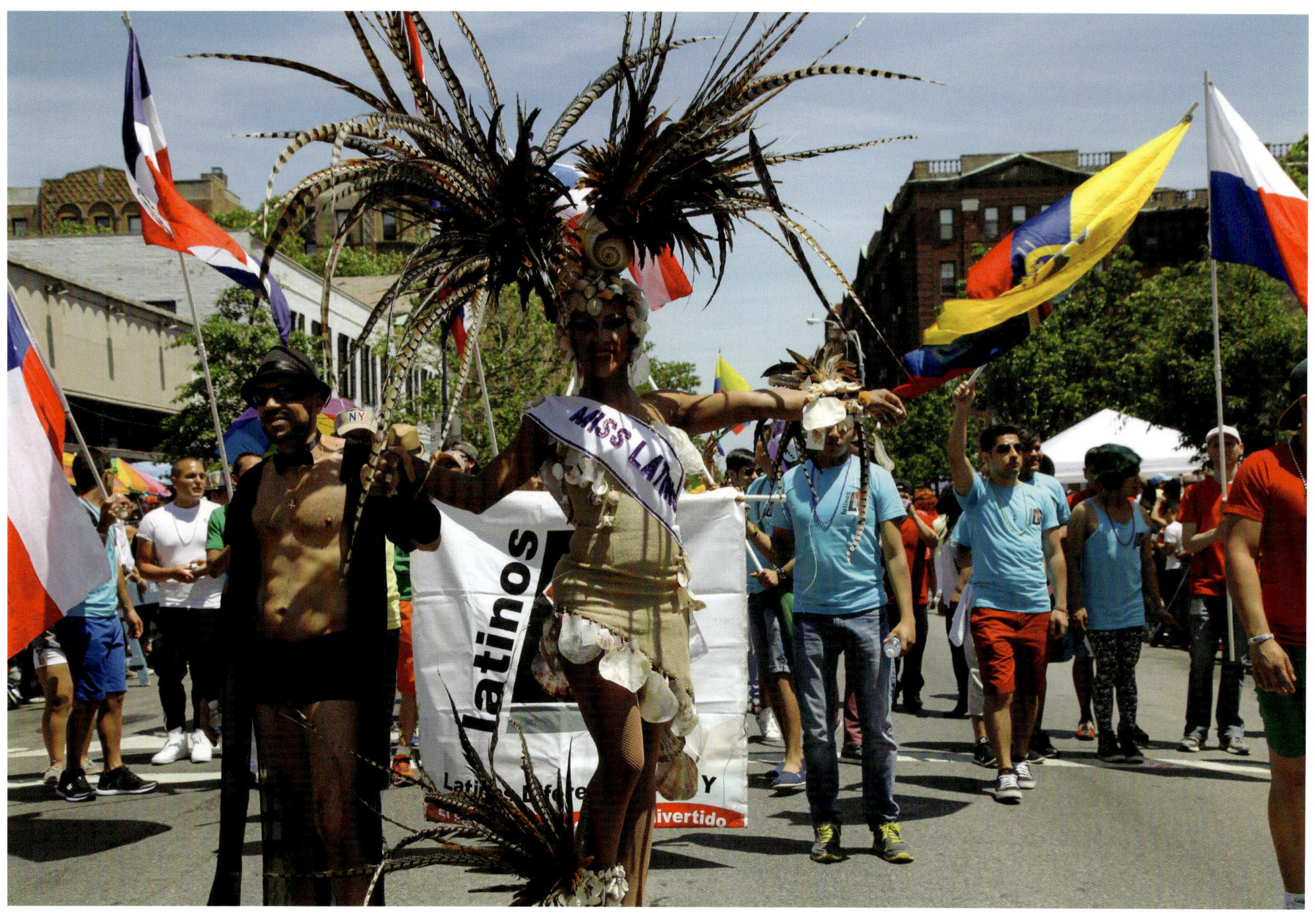

Miss Latinos, Pridefest, Jackson Heights

Western Queens is home to vibrant, multiethnic transgender and drag cultures, with many nightclubs, bars, and services concentrated along Roosevelt Avenue. Over the years, transgender people have experienced high levels of police repression as well as violence and harassment from residents in surrounding neighborhoods. In response, transgender activists have waged a determined campaign to counteract violence in their everyday lives as well as bigotry and prejudice in the law. Pridefest in Jackson Heights has become an important venue for the community to assert their presence on the landscape and their right to live without fear in the city.

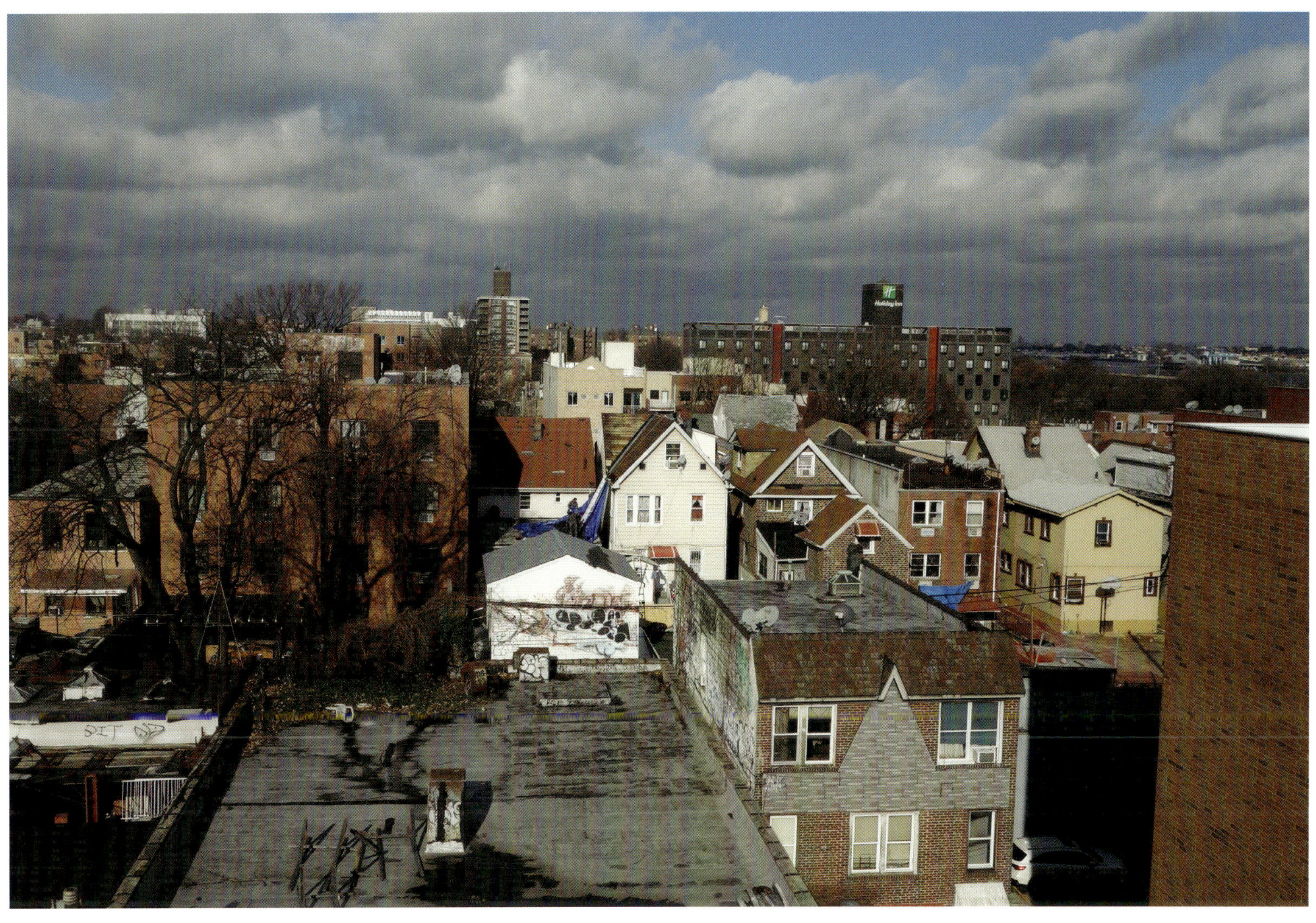

View over Corona from the 7 train

After passing through the mid-rise towers of Jackson Heights, a traveler on the 7 train might notice an abrupt shift, as the built environment hugs closer to the ground in Corona. Where Jackson Heights was developed as a cooperative apartment community, Corona emerged in fits and starts as a low-rise landscape of single-family homes and duplexes. The view in this photo takes in a sweep between 112th and 114th Streets, looking northward toward Flushing Bay. The severe lack of housing in Corona has led residents to subdivide homes into multiple units and to double up in apartments, making it one of the most overcrowded neighborhoods in New York.

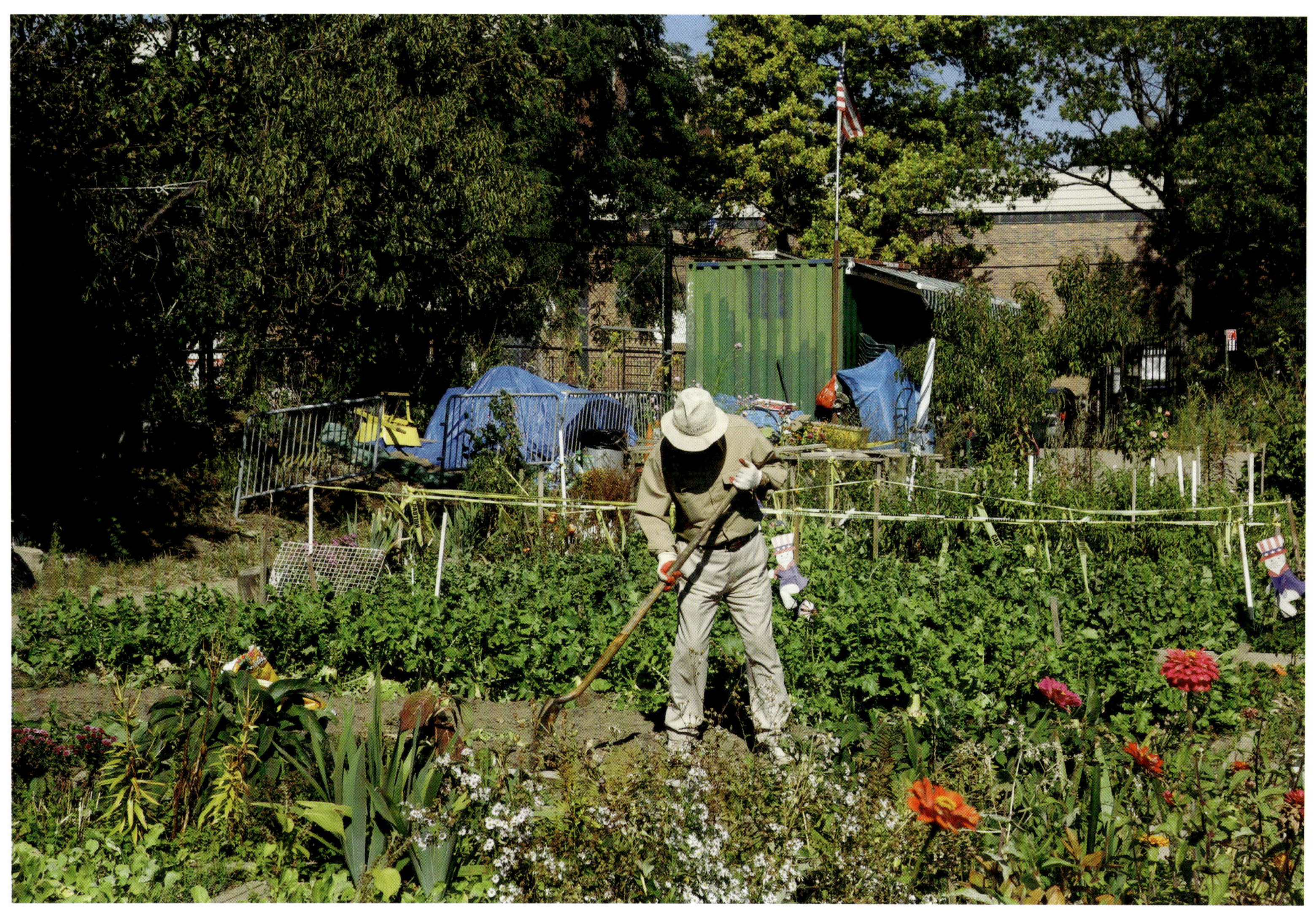

Evergreen Garden, Flushing

Evergreen is one of the largest community gardens in New York. A Korean-American senior citizen group established the five-acre garden in the early 1980s by cleaning up a trash-filled part of Kissena Park. They organized the garden into allotments leased by individuals and families. The city took over the garden in 2014 after alleging that gardeners were "illegally" selling produce. Today, the garden is operated by the city's Green Thumb program, which requires gardeners to maintain hours open to the public. Most of the gardeners are Korean or Chinese, using their collective horticultural wisdom to cultivate a great variety of vegetables, fruits, flowers, and other ornamentals.

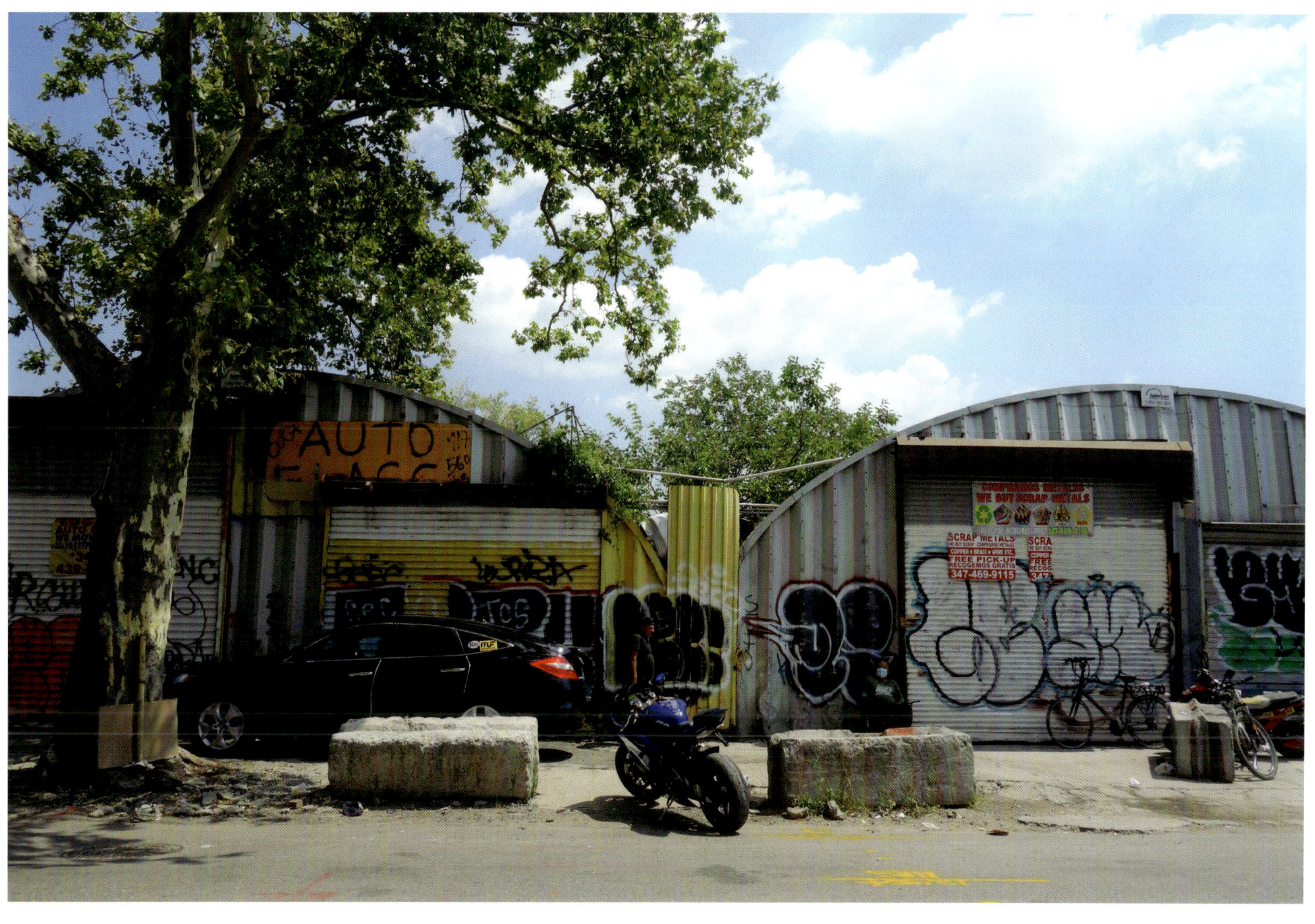

Remnant of the Iron Triangle, Willets Point

Willets Point is a spit of land jutting out into Flushing Bay, home to the Mets stadium, two large highway interchanges, and until recently, a zone of makeshift auto service shops known as the Iron Triangle. Spreading out over 45 acres, this shantytown of sheds, junkyards, and Quonset huts constituted the largest "chop shop" in New York. Hundreds of immigrant men and women, many undocumented, found employment here as mechanics, fabricators, haulers, food vendors, and sex workers. Transactions tended to be cash-only. City officials long targeted the Iron Triangle for demolition, citing the lack of sewer connections and frequent flooding, and in 2021 they finally cleared the area for redevelopment.

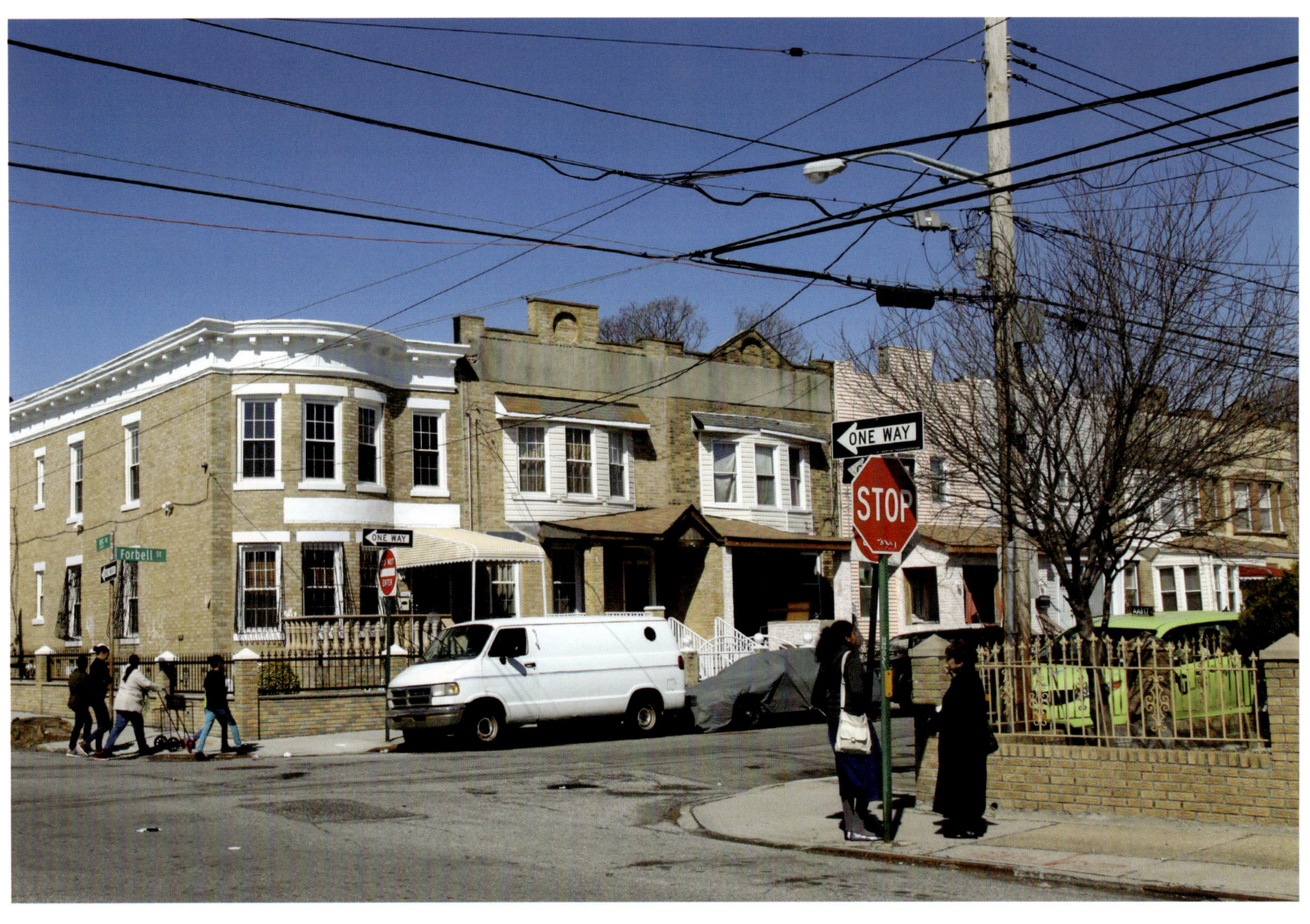

Spring in the Brooklyn-Queens borderlands

Neighbors stroll and chat at the corner of Forbell Street and 95th Avenue, where Cypress Hills, Brooklyn, and Ozone Park, Queens, collide. Cypress Hills has an old, settled middle-class Black community dating back to the 1920s. Ozone Park, however, remained defiantly White until the post–World War II decades. Throughout the 1950s and 1960s, civil rights activists pushed against racially restrictive housing, while real estate companies engaged in blockbusting and panic selling, leading to a rapid egress of White families. Today, few people here care about the exact boundary between the neighborhoods; the only difference here is whether or not your address is hyphenated.

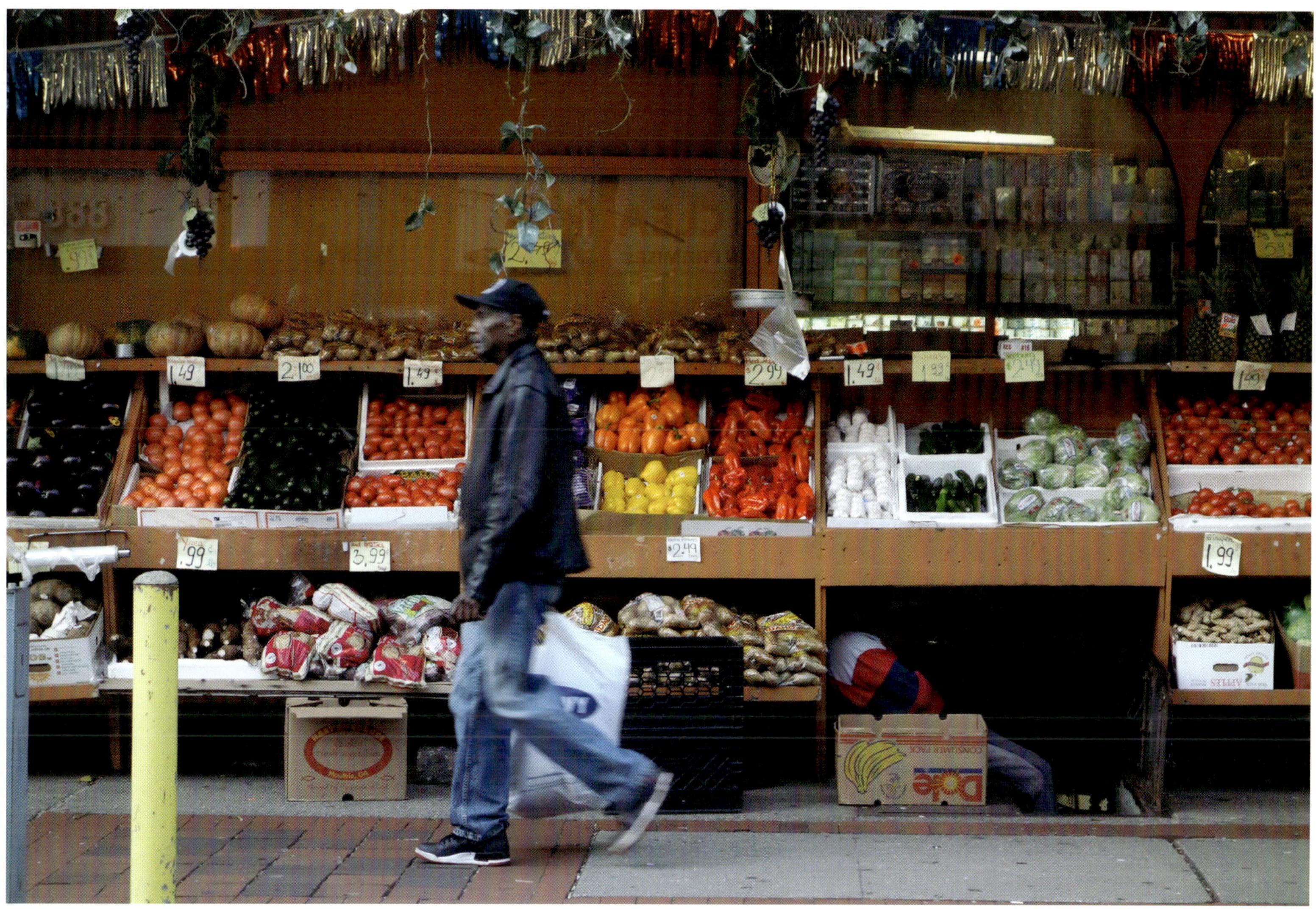

Grocer on Myrtle Avenue, Ridgewood

A man walks by the outdoor produce display of this grocery store in Ridgewood while a delivery worker takes a break below in the cellar doorway. New York City has over 5,000 grocery stores—with 1,200 in Queens alone, ranging from massive supermarkets to small bodegas and delis. In Queens, you can purchase a small grocery business of around four thousand square feet for as little as $500,000, not including monthly rent, though larger markets will cost upward of $2 million or more, depending on the location. Grocers have long provided entry-level employment for residents of Queens, and today more than eleven thousand people work in grocery retail in the borough.

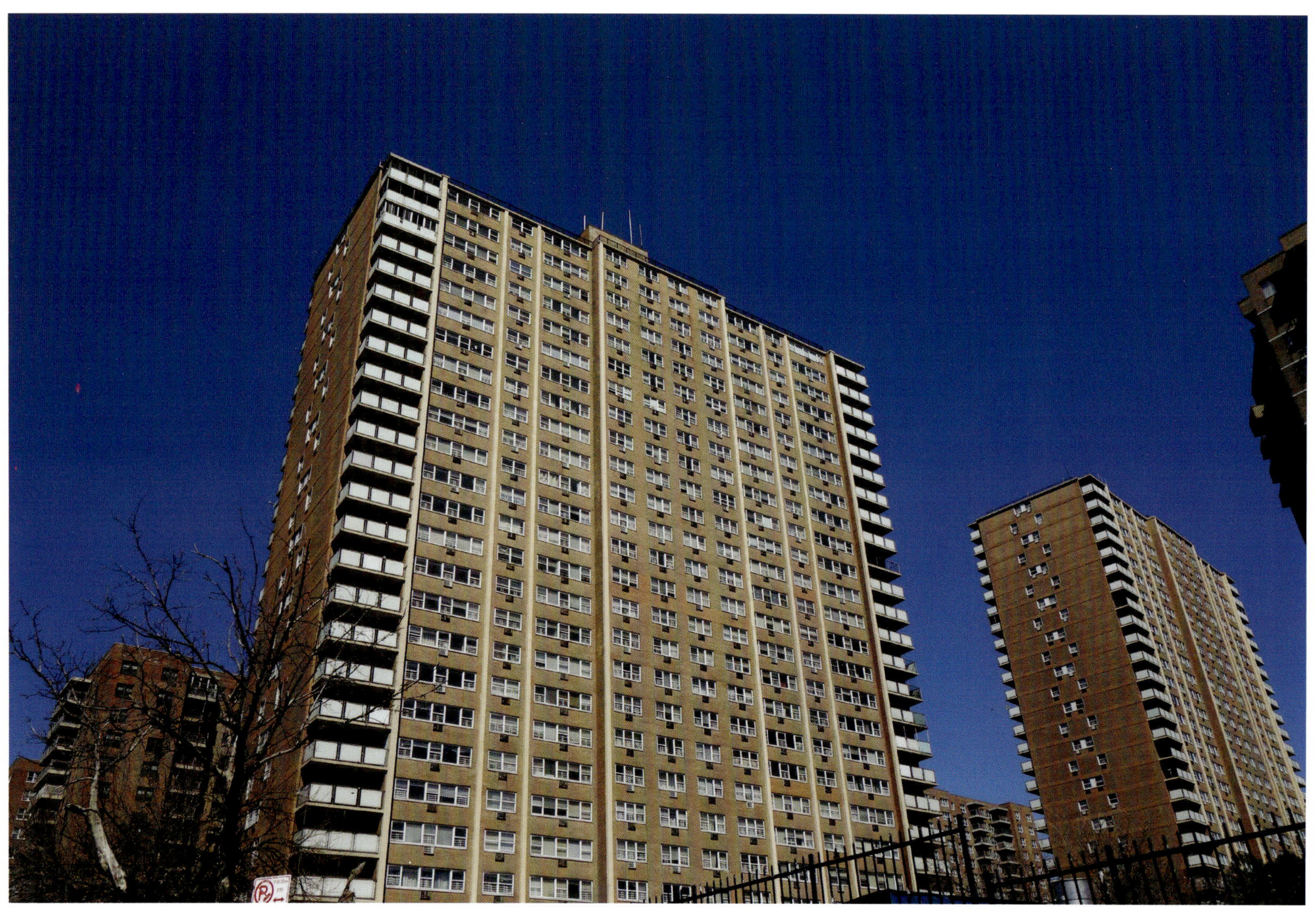

High-rise life, Flushing

While many people associate Queens with single-family homes, high-rise towers cluster in several neighborhoods, including Long Island City, Forest Hills, and Flushing. This photograph shows the massive 16-acre Carlyle Towers complex just north of Main Street in Flushing. Completed in 1962, the complex features seven 15-story buildings and two 24-story towers set in their own campus apart from the surrounding grid. Residents of the 2,700 apartments have access to underground garages, landscaped grounds, a swimming pool, and a gym. Since its completion, Flushing has accumulated dozens of mid-rise and high-rise towers in the blocks around Main Street, Parsons Boulevard, and Kissena Boulevard.

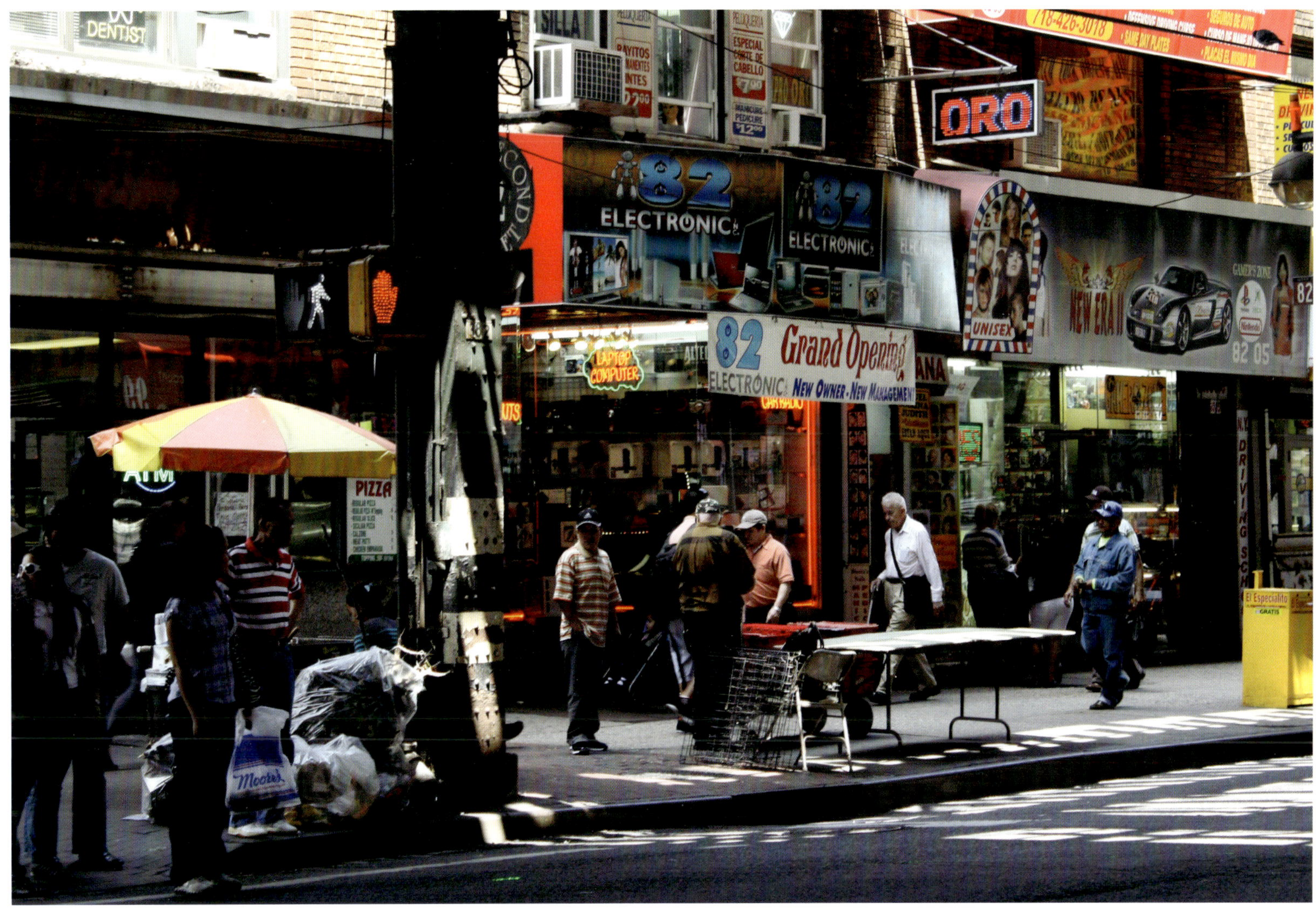

Glocal Commerce on Roosevelt Avenue

Roosevelt Avenue between 74th Street and Junction Boulevard is a classic "glocal" strip—that is, simultaneously global and local. Small family businesses here often sell products that swirl through global supply chains, such as cell phones, stereo and DJ equipment, cameras, watches, computers, and televisions. These are interspersed with more localized services, such as restaurants, bars, dentists, massage parlors, driving schools, hair salons, immigration law offices, and a multitude of other small businesses. Meanwhile, a few global chains have opened, primarily offering fast food, tax preparation, and banking. Nevertheless, most spaces continue to be occupied by family-owned single-location businesses.

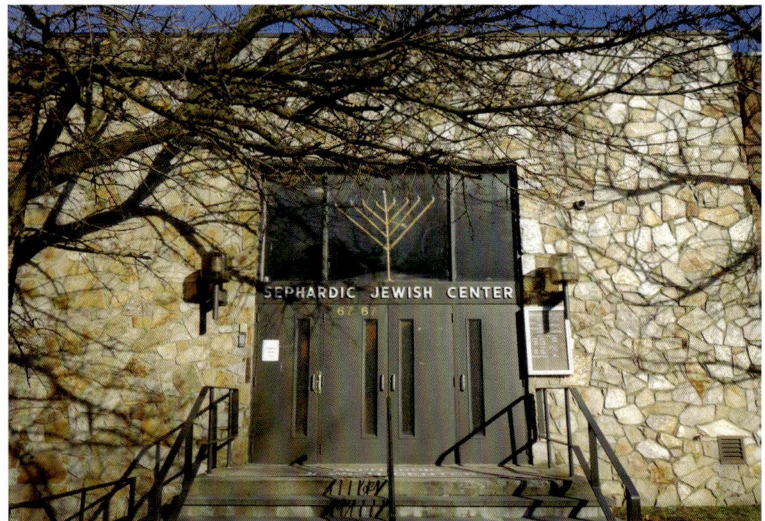

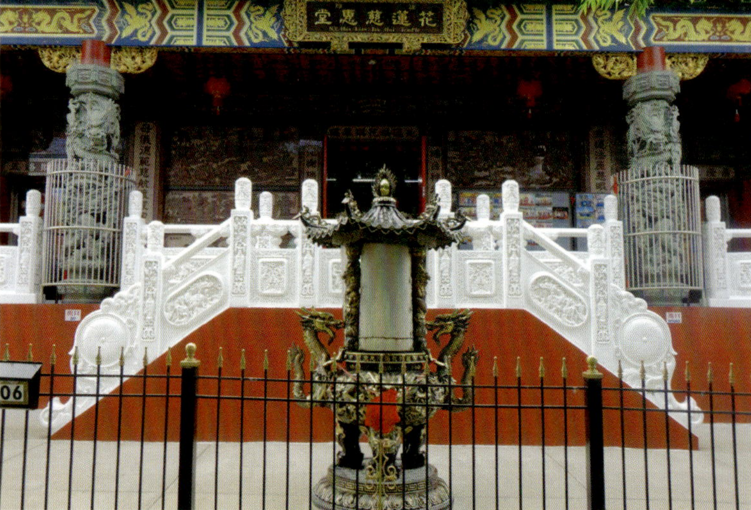

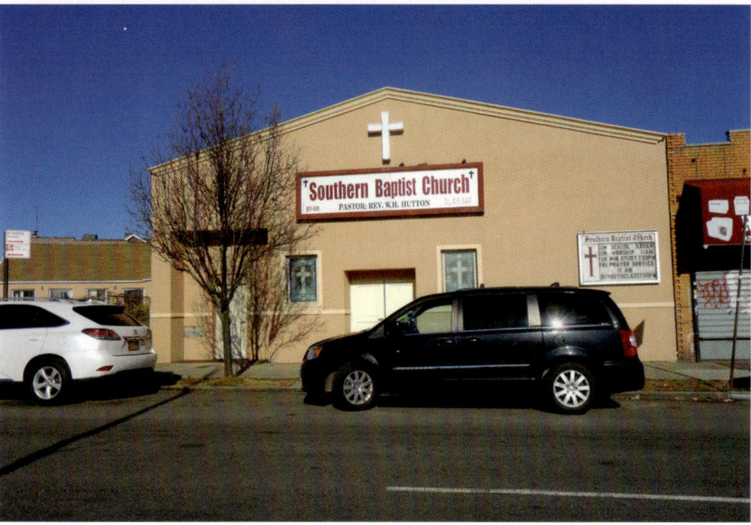

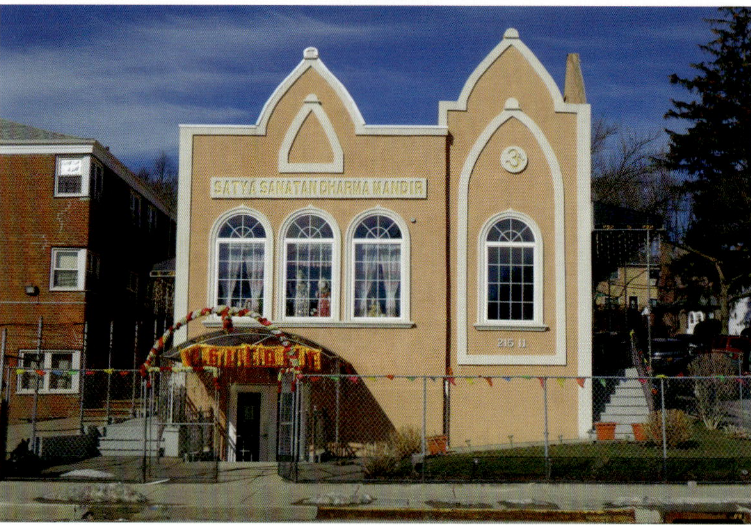

Purpose-built for devotion

Figures 55a–55h. Every group that establishes itself in Queens has laid down edifices to further the religious life of the community. Such buildings serve as a signal that a group has arrived and put down roots. Over time, hundreds of purpose-built religious structures, both modest and grand, accumulated on the urban landscape. Some continue to serve their original creeds, while others have been adapted for new ones. The result is an ever-changing religious geography, a mosaic of spiritual life for diverse communities of worship. Purpose-built religious buildings have left a rich and varied architectural legacy that often stands in contrast with the more mundane residential, commercial, and industrial landscapes surrounding them.

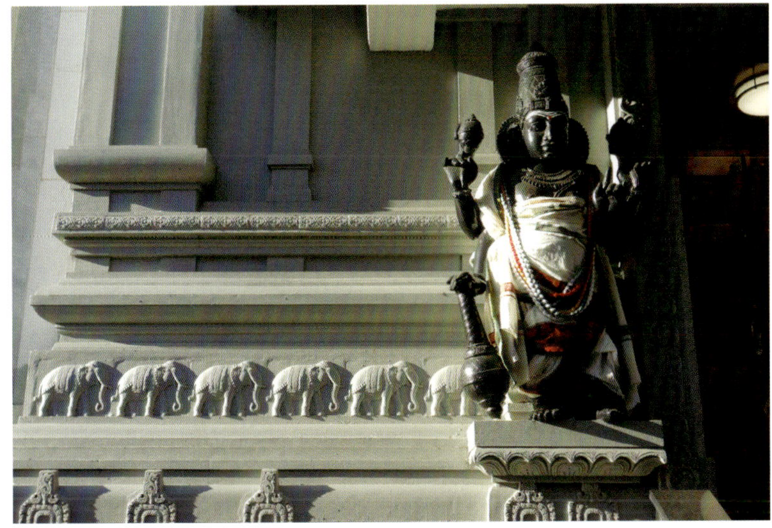

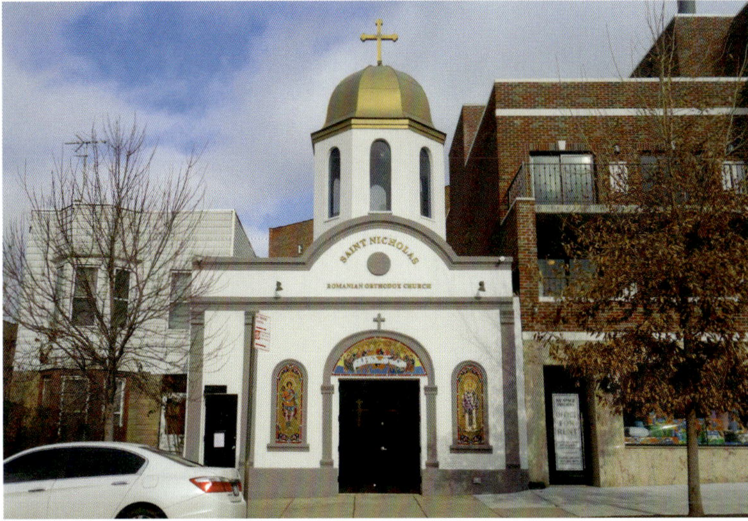

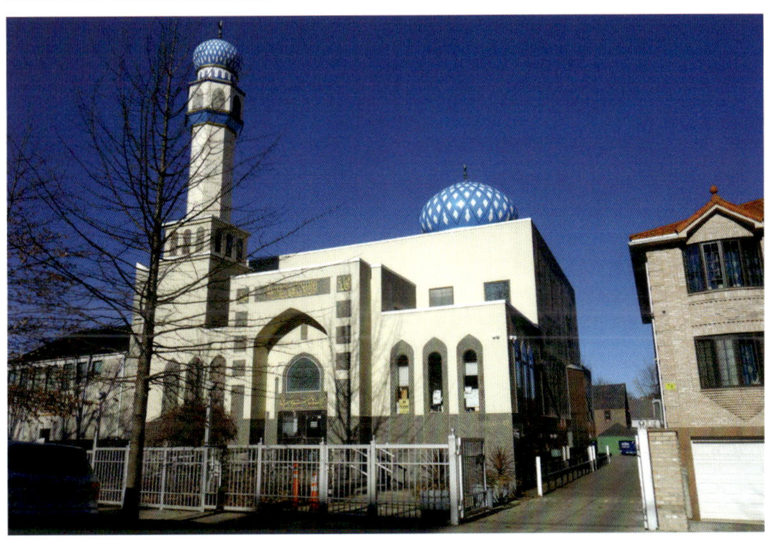

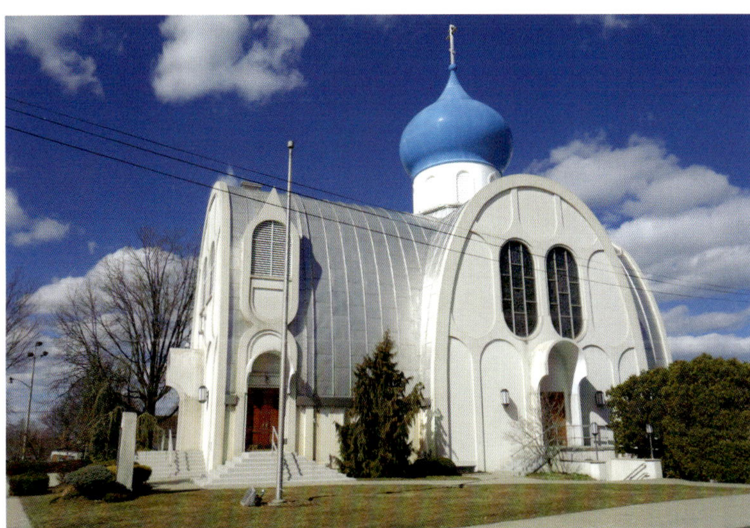

Opposite page, top left: Sephardic Jewish Center, Forest Hills. Top right: Hua Lian Tsu Hui Taoist Temple in College Point. Bottom left: Southern Baptist Church on Astoria Boulevard, part of the historic Black community of East Elmhurst. Bottom right: the Satya Sanatan Dharma Mandir, recently completed on Hillside Avenue in Queens Village. This page, top left: Hindu Temple in Flushing, devoted to Ganesh. Top right: St. Nicholas Romanian Orthodox Church in Sunnyside. Bottom left: Masjid Hazrati Abu Bakr Siddique, a mosque in Flushing founded by refugees from Soviet-occupied Afghanistan. Bottom right: St. Nicholas Greek Orthodox Church in Whitestone.

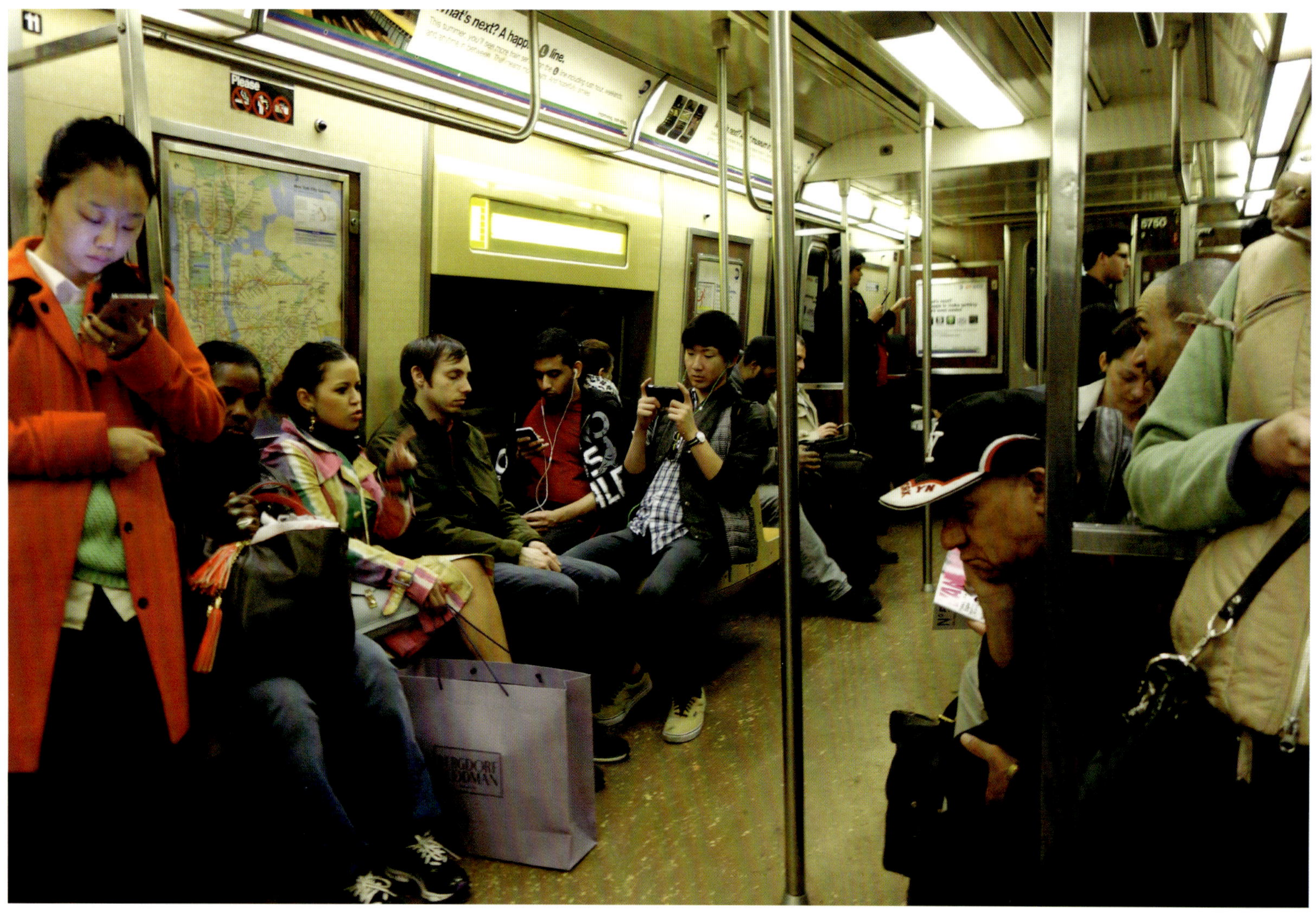

Homeward bound on the F train

Evening commuters and shoppers return home to Queens from Manhattan on the F train, shown here between 21st Street/Queensbridge and 74th Street/Jackson Heights. Subway service reached Jackson Heights in 1933, extending to Kew Gardens in 1936 and finally to Jamaica in 1950. The F train carries passengers daily along a 27-mile route from Coney Island through Manhattan and into Queens, where it runs express, making a total of forty-five station stops. The portion shown here runs underneath Northern Boulevard to Broadway until it turns onto tracks below Queens Boulevard, which carry the E, F, M, and Q trains to their various terminal points.

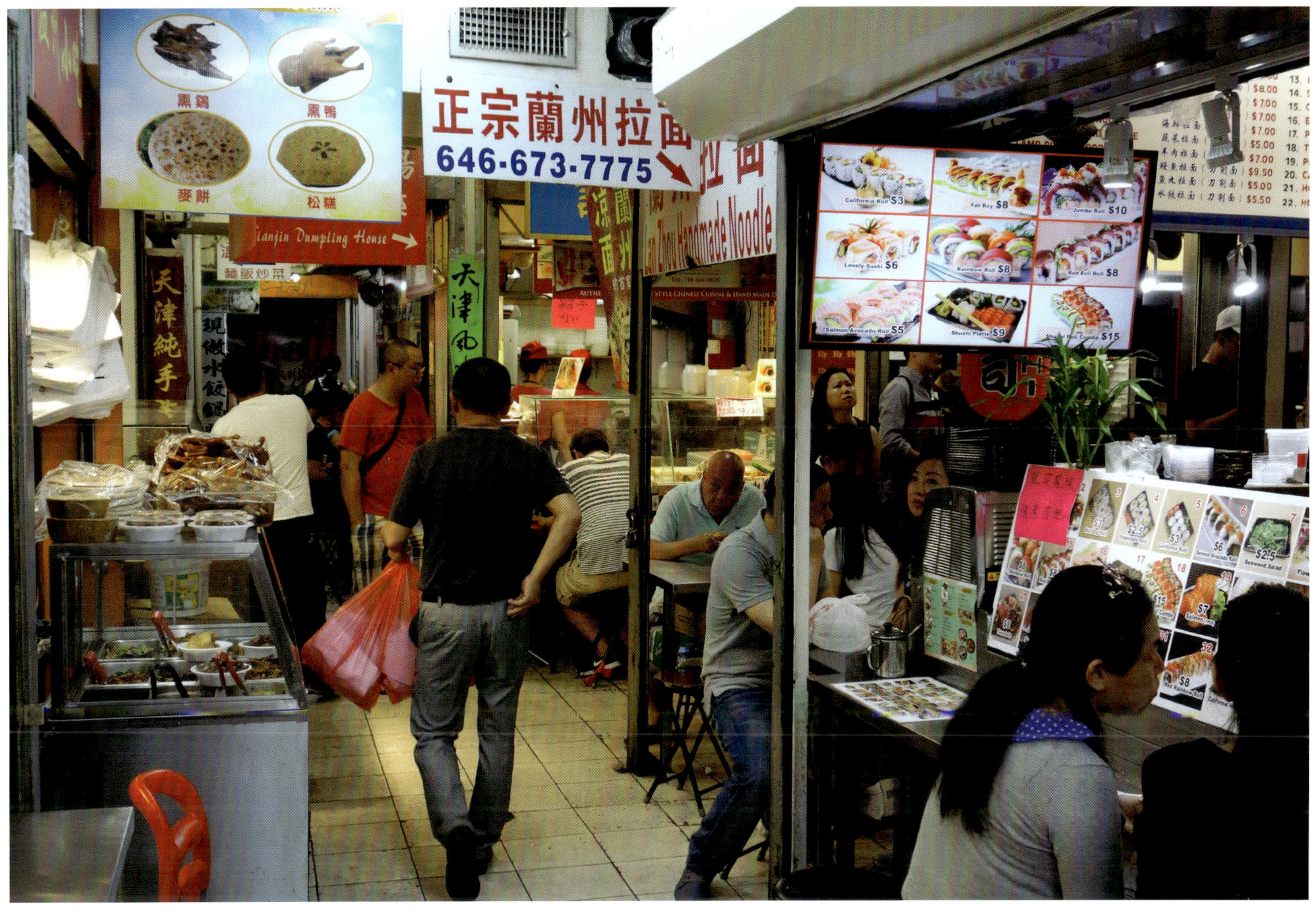

Golden Mall Food Court, Flushing

Entering through a nondescript door at street level and descending a flight of concrete steps brought you into the Golden Mall Food Court, a culinary gem of Flushing. Some dozen eateries folded themselves into the twists and turns of this small basement, where patrons sat cheek by jowl on small stools at narrow counters imbibing dumplings, noodles, rice, hot pots, and combination dishes. Flushing boasts several larger, fancier food courts, such as the massive New World Mall, but many loyal patrons swore by the offerings at Golden Mall. Lamentably, the operation closed in 2018 because of building code violations, though many of the businesses continue in other locations.

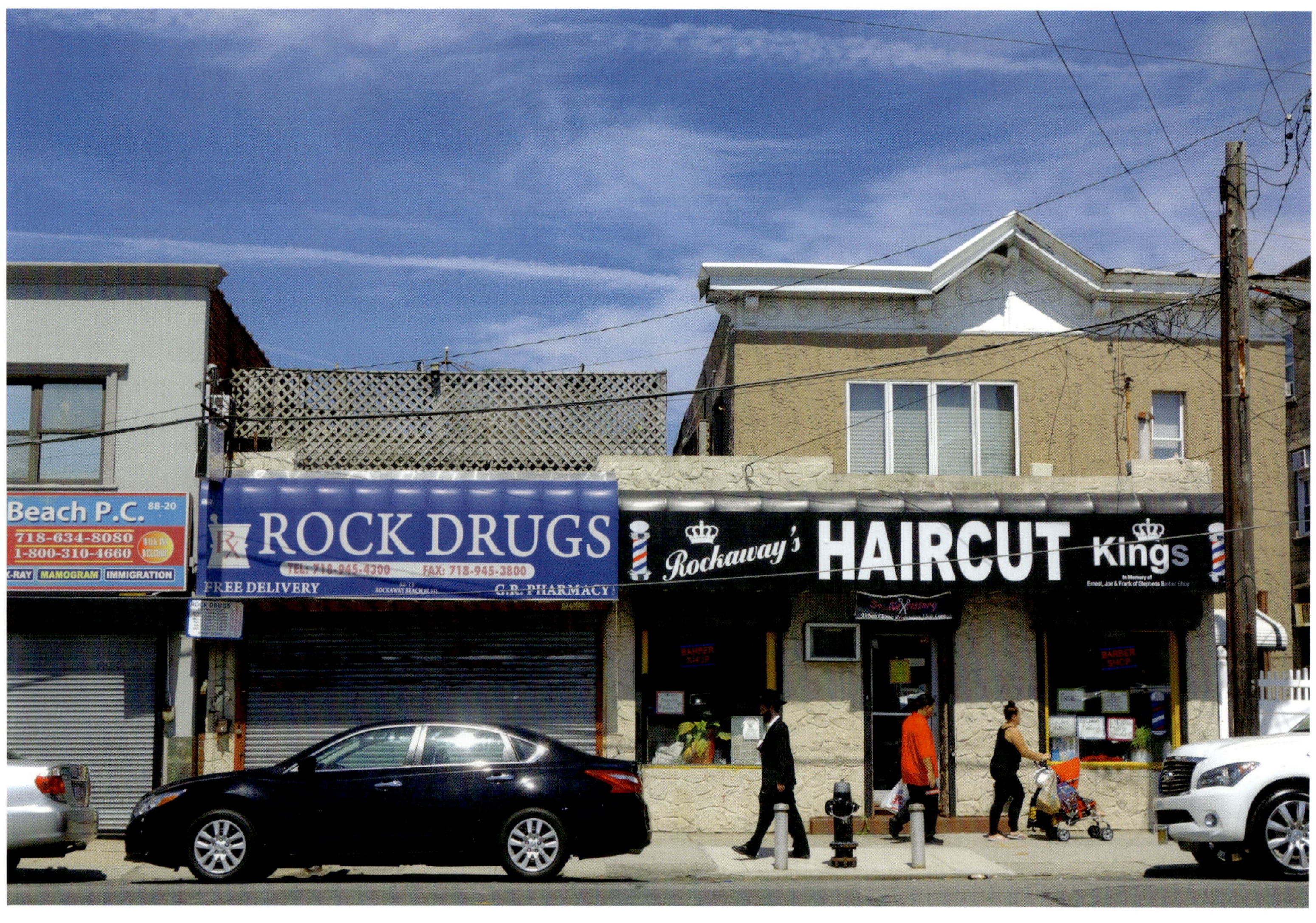

Rockaway Beach Boulevard

It looks like any ordinary Queens commercial street, but Rockaway Beach Boulevard, shown here, is only one block north of the Atlantic Ocean. Walking along this sidewalk, you can feel the salt in the air and smell the ocean. Rockaway is a 12-mile-long peninsula containing a succession of neighborhoods, from Breezy Point and Roxbury in the west to Arverne, Edgemere, and Far Rockaway at the Nassau County line. Community District 14, coterminous with the peninsula, is one of the few in the city with an even distribution of White, Black, and Hispanic residents—with all the diversity one would expect underneath such a mix. The area was hit hard by Hurricane Sandy in 2012 and was still in recovery when this photograph was taken in 2016.

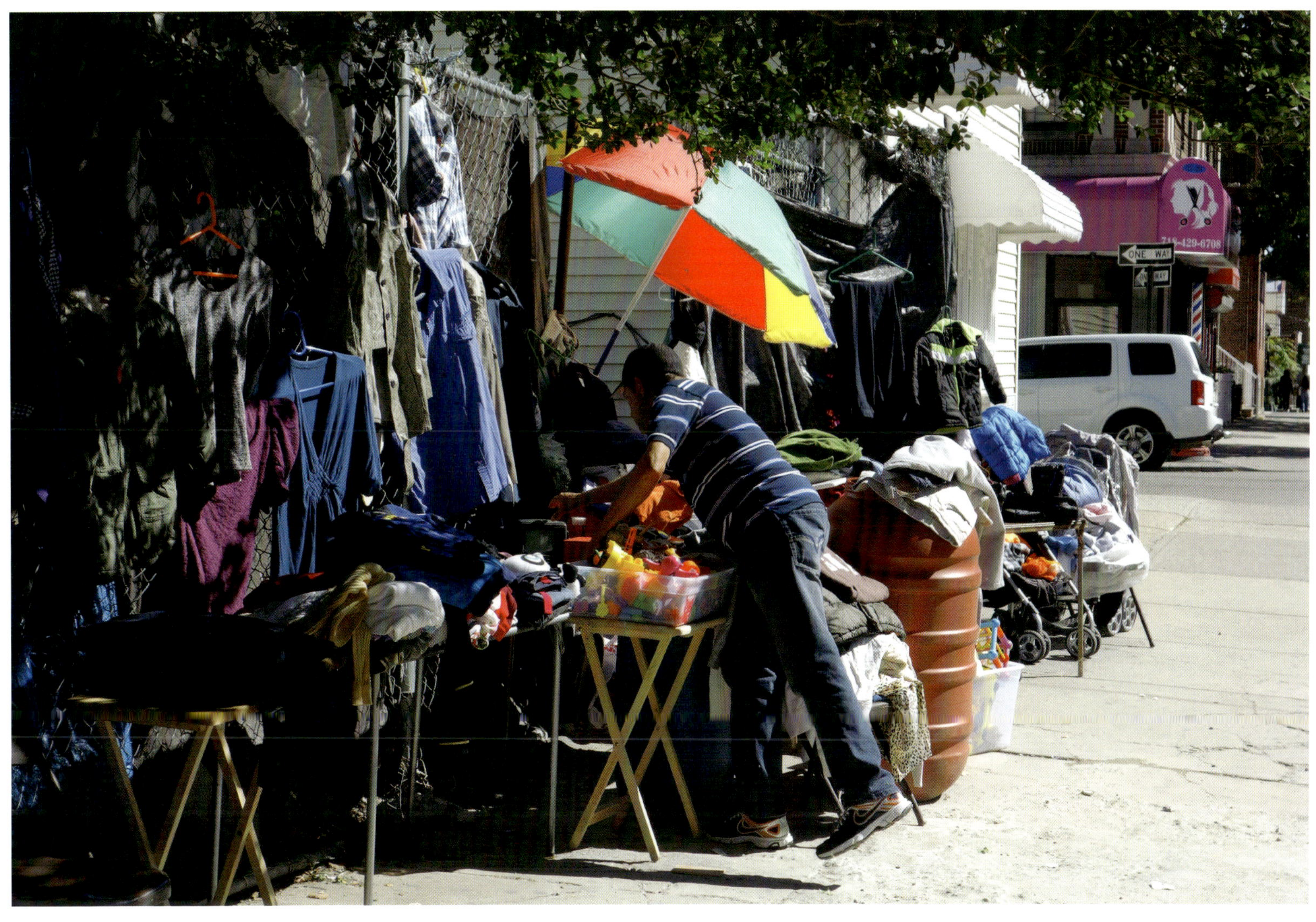

Sidewalk sale, Corona

While Brooklyn has its "stoop sales," people in Queens make do with selling items directly on the sidewalk since the borough has few stoops. Residents set up small tables, TV trays, and other flat surfaces to display their wares. They also hang items on fences and laundry lines for better viewing. Sidewalk sales typically include clothes, utensils, toys, CDs and DVDs, appliances, bicycles, and carriages. Some operate regularly, while others are temporary affairs meant to clean out a house or raise money. In any case, they are a common feature of life in working-class and immigrant neighborhoods throughout the borough.

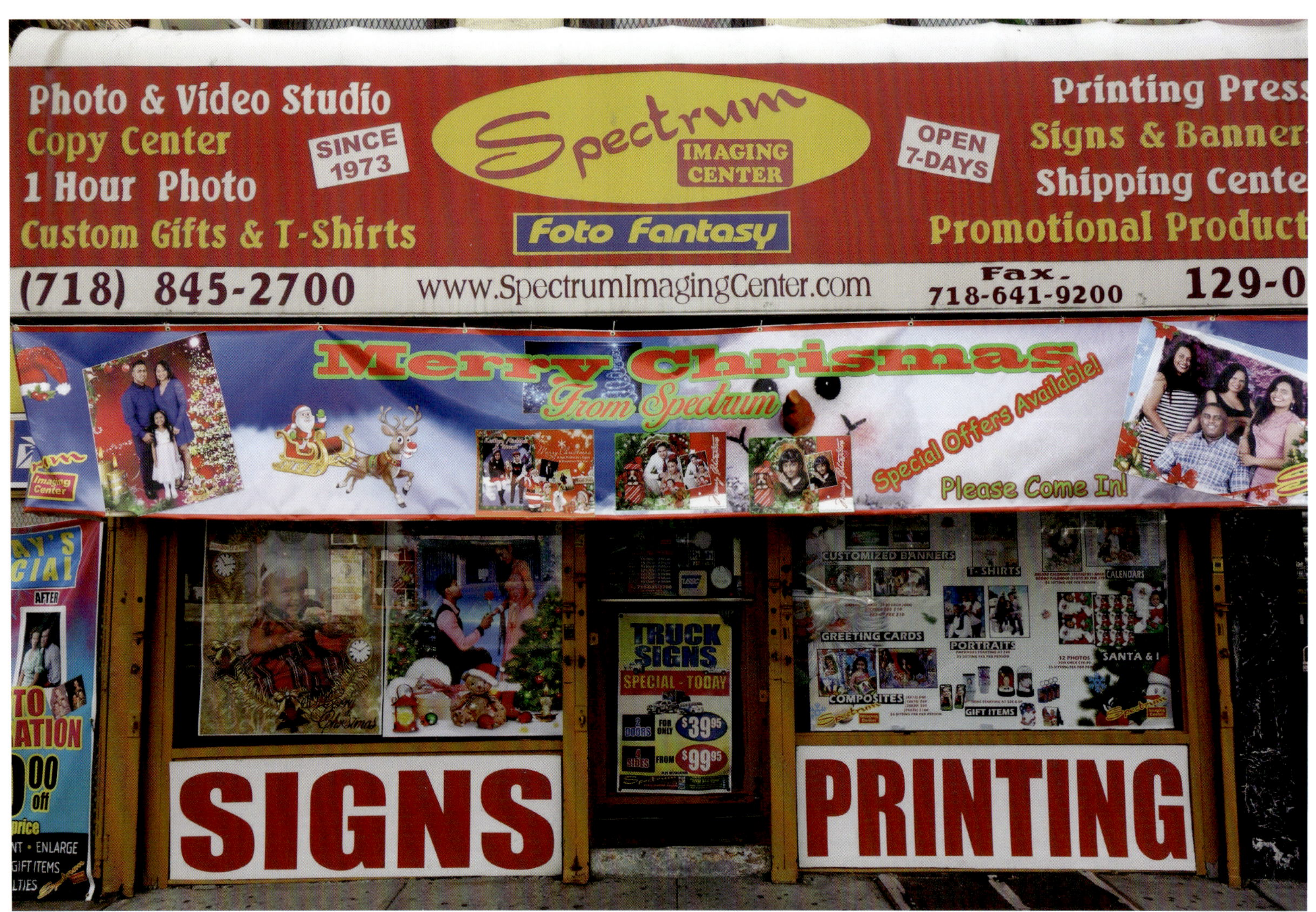

Since 1973, Richmond Hill

As neighborhoods transition culturally, so do the conventions of how residents represent themselves and form memories. Print shops are an important part of this process. Unlike corporate chains, locally-owned print shops and similar businesses readily optimize their services to match the aesthetic, financial, and cultural needs of the community. This shop offers residents of Richmond Hill a wide variety of services, from T-shirt and sign printing to video editing, studio portraiture, packaging, and shipping. The posters and banners adorning this façade show a mix of Latino, Indo-Caribbean, and Afro-Caribbean people, as befits a Richmond Hill clientele.

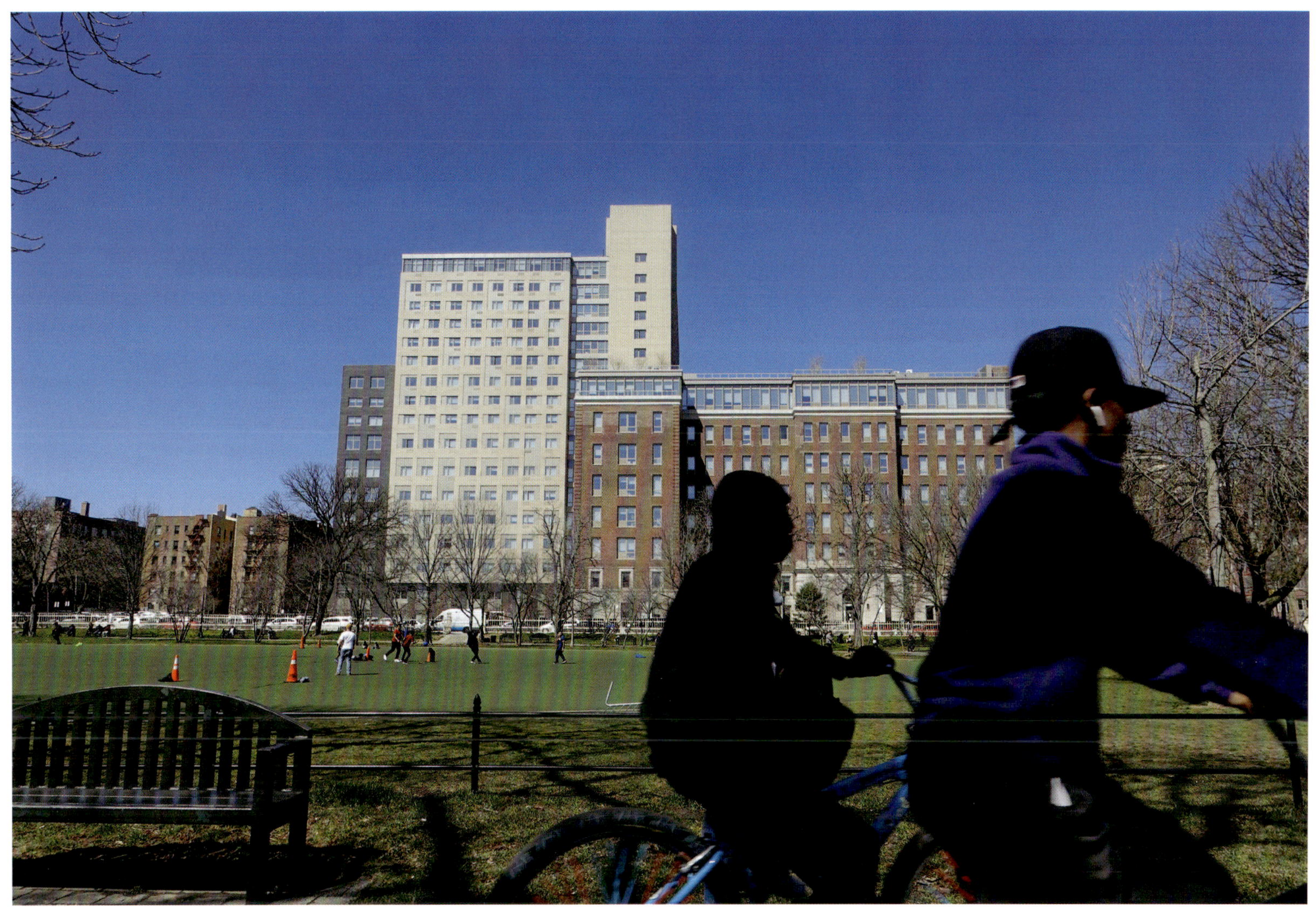

Rufus King Park, Jamaica

Two cyclists coast by a soccer match in progress on the astroturf field of Rufus King Park. At the northern edge of the park, new residential towers rise on the former campus of the Mary Immaculate Hospital. The southern edge runs along bustling Jamaica Avenue. The park has served as the public green for downtown Jamaica since the city acquired King's estate at the time of consolidation in 1898. Today, according to the Parks Department website, "Rufus King Park is a place of tolerance and independence, of sports and activity, and of natural beauty and wonder." In any case, it certainly is a beloved fixture of the neighborhood, used every day by a diverse cross-section of people.

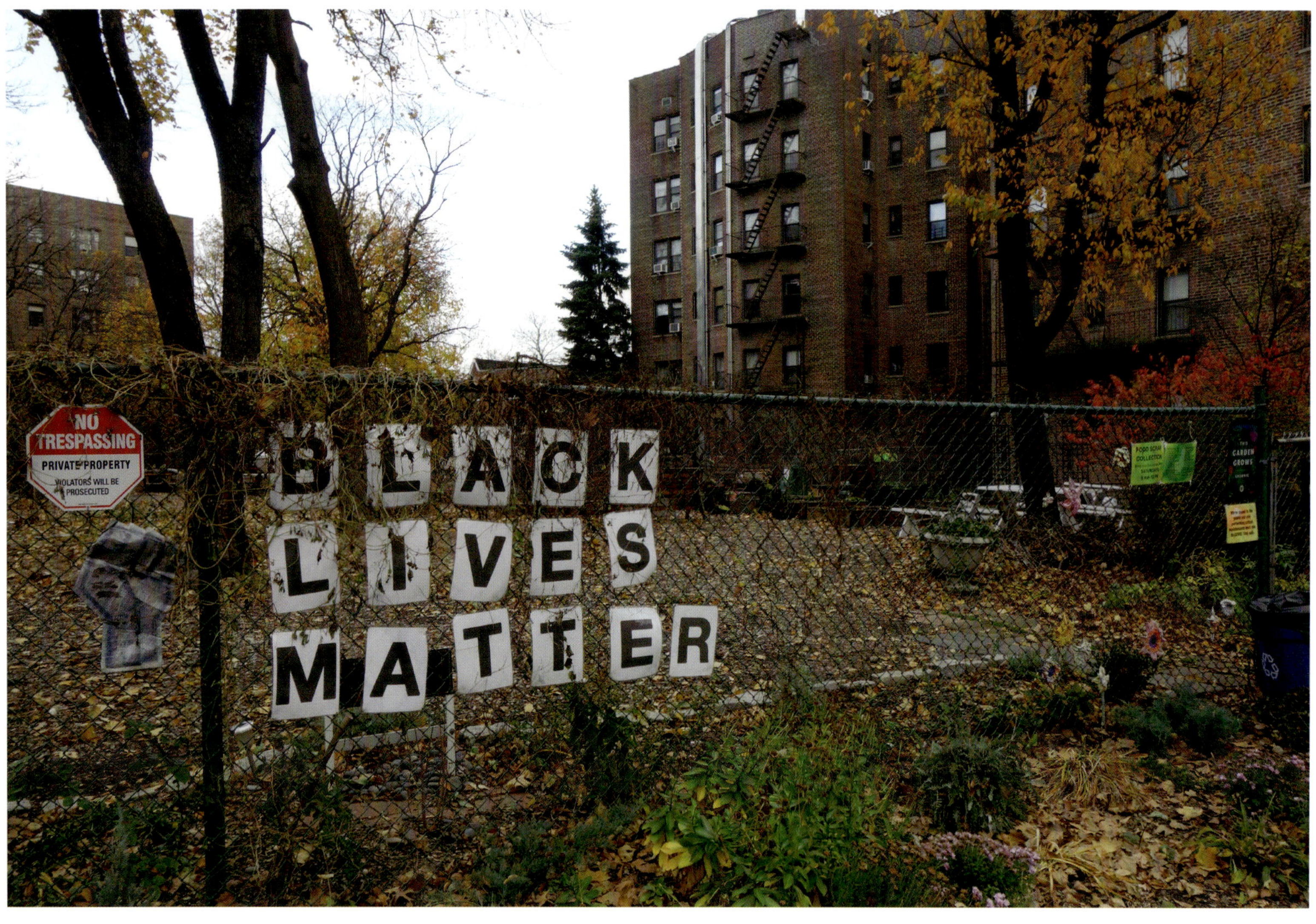

Black Lives Matter, Woodside

Gardeners at the Moore Jackson Community Garden in Woodside installed this Black Lives Matter sign in solidarity with the movement. The land under Moore Jackson was a Dutch cemetery from the early eighteenth century, and it remains protected against building encroachments. Local residents and activists launched the community garden in 2018 to create a green oasis in the formerly neglected plot. The garden is surrounded by Woodside Houses, a group of twenty 6-story buildings owned by the New York City Housing Authority. The 2,900 residents are predominantly African American, Afro-Caribbean, and Latino, with a large number of Dominican and Puerto Rican families.

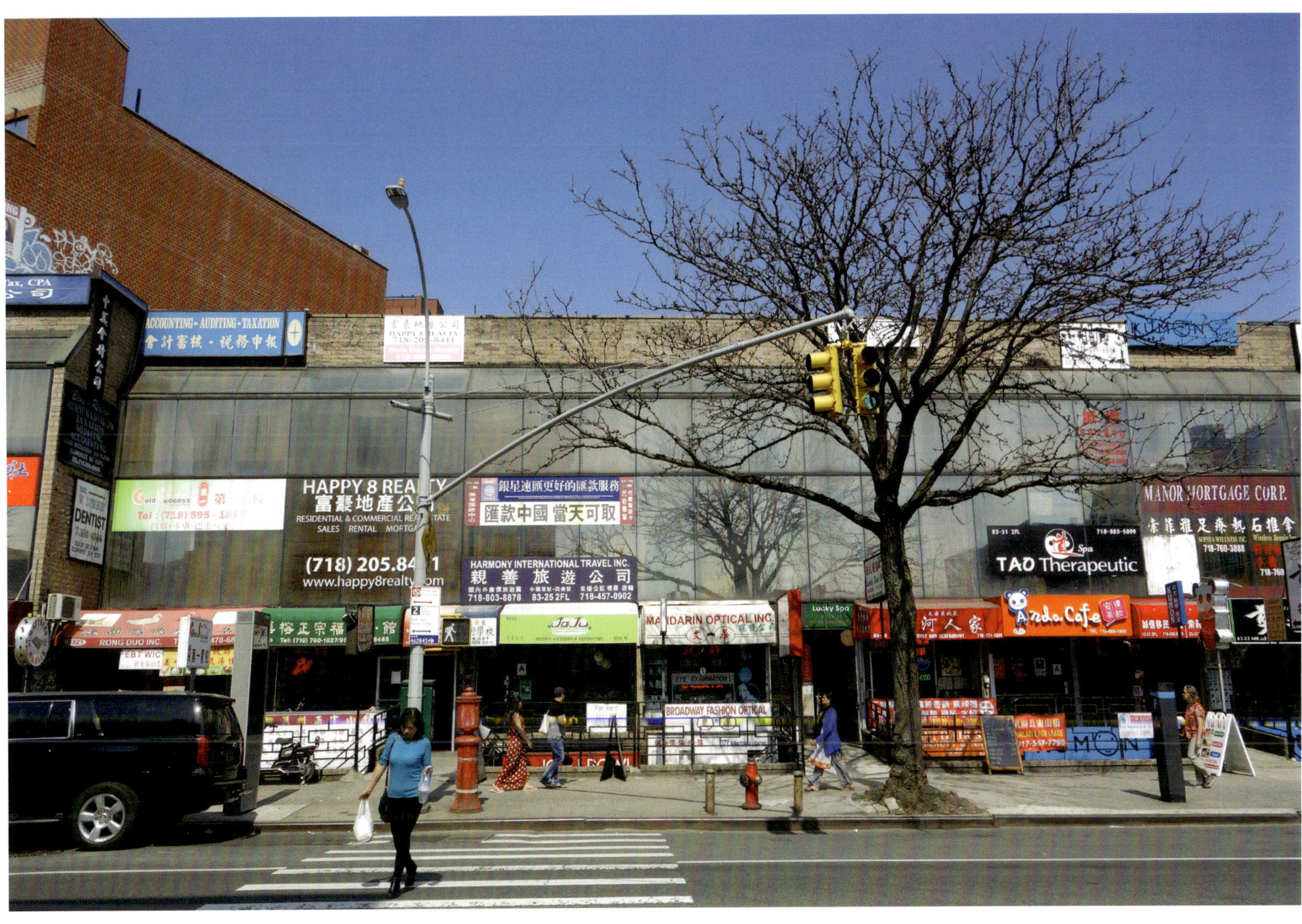

Broadway, Elmhurst

While many residents refer to the central business district of Elmhurst as "Chinatown," it is, in reality, home to a highly diverse mix of East and Southeast Asian people who have been settling here since the 1970s. Immigrants from Taiwan and Hong Kong predominate, while Mainlanders tend to be Min dialect speakers from Fujian Province rather than the more traditional Mandarin speakers. Since the early 2000s, an increasing number of Thai, Vietnamese, and Malaysian families have settled in the community, some of them of Chinese descent. The photograph shows a large commercial building along Broadway with a diverse mix of Chinese, Vietnamese, and Malaysian businesses.

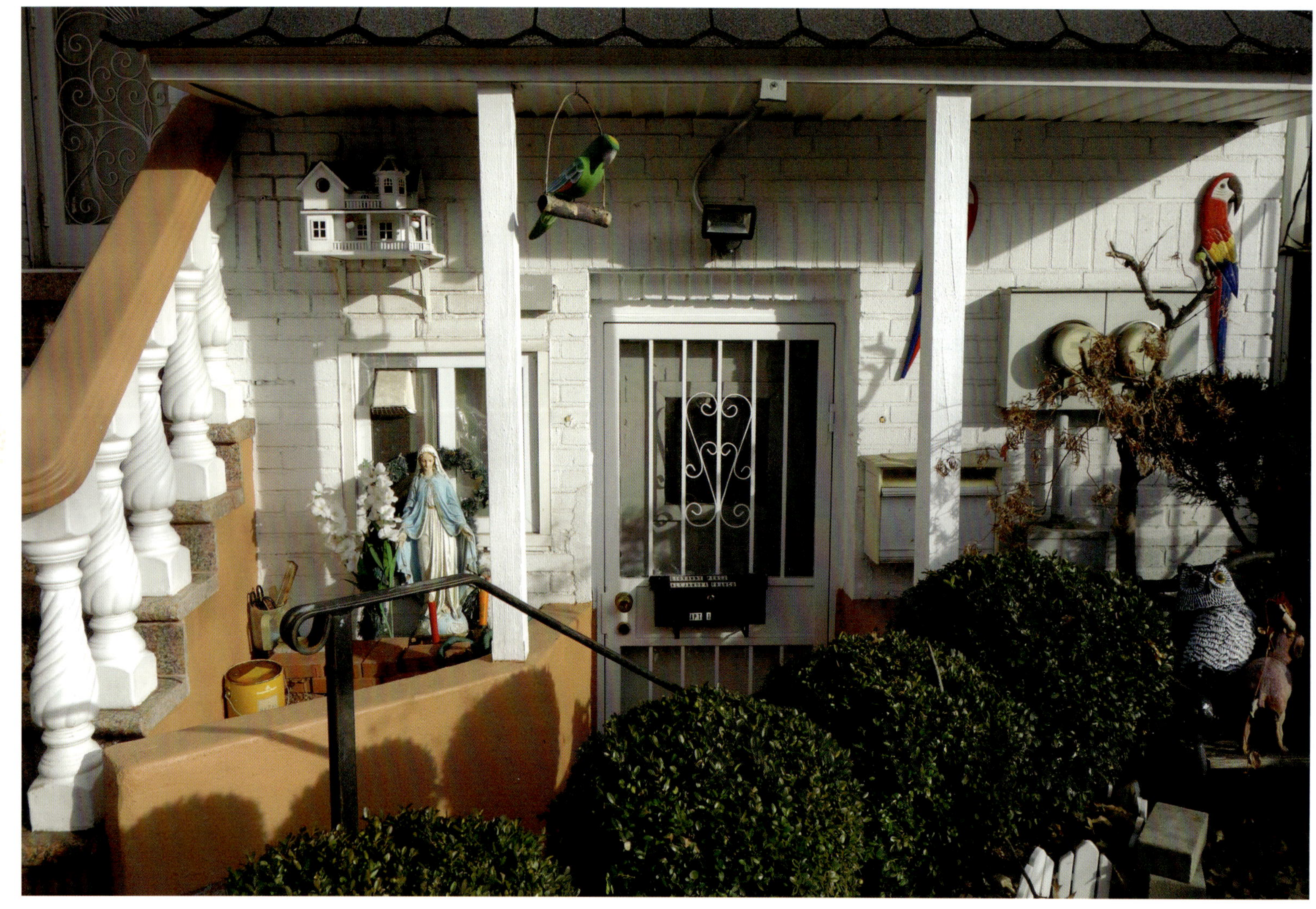

Yardscapes of Queens

Figures 64a–64e. Most yards in Queens are small, but people still decorate them in various ways. Residents use their yards to negotiate and display their sense of identity and belonging to a community, to show pride in place and home, and to extend a sense of welcome and care in the otherwise hectic city. This expression is especially significant for immigrant families who must re-orient themselves to new surroundings. This basement apartment entrance in Corona reflects one household's efforts to convey a sense of rootedness in place through planting and statuary. The Figure of Mary, in particular, provides continuity in Corona, which was once predominantly Italian and is now a Mexican and Central American enclave.

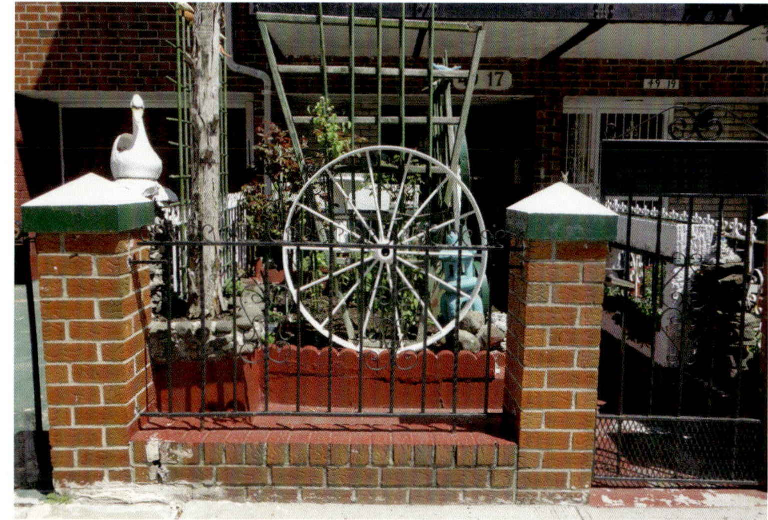

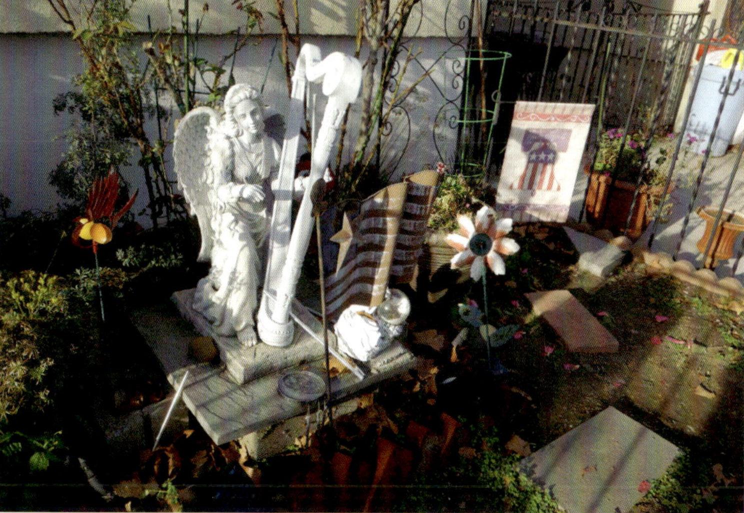

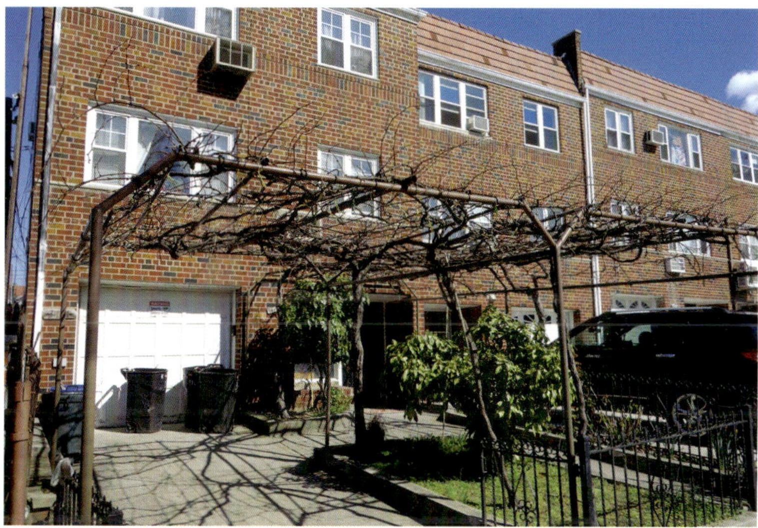

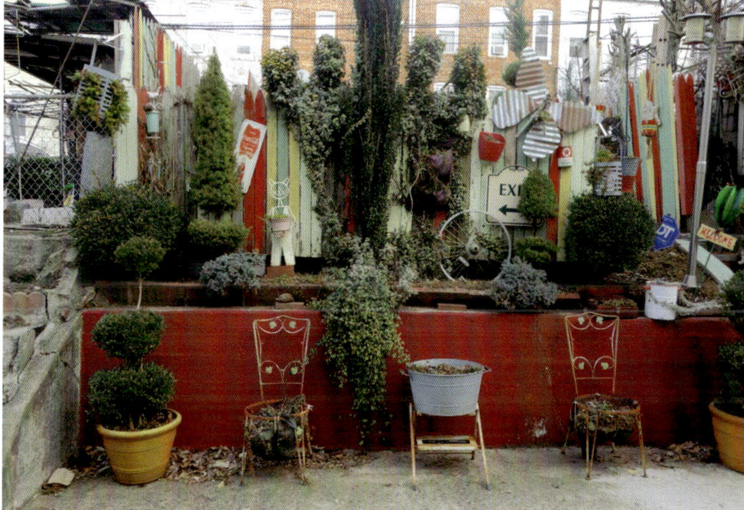

This page, top left: This household in Astoria has demarcated its front yard with a brick and iron fence and decorated it with statues, planters, a large wheel, and a rose trellis. Top right: A postage stamp–size front yard in Flushing displays an angel playing the harpsichord, decorative metal flowers and flag, and a "Never Forget" sign commemorating the 9/11 attacks. Bottom left: In East Elmhurst, the family in this rowhouse has covered their small driveway and walkway with a grape arbor. Bottom right: With no front yards, residents of this block in Jackson Heights use their alley (a rarity in New York City) as an outdoor space. The polychrome fence and shrubbery hide the parking space, while chairs offer a place to relax.

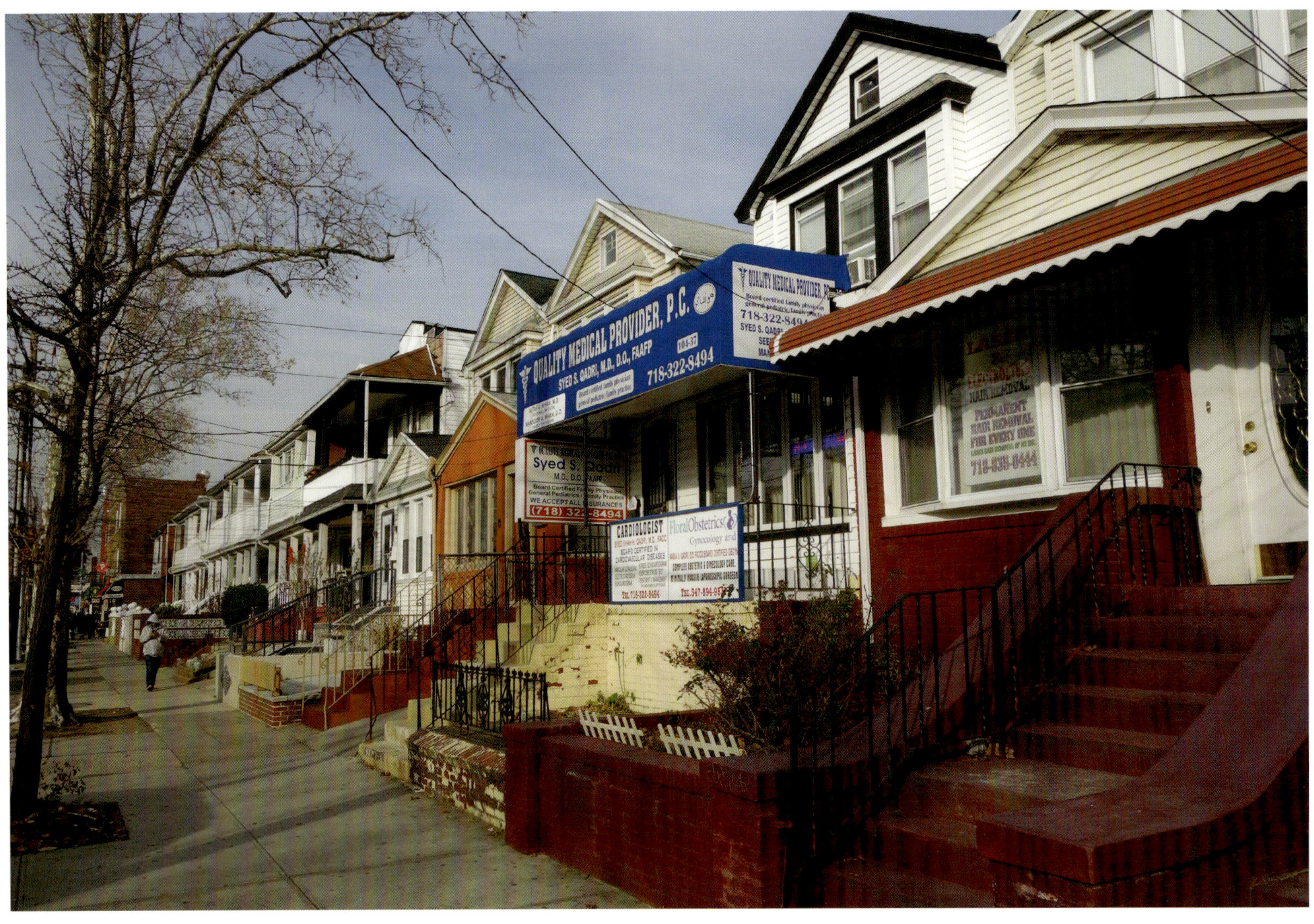

Doctors' offices in South Ozone Park

In Queens, many medical services operate out of converted houses, such as this family practitioner on Lefferts Boulevard in South Ozone Park. The rapidly expanding need for health care workers has opened opportunities for second- and third-generation family members to establish themselves in various private and institutional practices. Indian, Afro-Caribbean, Colombian, and Filipino people predominate in Queens medical services. Moreover, with commercial space at a premium, doctors, dentists, chiropractors, and veterinarians often set up shop in houses and storefronts. This also allows them to serve a close community with whom they may share language and cultural background.

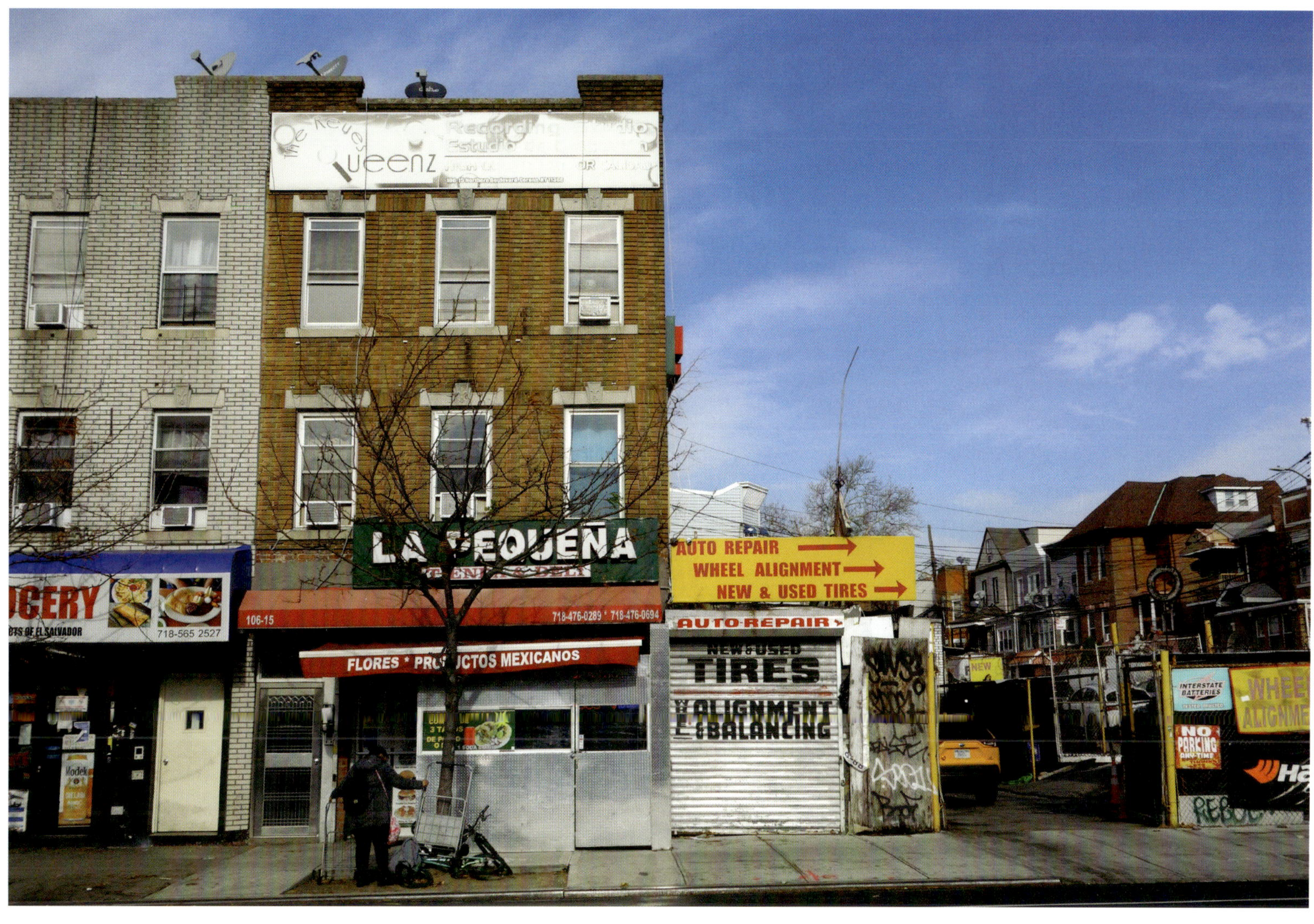

La Pequeña, Northern Boulevard, Corona

Jewish immigrants gave New York the Deli, Puerto Ricans bequeathed the Bodega, and Koreans saved the greengrocer from extinction. These are still three of the most important institutions of everyday city life, even if they have morphed and changed over the years. More recently, Mexican and Mexican-American families have established the Tienda, which typically combines a small grocery store with flowers and devotional objects for sale, as well as a steam table and grill for short-order dishes. They come in many shapes and sizes, but most advertise that they carry "productos Méxicanos." Here, La Pequeña is sandwiched between an auto repair shop and an El Salvadoran grocery.

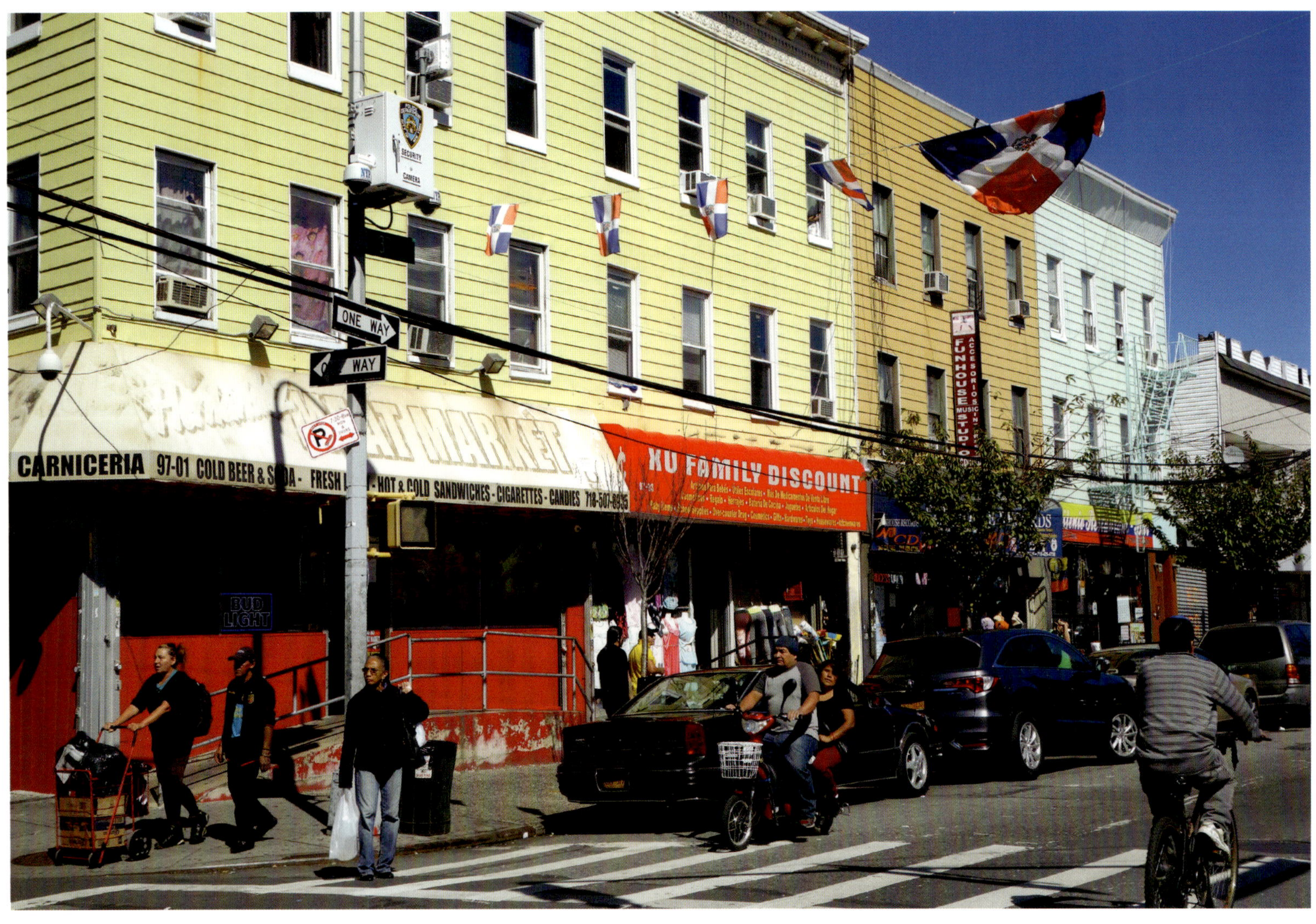

Corner scene in Corona

Corona residents go about their business at the corner of 37th Avenue and 97th Street. During the post-World War II decades, this part of Corona was largely Italian, Puerto Rican, and Dominican—D.R. flags fly above the street in this photograph. However, the neighborhood today is predominantly Mexican and Mexican-American, with many coming from Puebla State. New migrants are also arriving from El Salvador, Guatemala, Honduras, and Peru. There is even a small but prominent presence of Nahuatl, Quechua, Zapotec, and other indigenous groups. While highly diverse, the shared experience of Catholicism and Spanish language, to some extent, eased the process of coexistence and community building.

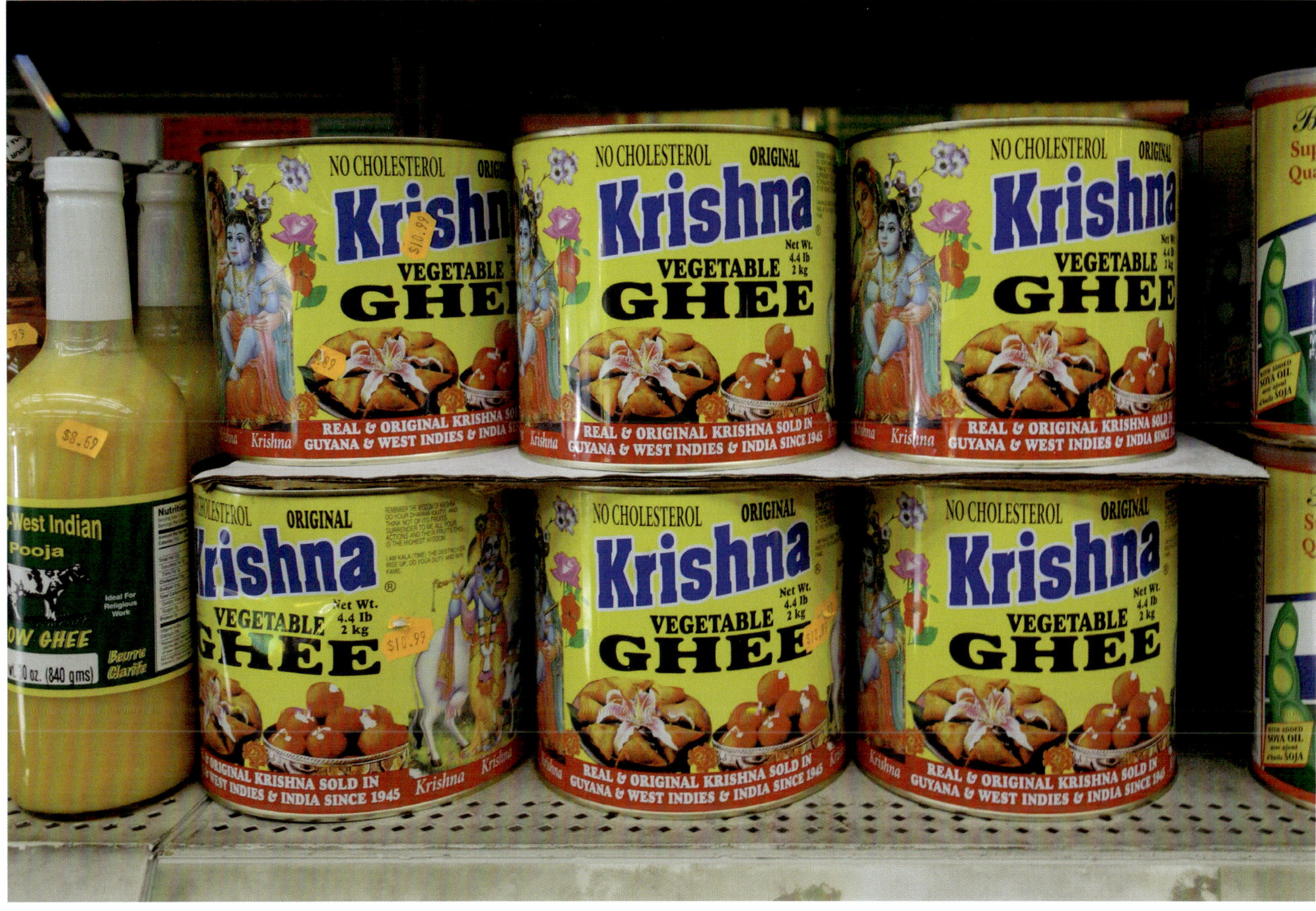

Krishna Vegetable Ghee, Richmond Hill

Indian and Indo-Caribbean products line the shelves of this grocery store in the southern part of Richmond Hill. Beginning in the mid-nineteenth century, large numbers of Indian migrants, especially Gujaratis and Punjabis, came to the Caribbean basin as soldiers, miners, field hands, and dockworkers in the British Empire. There they forged a highly distinct culture heavily influenced by the Afro-Caribbean population. In the 1970s, many of their descendants immigrated once again from Guyana, Trinidad, and Suriname to New York, settling in Richmond Hill. They have since been joined by Bengali immigrants from Bangladesh and West Bengal State in India.

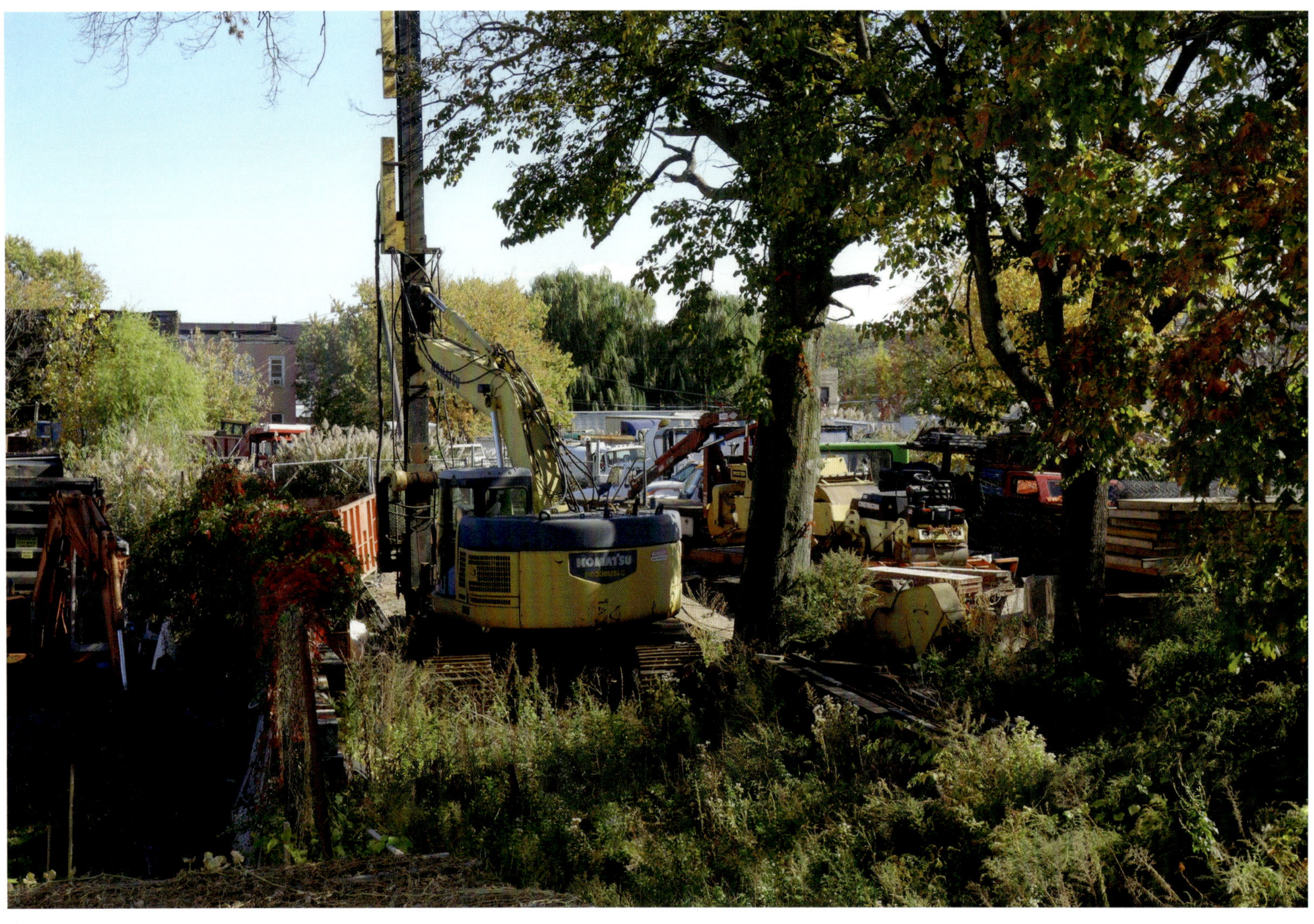

The Hole

Wedged between East New York in Brooklyn and Lindenwood in Queens is a neighborhood known as "the Hole," so named because it sits in a bowl surrounded by higher ground. With few connections to the city's sewer system, it floods continually, leaving the streets in a dilapidated condition. There is a large collection of semitrucks and trailers, broken-down buses, delivery vehicles, construction equipment, and campers lining the street. Residents of the Hole are fiercely committed to the neighborhood, united by their shared desire to be left alone by city officials. The community is home to the Federation of Black Cowboys, and it endures a reputation as a notorious mafia burial ground.

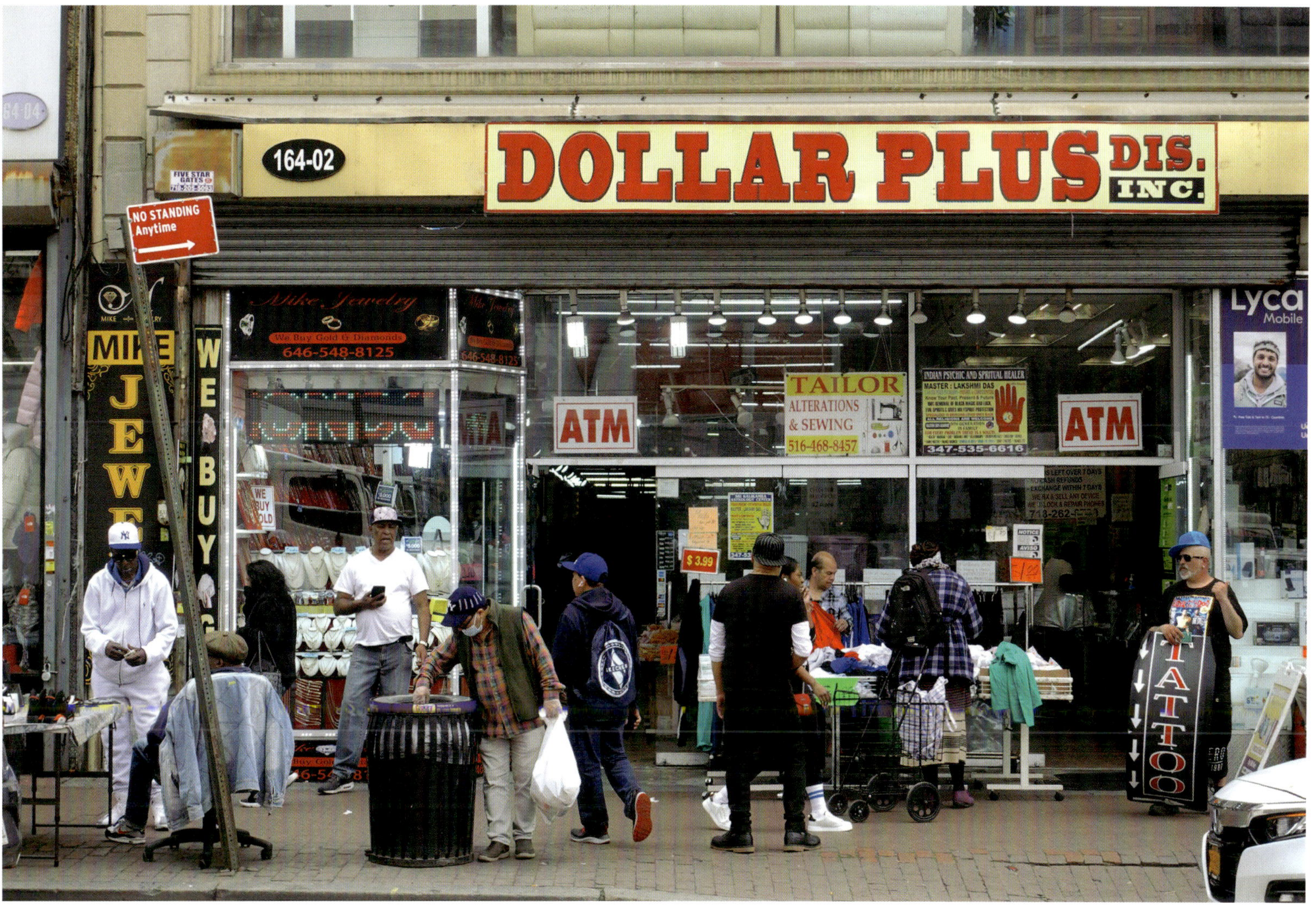

Street hustles, Jamaica

In the big commercial corridors of Queens, such as Jackson Heights, Corona, Flushing, and Jamaica, there is a constant hustle for trade in the streets and shops. Touts stand in front of stores to draw in customers and keep an eye on merchandise coming out. Vendors set up tables to hawk discount clothing, CDs, sunglasses, perfumes, cell phones, and other goods. Gleaners go through waste bins in search of cans and bottles to redeem for cash. Electronic shops send out high-decibel beats, providing a sonic backdrop for the action. These everyday practices create a vibrant street culture, but working-class life is hard in New York, often requiring long, tedious hours trying to make a living.

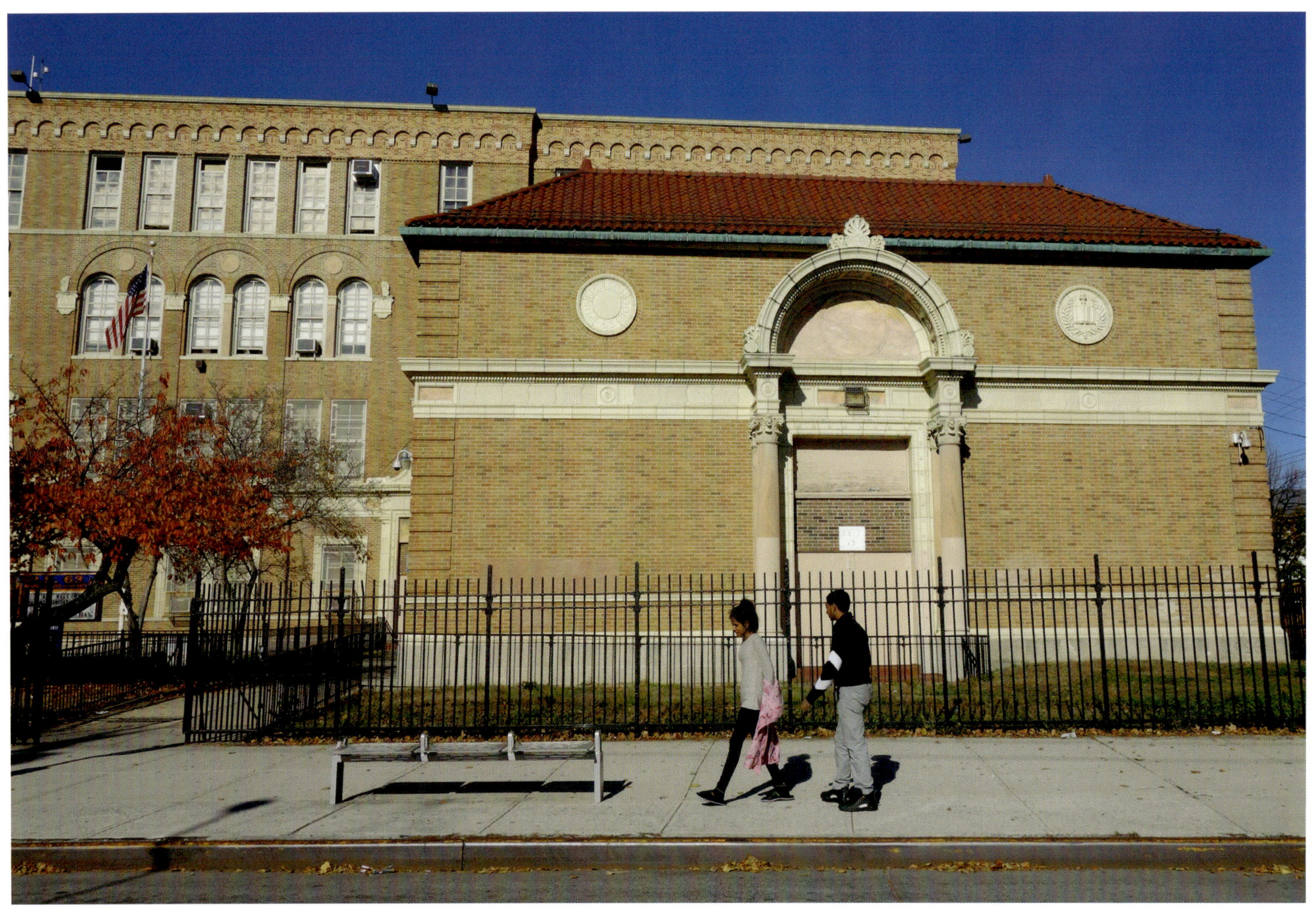

P.S. 63, Ozone Park

Just over a quarter of the city's one million K–12 students live in Queens, which has the most multilingual student body in the United States. As the student population changes unevenly, schools have had to expand, shrink, and expand again throughout the last hundred years. In one neighborhood, the public schools might become so empty that they rent space to charter and parochial schools—while schools in another neighborhood burst at the seams and must accommodate students in temporary facilities or new buildings. P.S. 63 in Ozone Park enrolls 1,100 students from prekindergarten through fifth grade under the school motto "A Rainbow of Possibilities."

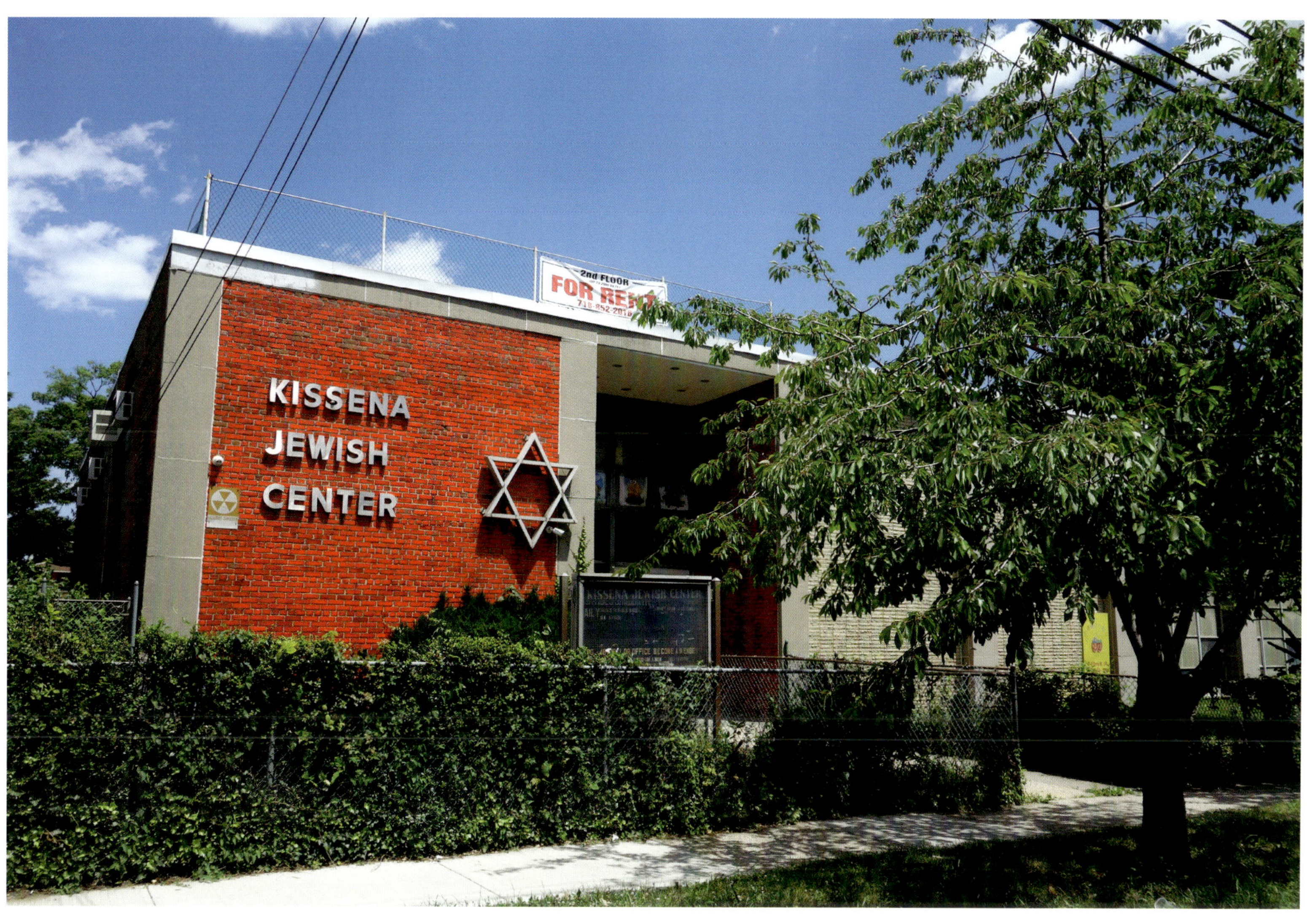

Kissena Jewish Center, Flushing

Since World War II, older Jewish and Catholic populations alike have been leaving Flushing for Long Island, Upstate, and Connecticut. Formerly Italian, Irish, and Polish Catholic parishes survived with an influx of the faithful from Puerto Rico, China, and Vietnam. However, apart from Bukharan Jews moving into Rego Park and some Orthodox families locating in Forest Hills, there has not been a corresponding influx of new Jewish congregants across Queens. As a result, many Jewish institutions in Flushing have been sold or rented out for other purposes. The Kissena Jewish Center on Bowne Street has been seeking a new tenant for several years now.

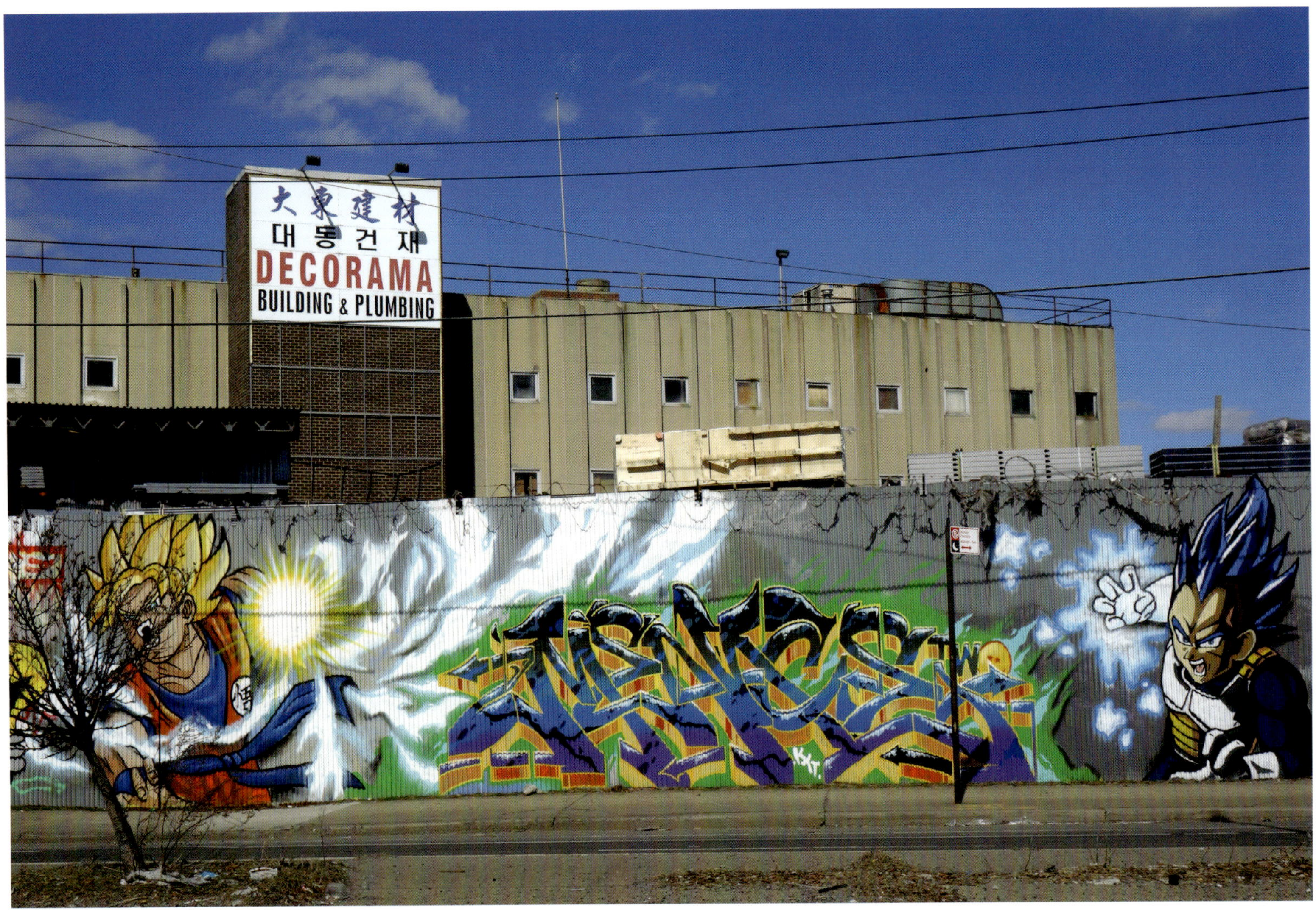

The Industrial Zones of Queens

Figures 73a–73q. While Queens is often linked in the popular imagination with sprawling residential communities, it contains many dense industrial zones. These tend to cluster along waterways and low-lying areas such as Long Island City, Dutch Kills, Steinway, Maspeth, Flushing, Jamaica, JFK Airport, and College Point. For much of the twentieth century, immigrant families gained a foothold in the economy through factory work. However, between 1974 and 2000 the city lost 25 percent of its manufacturing jobs. The losses were greatest in industries that tended to be more heavily unionized, such as textiles, chemicals, and machining. Still, Queens remains a home for thousands of industrial and warehouse operations, both union and nonunion.

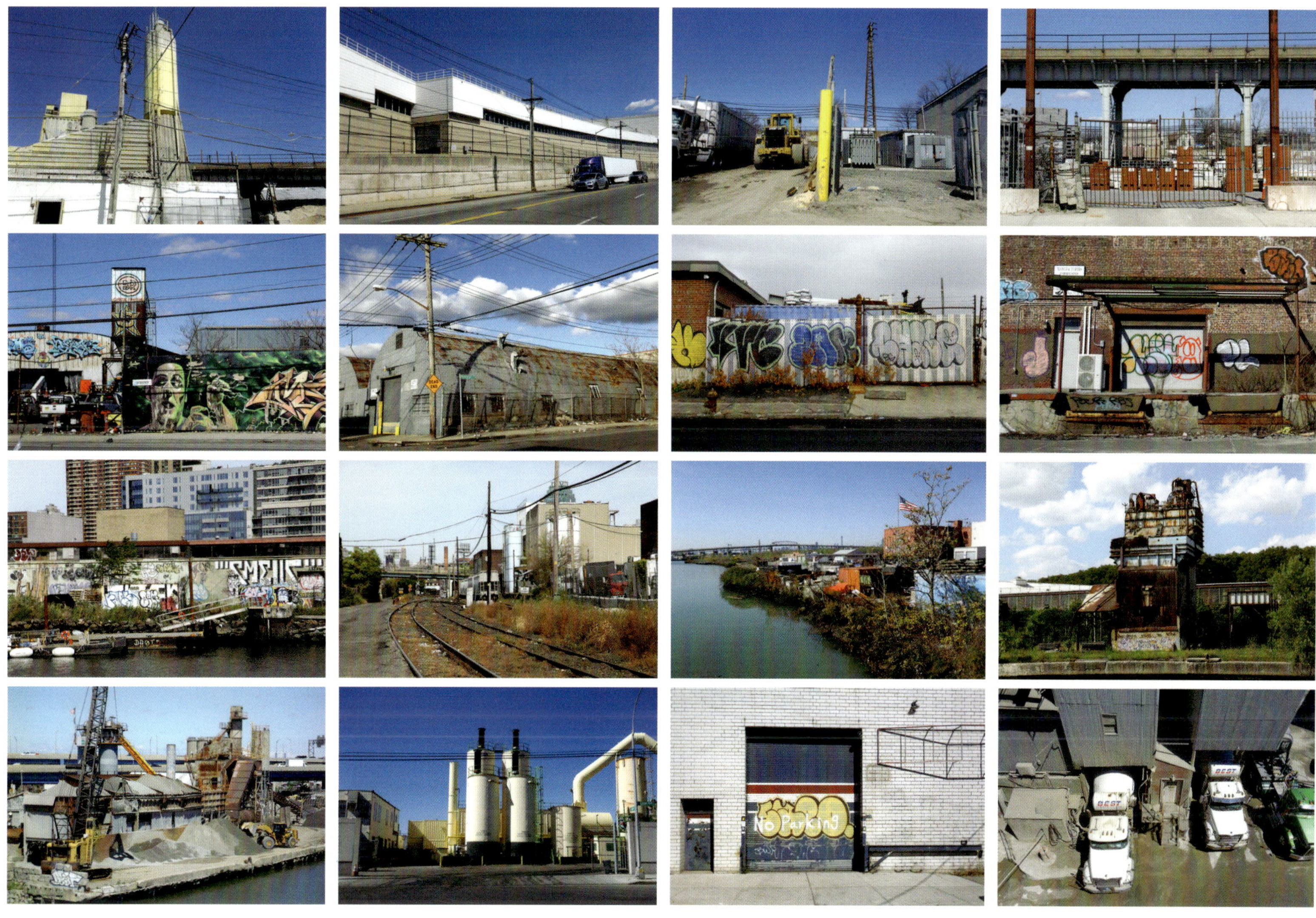

Opposite page: A former factory in Maspeth is now home to a large plumbing supply company. Storage and distribution of food, household goods, and building materials constitute the largest single sector of Queens's industrial economy. Meanwhile, the borough's "back stage" zones prove irresistible to graffiti artists, who ply their work on the walls, doors, and fences, creating a richly textured visual landscape. This page: Four industrial zones (top to bottom: Jamaica, Maspeth, Hunters Point, Flushing Bay). As an ensemble, they show the wide range of architectural and building types, from warehouses and factories to silos, storage tanks, loading elevators, gantries, docks, terminals, sheds, and supply yards.

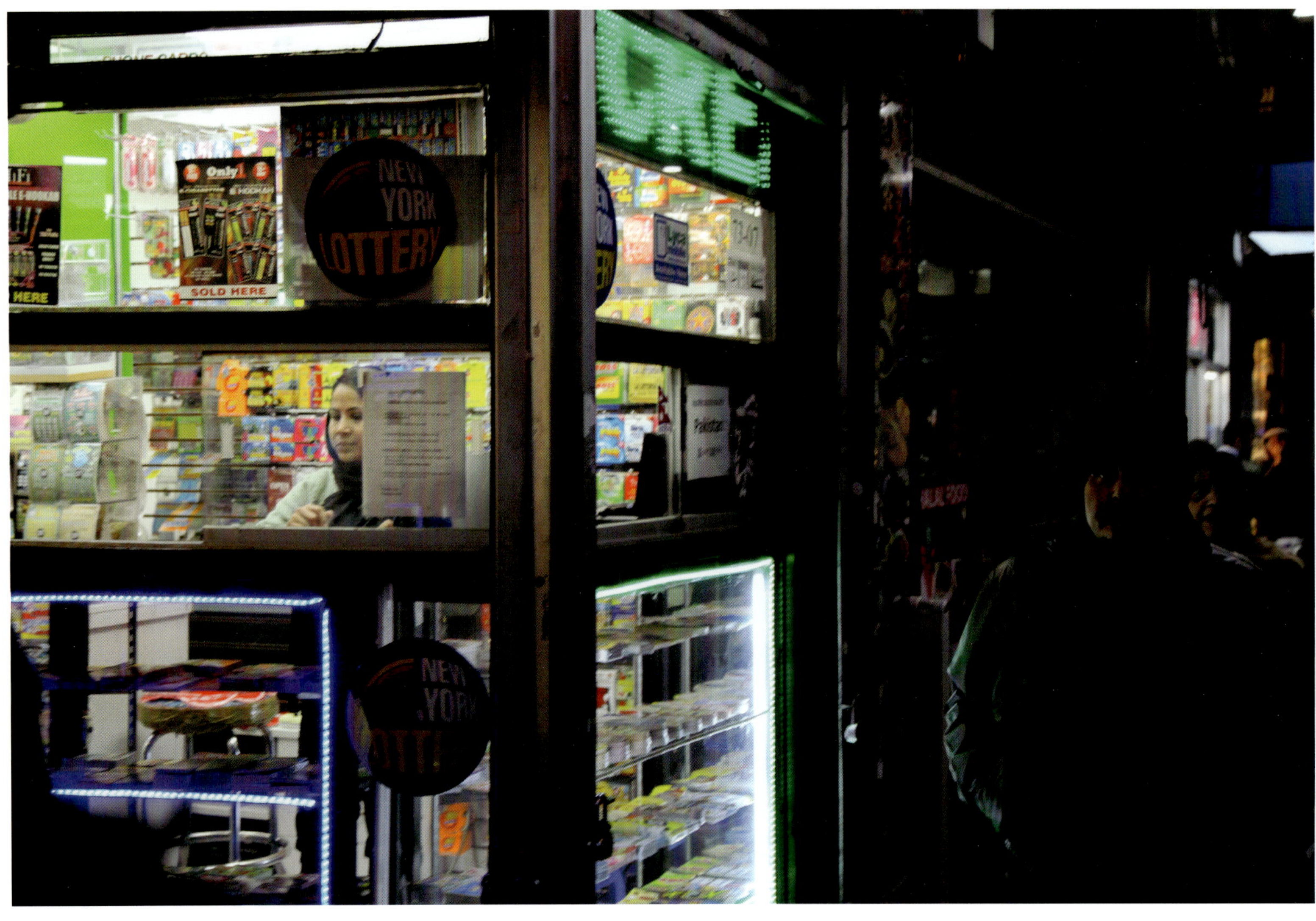

Night sales, Jackson Heights

Located at one of the entrances to the subway, this three-foot by five-foot shop sells a wide variety of small items, including lottery tickets, international phone cards, e-hookahs, lighters, and batteries. Because of the steep commercial rents in Jackson Heights, small business operators must carefully optimize their spatial footprint relative to the price and volume of the goods they sell. This frequently results in the division of storefronts into smaller spaces or even the creation of tiny cubicles such as the one shown here. Since this photograph was taken, the cubicle has been reabsorbed into a Bengali restaurant. Such architectural flexibility has been one of the keys to the success of small immigrant businesses in Queens.

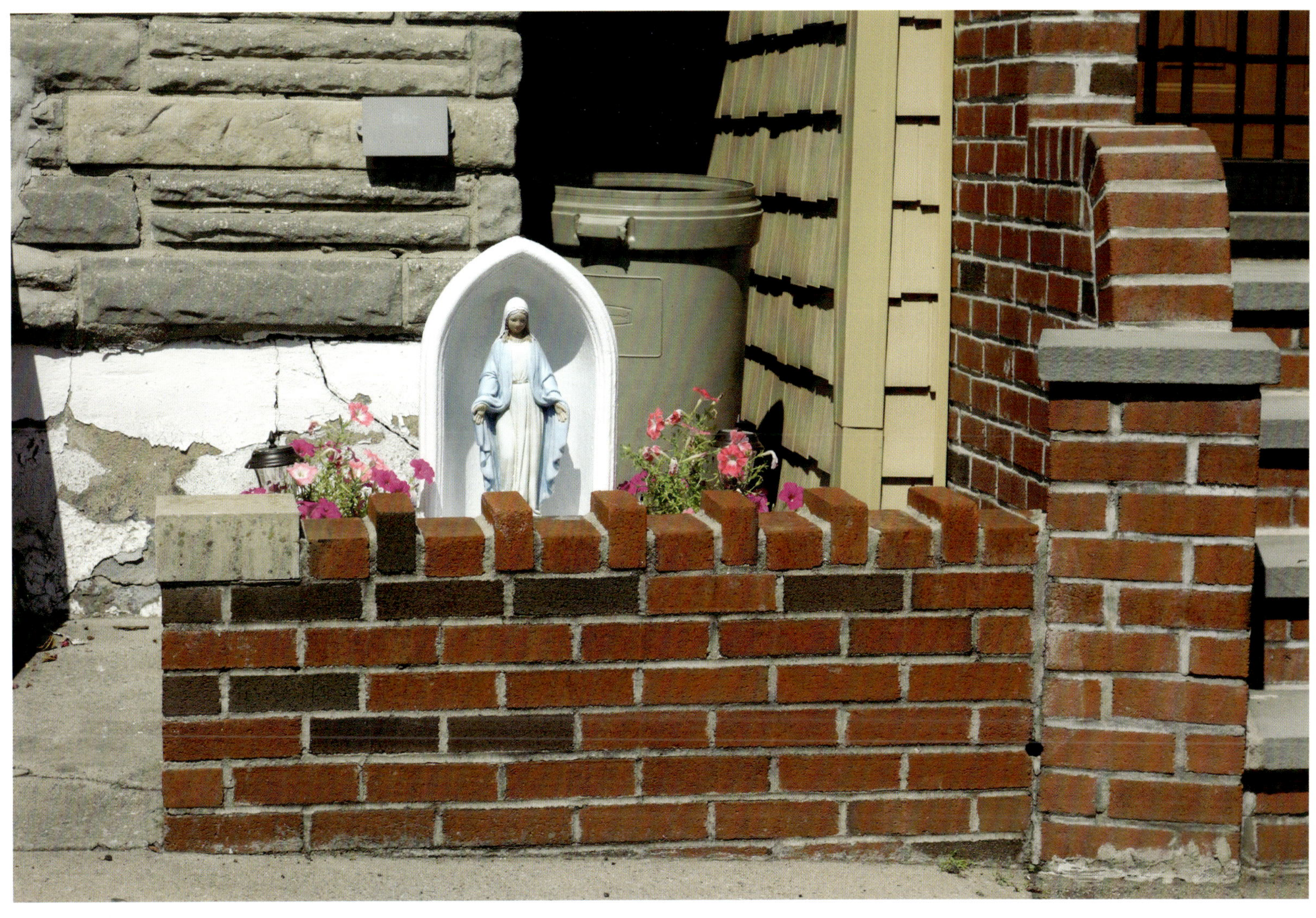

Blessed Virgin, Woodside

Somebody has repurposed the small storage niche in front of their house, typically used for garbage cans, into a shrine for Mary. Catholic residents often express their religious identity through statuary of saints placed in front yards, windows, doorways, and other visible locations. Some Catholics also bury statues of St. Joseph in their yards to help sell their house, and St. Francis, patron saint of animals and the environment, can be seen frequently in gardens. While Queens is not nearly as dominated by Catholicism as Staten Island, it is nonetheless the largest of the faith traditions in the borough. Queens also has the largest Hindu, Muslim, and Buddhist populations in New York City.

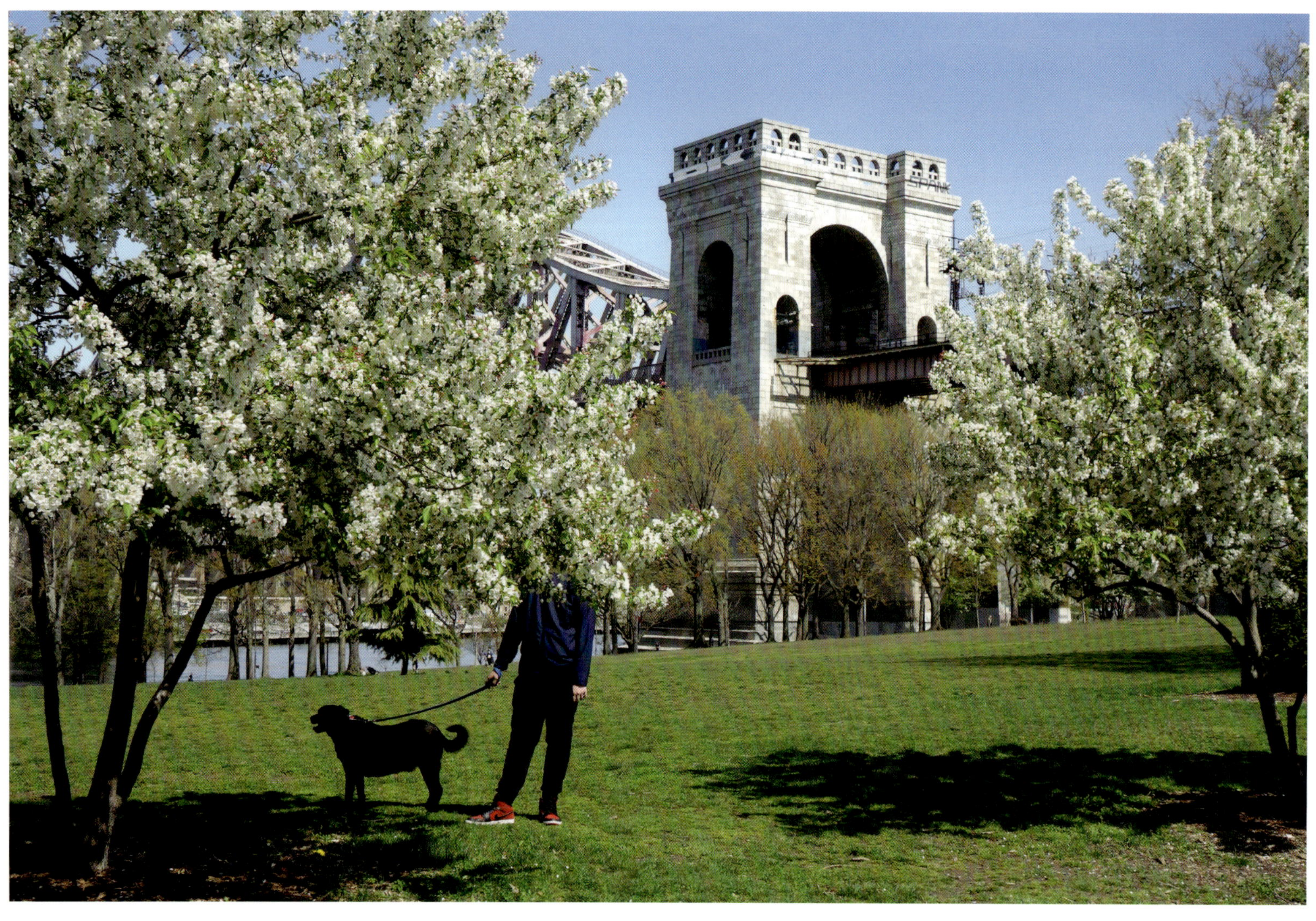

Springtime in Astoria Park, Astoria

Astoria Park is a popular 60-acre greensward stretched along the East River between the Hell Gate Bridge, shown here, and the Triborough Bridge. The park was designed by the city's chief landscape architect, Carl Francis Pilat, and opened in 1914. Many residents opposed the construction of the Hell Gate Bridge, which opened three years later. Today, however, the monumental bridge and its viaduct provide a strong visual definition and sense of place for park goers, even if the sonic clatter of the trains can be rather alarming. The park is also home to Astoria Pool, one of the great Works Progress Administration (WPA)–era public swimming facilities, completed in 1936.

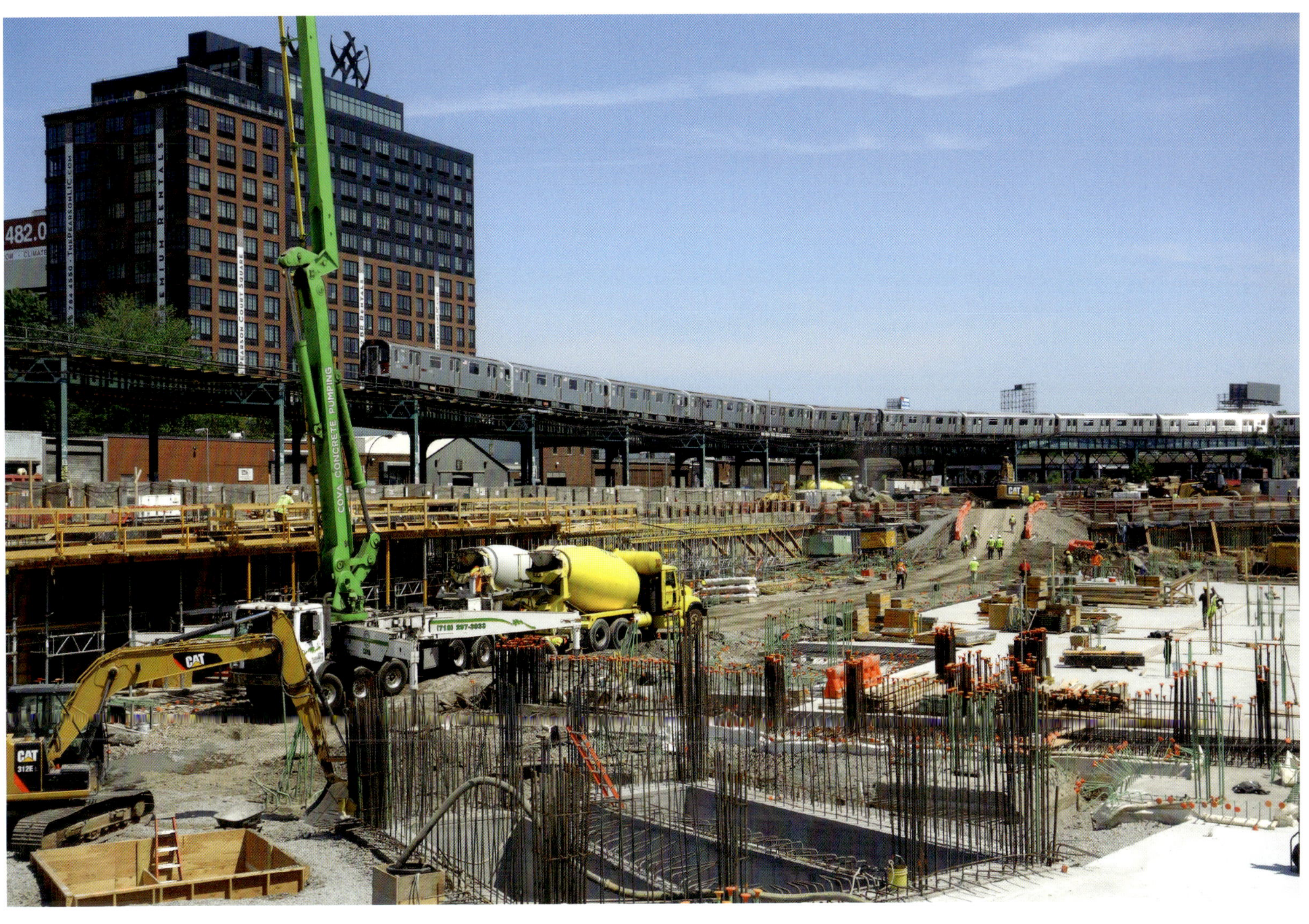

Construction site, Long Island City

The elevated 7 train winds around an immense construction site, indicative of the rapid transformation of Long Island City. Over the last twenty years, dozens of factories and warehouses of this once heavily industrial neighborhood have either been converted into luxury lofts or demolished to make way for high-rise condominiums, displacing many artists and small businesses in the process. This site once featured the 5 Pointz building, an old factory covered in graffiti murals by some of the leading aerosol artists in the world. After demolishing 5 Pointz, the property owner constructed two glass-and-steel residential towers that perfectly symbolize the rapid gentrification of Long Island City.

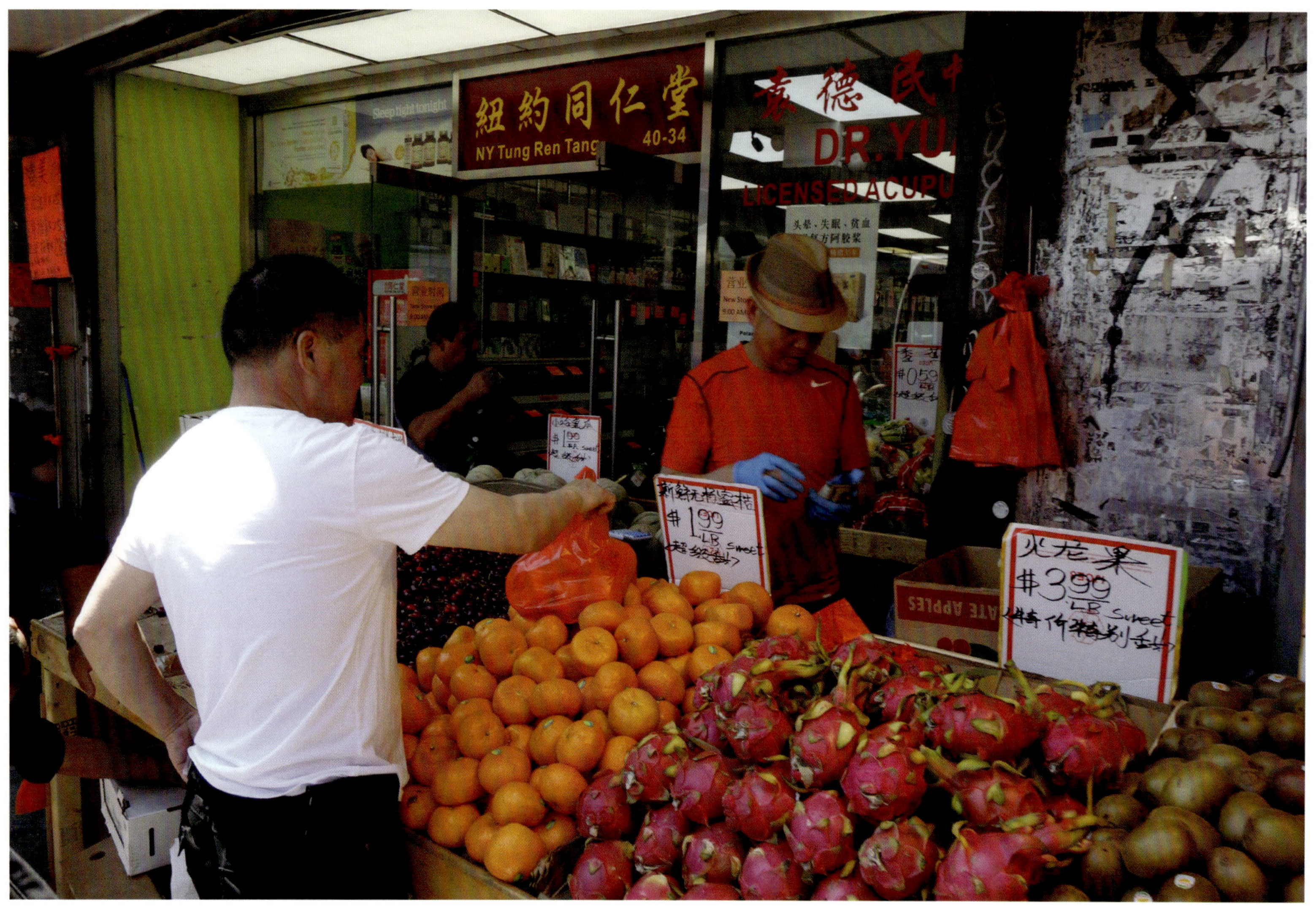

Food and healing on Flushing Main Street

A vendor sells fruit in front of a Chinese apothecary on Main Street. Apothecaries are an important part of everyday life in Flushing, as they sell a wide variety of ingredients for Chinese medicine. Staff members circulate among shelves lined with glass jars and bins containing roots, bark, flowers, seeds, and leaves, as well as fungi, insects, and animal parts. They mix these ingredients into teas, salves, boluses, oils, and other forms for bodily use. Apothecaries are also a hub of health practitioner services, including acupuncture, cupping, massage, and reflexology. Many Chinese immigrants use traditional and Western medicine in tandem, and area hospitals maintain connections to Chinese medicine specialists.

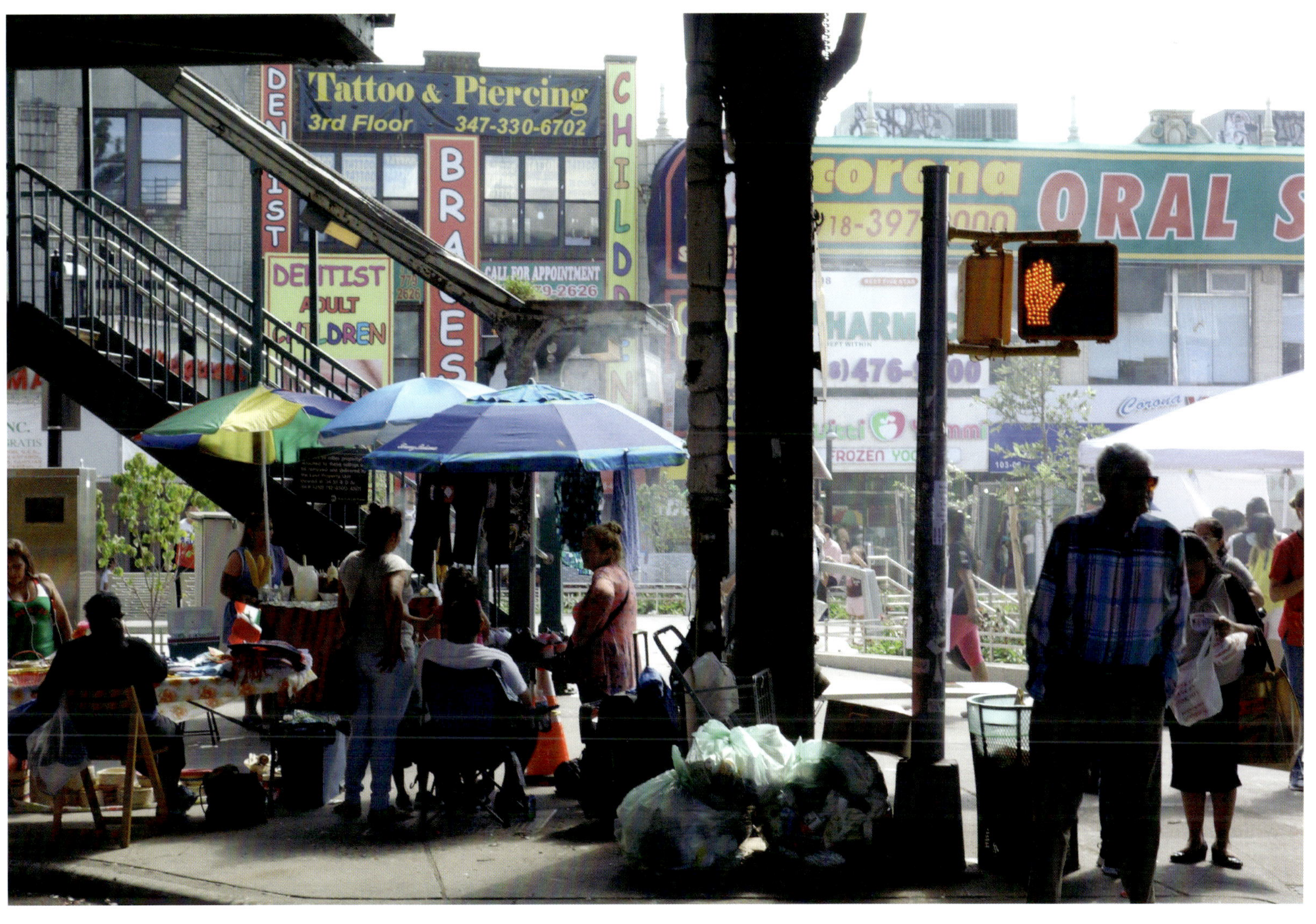

Scene at the 103rd Street–Corona Plaza station

A smoky haze of grilling meat from nearby food trucks wafts over the scene at the 103rd Street–Corona Plaza station. The stations along the 7 train route act as nodes for a wide range of activities. Here, vendors sell paletas, roasted corn, new and used clothes, jewelry, balloons, toys, and other goods. Small trailer trucks line up along Roosevelt Avenue offering hauling and delivery services for hire by the hour. Evangelical preachers frequently set up here, broadcasting the Good News over warbly PA speakers. Friends and families meet to hang out and share meals as children chase each other around the plaza. All this activity is punctuated by the periodic arrival and departure of the squealing and clacking 7 train overhead.

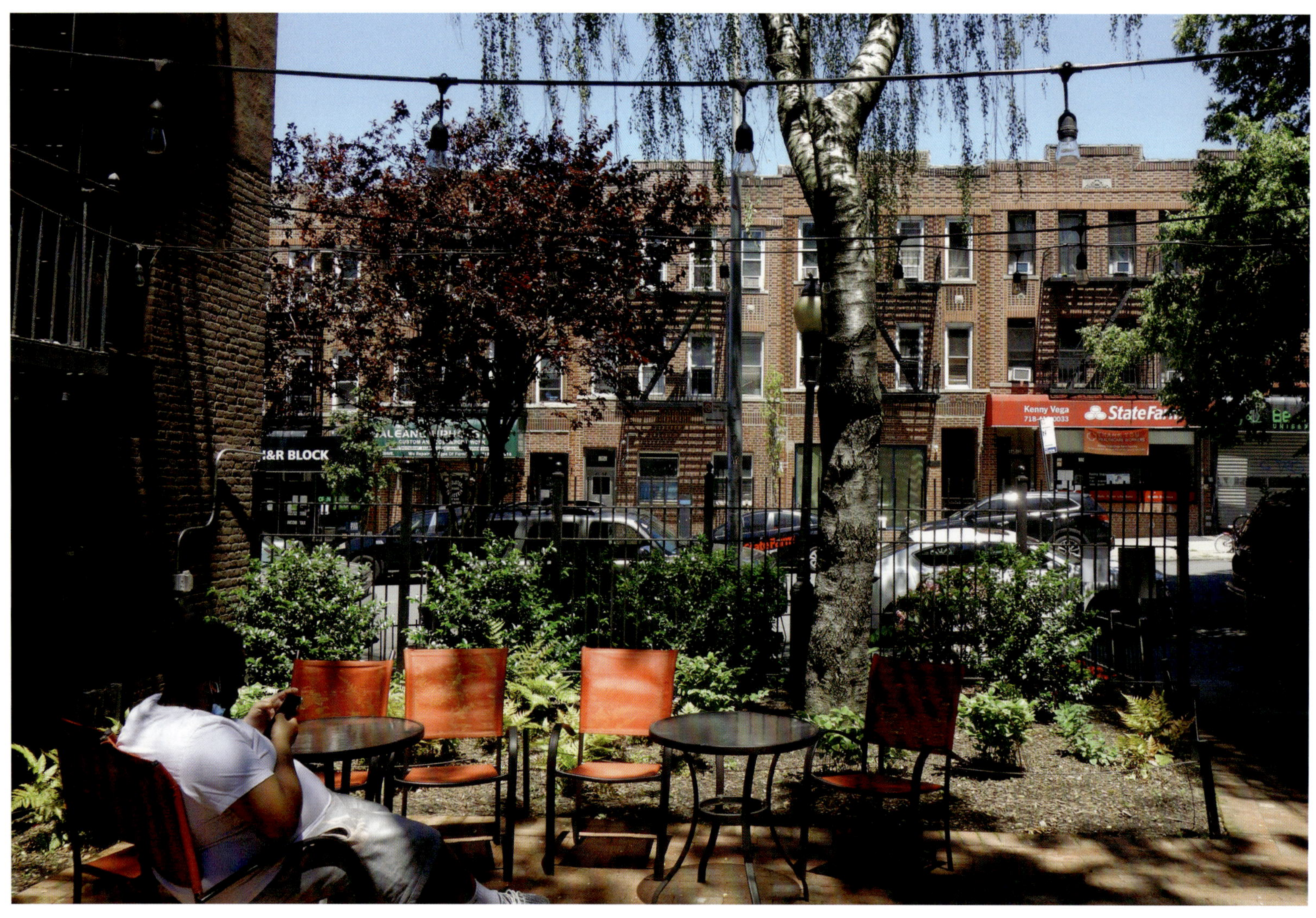

Courtyard at Metropolitan Houses, Sunnyside

The Sunnyside neighborhood was a kind of test bed for housing experiments in the 1920s and 1930s. Clarence Stein and Henry Wright designed Sunnyside Gardens in 1923, as well as the Phipps Houses, a model tenement completed in 1931. The courtyard in this image belongs to the Metropolitan Houses, a block of fourteen U-shaped apartment buildings designed by Andrew Thomas and financed by the Metropolitan Life Insurance Corporation for working-class residents. It reflects the architect's desire to create dwellings at minimum cost with maximum light and air. Today the complex, upgraded to "Cosmopolitan Houses," continues to function as a source of affordable housing for residents of Sunnyside.

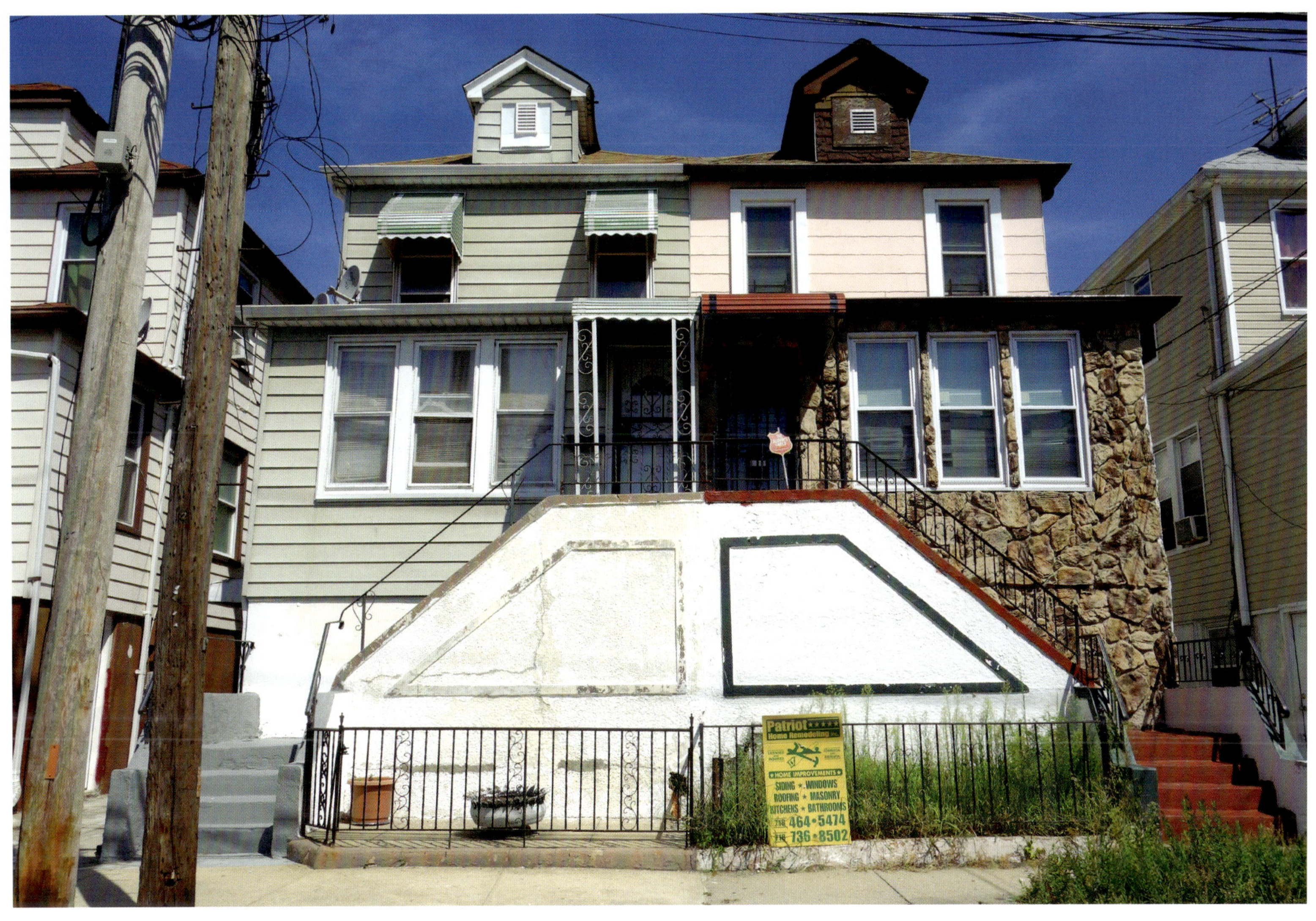

Twin Studies, Arverne

Rare in most U.S. cities, the semi-detached house is a staple part of the residential stock of Queens, with thousands built throughout the borough. Sharing a wall reduces construction costs, making housing more affordable for young families. While born identical but separately owned, they also provide a record of their divergent histories, as successions of owners have made choices about style, form, and adornment. Changeable elements include porch enclosures, window and door treatments, siding styles and colors, awnings, stairs and rails, fencing, yards, and plants. These two houses are part of a group built in the 1920s in Arverne, a historically African American neighborhood on the Rockaway peninsula.

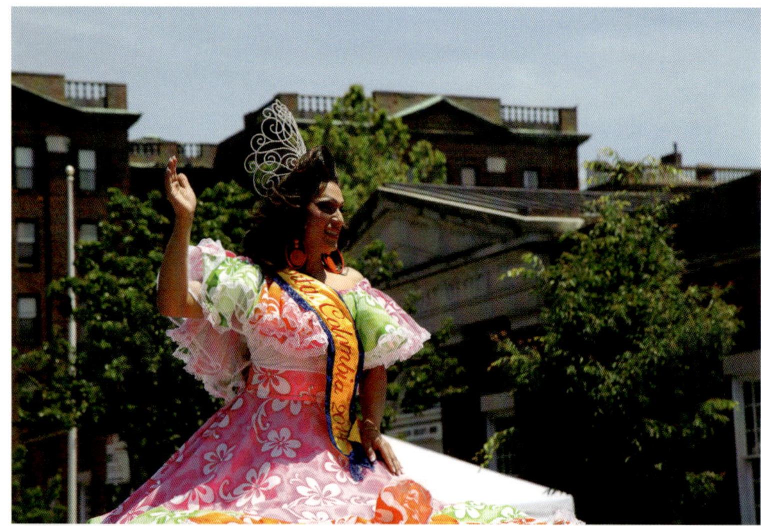

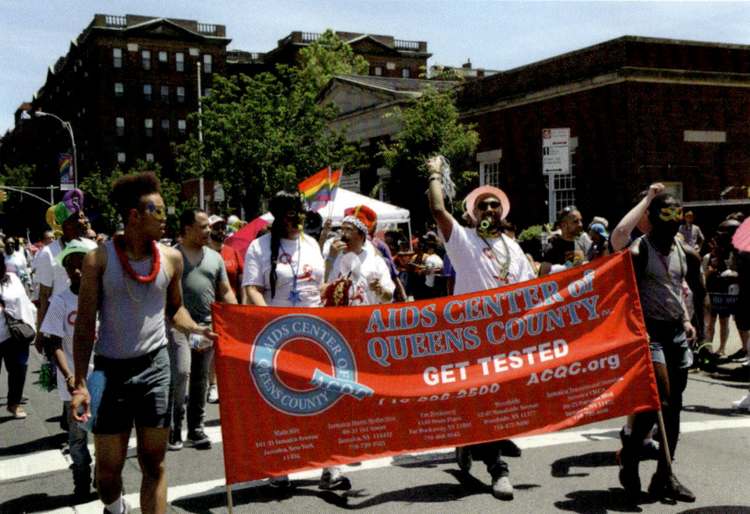

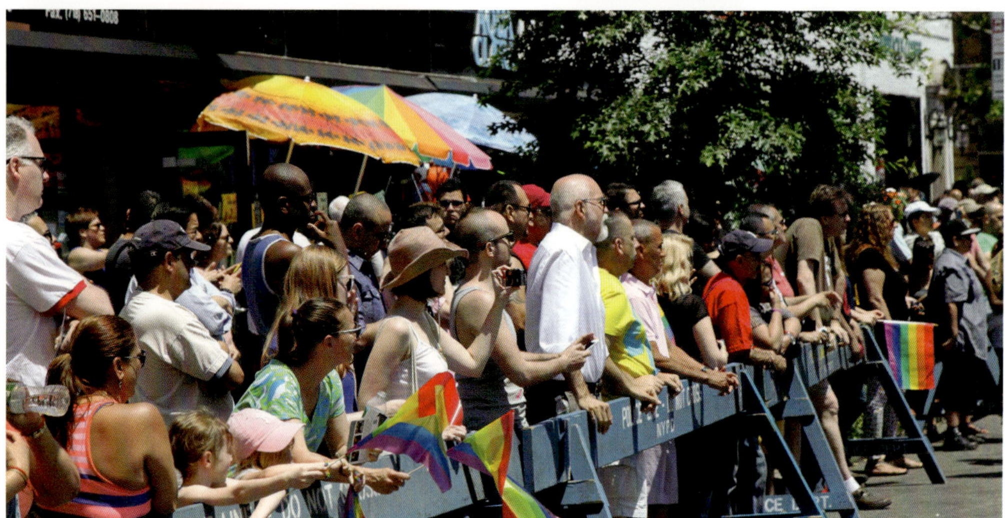

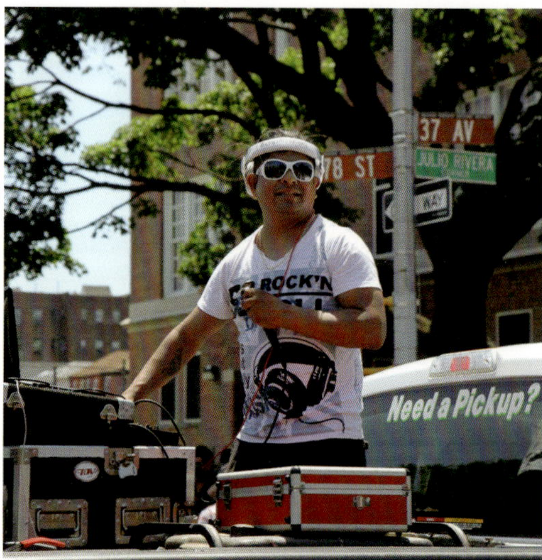

Pride Parade, Jackson Heights

Figures 82a–82g. From its early days, Jackson Heights has been home to a large gay and lesbian population. In the 1970s and 1980s, Latino immigrants began opening gay bars and clubs along Roosevelt Avenue. However, the LGBTQ community experienced harassment from both the neighborhood and the police. In 1990, Julio Rivera, a gay Puerto Rican bartender, was beaten and stabbed to death in the P.S. 69 schoolyard. To commemorate his life and resist the violence, Cuban-born LGBTQ activist Maritza Martinez and public school teacher Danny Dromm (future city council member) founded the Queens Pride Parade. Today, Jackson Heights hosts the largest Pride Fest outside of Manhattan, and the neighborhoods of Western Queens constitute the center of Latino LGBTQ activism in New York.

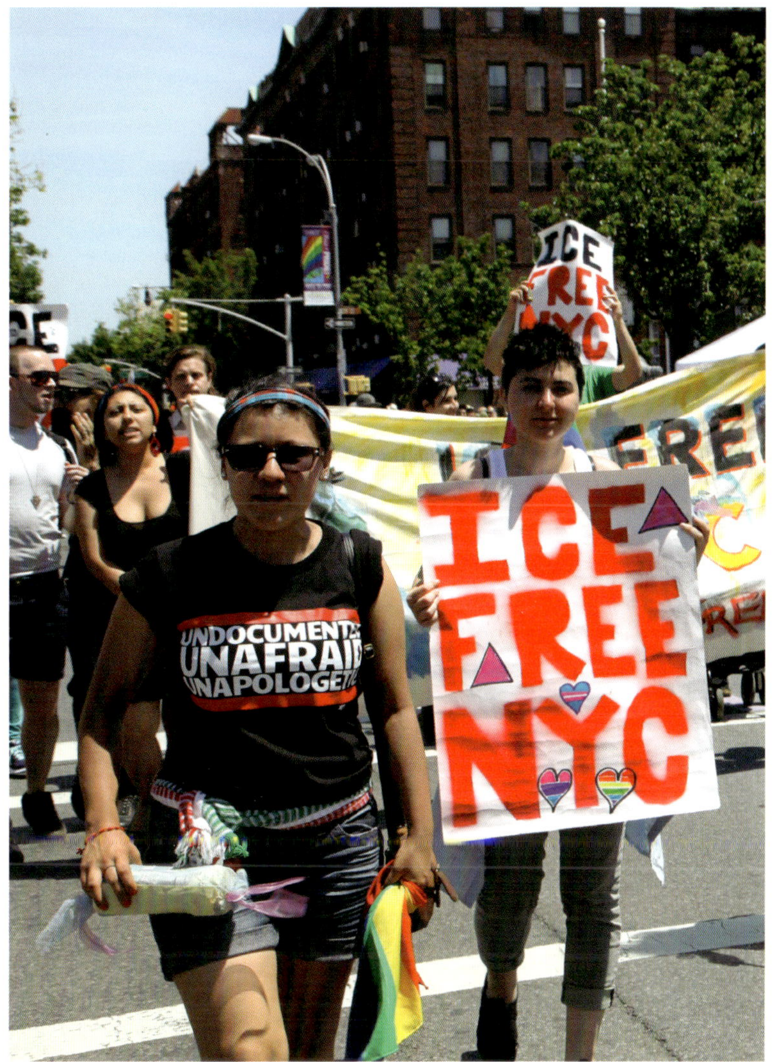

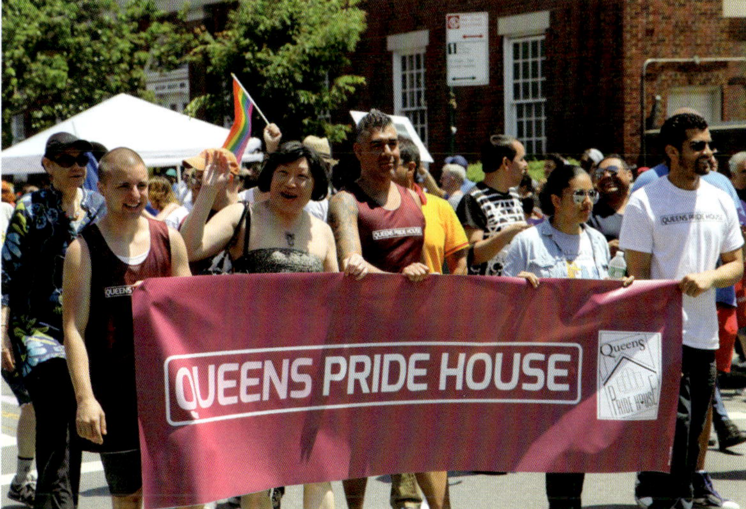

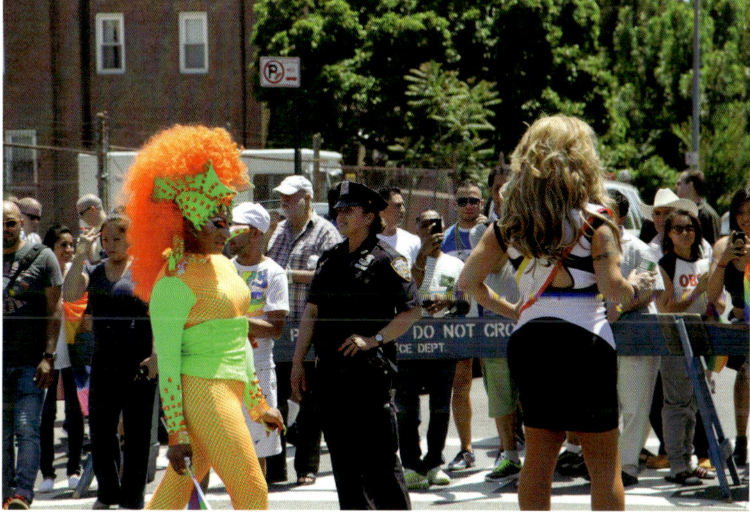

The parade provides an opportunity for a wide range of local, citywide, and national organizations to make their presence known, such as Queens Pride House, the Queens AIDS Center, the Gay Seniors of Queens, the Stonewall Democrats, and Generation Q, a queer youth program. The parade is also a moment for LGBTQ communities of Queens to show solidarity with other groups and struggles. In recent years, LGBTQ activists have demonstrated common cause with the Black Lives Matter movement as well as the fight against the Immigration Control and Enforcement agency and its harassment, intimidation, and deportation of undocumented people. Meanwhile, politicians at the borough, citywide, and state levels march in the parade both to show solidarity and to court votes.

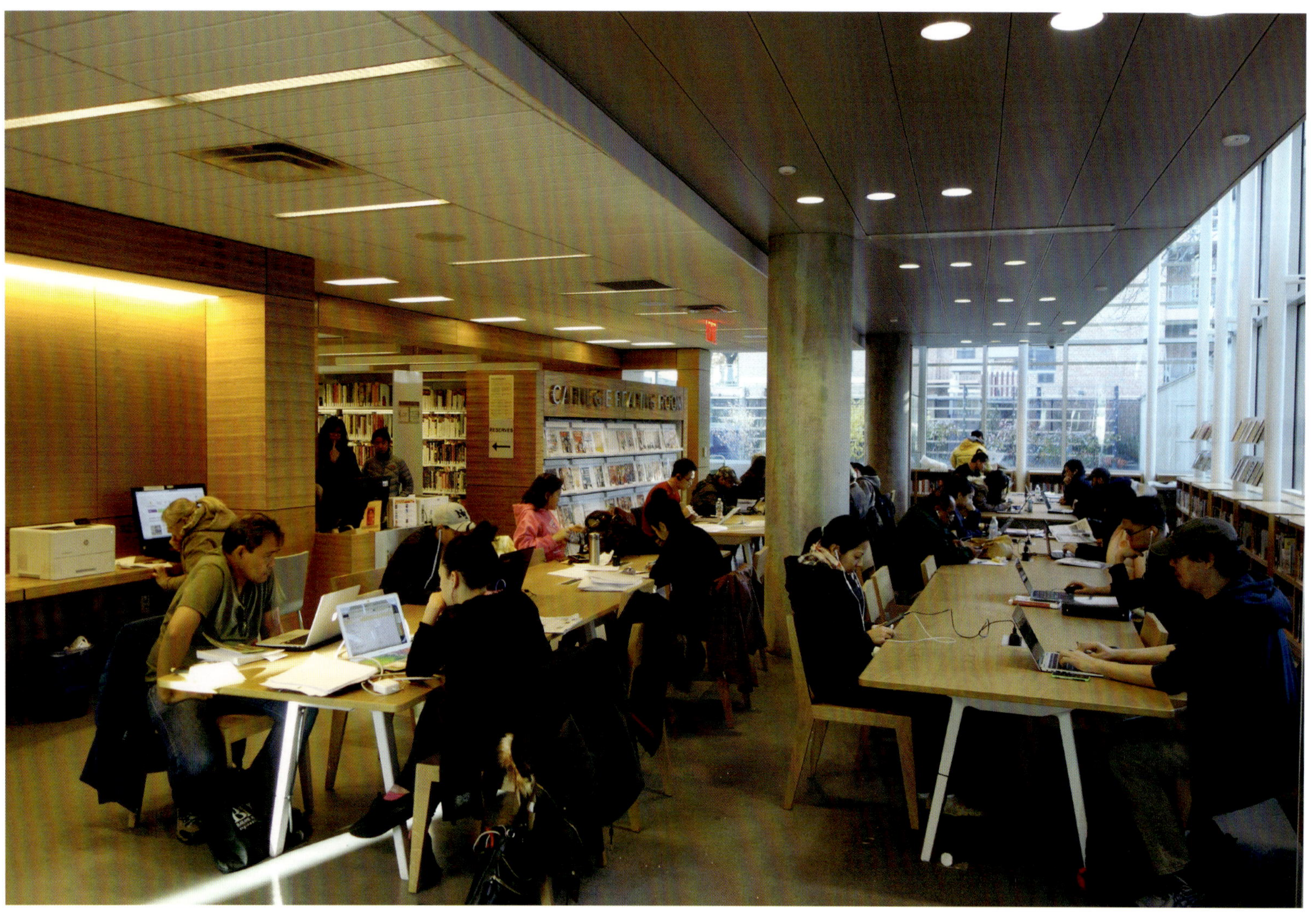

Reading room at Elmhurst Library

With the advent of the Internet, many questioned the ongoing relevance of physical libraries. The Queens Library system, however, puts paid to such pronouncements. In neighborhoods like Elmhurst, many residents live in cramped apartments with unreliable Internet and depend on the library for space and connectivity. The libraries also offer a wide range of services for new immigrant families, lectures and concerts for multiple audiences, and programming for children and older adults. Unfortunately, library officials had to demolish the historic Carnegie branch that once stood here, but the neighborhood desperately needed the larger building that took its place.

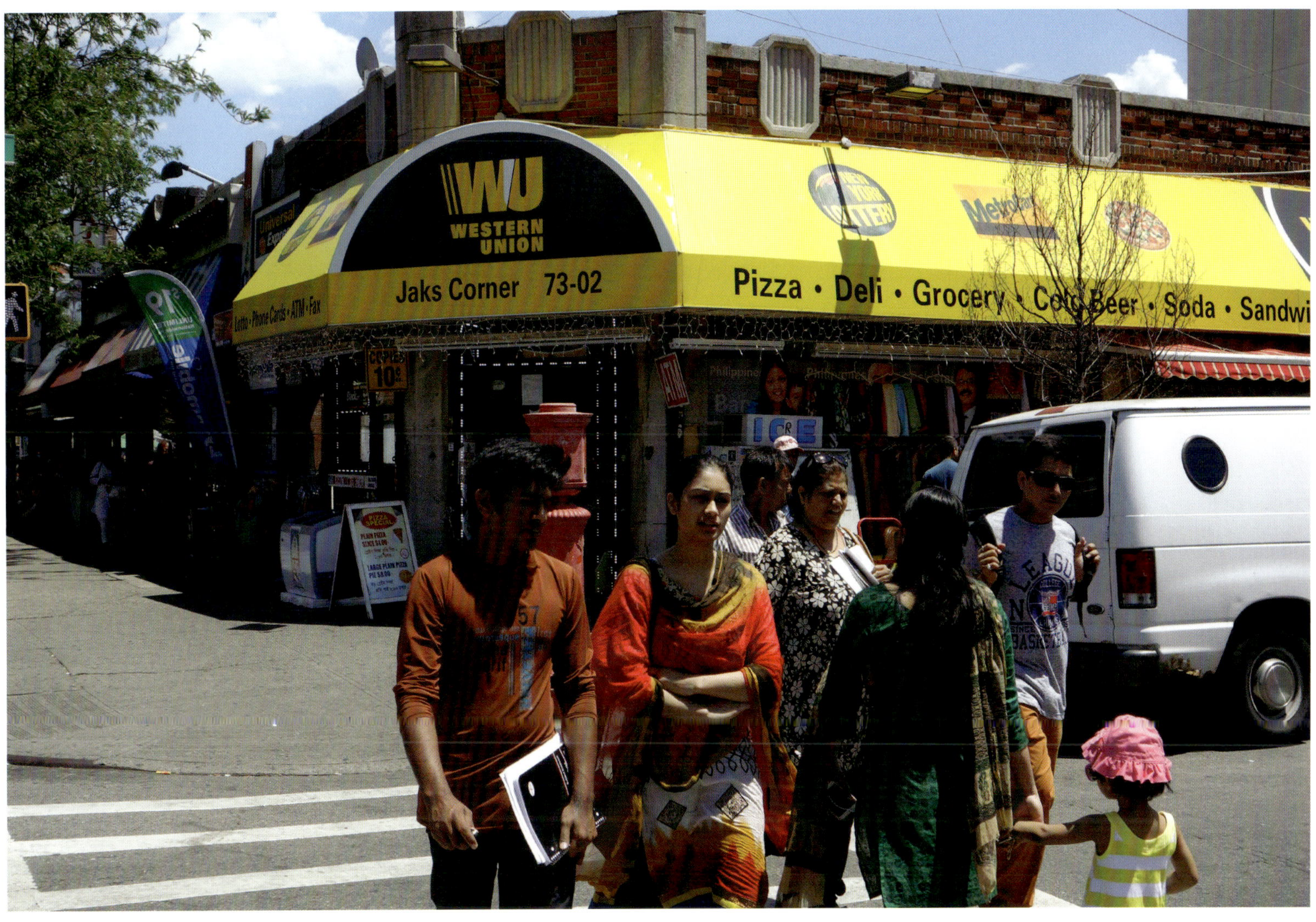

Remittance economy in Jackson Heights

Pedestrians walking along 37th Avenue cross 73rd Street in the Jackson Heights South Asian district. In the background, Jaks Corner offers Western Union wire services, a crucial function in the immigrant communities of Queens. Wire transfers are the lifeblood of the remittance economy—money earned in the United States and sent to families in countries of origin. Every year, New York City residents send more than $10 billion to relatives abroad, with India, China, and Mexico being the lead recipient countries. Families in recipient countries may save the money or very often spend it on purchasing property, building homes, paying school and college fees, supporting elders, and many other crucial needs.

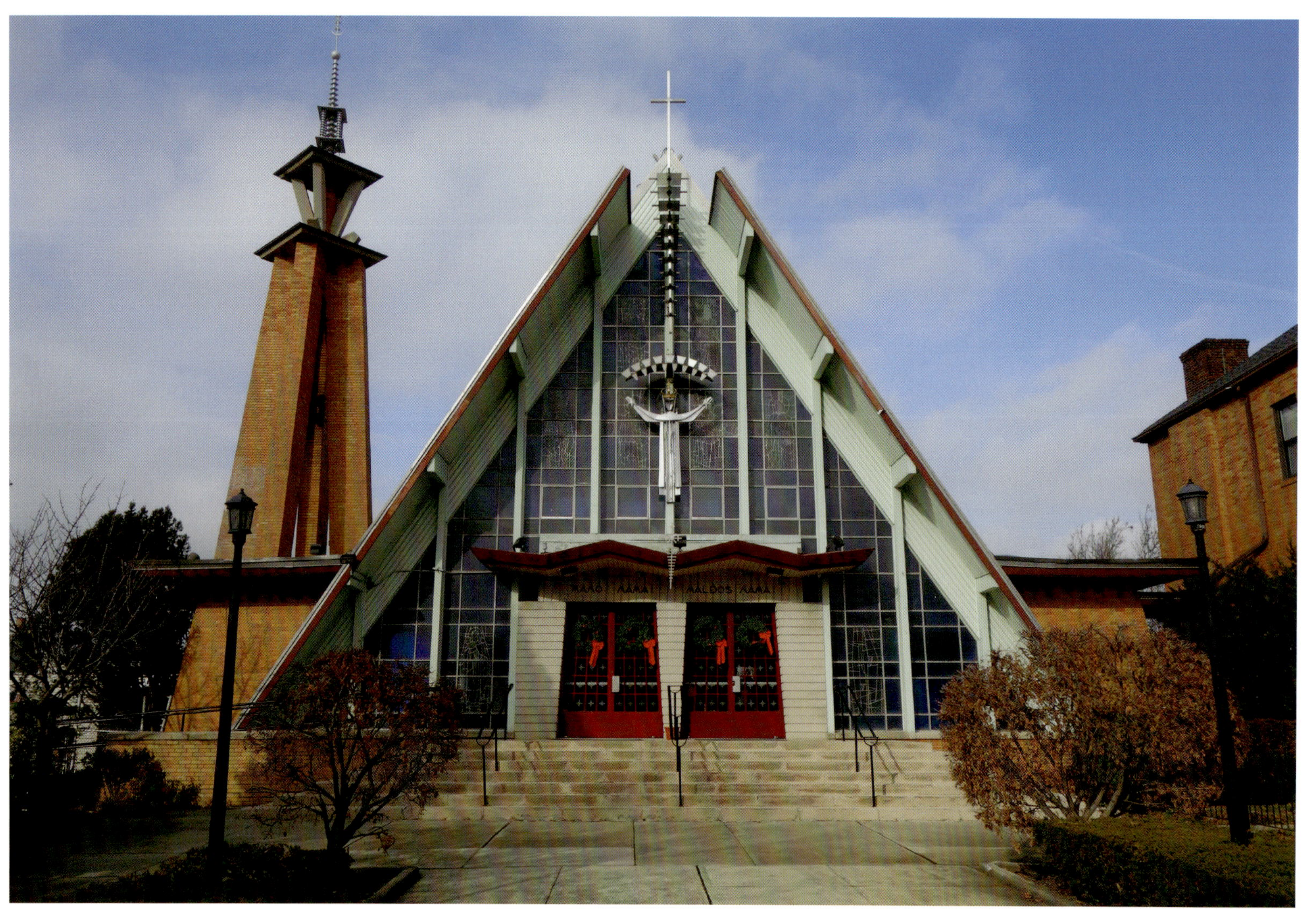

Transfiguration Roman Catholic Church, Maspeth

Maspeth has long been home to an ethnically diverse Catholic population, with parishes established by Irish, Italian, German, Bohemian, and Polish immigrant communities. They built their churches in the traditional styles of Gothic and Italianate, with a few Neoclassical examples for good measure. After World War II, the Catholic Church embraced Modern architecture to connect with the contemporary world. Transfiguration Church is one such effort, completed in 1962 to serve a Lithuanian parish. The congregation has dwindled over the last few decades, and today the church offers Lithuanian mass only once per week. In 2019, it merged with a shrinking Polish congregation, St. Stanislaus Kostka.

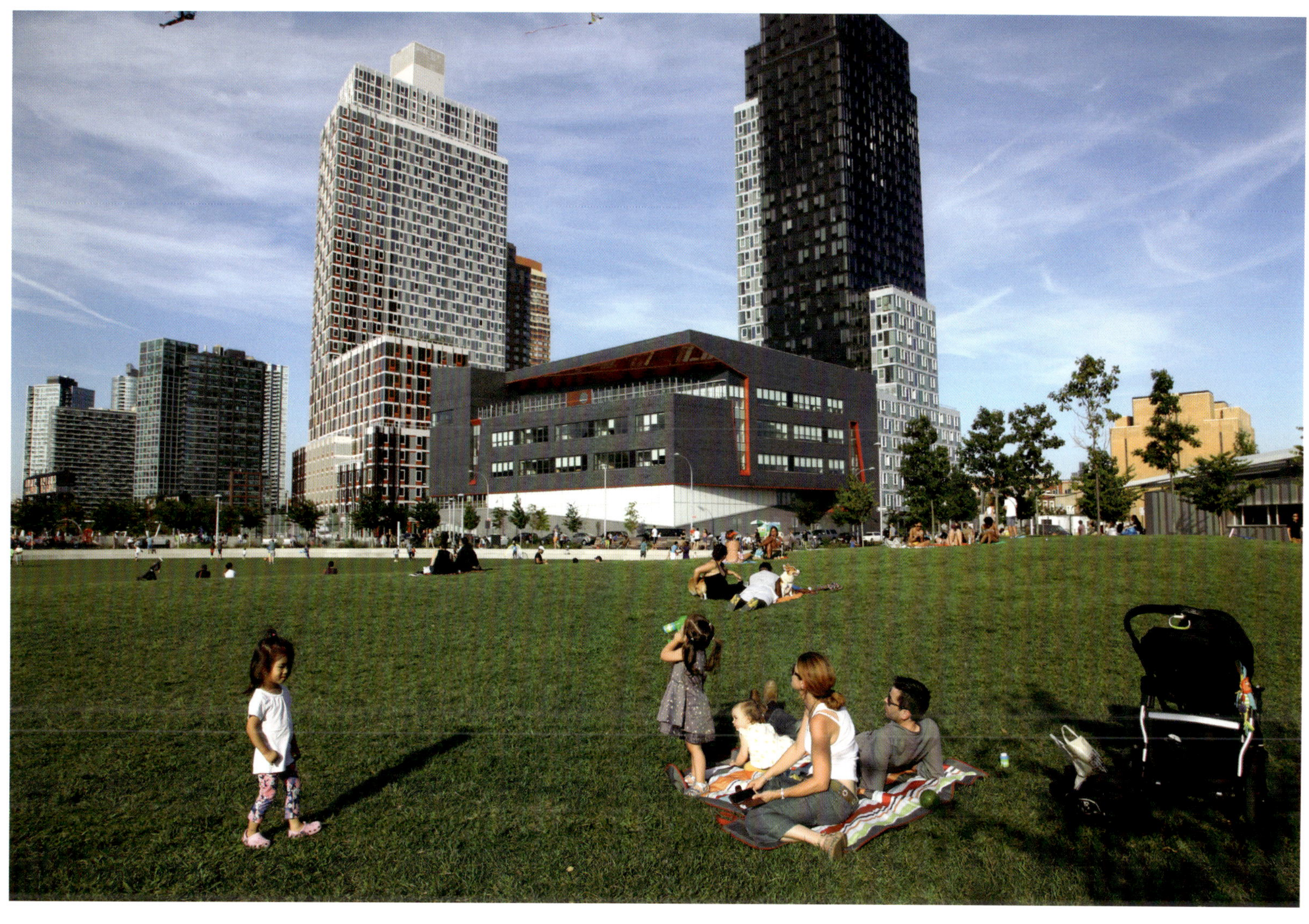

Hunters Point Park, Long Island City

The large oval lawn shown here is part of a decades-long effort to reclaim the East River Waterfront for public space and recreation. Long given over to factories, warehouses, piers, and dry docks, today the waterfront offers green spaces, promenades, playgrounds, exercise stations, and tidal marsh restoration zones. The park has undoubtedly played a part in the broader gentrification of Long Island City through the uneven provision of green amenities. Most of the new glass-and-steel condominium towers shown here feature luxury high-end housing. On the other hand, Queens residents are desperate for additional green space, and the park is well used by a diverse array of people.

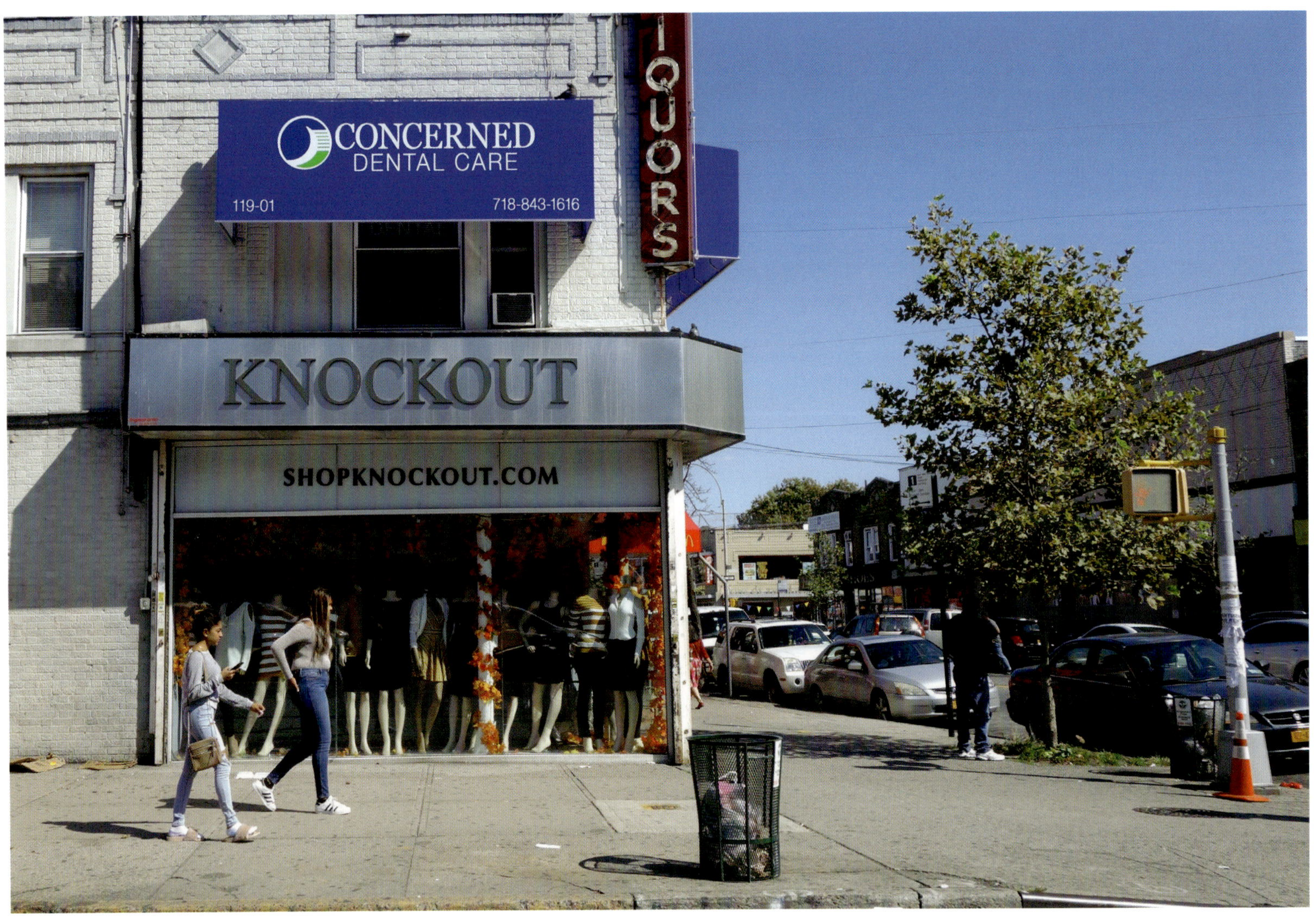

Richmond Chill

A quiet corner on a quiet afternoon in Richmond Hill. The neighborhood is known for having a low-key vibe and easygoing atmosphere. Residents attribute this to the large Indo-Caribbean and Afro-Caribbean population, mostly hailing from Guyana and Trinidad. They maintain that the island cultural practices they have brought with them help to counter, or at least restrain, the more hectic pace of New York City. Richmond Hill is also more racially diverse than other Queens neighborhoods. Nearly one-third of the neighborhood's 52,000 residents identifies as Asian or Asian descent, 12 percent as African descent, 12 percent as White, 30 percent as Hispanic, and 7 percent as mixed race.

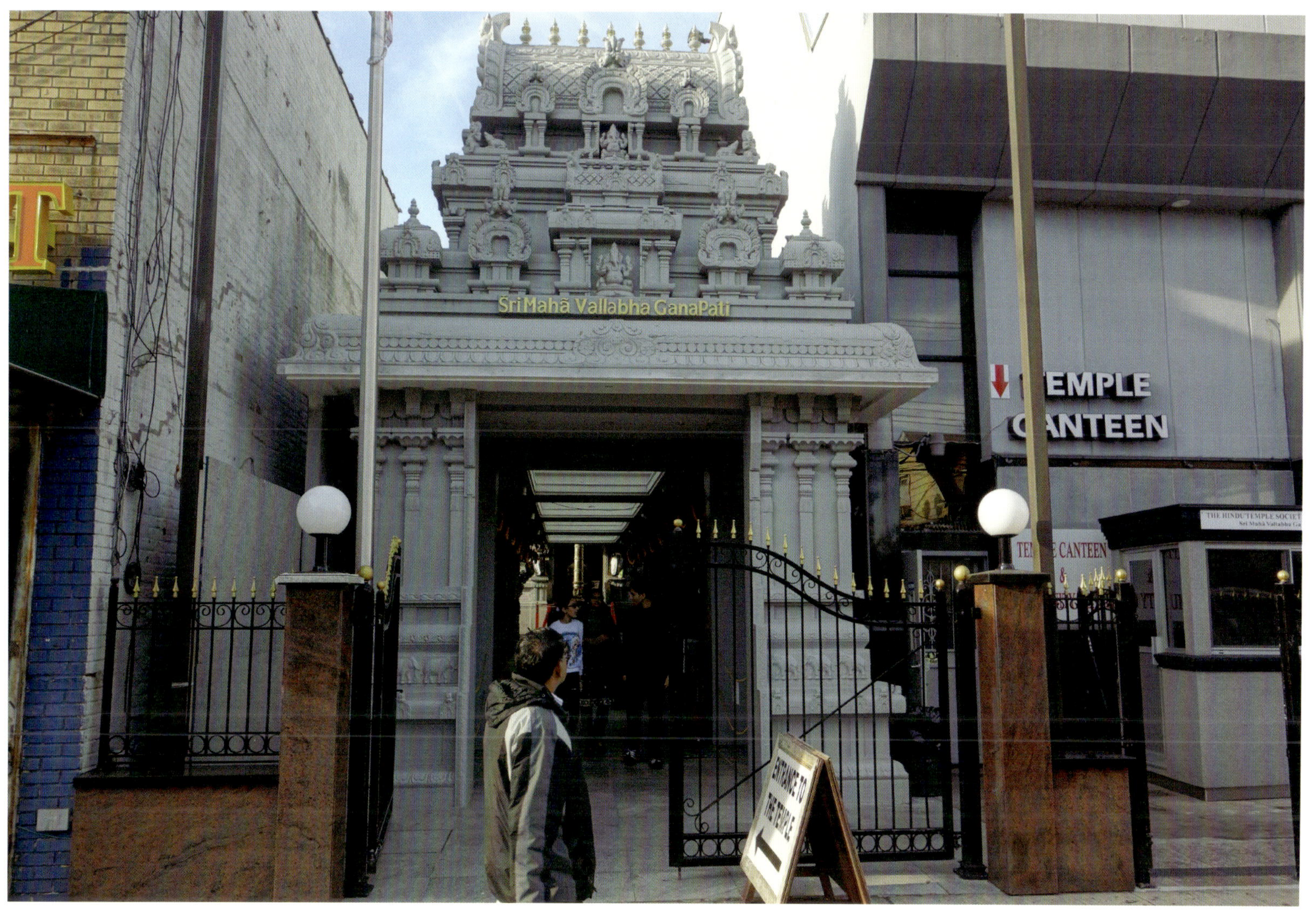

SriMaha Vallabha GanaPati Temple, Flushing

Home to the Hindu Temple Society of North America, this building complex in Flushing is a major hub of the Hindu community in Queens. The society was founded in 1970, and members raised funds to purchase a lot formerly occupied by a Russian Orthodox church to build the current temple. Completed in 1977, the design leans heavily toward South Indian Dravidian architecture. In addition to the worship space, dedicated to Ganesh, the temple has a popular basement canteen serving lunch every day of the week. There are also meeting rooms, offices, youth activity spaces, and large event rooms for weddings, banquets, and traditional dance classes. Priests rotate from India to serve at the temple.

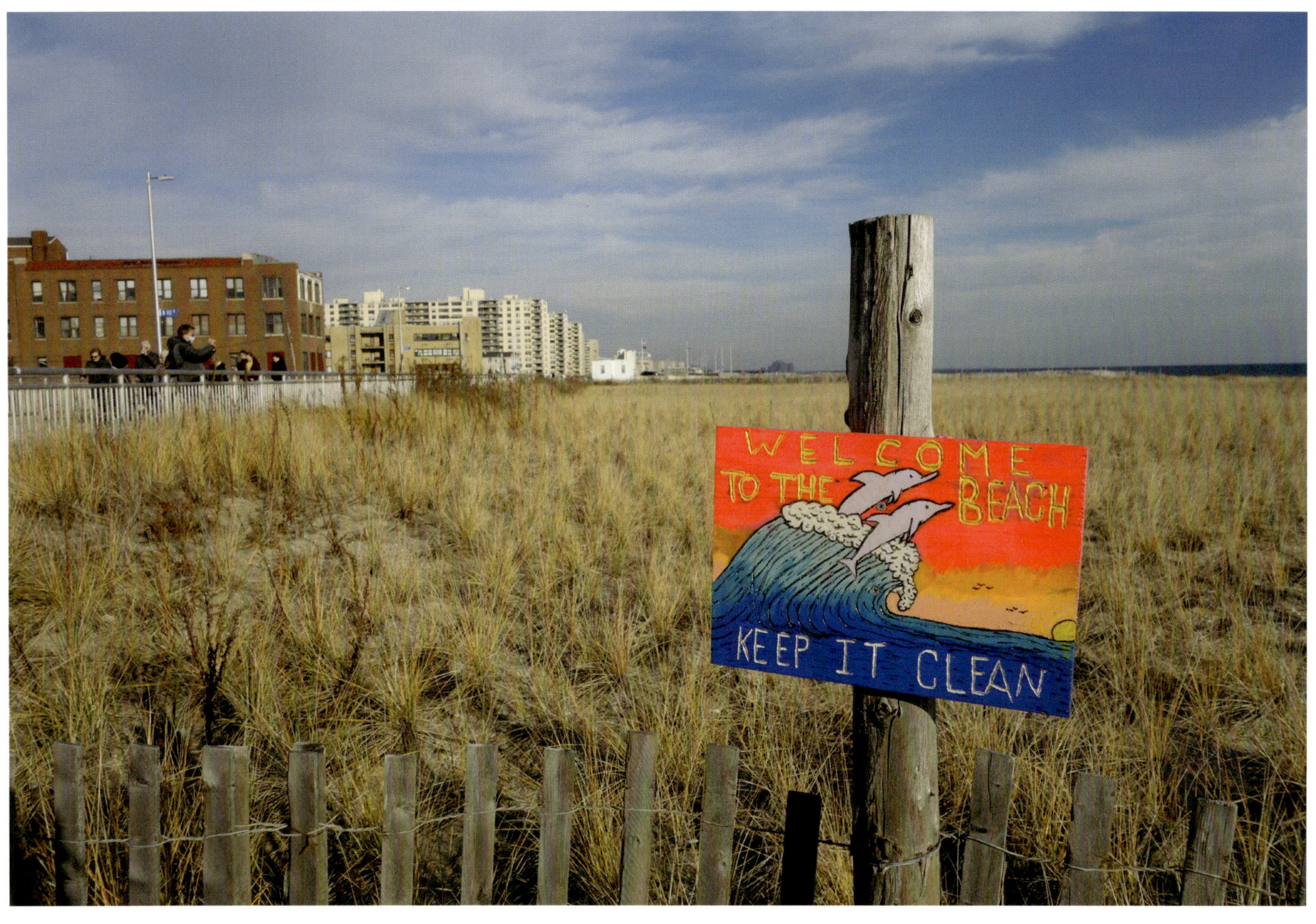

Dune restoration, Rockaway Beach

The seven-mile-long Atlantic coastline at Rockaway is subject to constant erosion from wind and surf and sudden dramatic alterations from storm surges. Hurricane Sandy took its toll on the beach and surrounding communities, destroying many of the dunes vital for protection against flooding. Here at Beach 114th Street, the Parks Department has undertaken to restore the fragile ecology by planting native grasses, such as American Beach Grass (Ammophila breviligulata). As prevailing winds blow over the beach from the oceanfront, the grasses provide structure to trap sand so that dunes will form over time. Restoration comprises a never-ending environmental project along the Rockaway coast.

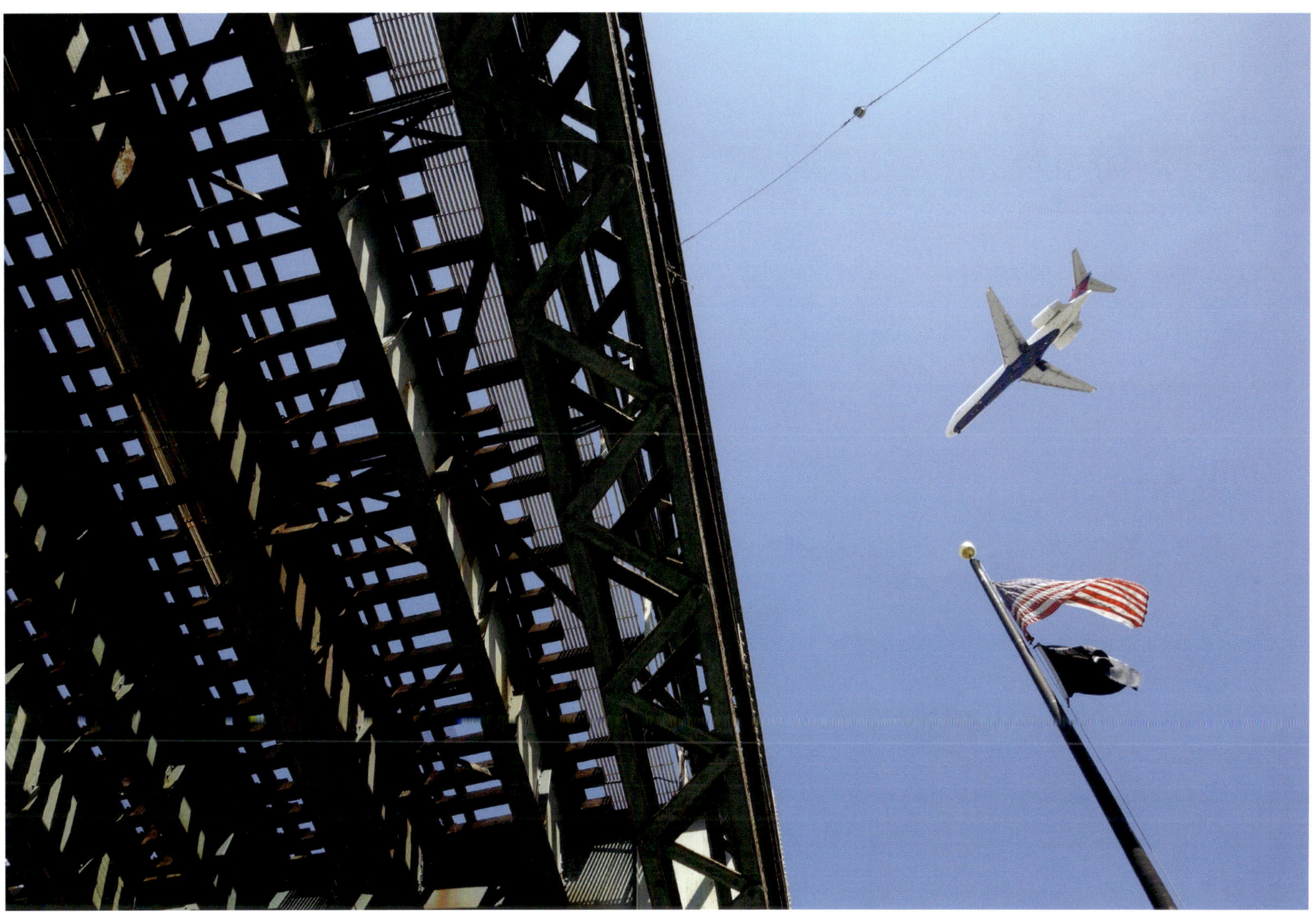

The Airport Borough

A commercial jet flies over the tracks of the 7 train on its approach to La Guardia Airport. With LGA on the borough's northern extremity at Bowery Bay, and JFK on the southern edge along Jamaica Bay, Queens has earned its nickname as the "Airport Borough." The Federal Aviation Administration and the Port Authority maintain strict regulations on air traffic in this dense corridor, which sees thousands of flights every day. JFK is the busiest international gateway to the United States, a role once played by Ellis Island when people arrived on transatlantic steam ships and ocean liners. Since Ellis Island closed in 1954, the great majority of immigrants to New York City have arrived by airplane.

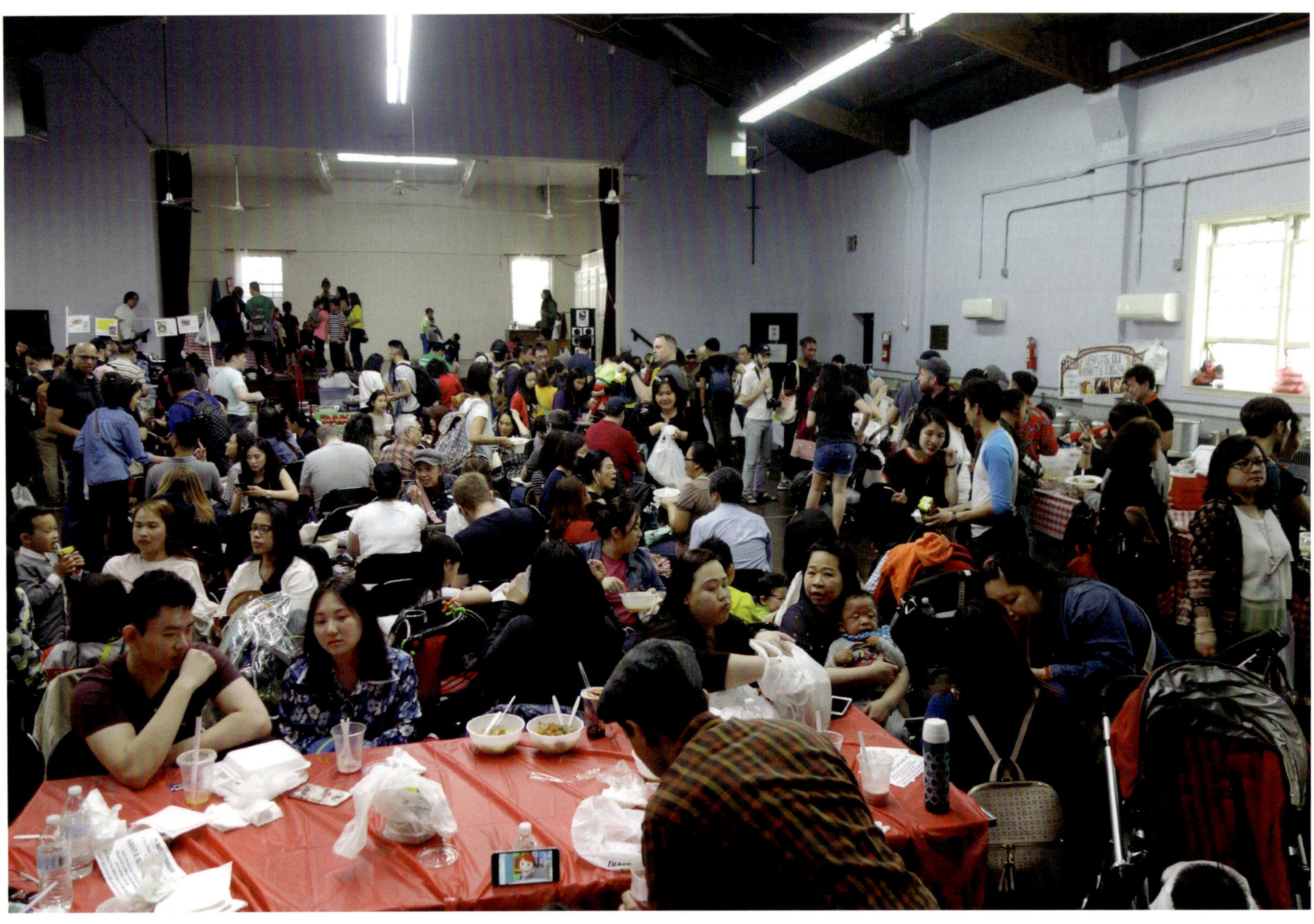

Indonesian festivals

Figures 91a-91e. From the Festival of San Gennaro in Little Italy to the West Indian Day Parade in Crown Heights, ethnic celebrations make up one of the great traditions of New York City. Given its unparalleled diversity, Queens features scores of celebrations for groups to mark important dates, or just to share food, music, dance, and other cultural forms. As one of the newest immigrant groups in Queens, Indonesians have only opened a few groceries and restaurants so far, compared to more well-established immigrants from China, Thailand, and Vietnam. As an interim solution, Indonesian civic organizations have established several monthly festivals running from April through October in Elmhurst and Woodside.

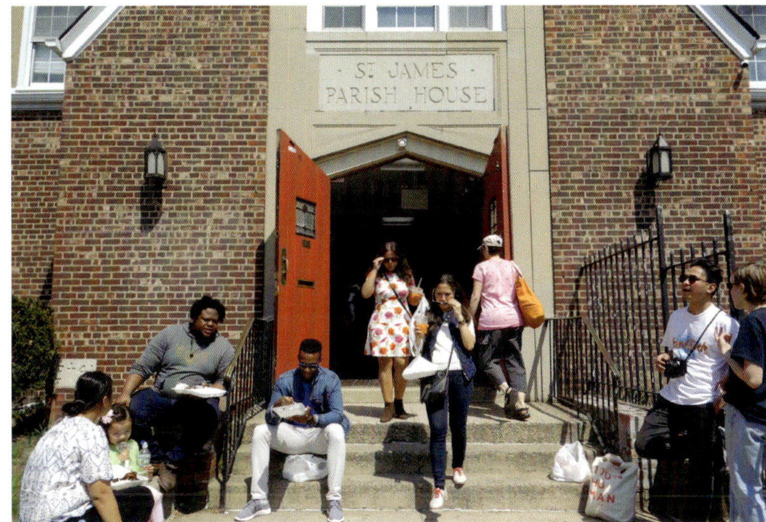

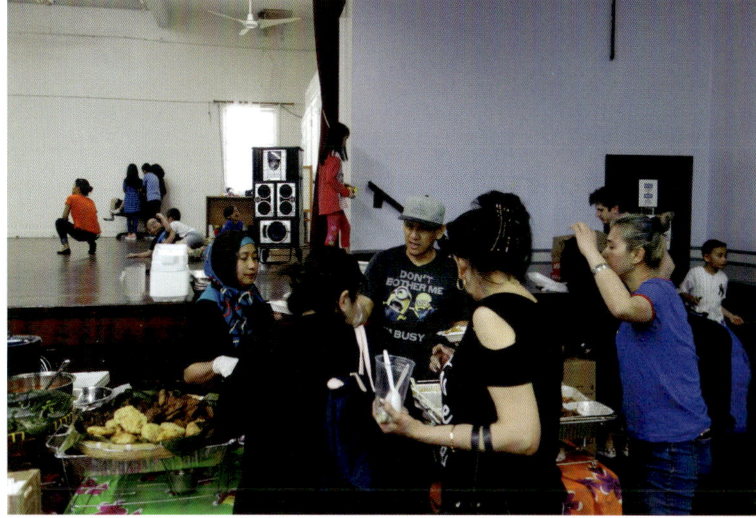

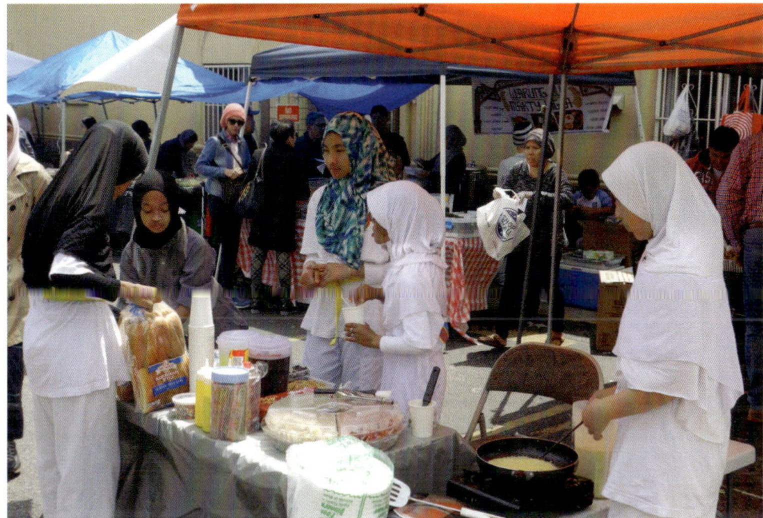

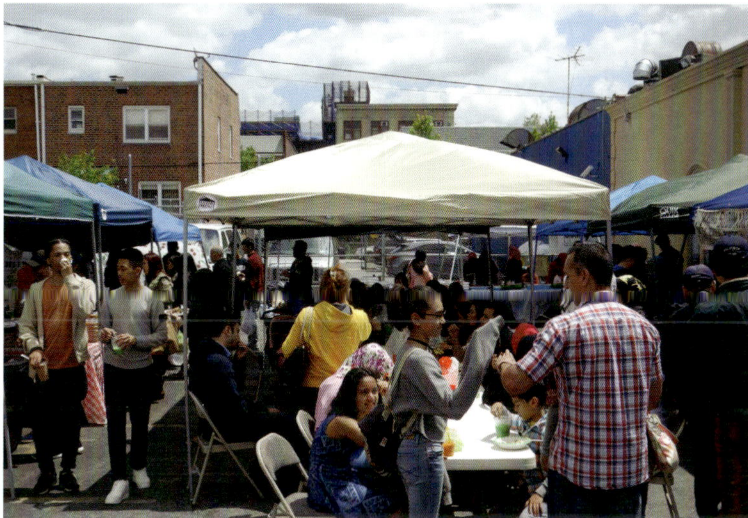

Opposite page: Festival goers enjoy food and lively company at the Indonesian Festival held at St. James Parish House in Elmhurst. This page, top left: Entrance to the St. James Indonesian Fest, with participants spilling onto the front steps and yard. Top right: Vendors at St. James serve Indonesian meals as children play on the stage in the background. Bottom left and right: The monthly Indonesian Festival at the Masjid Al-Hikmah in Woodside. Here, organizers set up tents, tables, and chairs in the parking lot. Around a dozen vendors bring grills, hot plates, and tables to sell a wide variety of dishes from Java, Sumatra, and Sulawesi. Many families bring boxes to take out quantities of prepared food.

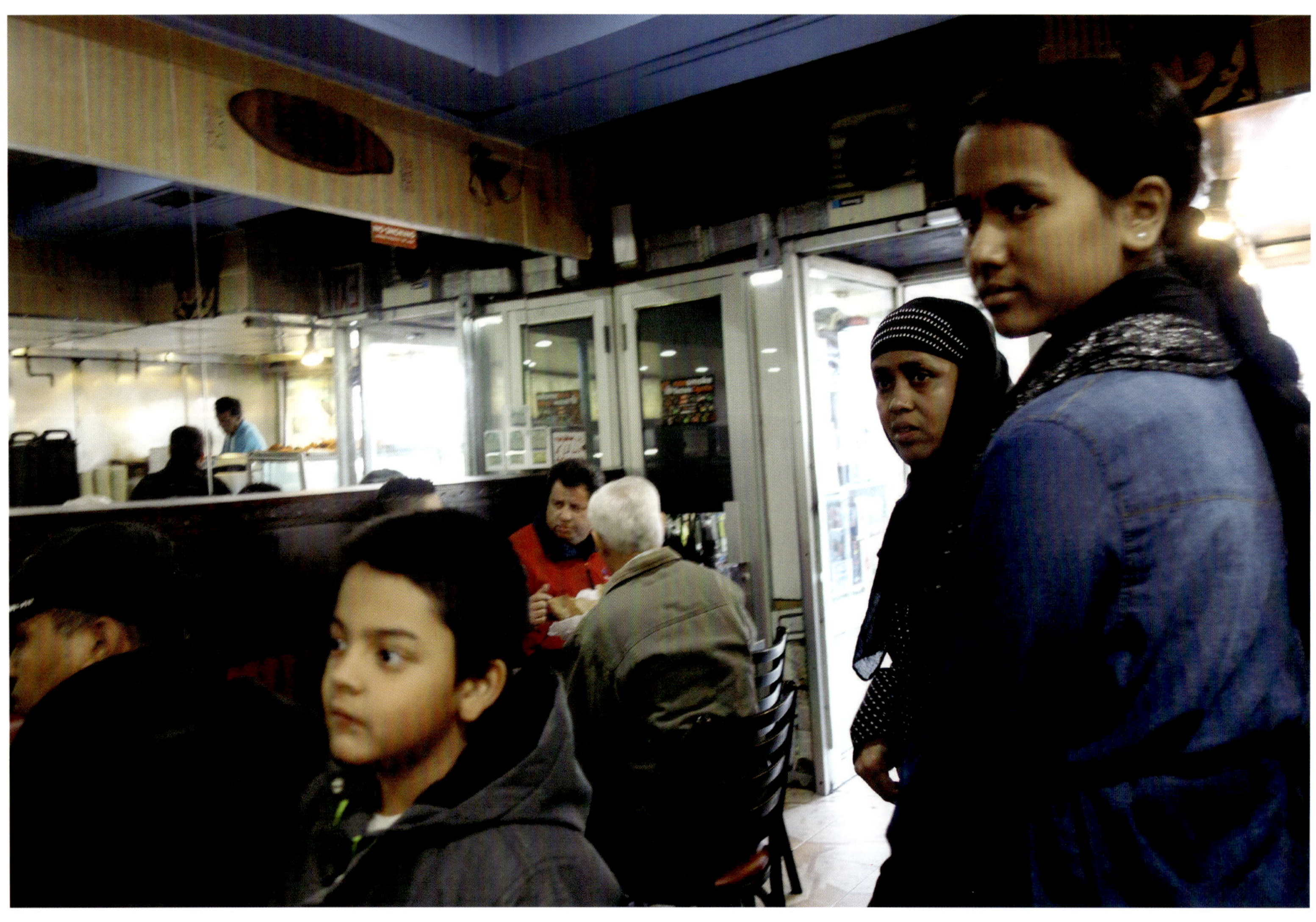

Waiting at Merit Kabab, Jackson Heights

A family waits for a table at Merit Kabab, a popular Bengali diner in Jackson Heights located right near the staircase of the 7 train station. On any given day, the seats are packed with locals as well as cab drivers and traffic wardens working the area. Despite its name, Merit Kabab specializes in fish dishes and biryani, with a long steam table bearing multiple mounds of rice and meat combinations. To increase trade, the proprietors made room for a small Nepalese-Tibetan food service in the back of the diner, which serves assorted momo, laphing, thenthuk, and other specialties. The two operations share one kitchen, and have had to carefully work out routines of preparation, cooking, storage, and staging.

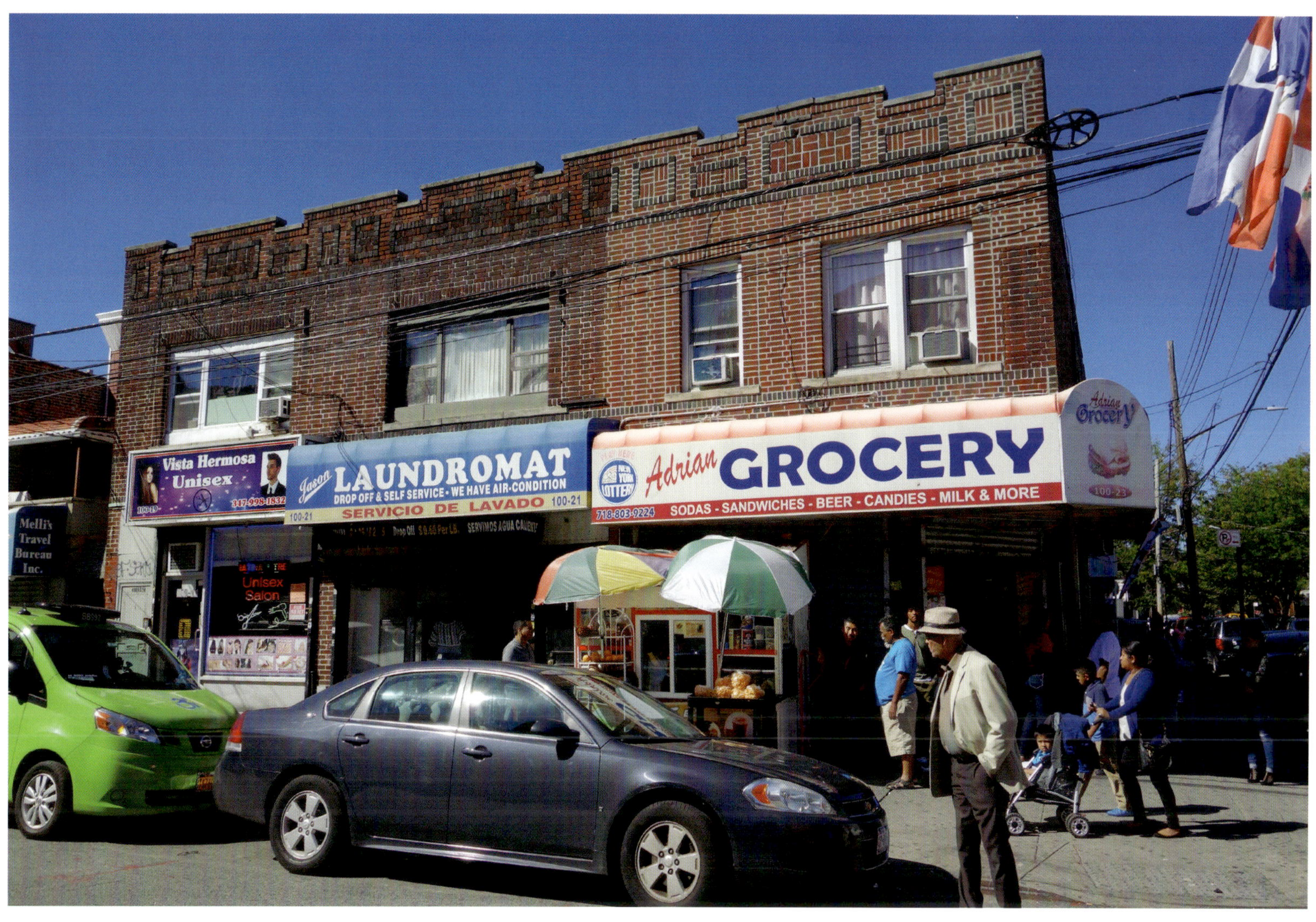

Street scene in Corona

On a warm afternoon in early autumn, residents go about their business on 37th Avenue at 101st Street in Corona. This part of the neighborhood is often referred to as "North Corona," as it sits to the north of Roosevelt Avenue. There is the usual mix of a bodega, laundromat, hair salon, and travel agency that you can find on hundreds of street corners around Queens. But to appreciate this scene fully, you have to imagine the sounds of animated conversations in Spanish, the yells and laughter of children, the sweet-sour flavor of a mango orange juice from the little juice bar, the smells of delivery truck exhaust and grilling meat, and Bachata music blaring from speakers of passing cars.

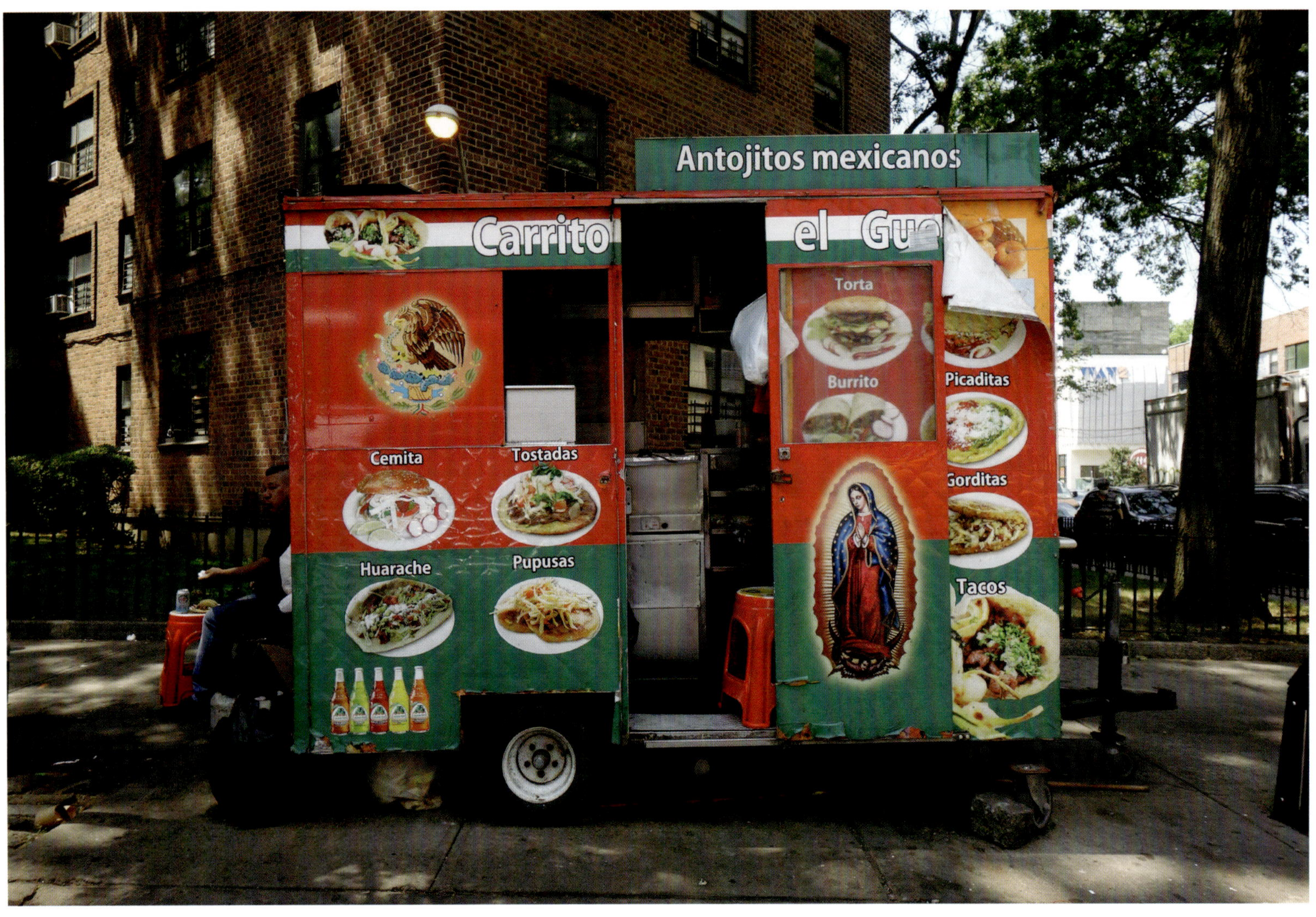

Food truck at the James A. Bland Houses, Flushing

This Mexican food truck might seem out of place in a predominantly Chinese neighborhood, but it draws a loyal crowd of Chinese American youth who grew up eating Mexican food. It also draws many Latino workers from the kitchens and construction sites of the neighborhood, though many of them may also enjoy Chinese food; Chinese takeout is a popular option in most Latino communities. The "Carrito el Guerrero" truck can be found most days parked on Prince Street where it bends into 40th Road near the James A. Bland Houses, seen here in the background. Bland Houses is a large NYCHA-owned complex named for an African American musician and performer who grew up in Flushing in the nineteenth century.

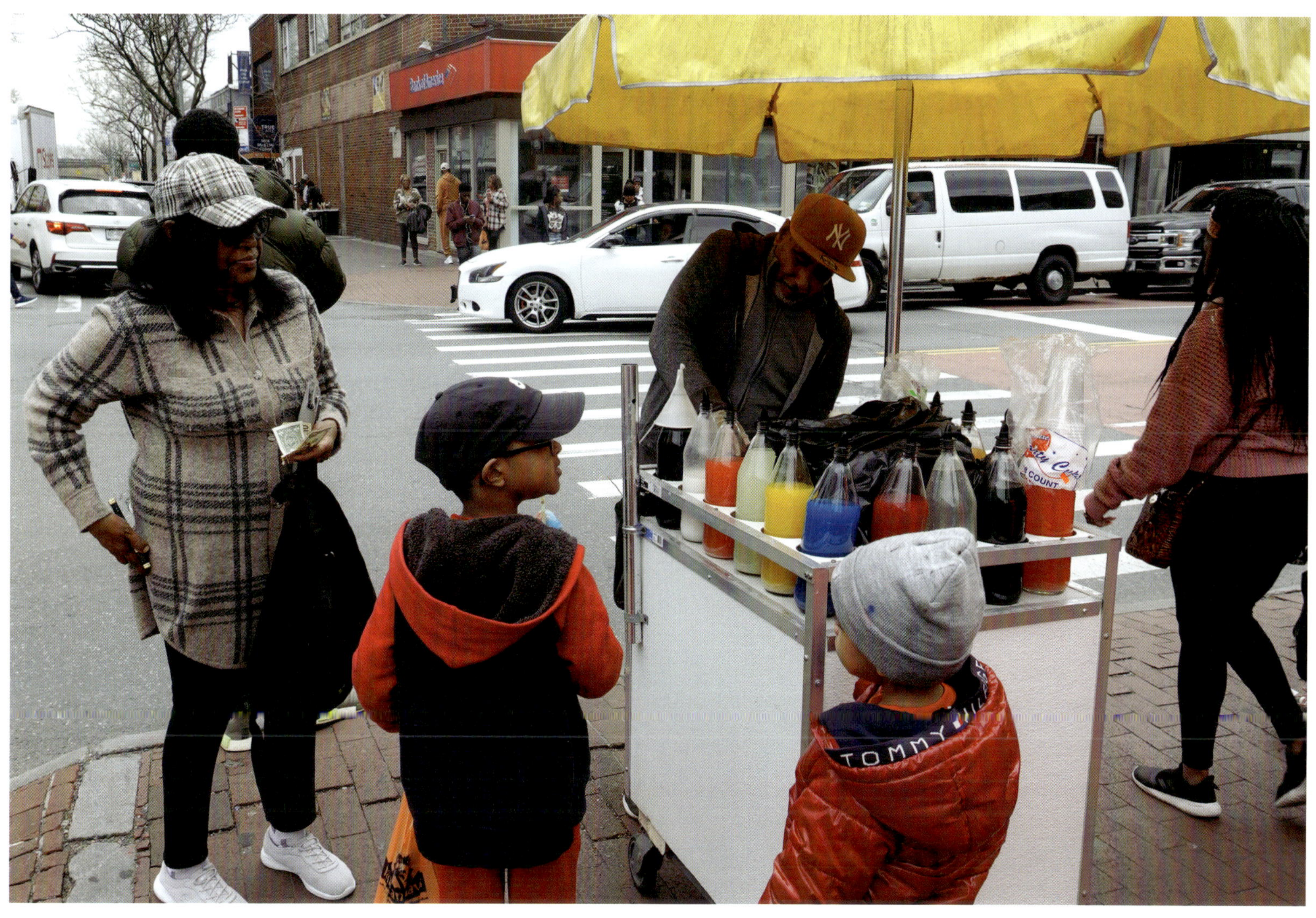

Snow cones after school, Jamaica

After-school treats are a staple in many neighborhoods of Queens, often purchased from street carts like the one shown here selling snow cones. The vendor shaves ice from a large block into a paper cone and adds one or more of a variety of flavors, including mango, tamarind, strawberry, coconut, cherry, blue raspberry, lime, passion, and grape. Some vendors will even add cream, sliced fruit, and nuts. There is a long tradition of shaved ice concoctions in Queens, from Italian ices to Puerto Rican piraguas to Mexican raspados. Popular after-school snacks differ from one neighborhood to the next but might include paletas (popsicles), elote (grilled corn with mayo and chili), jalebi (sweet crunchy spirals), and Dou Sha Bao (red bean buns).

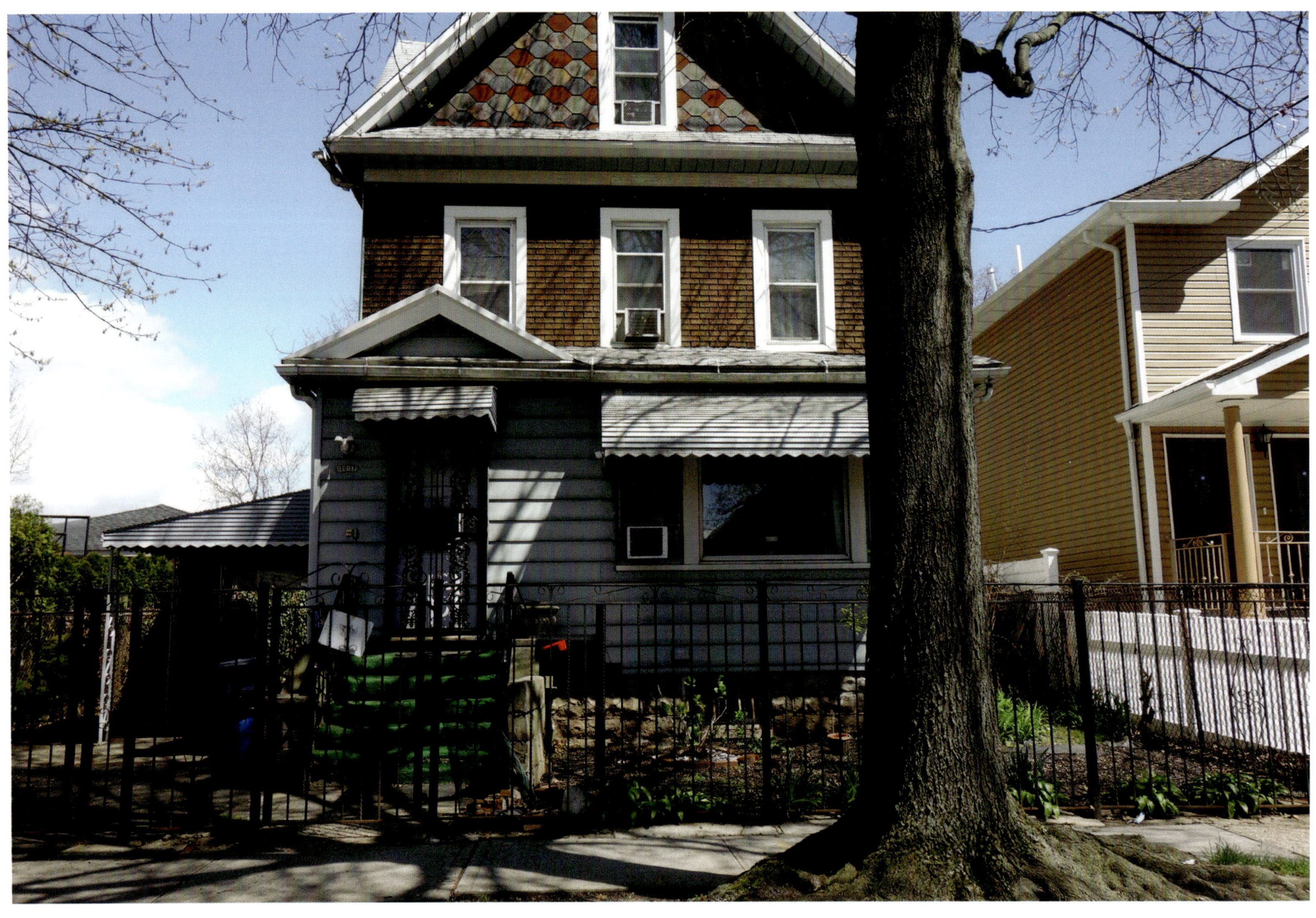

House in South Jamaica

This residence in South Jamaica shows all the signs of incremental adaptation and multigenerational care typical of many older single-family houses in working-class neighborhoods. Built in the 1920s with wood frame on a stone foundation, over time the house has accumulated vinyl and asphalt siding in varied styles, astroturf covering front stairs, an iron fence, and seemingly tacked-on awnings and carport. This cumulative aesthetic contrasts sharply with the relative blandness of the new house next door. Many of these older town houses are considered "tear downs," meaning that buyers will demolish them to make way for larger homes or even apartment buildings.

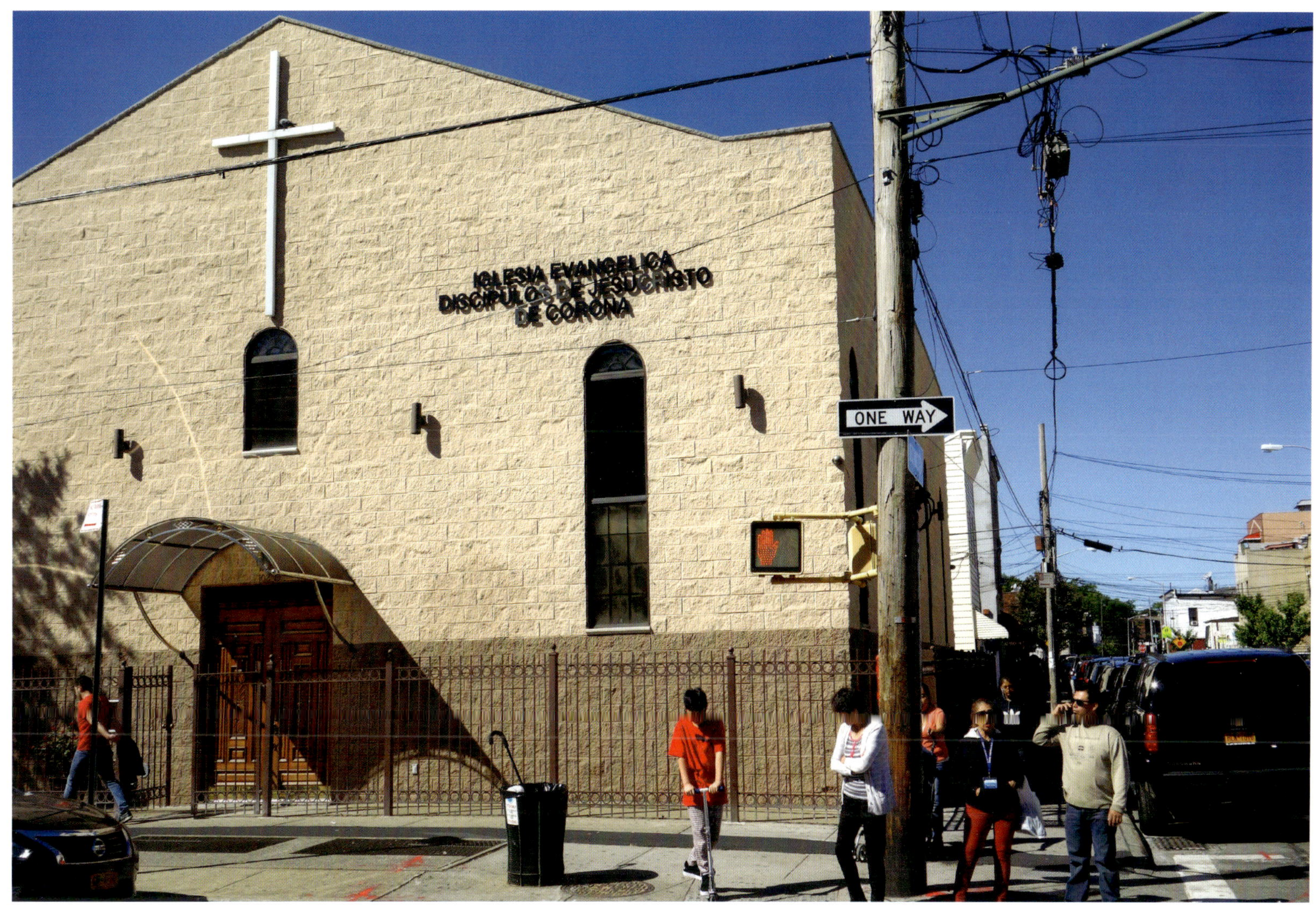

Evangelical Church, Corona

Pedestrians wait at a crosswalk near the Iglesia Evangélica Discípulos de Jesucristo de Corona. Over the past few decades, charismatic denominations, including Evangelicals, Pentecostals, Jehovah's Witnesses, and Seventh-Day Adventists, have made inroads into once staunch Catholic communities—in Queens and throughout Latin America. A global phenomenon, they do particularly well with newcomers to urban life, who tend to be poorer and less connected, and who feel heavily exploited in their precarious and unfamiliar circumstances. They have also made significant inroads into Indo-Caribbean and Afro-Caribbean communities in Queens.

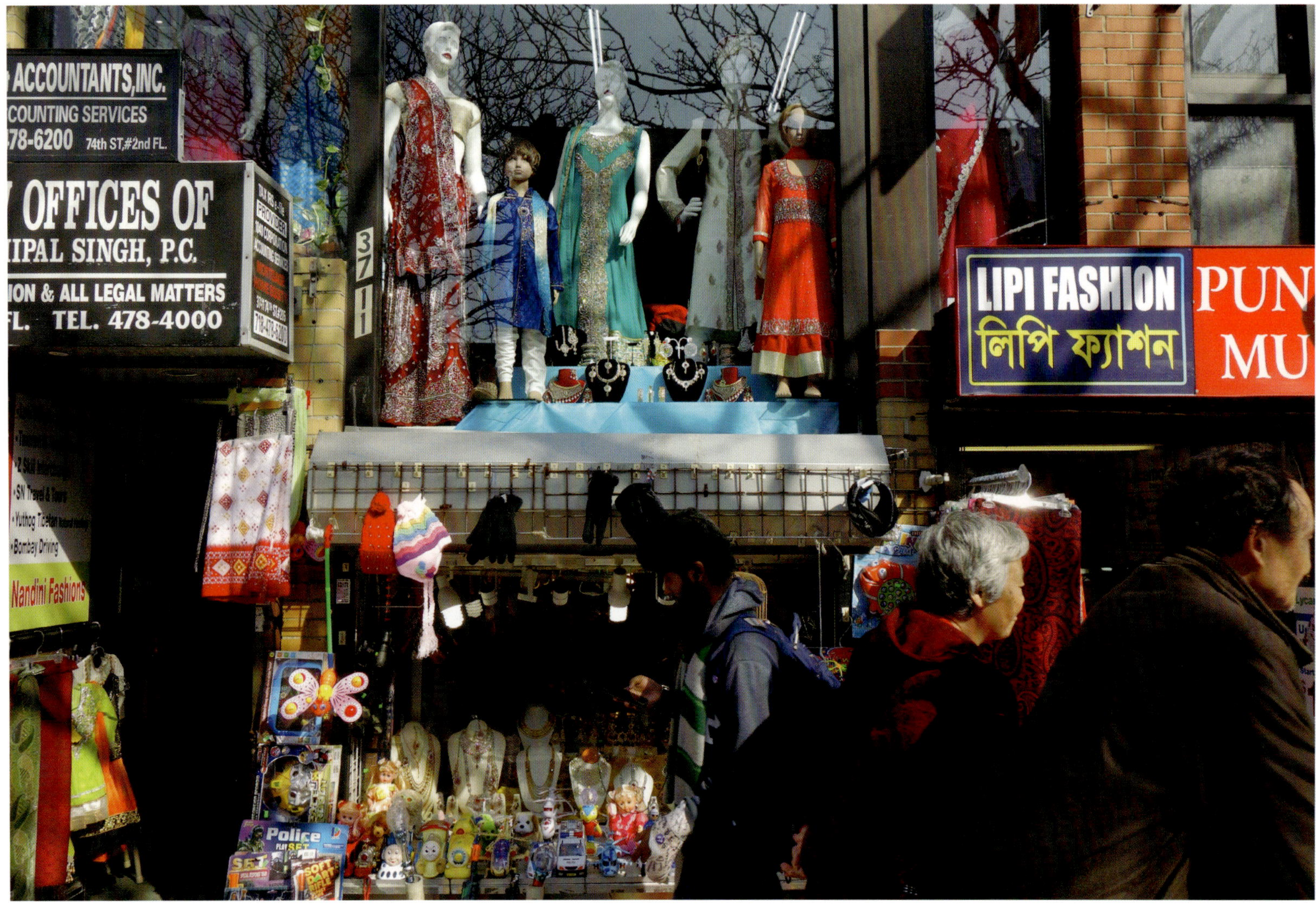

Sari shops in Jackson Heights

The stretch of 74th Street between Roosevelt Avenue and 37th Avenue is renowned as a regional destination for South Asian wedding planners and shoppers. Here they can consult with multiple caterers, sweet shops owners, music vendors, grocers, jewelry and sari sellers, and—importantly—astrologists. Additionally, families may bring along their gold, stored in the form of jewelry, to one of the many gold dealers on the street to raise cash to pay for weddings and other major events. Many of the shop owners are Bengali Muslims, but they all cater to the needs of Hindu, Muslim, Jain, and Sikh celebrations across the varied South Asian diasporic communities.

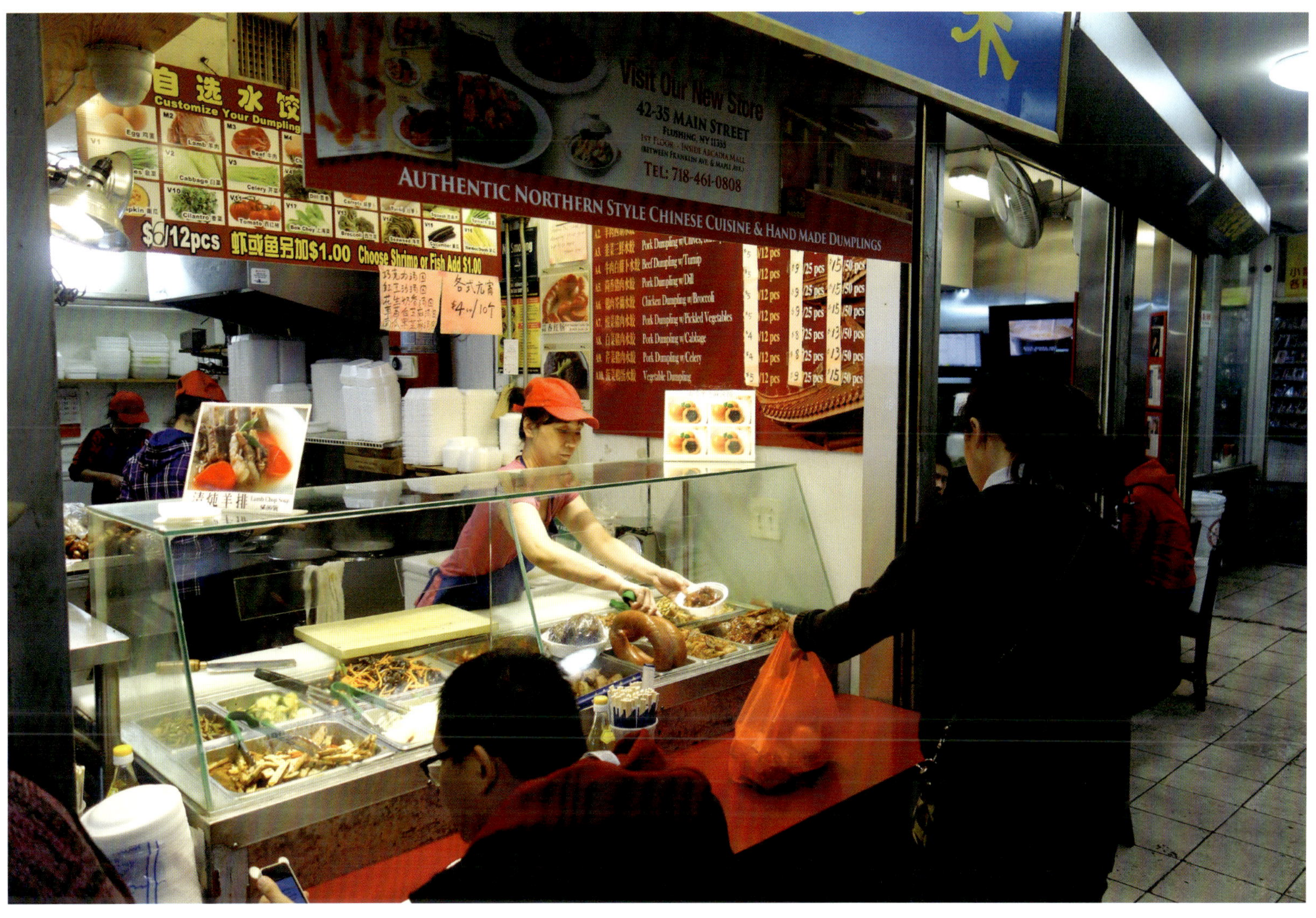

Tian Jin Dumplings, Flushing

One of a dozen businesses crammed into the now closed Golden Mall Food Court in Flushing, Tian Jin served ten delicious varieties of dumplings for short order, or in special orders choosing from a list of twenty-four ingredients. They also maintained a steam table of over a dozen side dishes, such as marinated tofu, liver sausage, bok choy, and pigs' feet. And the family-operated business accomplished all of this in a one hundred–square-foot kitchen, proving themselves to be masters of spatial utility. If one generalization holds among the otherwise diverse Chinese community, it is that they are very serious about their cuisine. And many dumpling connoisseurs considered Tian Jin to be among the very best dumpling restaurants in New York City.

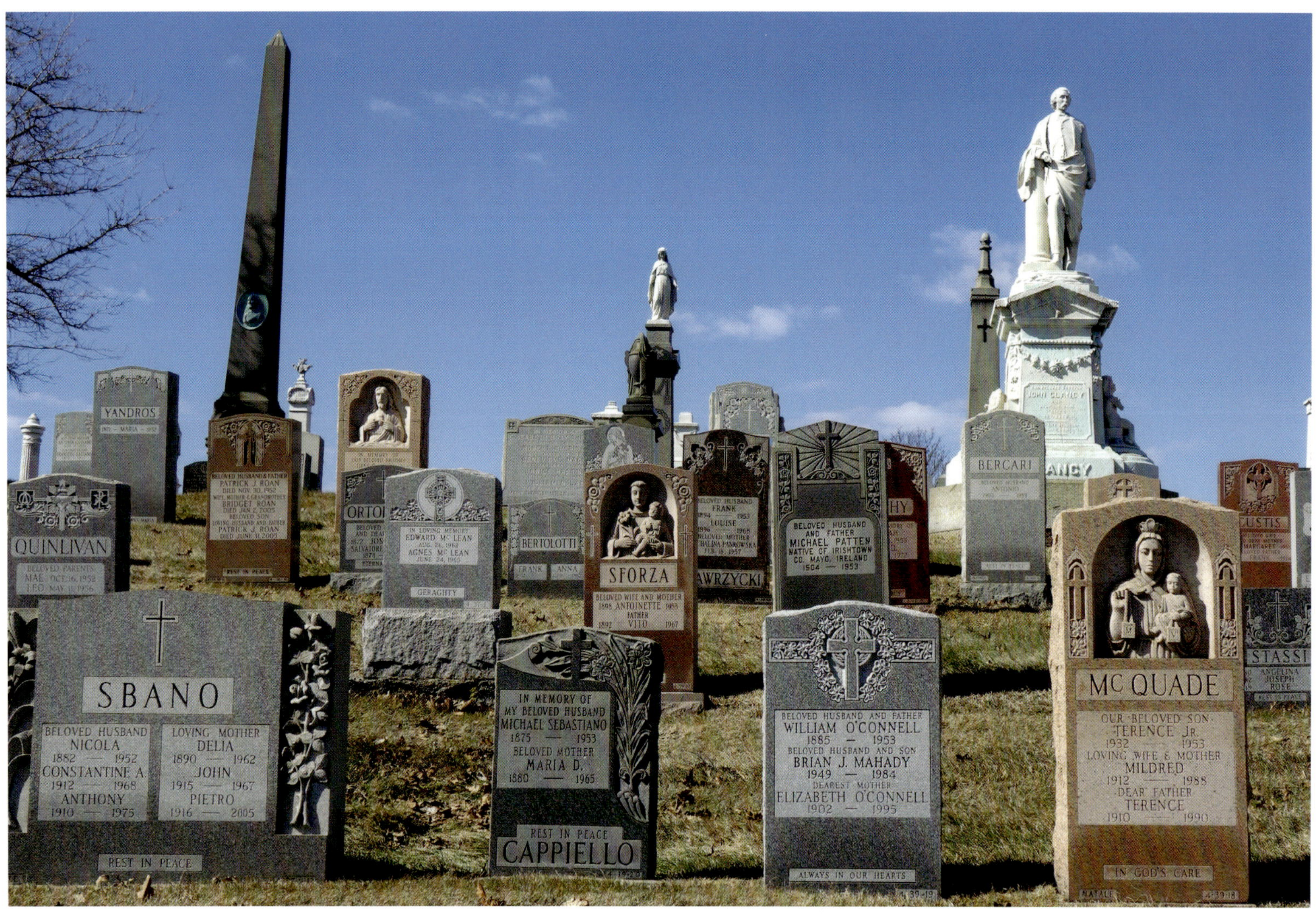

Borough of the Dead

Figures 100a–100e. Because new burials in Manhattan were curtailed in the mid-nineteenth century, rural cemetery development became a big business. State law limited ownership to 200 acres in any county, so many enterprising developers sited their cemeteries on the Brooklyn-Queens border so they could double the size of their cemeteries. And the availability of cheap land made Queens the obvious choice for the location of new cemeteries. Up until World War II, most burial grounds were religiously restrictive, until several large nonsectarian cemeteries opened from the 1920s to 1960s. Today Queens has twice as many people interred below ground as residents above ground, making the borough a true necropolis.

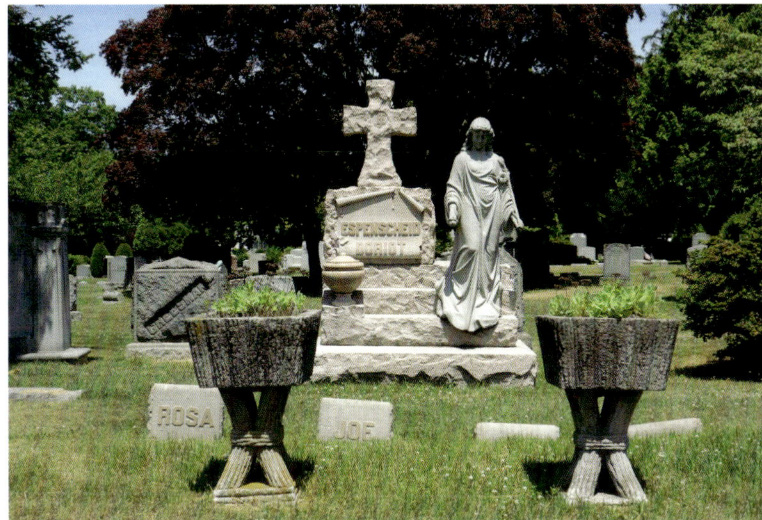

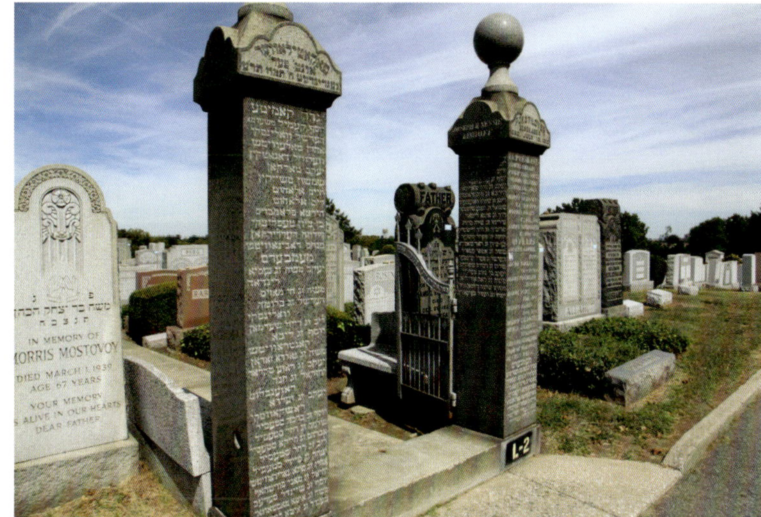

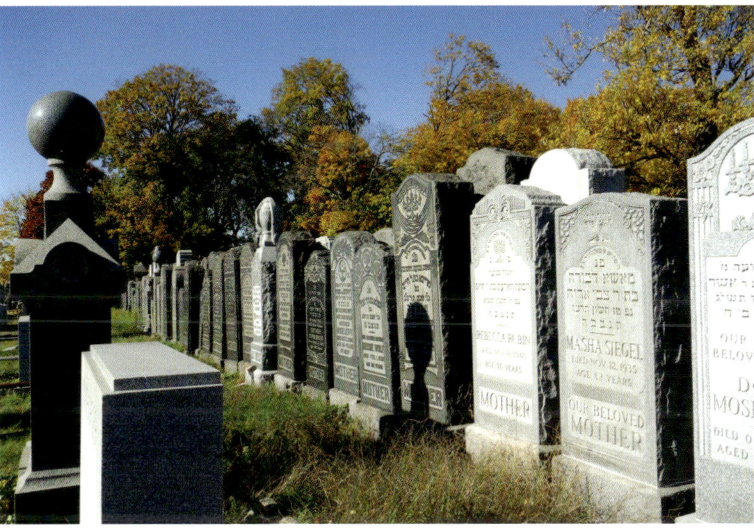

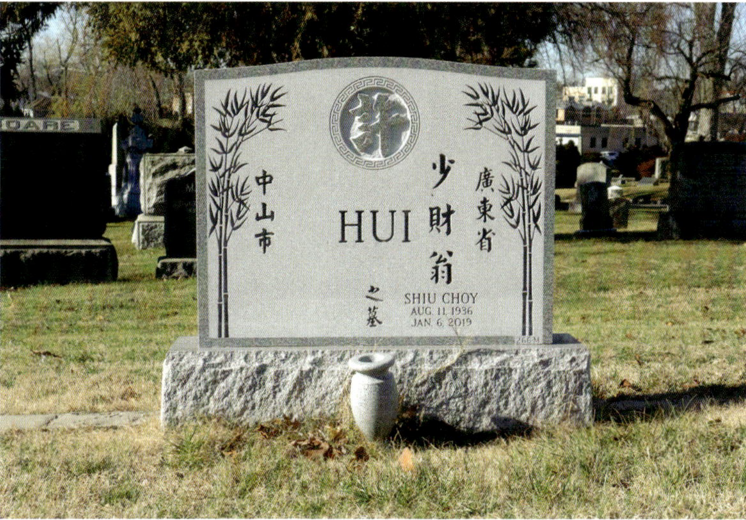

Opposite and this page, top left: With its three million graves, the Roman Catholic Cavalry Cemetery in Maspeth is the most populous burial ground in the country. This page, top right: Mount Lebanon Cemetery was established in Glendale in 1914 for Jewish families. Today it has over 92,000 graves, many of which are cared for through family endowments. Bottom left: One of the oldest Jewish cemeteries in New York is the Acacia Cemetery in Ozone Park, founded by the Pike Street Synagogue in 1891, now run by the Congregation Shaare Zedek. Bottom right: Flushing Cemetery, established in 1853, is a nonsectarian burial ground, with headstones reflecting the area's changing demographics over the last 150 years.

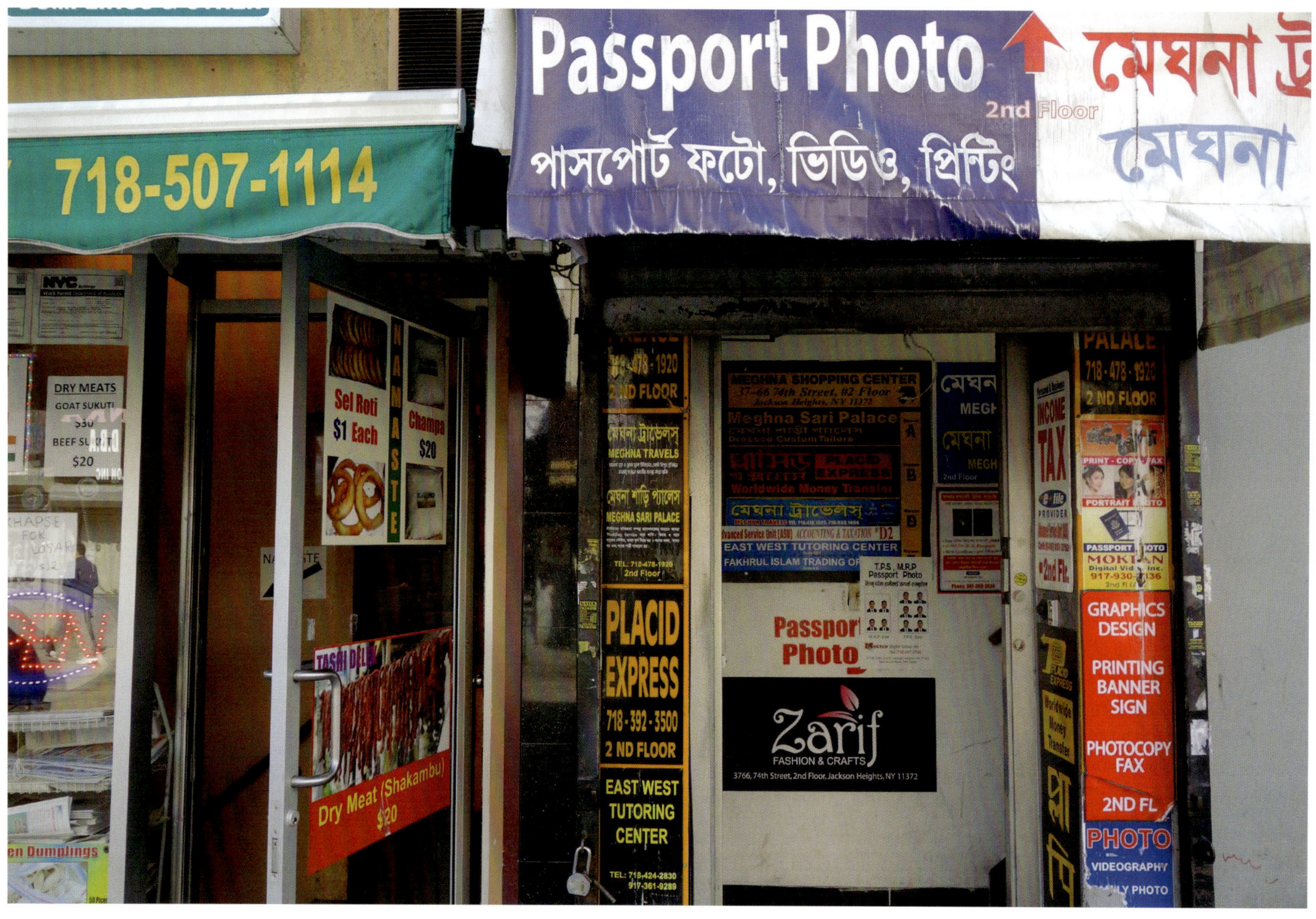

Diaspora text, Jackson Heights

We can read the needs and desires of diasporic communities by the texts they apply to the surfaces of the city. On the left, the entrance to a downstairs restaurant shows an Indian flag as well as an advertisement for Indian and Nepalese dishes such as roti, dumplings, and dried meats. On the right, the entrance to a stairwell to the second story advertises a range of services in both English and Hindi, including travel agents, tutoring center, passport preparation, graphic design, income tax preparation, wire transfer, and a fashion and craft shop. Each shop and service represents an immense amount of time, labor, and care devoted to the establishment of a foothold in this country.

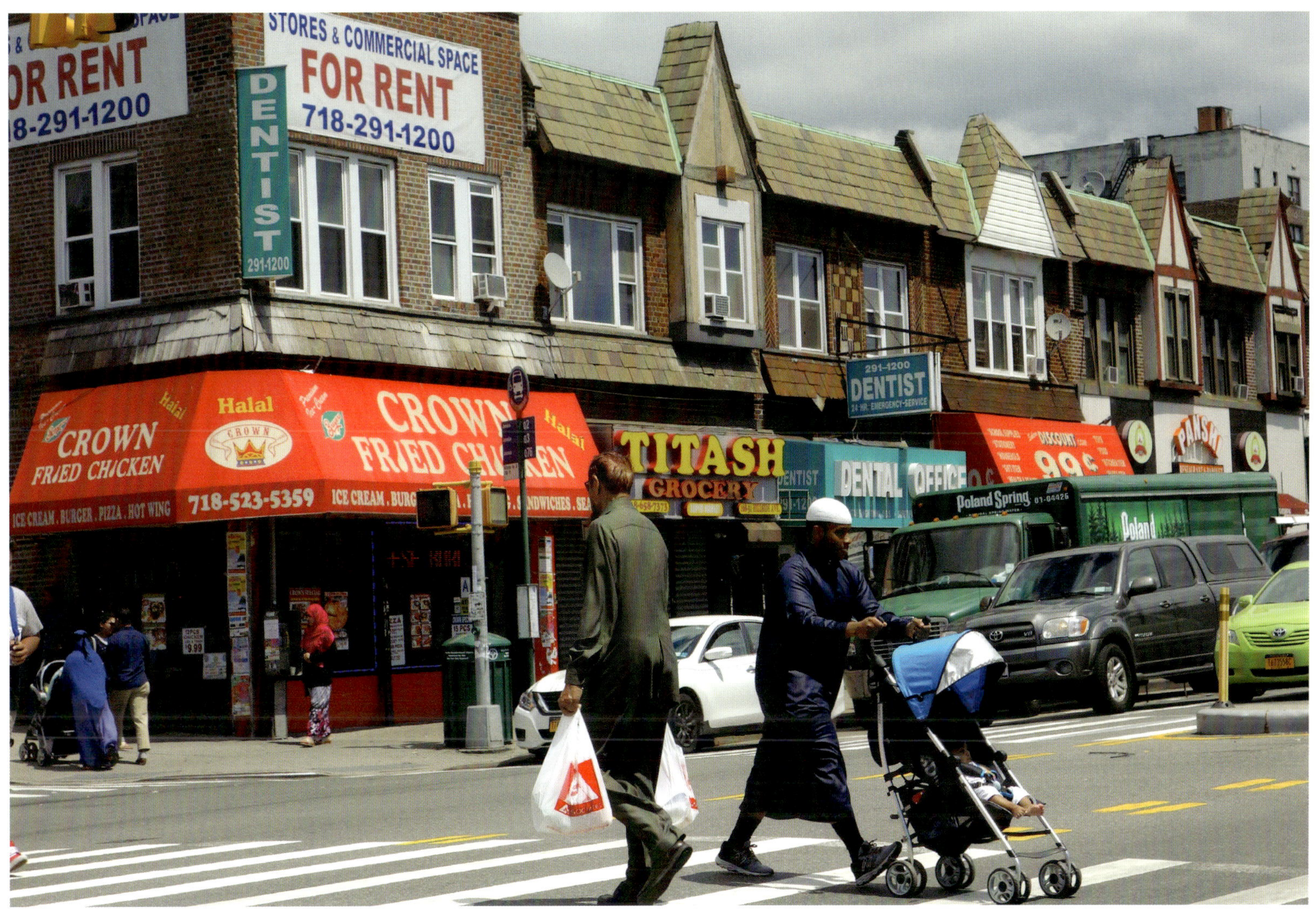

Street scene on Hillside Avenue

A father pushes a stroller across Hillside Avenue on the border between Jamaica Hills and Jamaica. In the background is Crown Fried Chicken, a rival to the older Kennedy Fried Chicken. Kennedy and Crown are neither chains nor franchises, but a blueprint shared among Afghan immigrants since the 1970s as a way to establish businesses in the United States. Their menus feature a mix of American, Caribbean, and Middle Eastern dishes, with a distinct African American influence in the preparation of fried chicken (skin on, lightly battered, heavily seasoned). Crown Fried Chicken launched in the 1990s, and now there are dozens of Crowns and Kennedys across New York and New Jersey.

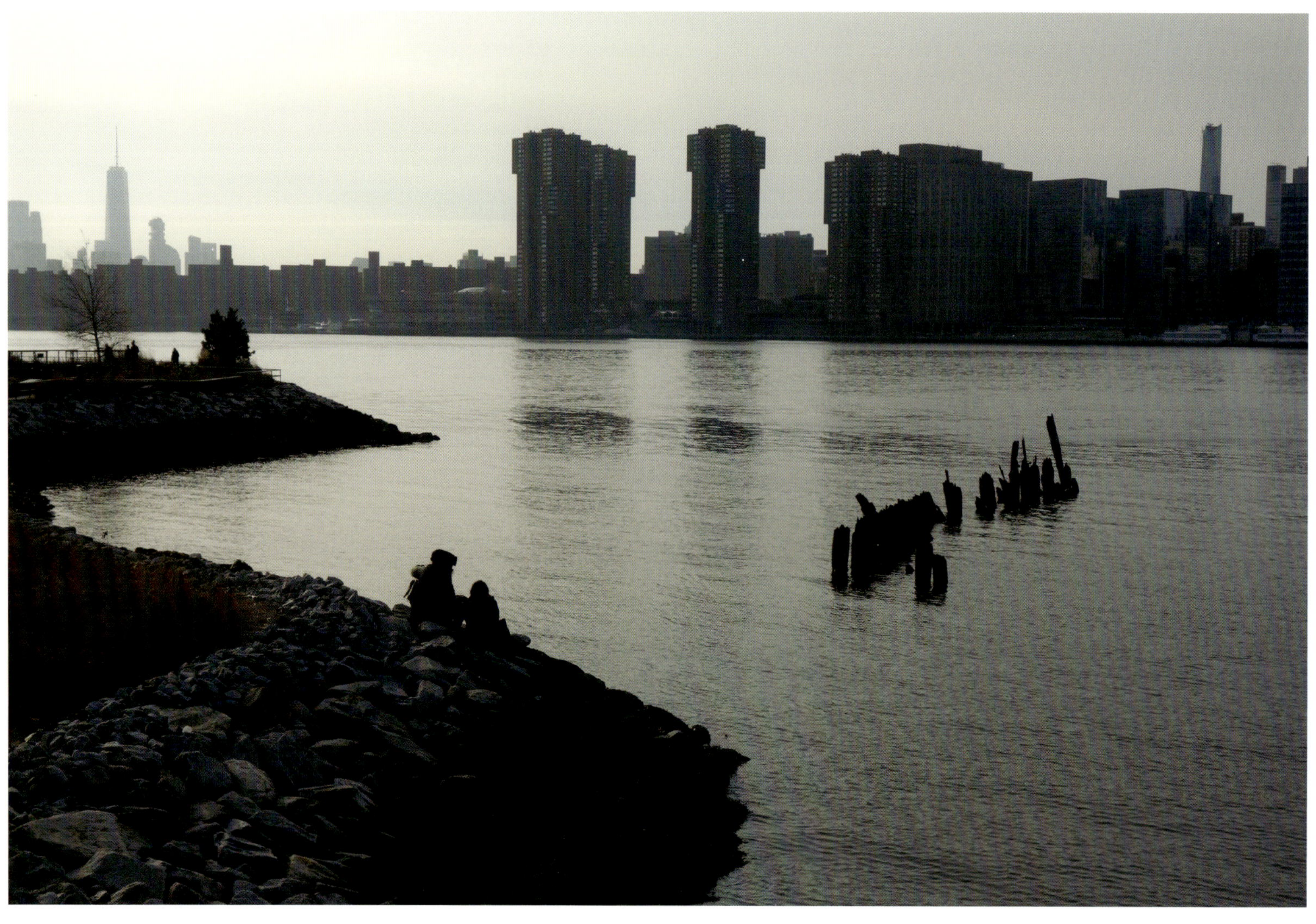

Dusk on the East River, Long Island City

For over a decade, city officials, environmental activists, and local residents have been engaged in an effort to reclaim portions of the East River waterfront. For centuries, the coastline of this tidal estuary served primarily industrial and shipping uses, with numerous piers, dry docks, and material conveyors. Since 2010, the waterfront has been redesigned with resilience in mind. The built-up shoreline and native marsh plant restoration will help mitigate storm surges, which are increasing in frequency and strength because of climate change. The project has also provided much-needed recreational space for Queens residents and visitors, including large open areas, exercise stations, playgrounds, and garden walks.

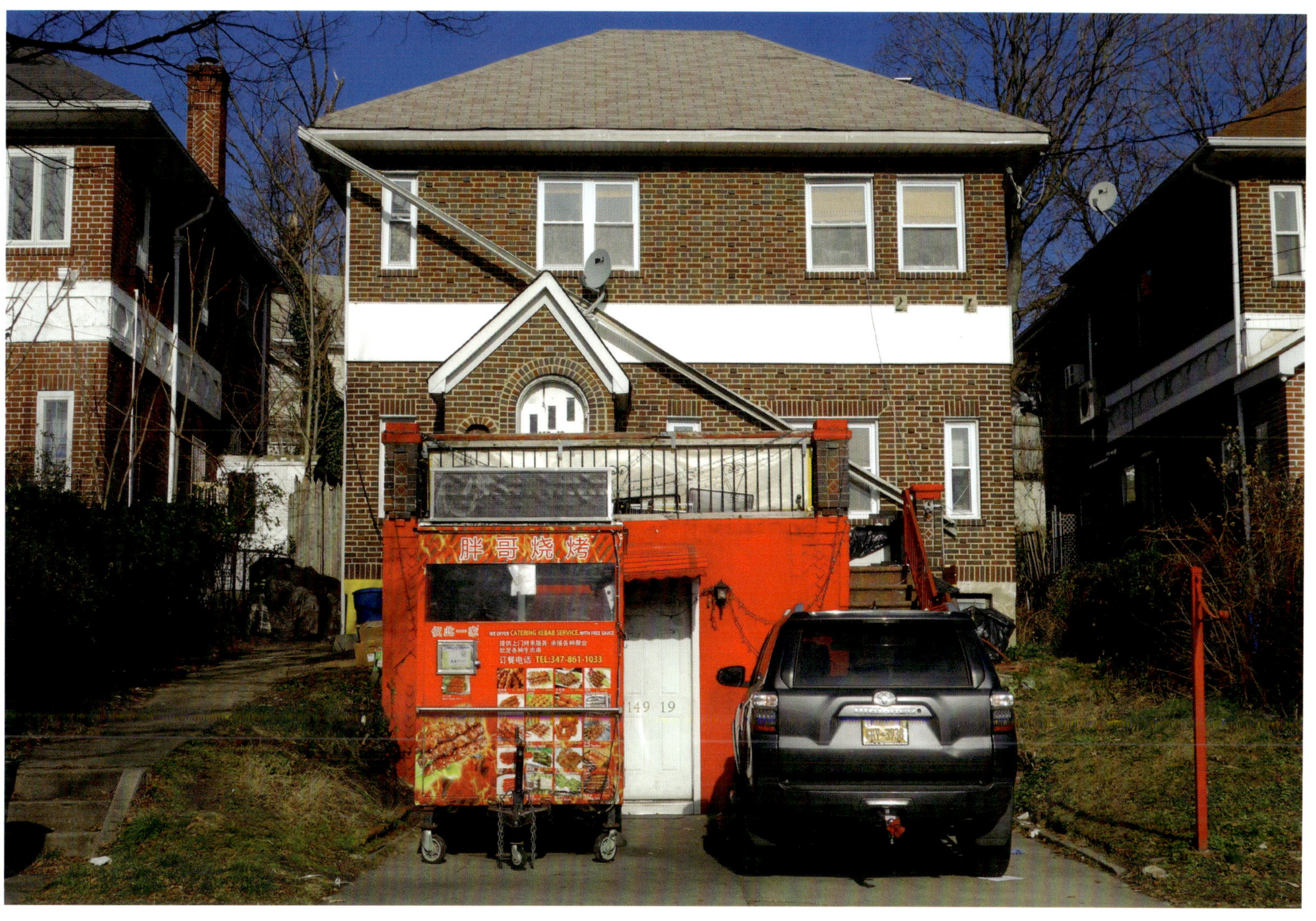

Vendor cart in driveway, Murray Hill

Vendor carts and trucks have a wide range of owner, operator, and storage arrangements. Some are owned and operated by the same person, while others are owned by an individual or company that either employs people to work the carts or leases them to operators. They may be stored at the owner or operator's home, as seen here, or for a fee, they can be stored in one of the many vendor cart garages scattered throughout the borough. The garages typically include parking spaces, propane and generator fuel stations, maintenance services, and even kitchens. Meanwhile, some carts move around the borough to different sites each week, while others establish themselves in one location to build up a loyal clientele.

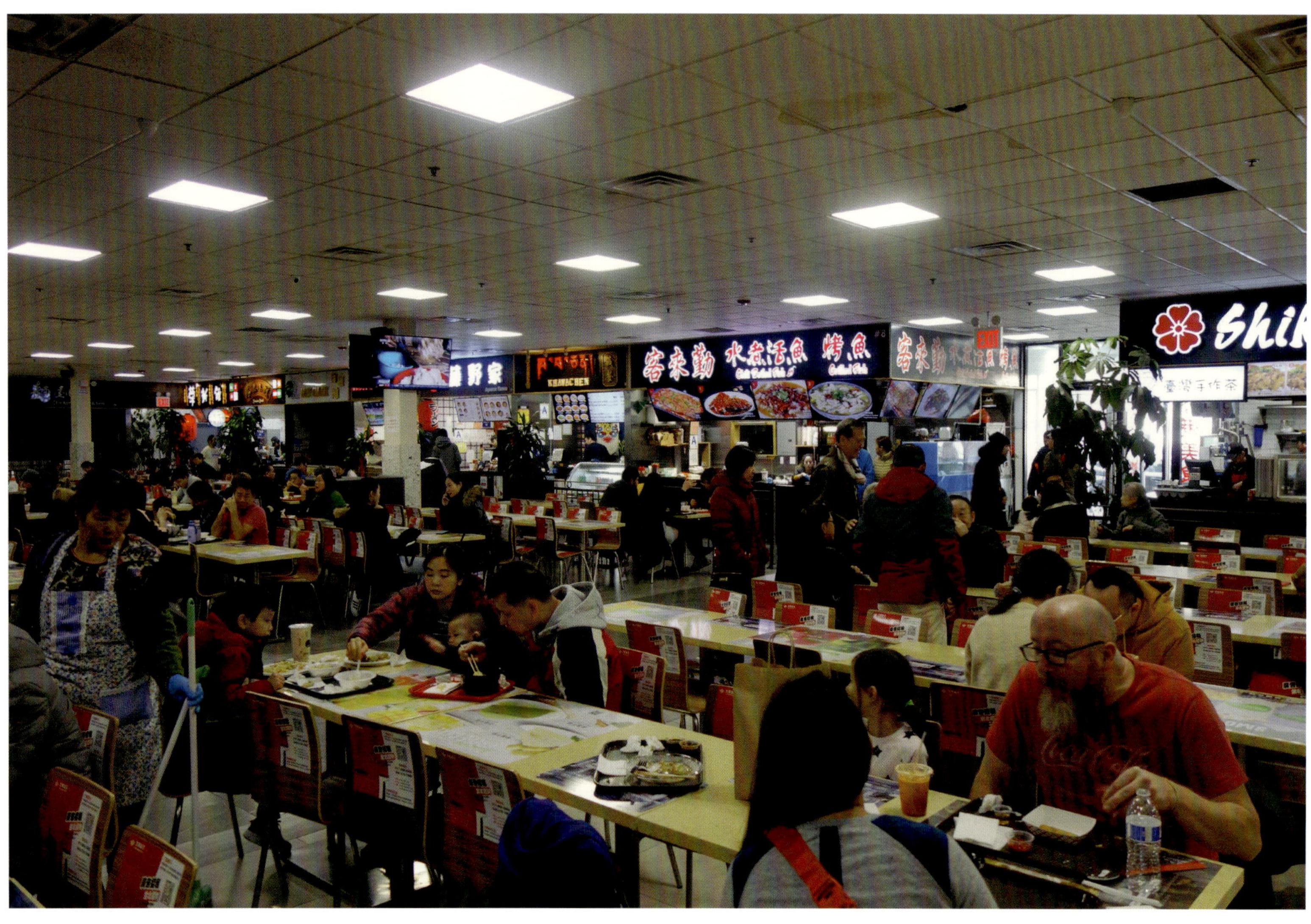

Food court, Elmhurst

Food courts are very popular in Chinese communities. While the American food court faded with the shopping mall, Chinese food courts do not require an adjacent mall to be a sought-after dining option. They offer visitors a wide selection of dishes from various regions of Mainland China, Taiwan, and Hong Kong. They also provide vendors with space to operate their businesses at a far lower cost than a storefront or stand-alone building. This is especially important in neighborhoods with rapidly rising commercial rents, few available spaces, and new immigrant groups looking for business opportunities. The Hong Kong Food Court, pictured here, opened in 2018 in a former supermarket on 45th Avenue in Elmhurst.

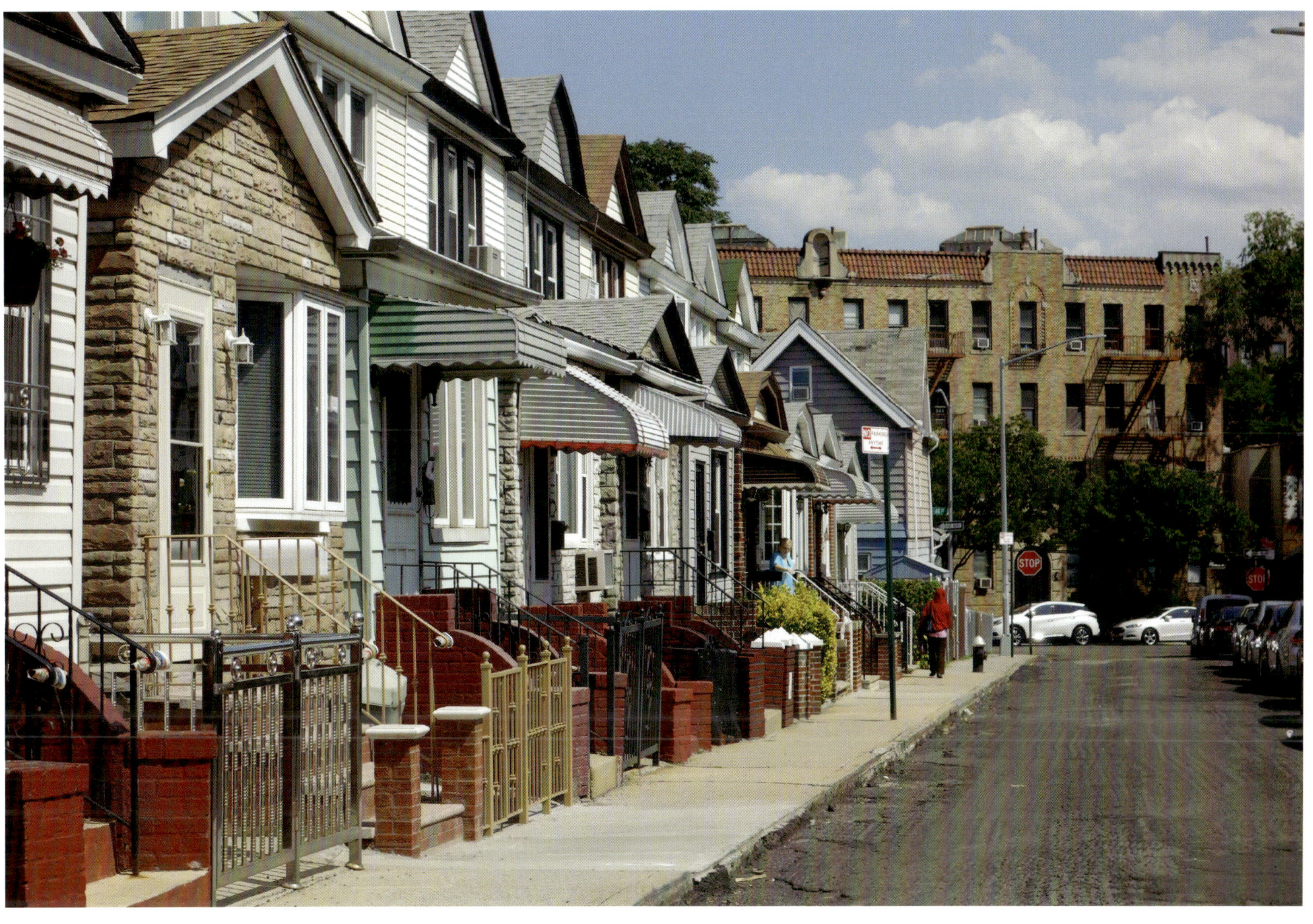

Narrow side street in Woodside

A group of row houses along 41st Drive slopes down toward 60th Street in Woodside. There are 52 houses on this tightly packed block, including 20 narrowly-spaced detached houses and 32 row houses (shown here). Woodside grew rapidly during the 1910s and 1920s, as speculators targeted middle-class families searching for low-cost home ownership options outside of Manhattan. This resulted in a jumbled mix of low-slung single-family houses and large apartment buildings. Today, it is one of the most ethnically diverse neighborhoods in the United States, with immigrants from the Philippines, Thailand, Indonesia, Ecuador, Peru, Colombia, and many other countries.

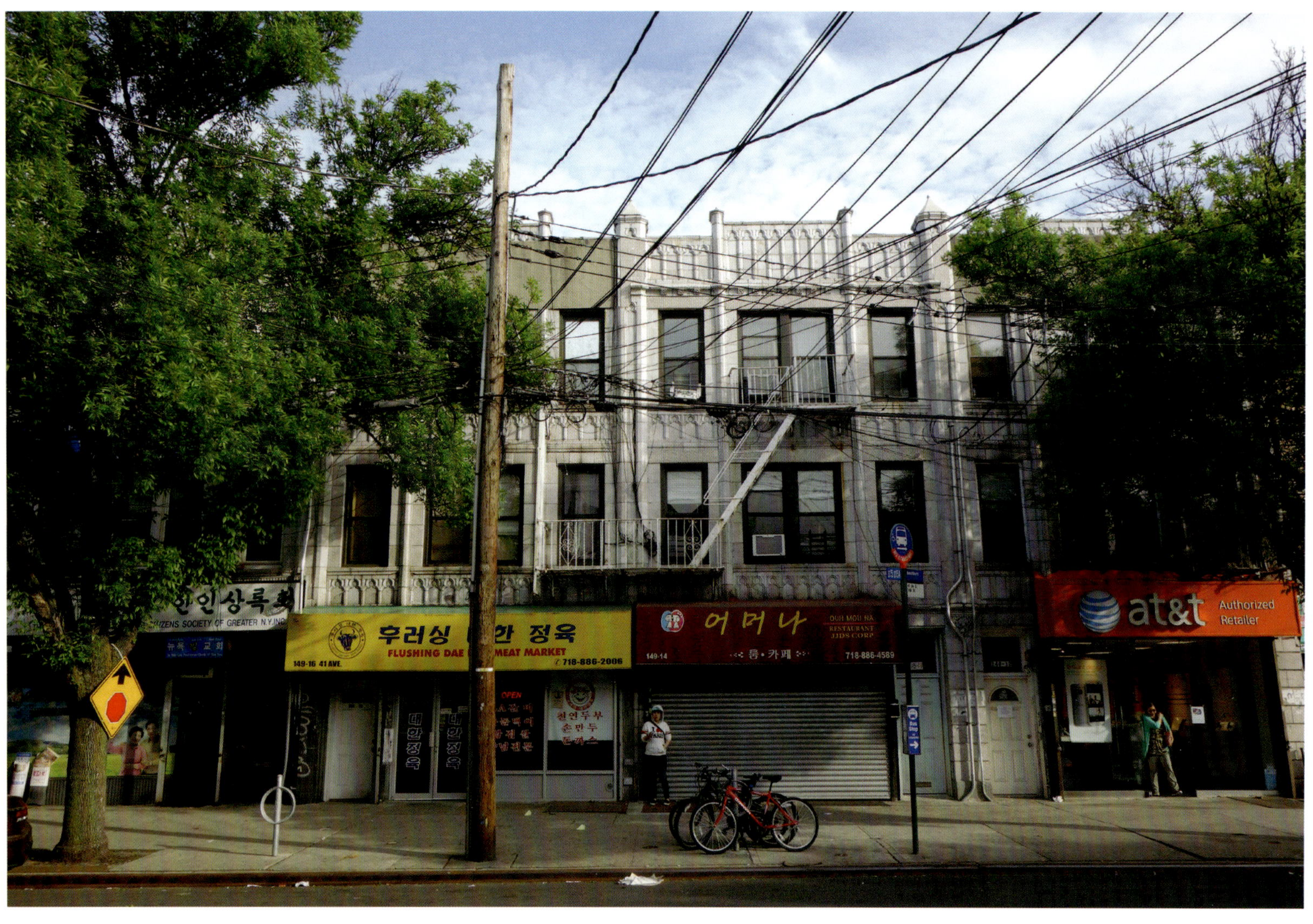

Korean shops along 41st Avenue, Murray Hill

As Korean-American and Korean immigrant families began moving out of crowded downtown Flushing in the 1980s and 1990s, they reestablished an enclave to the east in Murray Hill. Here they purchased large single-family houses and set up restaurants, groceries, hair salons, law and accounting firms, and other businesses. Located astride Northern Boulevard, the neighborhood is served by the Murray Hill stop on the Long Island Railroad, which connects it to Penn Station in Manhattan. Commercial revitalization and proximity to mass transit has made Murray Hill increasingly popular, resulting in many tear downs over the last decade, with owners demolishing hundred-year-old houses to build multifamily units.

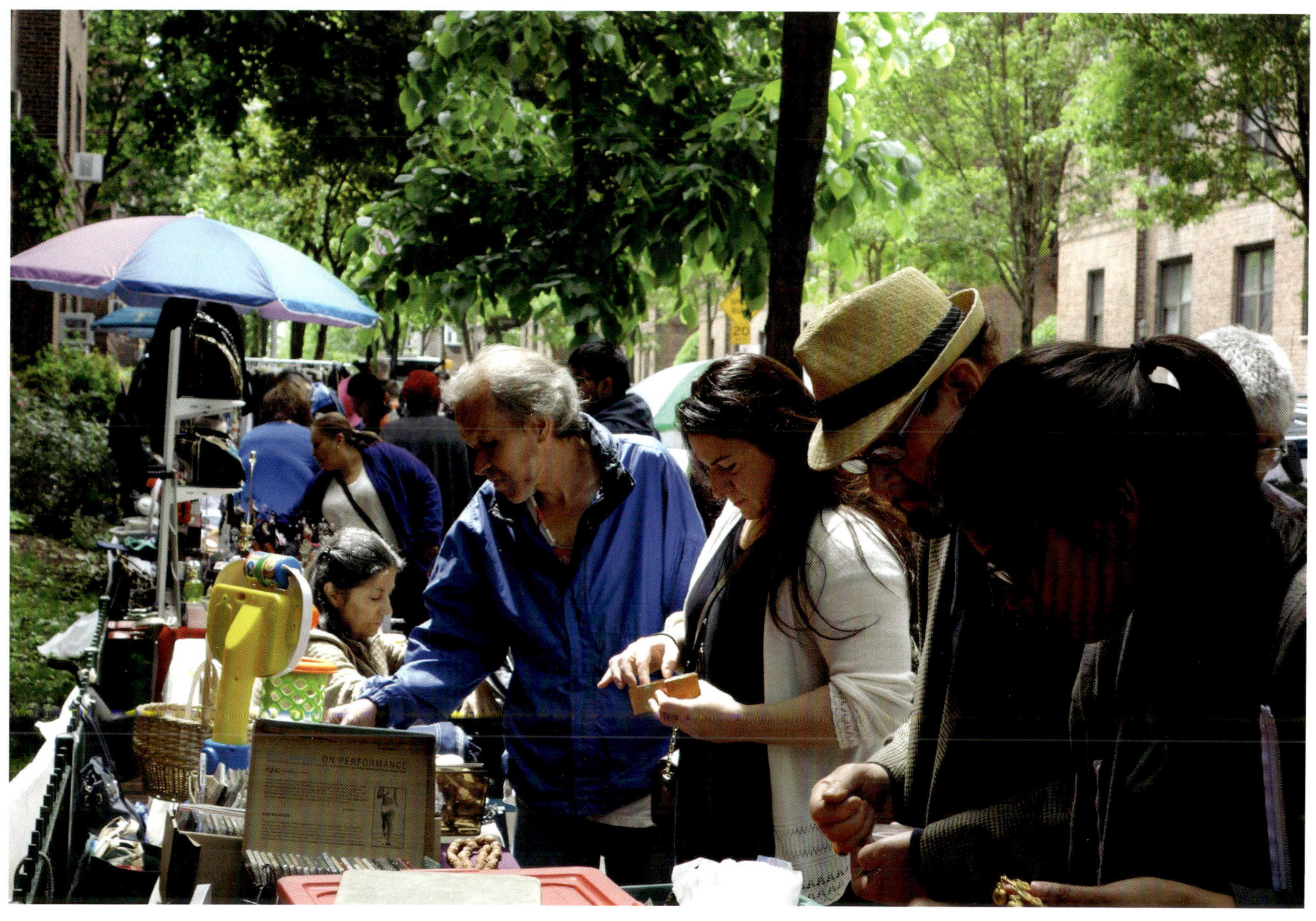

Outdoor flea market, Jackson Heights

Flea markets are a popular weekend pastime in Jackson Heights and a source of revenue for many of the large co-ops and churches that operate them. They rent space to vendors, who in turn set up tables with mostly used items—everything from clothes and household goods to CDs, records, DVDs, toys, books, appliances, electronics, and antiques. Some vendors are co-op residents who take the opportunity to clear out the closets, while others live in the neighborhood or nearby and sell items as a source of income. Many co-ops also sell coffee, pastries, and even lunch. There are usually at least two or three flea markets a week going on in the neighborhood from late spring to early fall.

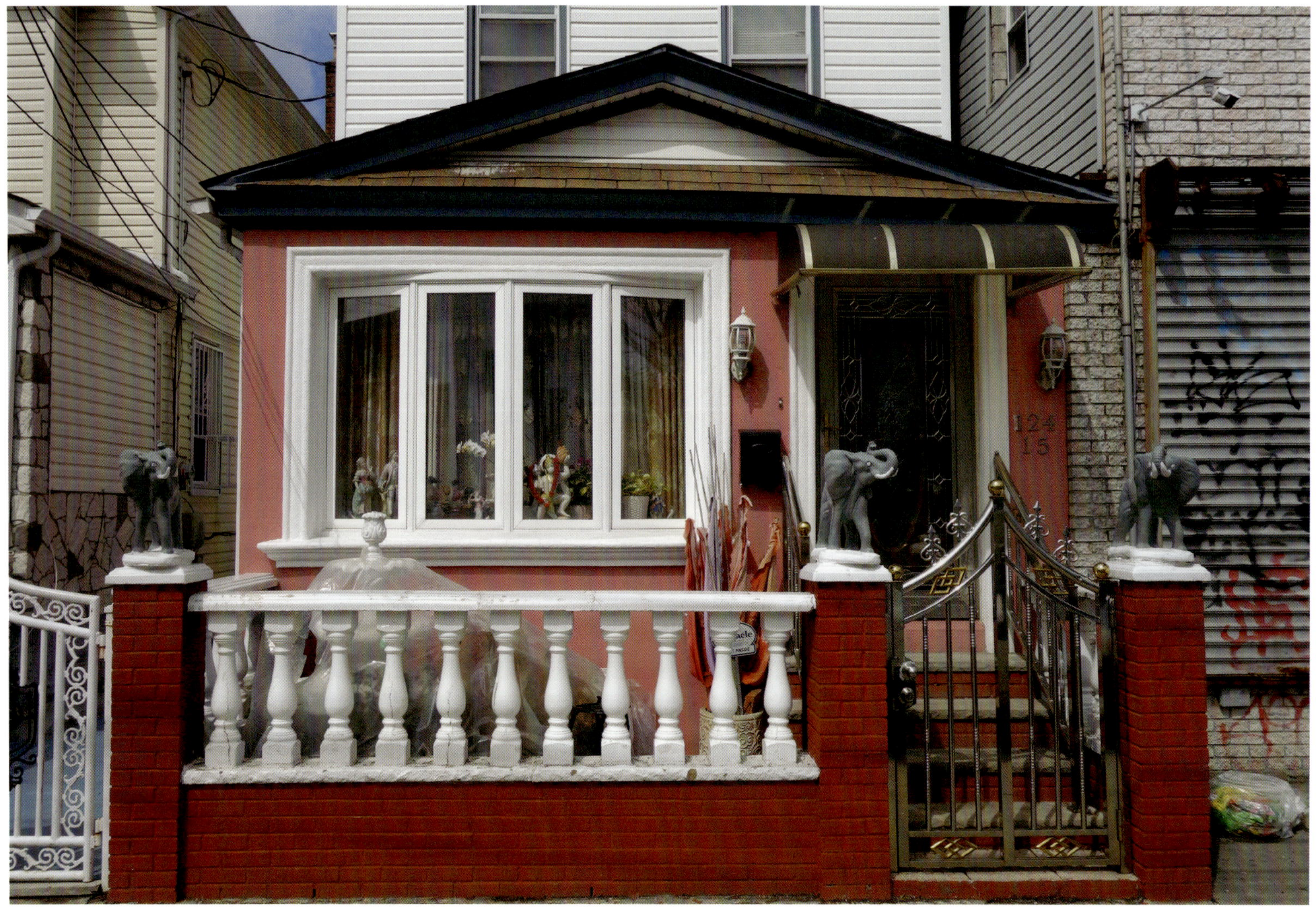

Focus on façades

Figures 109a–109q. Façades are the public face that buildings show to the world. Residents shape and reshape their façades to express their identity and articulate their relationship with the broader community. This includes a wide range of interventions over time, such as tuck-pointing (new mortar colors can completely change a building's look); re-siding; adding porches, awnings, and new coats of paint; and changing styles for doors, windows, and trim. Adornments can evoke ties to home places, such as those displayed in the photo above of a house in Ozone Park. In all cases, the façades of Queens present an incredibly diverse array of elements, textures, styles, and symbols, creating an ever-changing collage of surfaces.

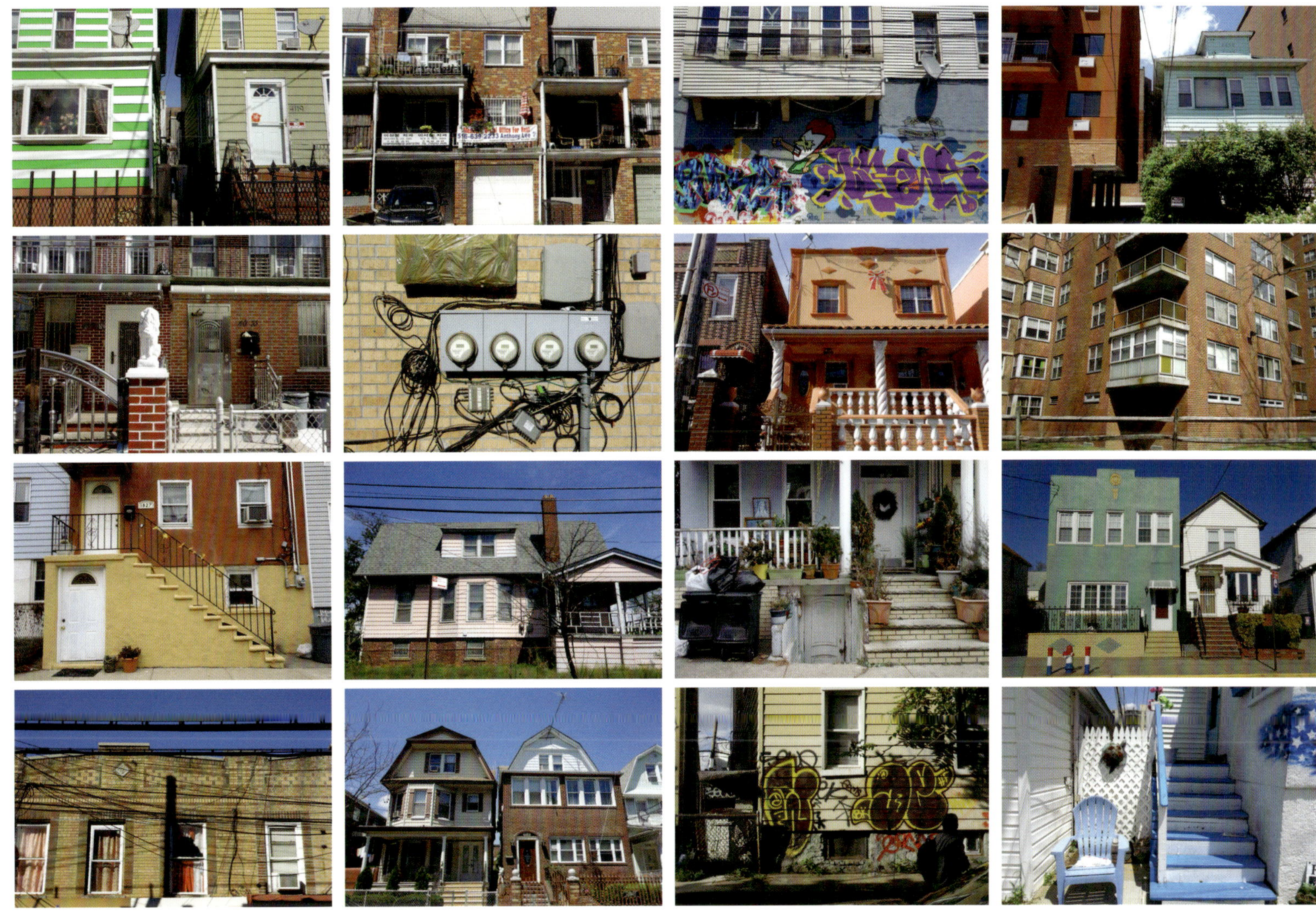

Top row (l to r): Green stripes in Elmhurst; mixed-use apartment building, Flushing; apartment above a graffiti mural, Rockaway; last remaining single-family house on the block, Flushing. Second row: Chrome and statuary are all the rage in Elmhurst these days; bundle of utilities on an apartment building in Ozone Park; ornate renovation increasingly common in Richmond Hill; enclosed balcony at Rochdale co-op; Third row: Projecting stairwell provides vestibule for lower apartment in Long Island City; pink house, Arverne; lived-in porch, Ditmars/Steinway; Ozone Park renovation featuring bold neo-Babylonian look. Fourth row: Curtains animate this stolid façade on Jamaica Avenue; built identically, these two houses in Corona took divergent paths; tags on a house facing Roosevelt Avenue; beach mode, Rockaway.

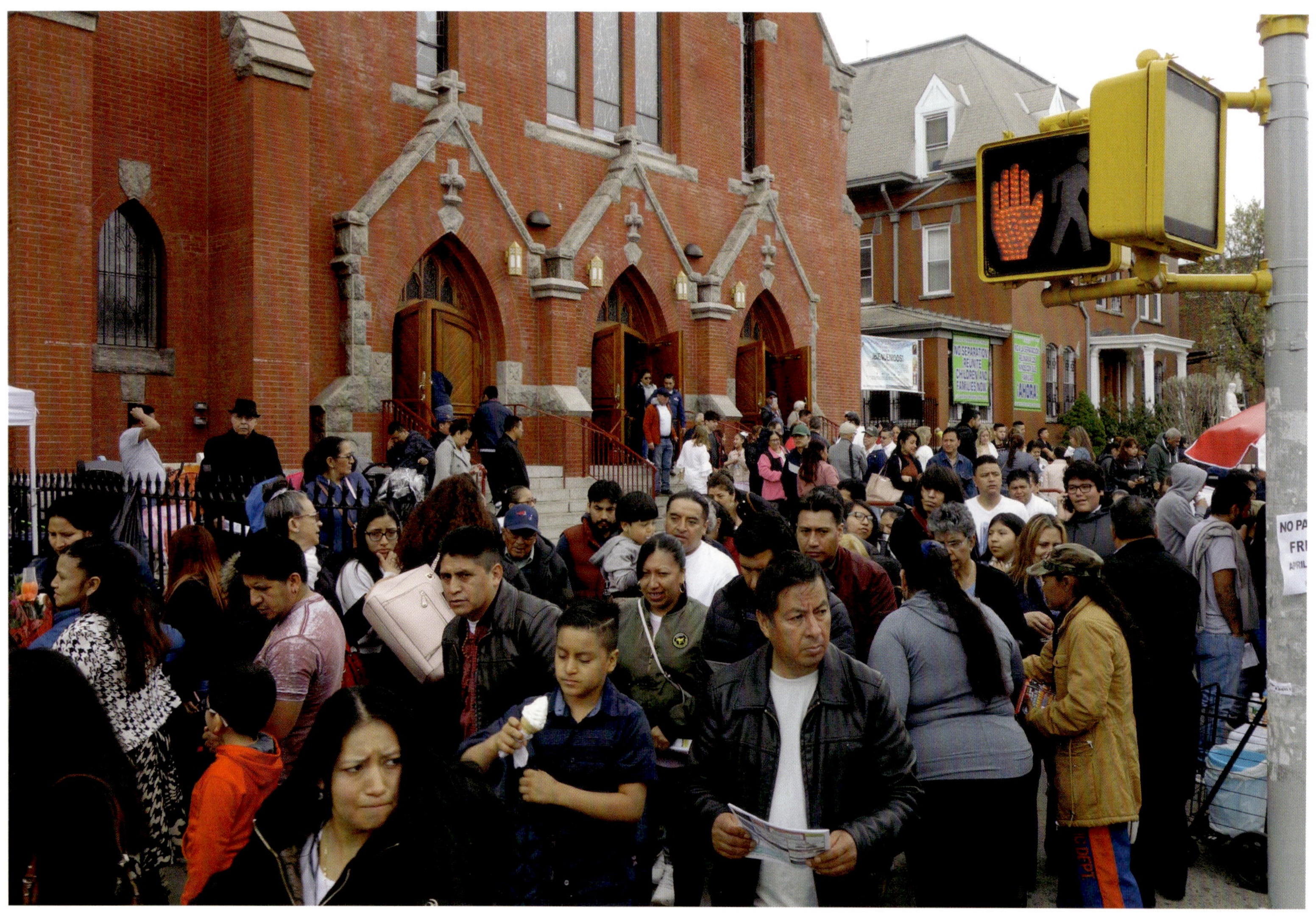

After mass at Our Lady of Sorrows, Corona

Congregants stream out of Our Lady of Sorrows church after Sunday mass in April. The parish was established in 1872, and through much of the twentieth century, it served a large Italian population. In the 1940s and 1950s, Puerto Rican and Cuban families settled in the neighborhood and joined the parish. Today the congregation is predominantly Mexican and Mexican-American, with an increasing number of Central American immigrant families attending. This kind of neighborhood succession by co-religious groups has saved many urban Catholic parishes in Queens. The Our Lady of Sorrows campus includes the church, a large rectory, a school, and an office and event annex.

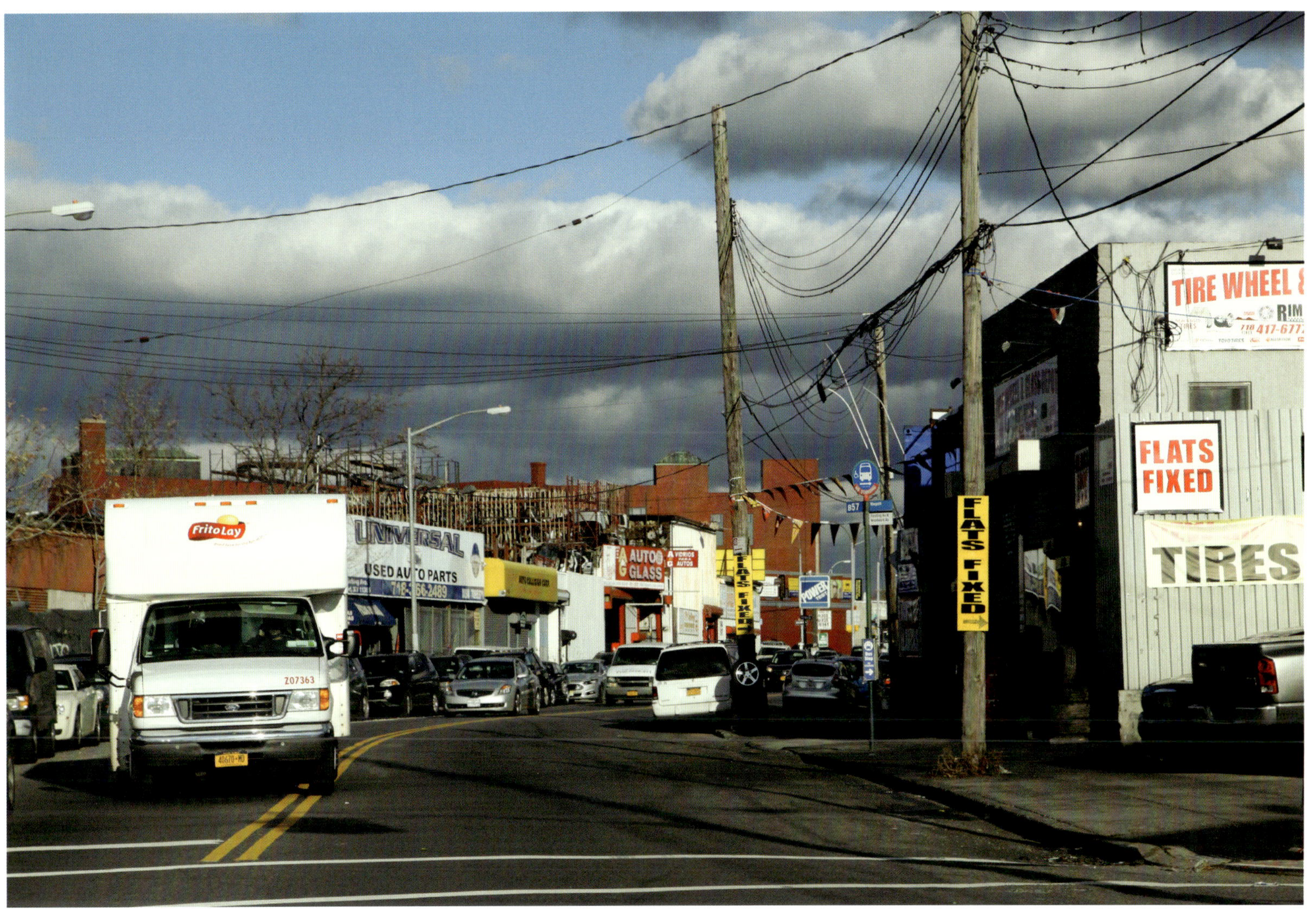

Auto row on the Brooklyn-Queens Border

One of several automobile rows throughout New York City, this one stretches for nearly a mile along Flushing Avenue through Queens and Brooklyn. This strip, interspersed with warehouses and haulage companies, includes body and engine repair garages, parts and tire shops, glass installation services, and towing and wrecking yards. Auto services benefit from this kind of agglomeration and provide crucial employment opportunities for tens of thousands of workers—in this case, Mexican and Central American immigrants. Mixed into this landscape are the usual delis, bodegas, gas stations, bars, laundromats, Chinese takeout, and other services found in similar working-class industrial areas of Queens.

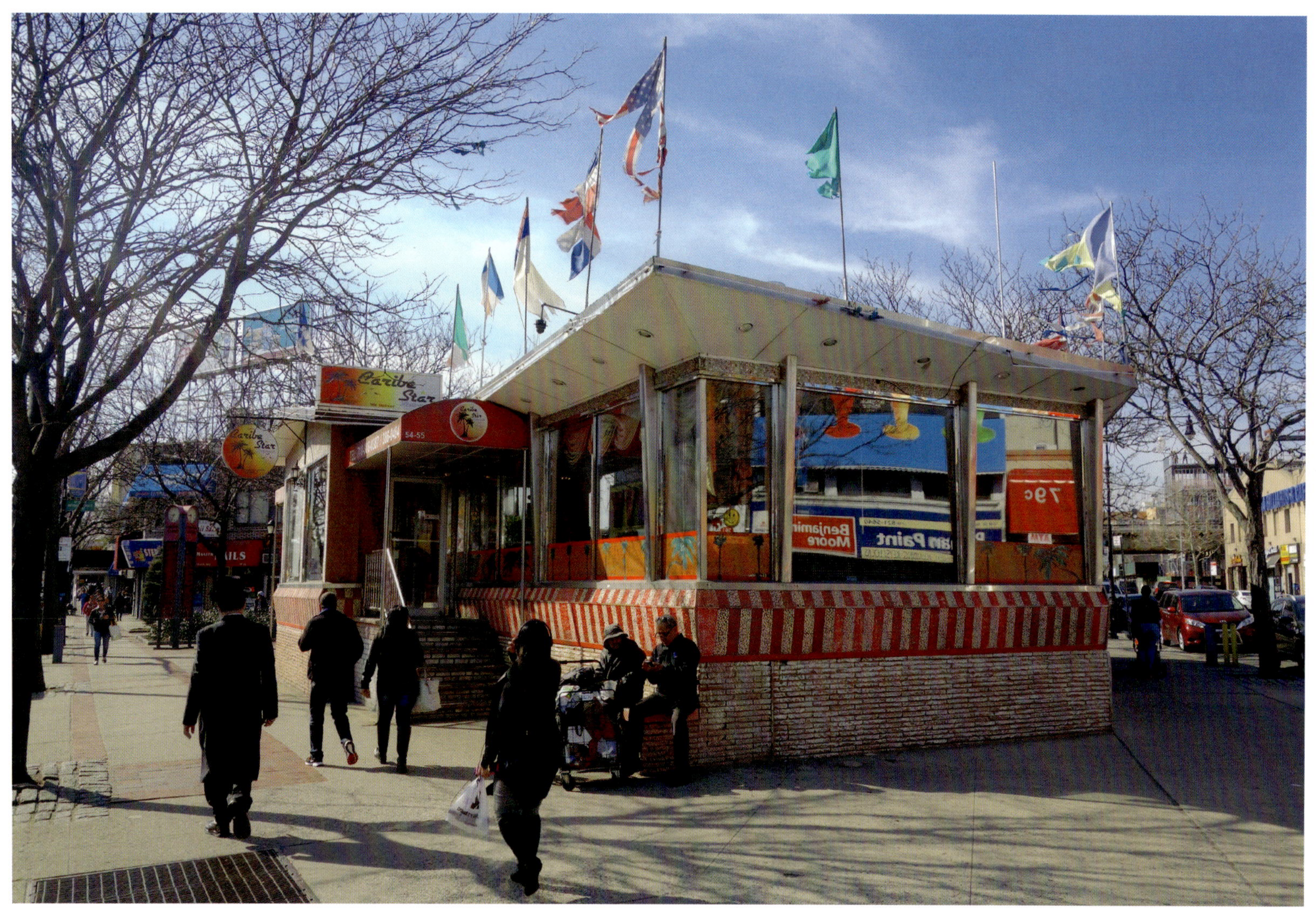

Venditti Square, Ridgewood

Like many "squares" in Queens, Venditti Square is actually a triangle, in this case formed by the diagonal cut of Myrtle Avenue as it meets St. Nicholas Avenue. The block sits right on the border with Brooklyn. The square was named for Anthony Venditti, an NYPD detective gunned down by members of the Genovese crime family right outside of this diner in 1986. His partner, Karen Burke, was also shot but survived. While the mob and the violence it wrought once seemed endemic to Queens, its hold on the borough has faded over time as members age out and move to Nassau County and Staten Island. And while the diner once served Italian and Greek fare, today it is run by a Dominican family serving Caribbean food.

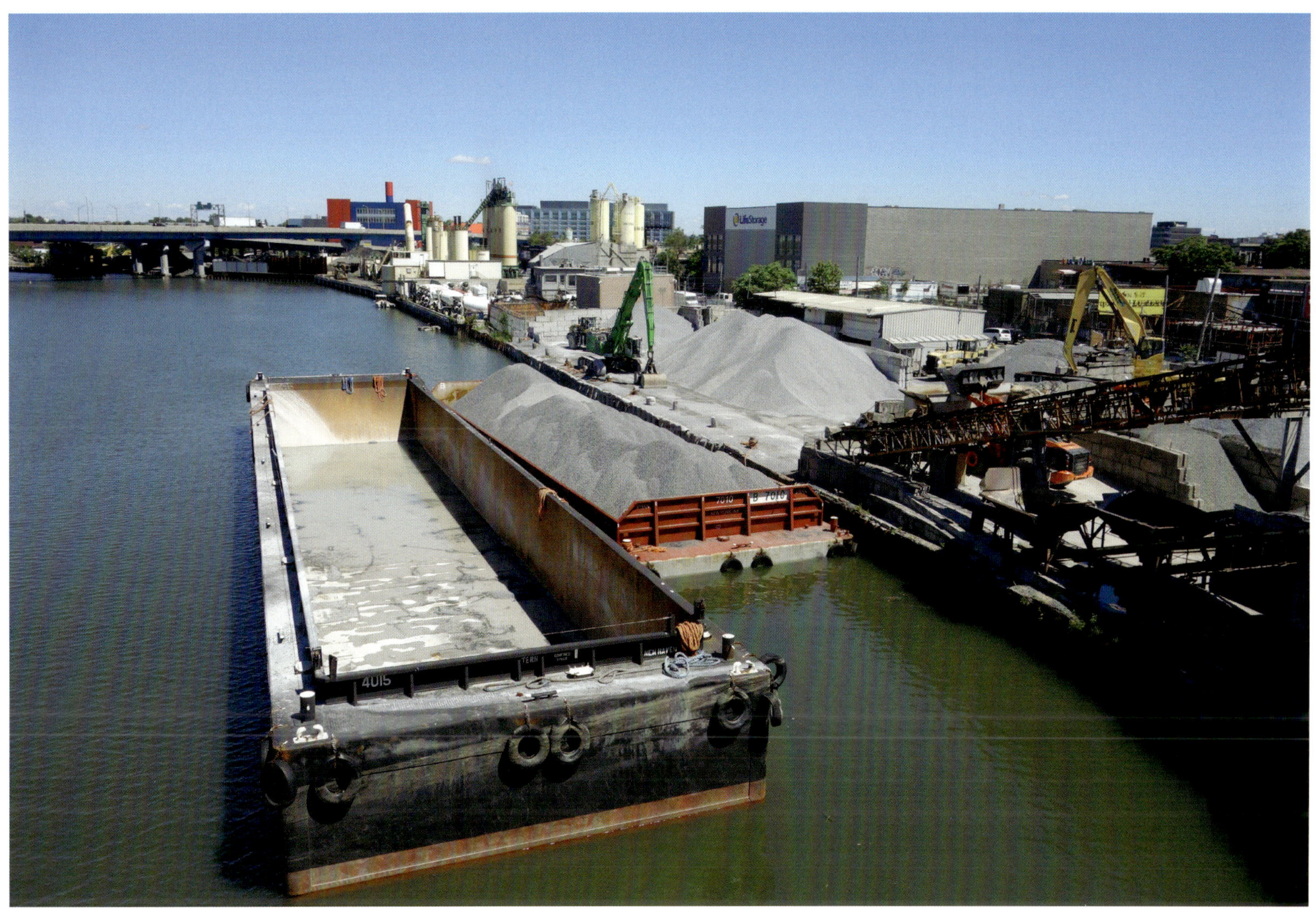

Flushing Creek

View of Flushing Creek from the Northern Boulevard bridge, looking northeast toward the Whitestone Expressway. Flushing Creek, much of which has been channeled underground, runs for several miles through northern Queens. While it empties into Flushing Bay, it also receives tidal backflow from the East River and Long Island Sound. Like most waterways in Queens, the creek was given over to heavy industrial use in the early twentieth century and remains a heavily polluted tributary today. Along the stretch, shown here, are asphalt plants, gravel yards, cement works, and other operations that benefit from barge transport. Much of the hard and dangerous labor is undertaken by Chinese and Latino immigrant workers.

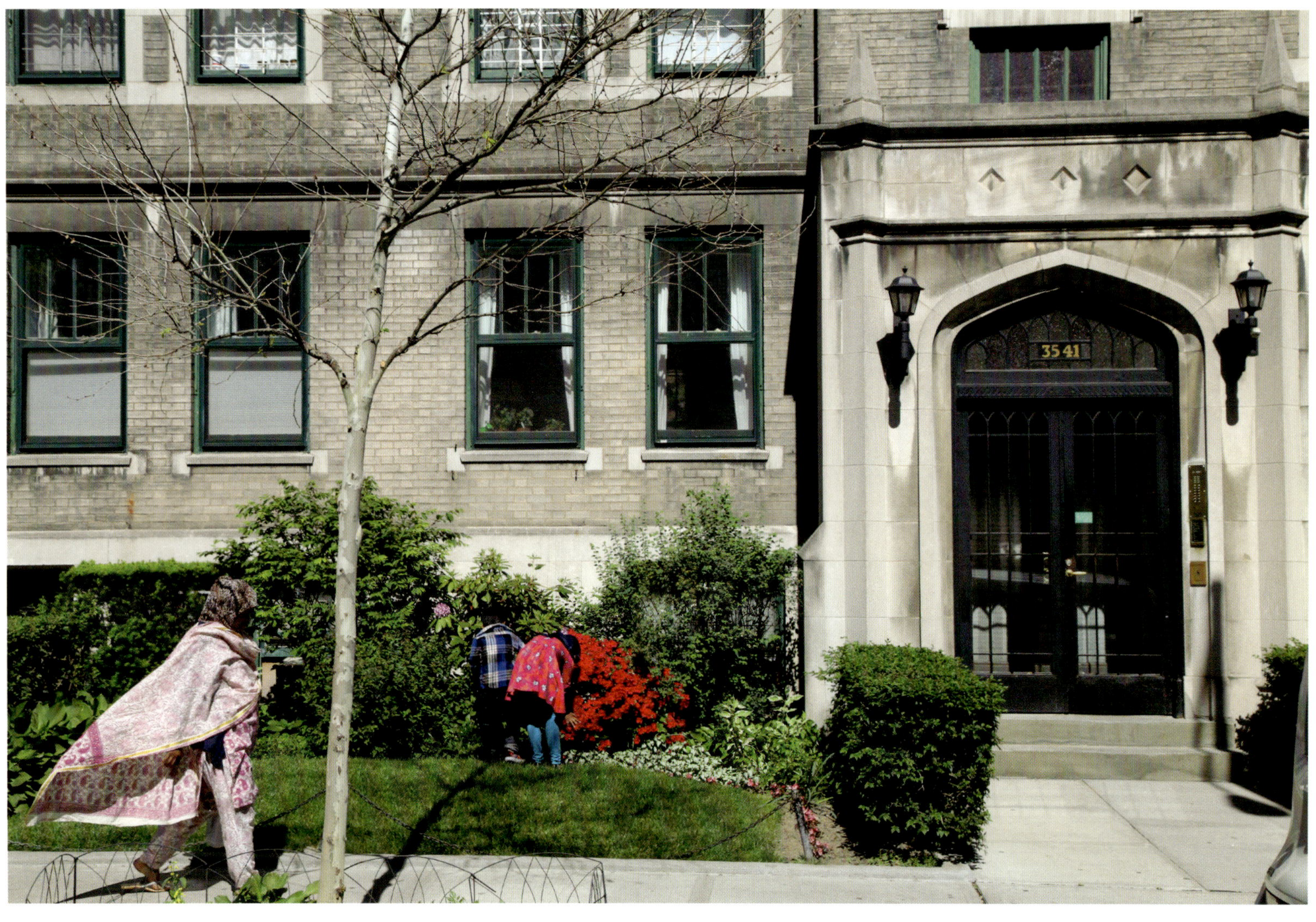

Greystones co-op, Jackson Heights

Kids inspecting flowers in front of the Greystones Co-op. Completed in 1917, Greystones was the first of over a dozen large cooperative complexes built in Jackson Heights by the Queensboro Corporation under the direction of Edward MacDougall. After experimenting with row houses and stand-alone apartment buildings, MacDougall settled on a "garden apartment" model in the 1920s, grouping mid-rise towers around block perimeters to enclose long, internal courtyards. While MacDougall and his backers originally envisioned Jackson Heights as a haven for middle-class White Protestant families escaping overcrowded Manhattan, today it is the most ethnically diverse neighborhood in the United States.

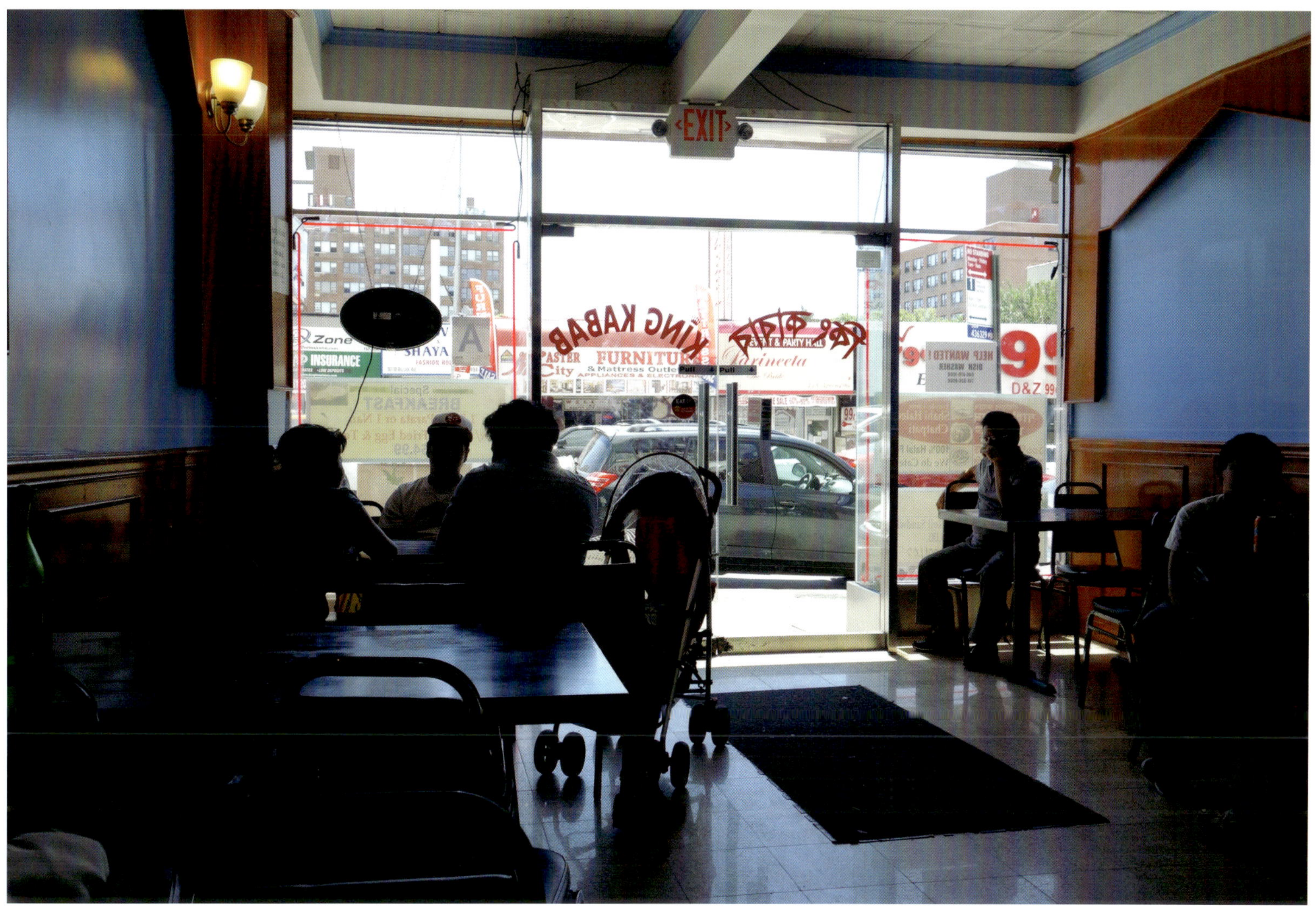

Hanging out at King Kabab, Jamaica

This kebab shop on Hillside Avenue is a popular neighborhood spot. Families come here for meals, especially in the summer when apartments are hot and crowded. Cab drivers sit around in between shifts drinking chai, a hot milky black tea with sugar, cardamom, cloves, and other spices. Kids from nearby Jamaica High School hang out after the last bell, eating snacks and raising the interior volume. The shop also does a brisk takeout business, as a steady stream of people from the surrounding neighborhood comes in to pick up orders. They also deliver food to local homes and offices. In many ways, it is the quintessentially neighborhood-focused business so typical of Queens.

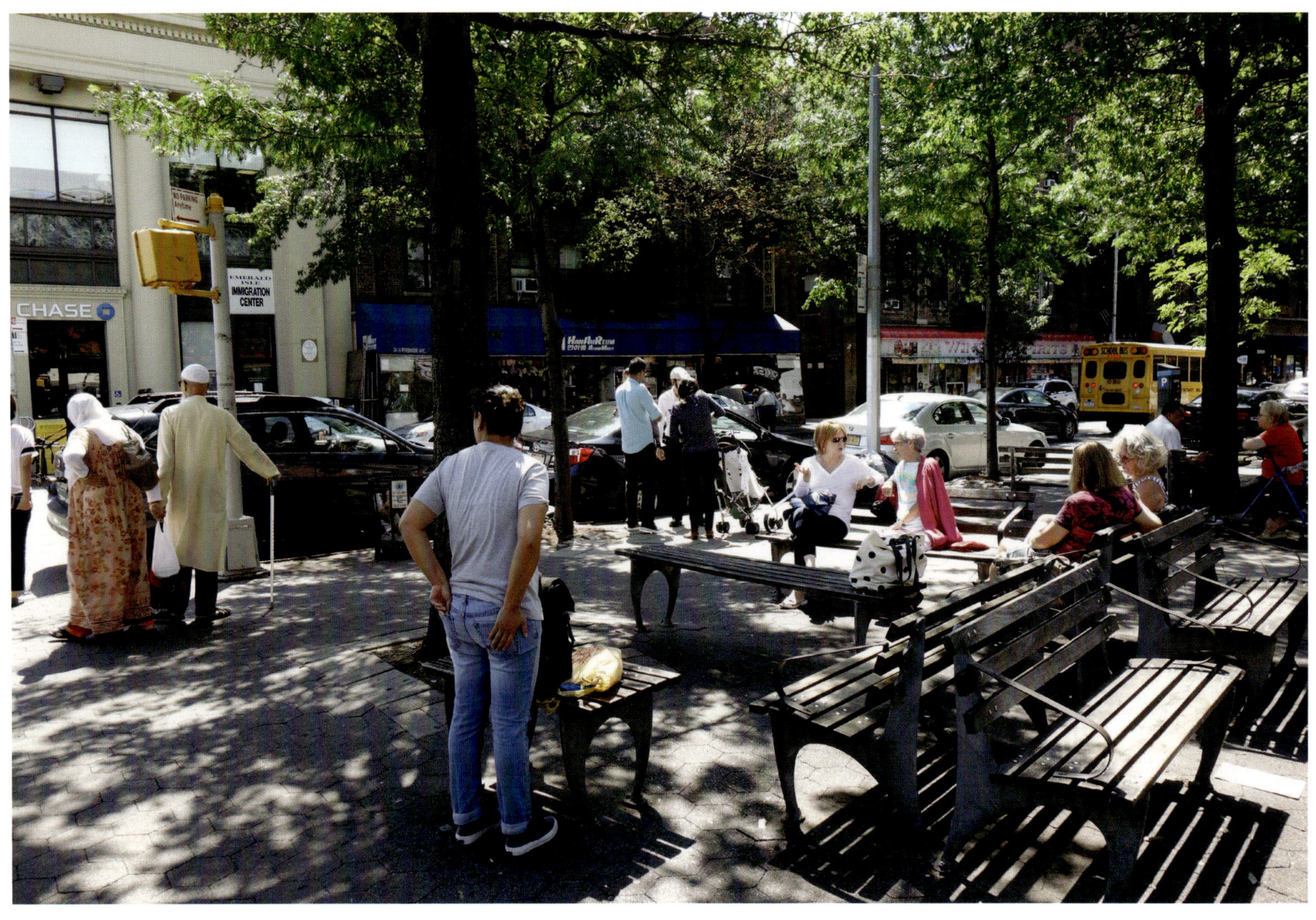

Memorial Plaza, Woodside

On a hot summer day in August, residents of Woodside seek shade beneath the large trees at Memorial Plaza. The plaza commemorates soldiers from the neighborhood who died in twentieth-century wars. The triangular space is formed by the diagonal cut of Roosevelt Avenue as it crosses 60th Street and Woodside Avenue. While the neighborhood has an older population of Irish-American and Korean-American families, it is now home to a diverse array of people from the Philippines, Indonesia, Afghanistan, and Central America. The original Han Au Reum Korean grocery store, otherwise known as H-Mart, can be seen under the blue awning in the background.

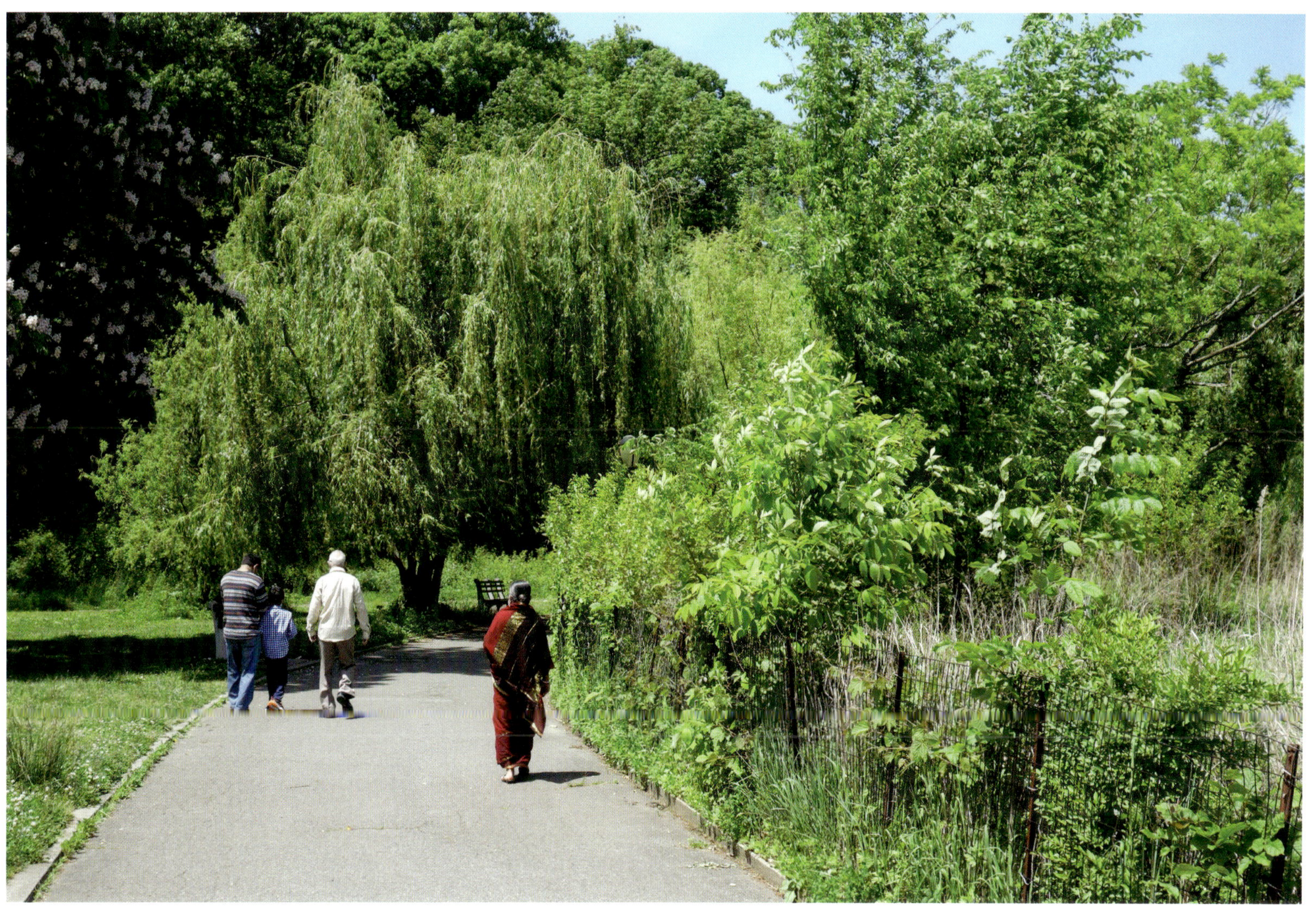

Strolling around Kissena Park, Flushing

Kissena is an Algonquian word meaning "place of cool waters." In the nineteenth century, Samuel Parsons operated a large orchard and nursery here to supply street trees in New York City, part of Flushing's rich horticultural heritage. In 1910, the Parsons family transferred the land to the city to create the 265-acre Kissena Park, with woodland paths encircling a small natural lake. Today the park is one link in a chain of green spaces stretching eastward from Flushing Meadows and the Queens Botanical Garden to Cunningham and Alley Pond Parks. The greensward travels through some of the most diverse "suburban" communities in the country, with large numbers of South and East Asian residents.

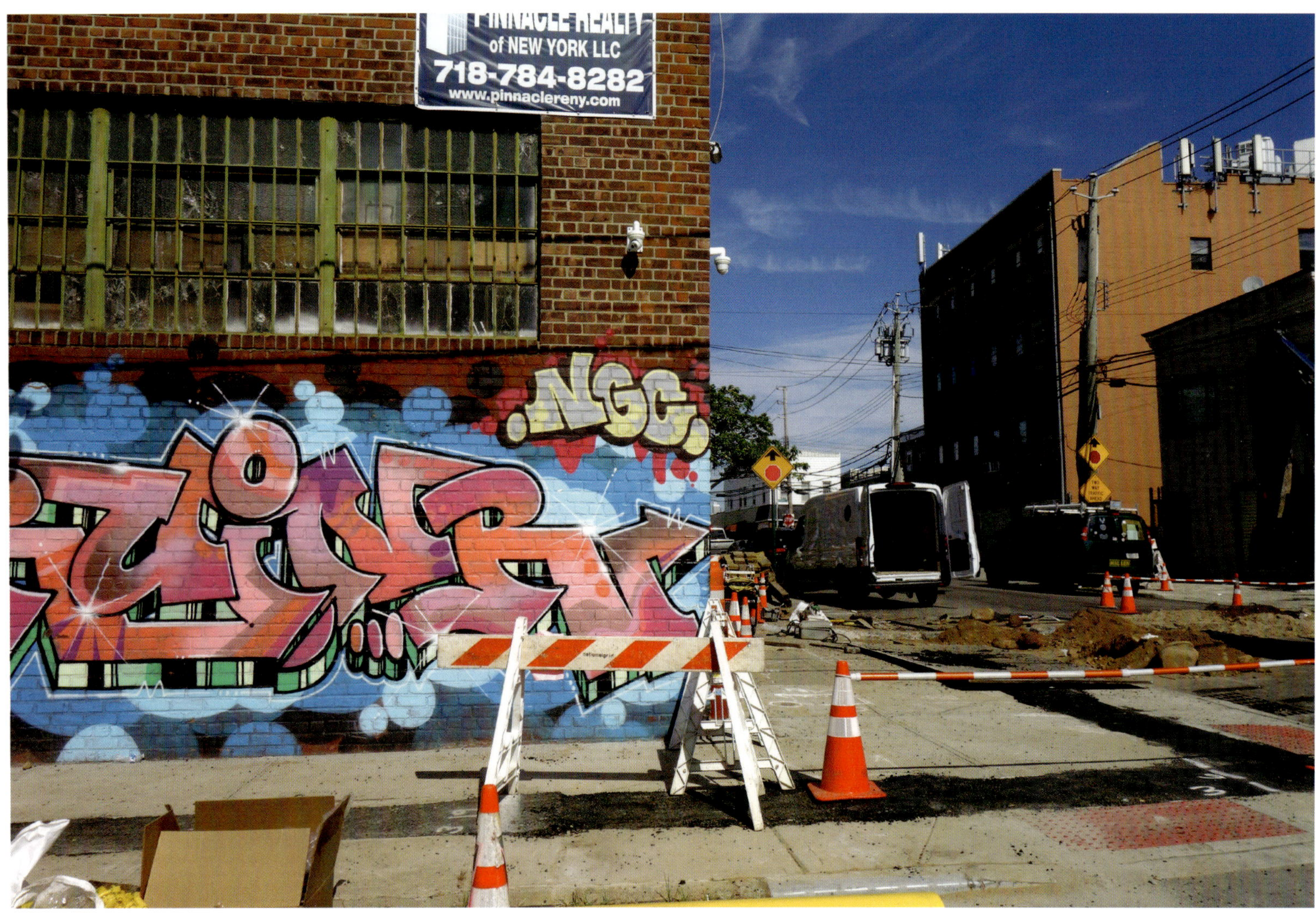

Urban hieroglyphs

Figures 118a–118g. Queens is replete with graffiti, those exuberant arcs, jags, swirls, and colors that form a kind of urban hieroglyphic. This graphic art form ranges from highly stylized and elaborate aerosol murals to bubble-lettered messages to hastily scribbled tags. While there are many superb aerosol murals scattered throughout the borough, it is the humble "tag" that suffuses the everyday landscape of most neighborhoods in Queens. Like murals, tags are a signaling system, a way for young people to make space for themselves in a world that often denies it to them. Some mark out gangland terrain, others simply telegraph who passed this way. Many residents view murals and tagging as a scourge, an unwanted bit of visual noise that damages buildings and lowers property values. But young men and women see it as a vital way to connect themselves to the city.

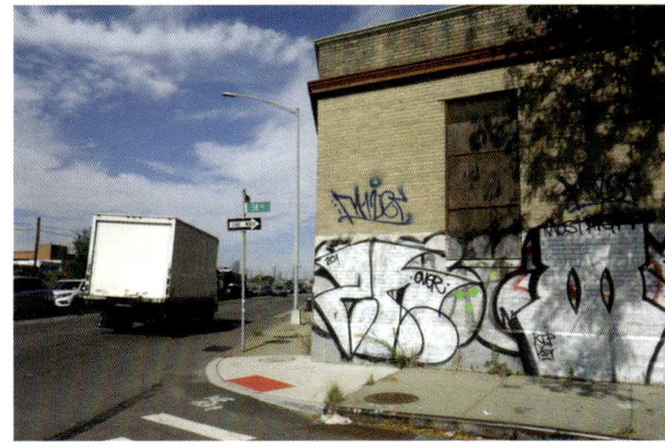

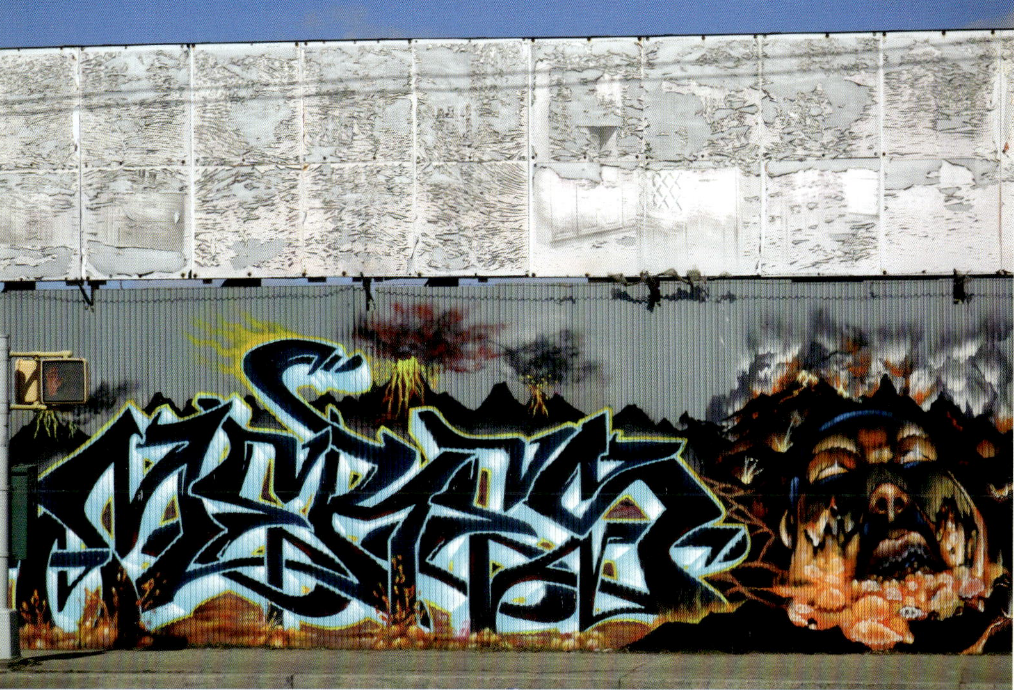

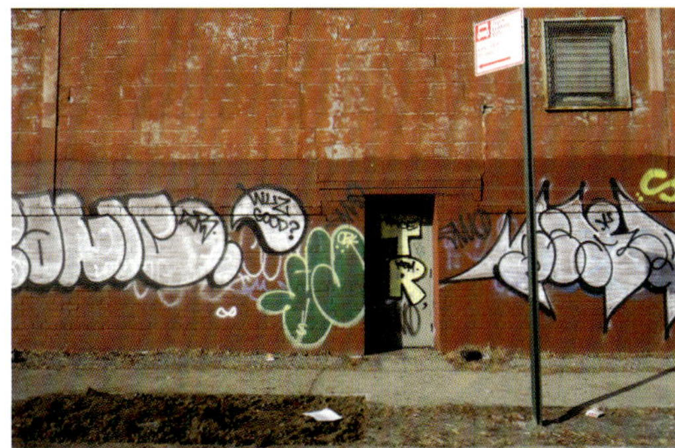

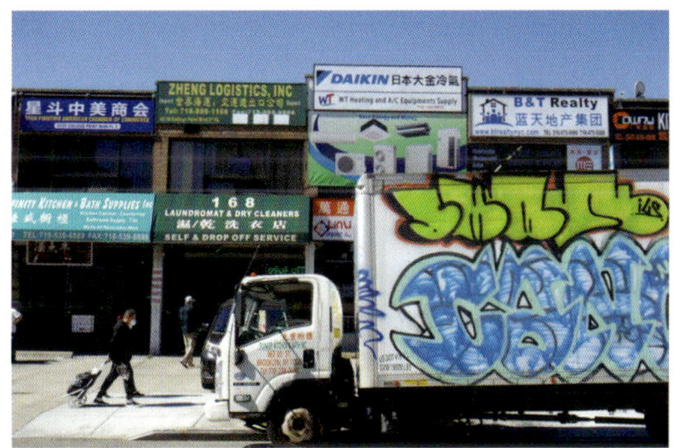

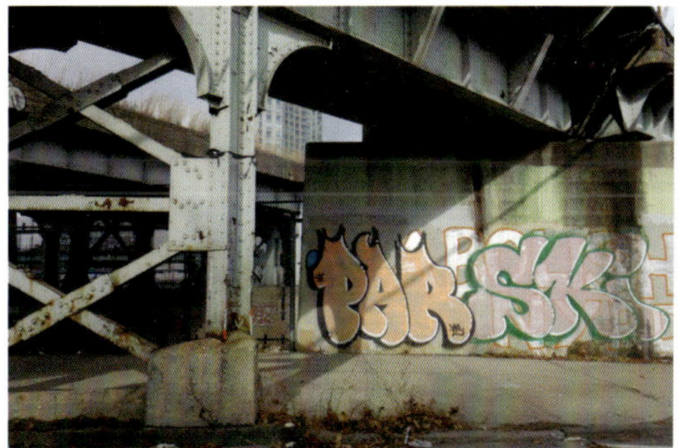

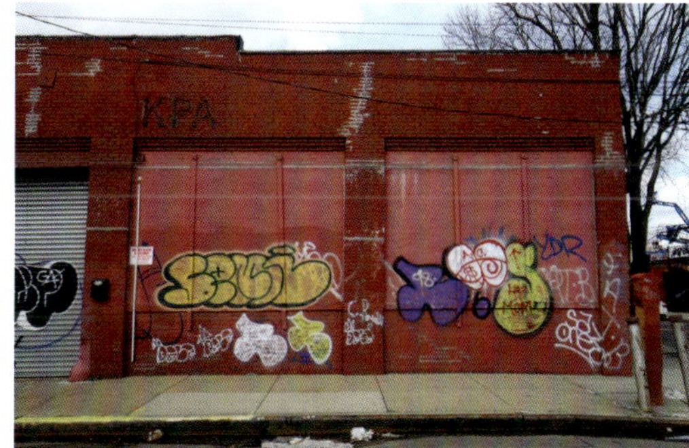

Opposite page: Highly stylized aerosol mural with anime influences on a vacant warehouse in Maspeth. This page, top left: Factory at 58th Avenue and the appropriately named Rust Street, looking northeast. Middle left: Former book depository building in Ravenswood. Bottom left: Graffiti on a delivery truck trailer in Flushing. Top right: Wild style mural on a fence in the Maspeth industrial zone. Middle right: Bubble letters under a train viaduct on 49th Avenue in Hunters Point, Long Island City. Bottom right: Warehouse building at the corner of 92nd Avenue and 130th Street in Richmond Hill.

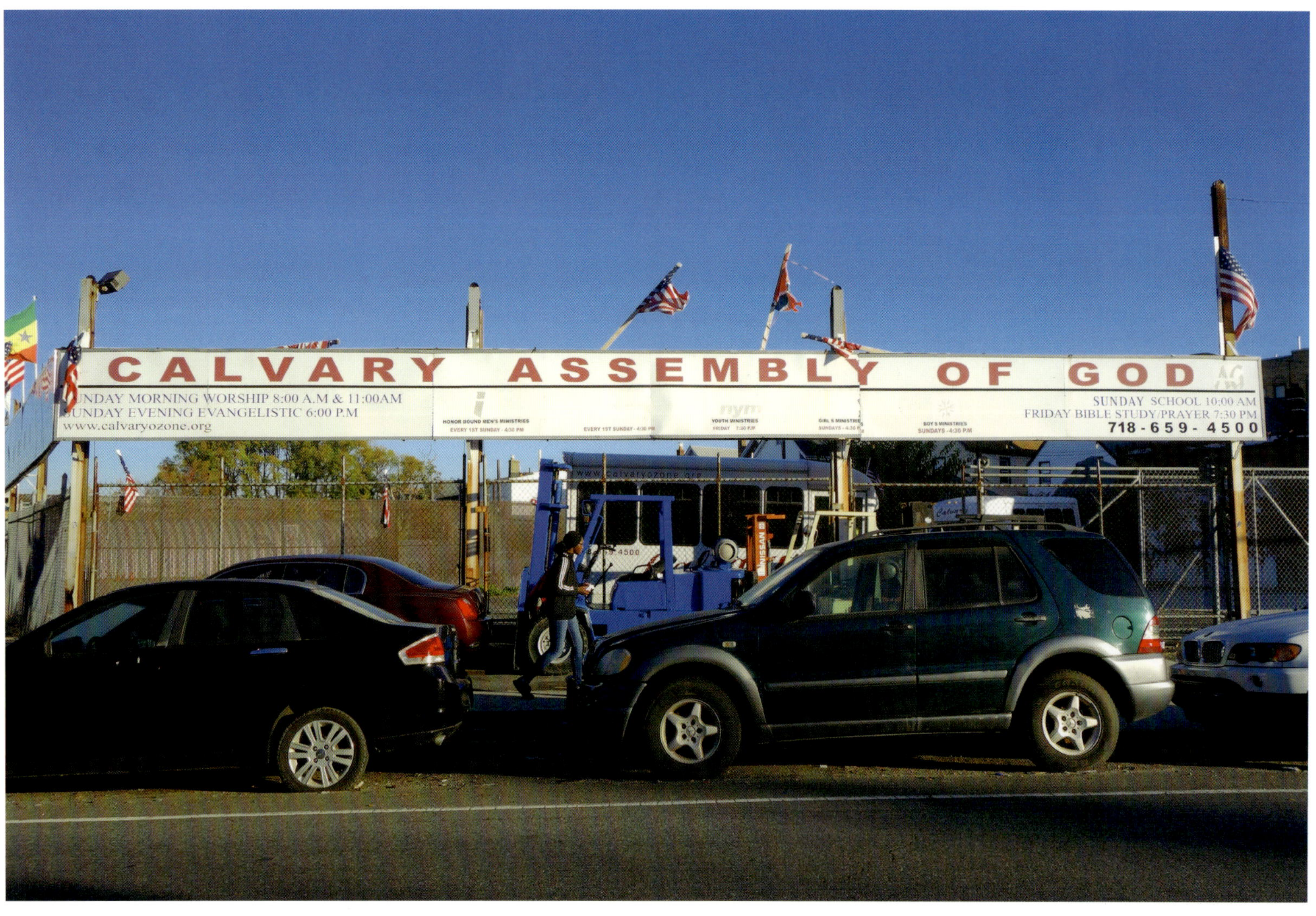

Calvary Assembly of God parking lot, South Ozone Park

Calvary is a charismatic Evangelical church on Rockaway Boulevard in South Ozone Park. The congregation is a mixture of Indo-Caribbean and Afro-Caribbean families—mostly from Guyana, Suriname, and Trinidad. They use this parking lot for Sunday overflow and to store their vans. Like many Protestant churches outside the mainstream denominations, Calvary is embedded in its community, with multiple ministries and outreach programs for youth and the elderly. Charismatic Christian churches have made dramatic inroads among Central American and Caribbean communities in Queens. Many congregations begin in storefronts before moving on to purpose-built houses of worship.

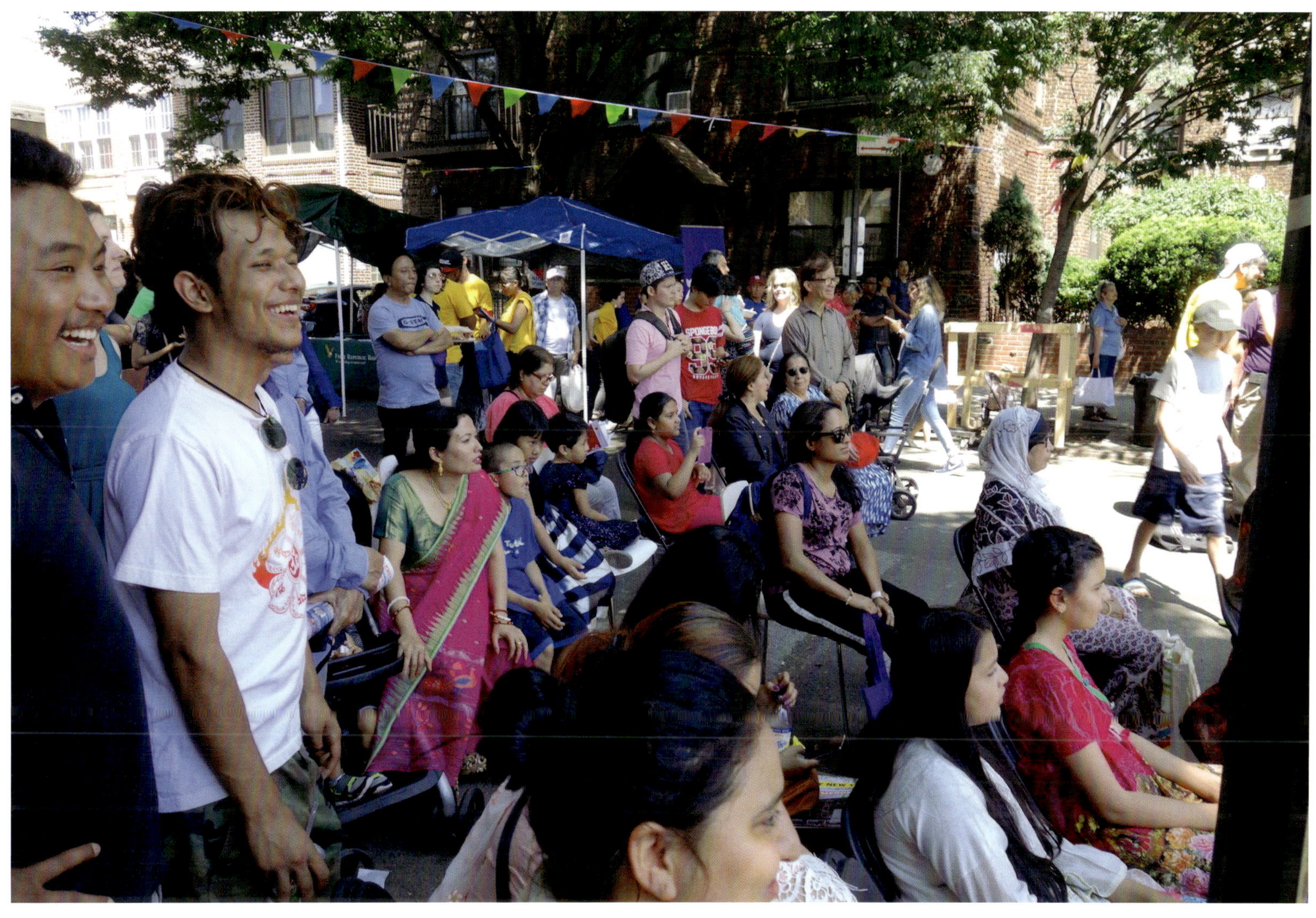

Chhaya street festival, Jackson Heights

A crowd of people enjoys Bollywood dancers at the Chhaya Street Festival in Jackson Heights. Chhaya is a nonprofit organization founded to empower South Asian communities in Queens, particularly on issues of housing and labor justice. They have also been on the front lines in the fight against the harassment of immigrant communities by authorities, especially the intrusion into neighborhoods of federal agencies such as Immigration Control and Enforcement (ICE). The annual street festival celebrates South Asian cultures through music, dance, food, and storytelling, and it provides an outlet for campaigns such as the mobilization efforts around the 2020 U.S. Census.

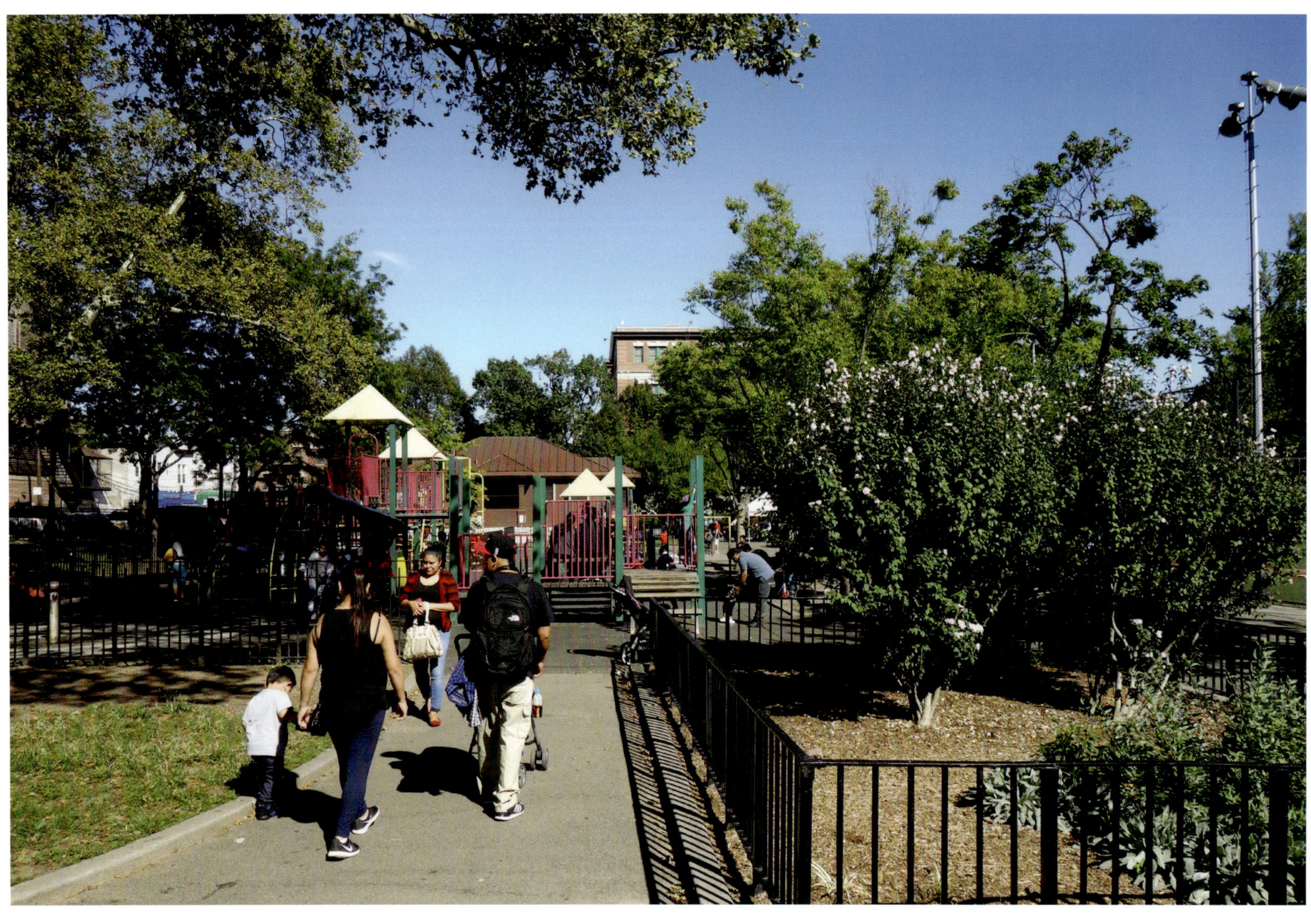

Sunny day at Park of the Americas, Corona

A family strolls into the Park of Americas, formerly known as Linden Park. This square has been a green commons since the mid-nineteenth century when residents brought livestock here to drink water from a small lake. The lake was drained after World War I to make way for a new park, part of the broader small parks movement of Progressive-Era New York when the city set aside dozens of one-block square spaces for public recreational use. Today it features playgrounds, basketball courts, walking paths, a "comfort station" (bathrooms), and a small baseball diamond. In 2004, it was renamed Park of the Americas in recognition of the diverse Latino communities that have established themselves in Corona.

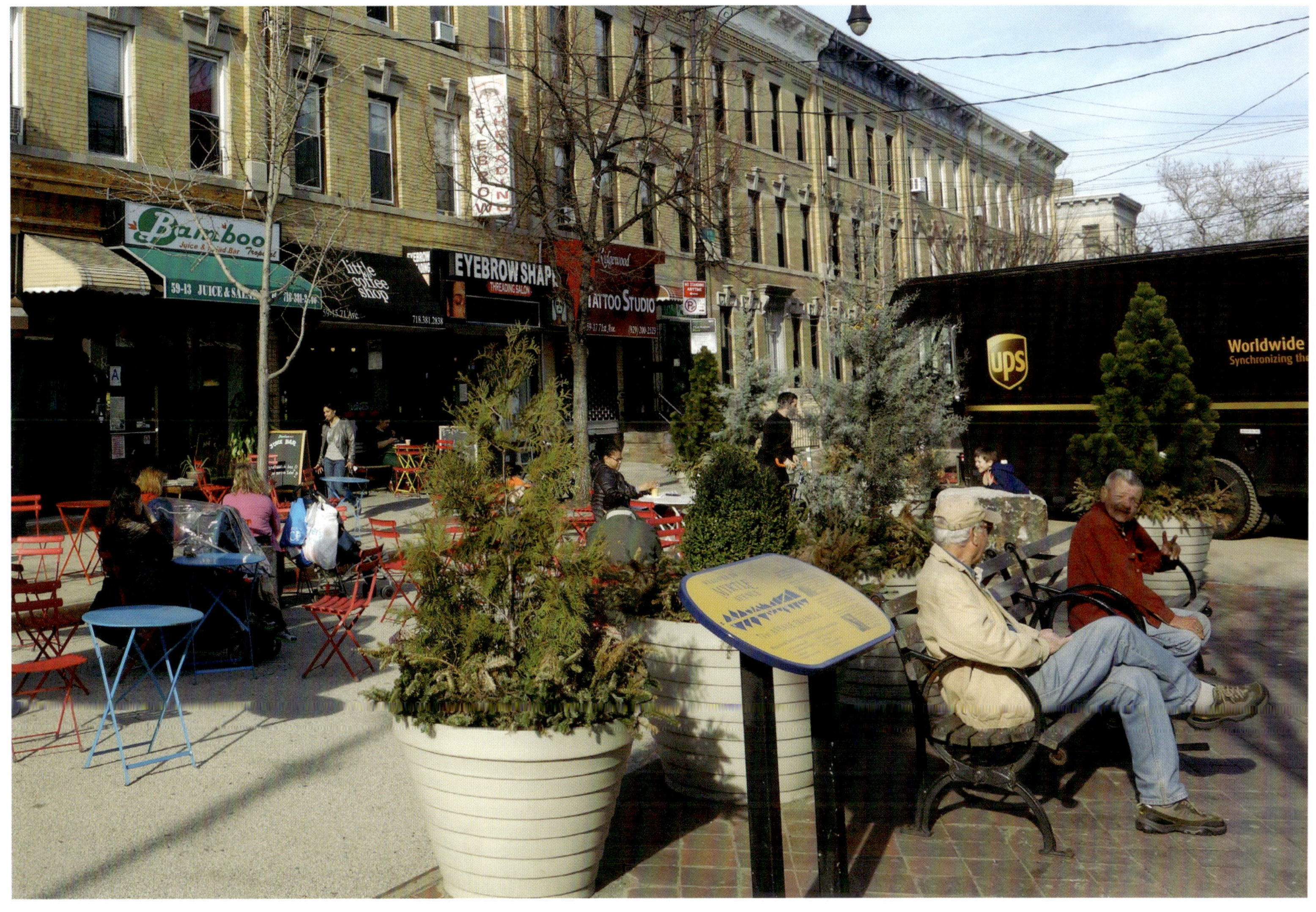

71st Avenue Plaza, Ridgewood

The handsome block of Federal-style row houses forms one side of the triangular block in Ridgewood. Here the Department of Transportation (DOT) has installed a permanent plaza to serve the neighborhood by blocking off 71st Avenue, where it once connected to Myrtle. To date, the DOT's Plaza Program has led to the creation of seventy-one such installations throughout the city, thirteen of which are in Queens. Here, residents and shoppers take advantage of the benches, chairs, and tables to hang out, have a cup of coffee, and talk. Ridgewood, and its conjoined neighborhood of Bushwick, Brooklyn, are both notably deficient in adequate public space, so the plaza is a welcome addition.

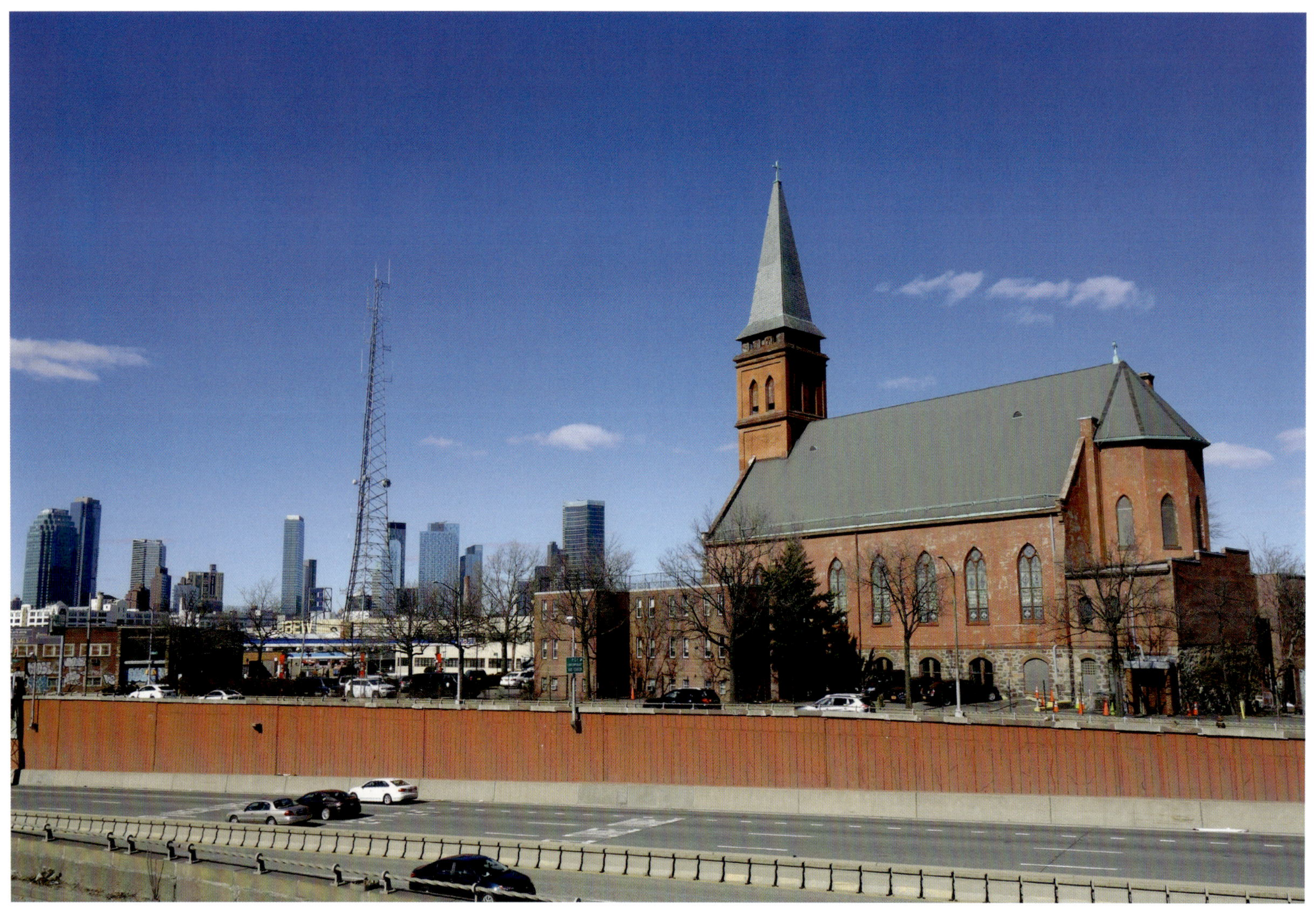

Long Island Expressway

Although known colloquially as the Long Island Expressway (LIE), the stretch of Interstate 495 that runs through Queens is officially titled the Queens-Midtown Expressway for one portion and Horace Harding Expressway for another. Completed in stages in the 1940s and 1950s under the direction of Robert Moses, the road cut a destructive 260-foot-wide swath through Queens, a veritable "Maginaux Line" that severed older relations of place and memory. Of all the boroughs, Queens has the most miles of interstate, although the Bronx arguably was even more transformed by the highway era. The image here was taken in Maspeth looking across the expressway toward St. Raphael Roman Catholic Church in Sunnyside.

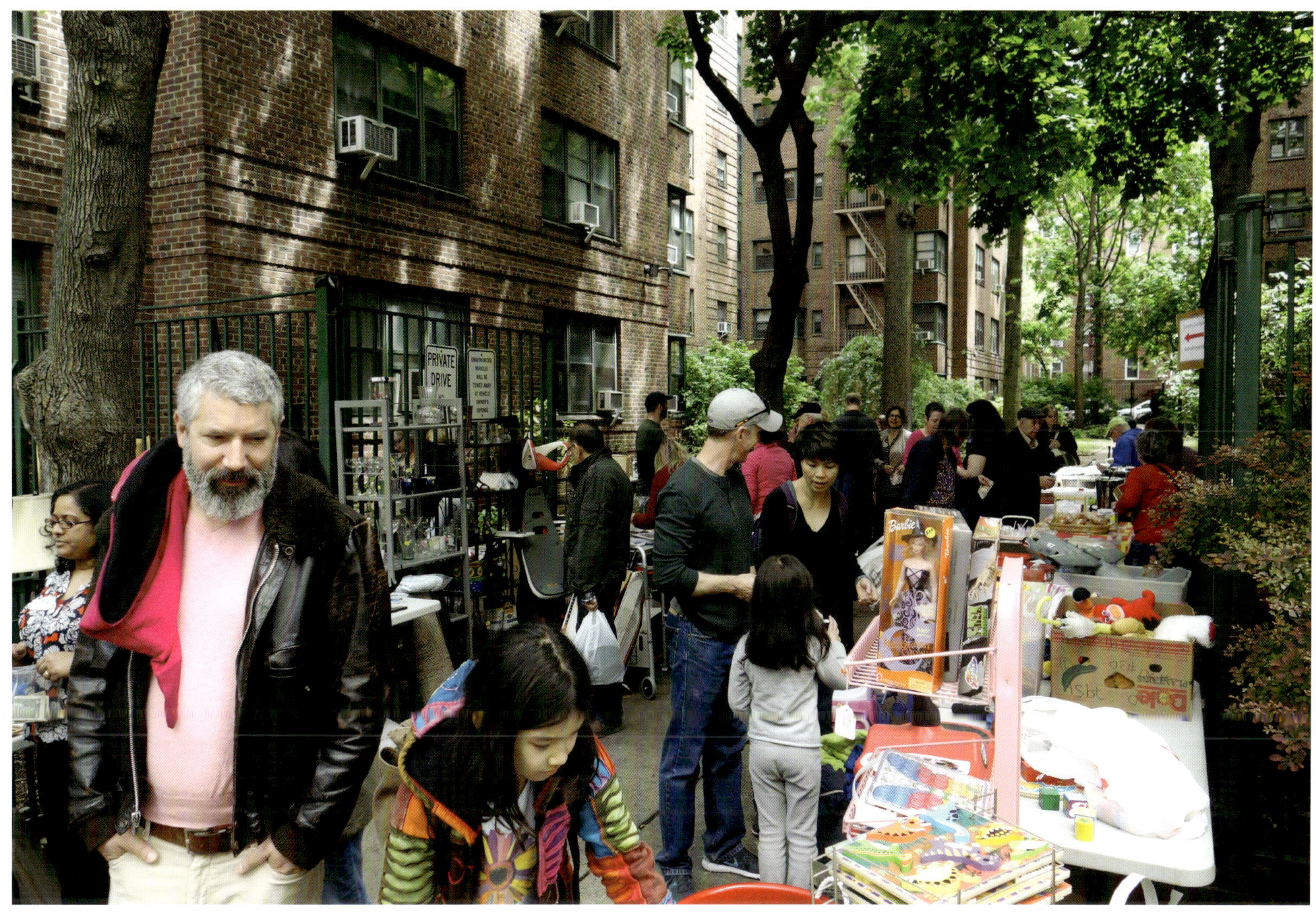

Under the tree canopy, Jackson Heights

Browsers at a flea market in Jackson Heights enjoy the canopy provided by the street and courtyard trees of Dunolly Gardens cooperative. Queens has a disproportionate share of trees: More than 40 percent of the city's seven million trees are in Queens, even though the borough only accounts for one-third of the land mass. Of the five boroughs, Queens has the most acreage of tree canopy, and only Staten Island has a greater density of canopy coverage. Common species include Norway Maple, Horse Chestnut, Pin Oak, Green Ash, Callery Pear, Honey Locust, and London Plane. Dunolly Gardens alone has eighty trees, including those on the co-op property and the "street trees" around the perimeter.

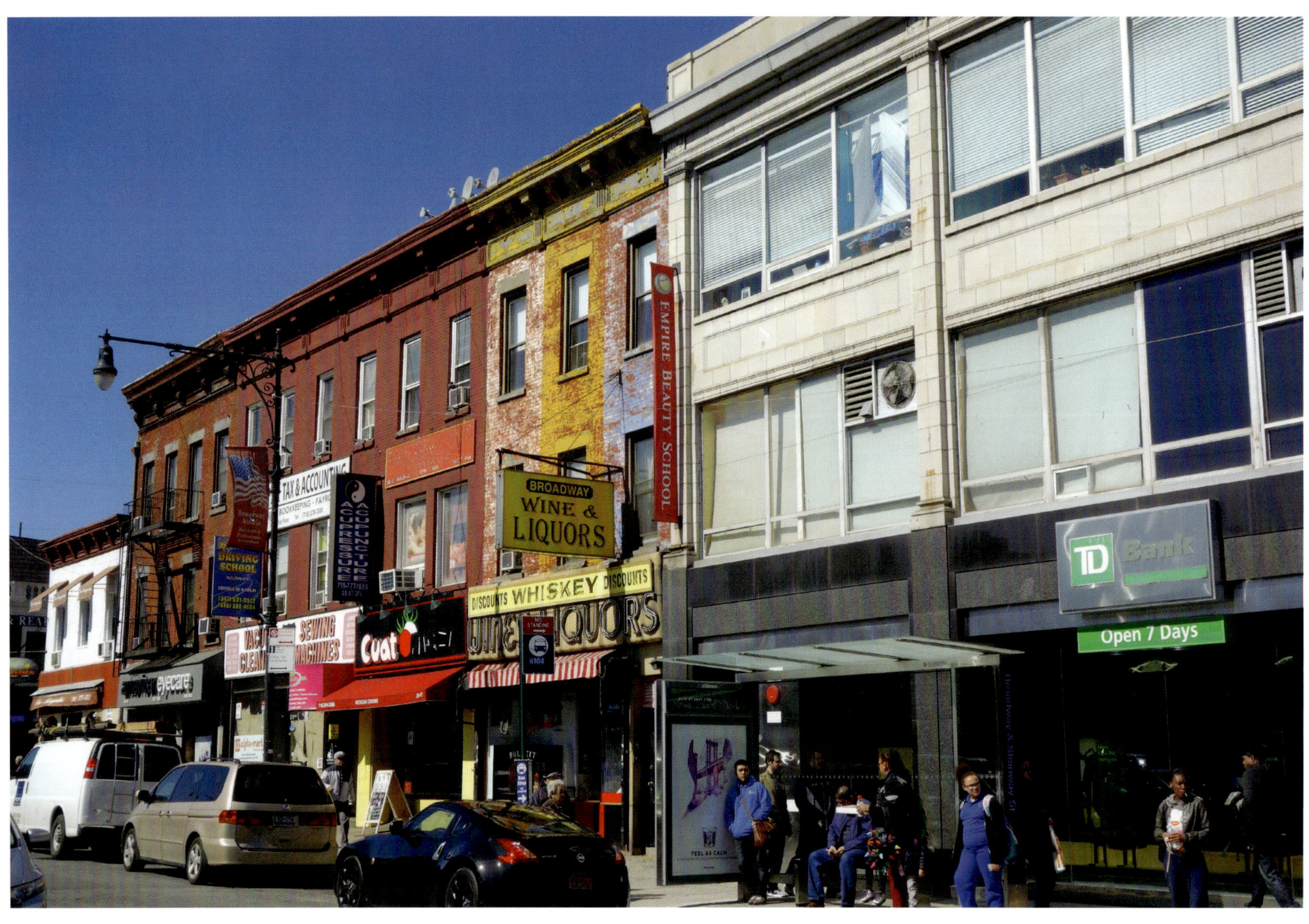

Broadway at Steinway Street in the heart of Astoria

Astoria became the hub of Greek life and culture in New York in the early twentieth century, and it remains one of the largest Greco-American enclaves in the country. Since the 1960s, many actors, dancers, musicians, and other performing arts workers priced out of Manhattan began moving into Astoria, which offers excellent train connections to Times Square and the Theater District. And over the last forty years, a large number of immigrants from Egypt, Yemen, Algeria, and Morocco have settled into the northern part of the neighborhood, opening restaurants, groceries, and mosques. All of this gives Astoria a unique mix of people living and interacting in the same community.

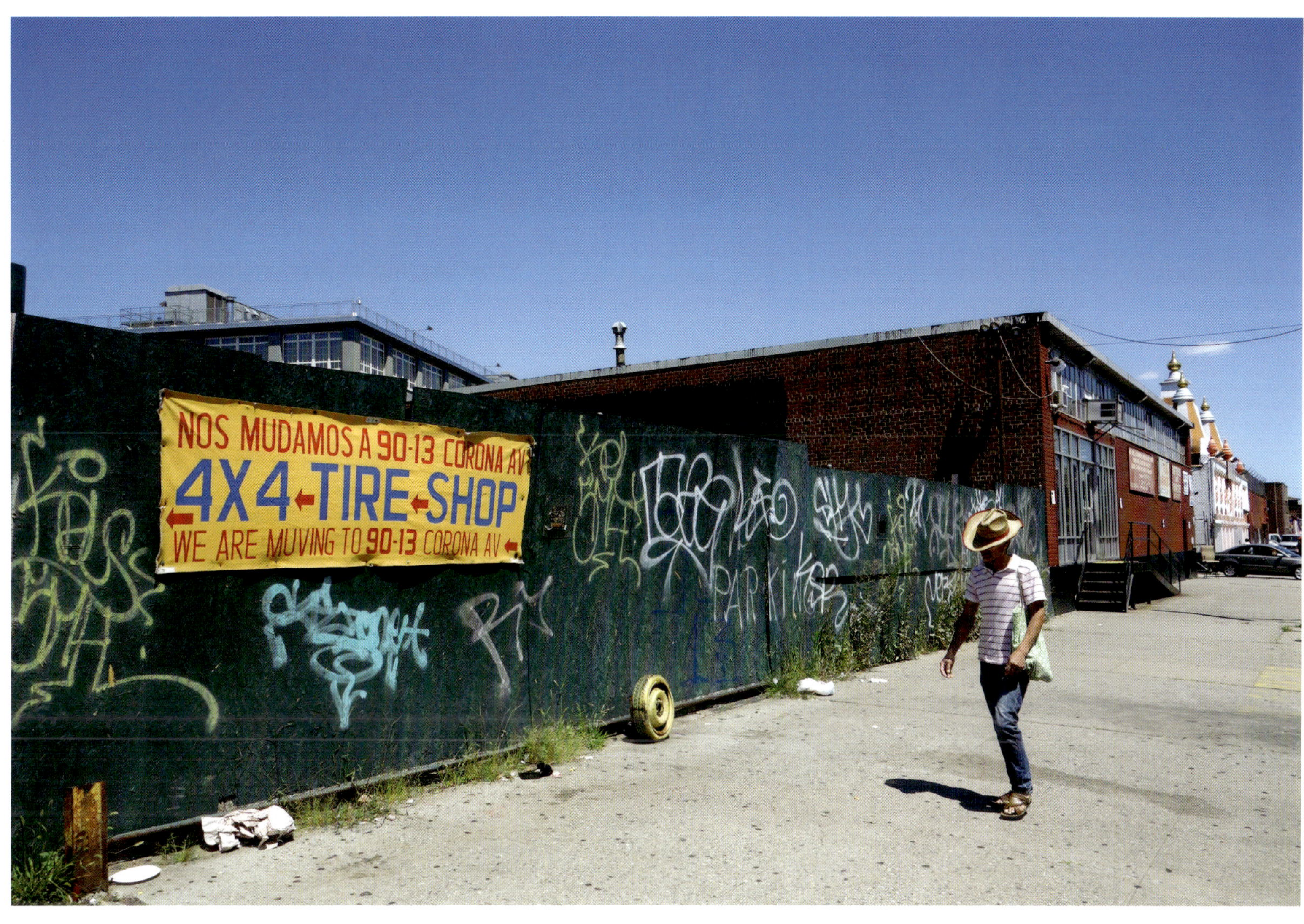

The 4x4 Tire Shop Is Moving, Elmhurst

On a scorching July day, a man strolls along a street in Elmhurst shaded by the brim of a straw cowboy hat, a style popular among immigrants from rural areas of Central America and Mexico. The bright Spanish and English sign announces the relocation of the Chinese-owned tire shop that once stood here. Down the street, the orange and white sikhara (spires) of the Geeta Hindu Temple rise in the background. The 4x4 Tire Shop had to move when the lot was purchased and cleared in 2016 to build an apartment building, a sign of rising property values in the neighborhood. All that remains from the former land use is the capacious curb cut that once facilitated the entrance and exit of cars.

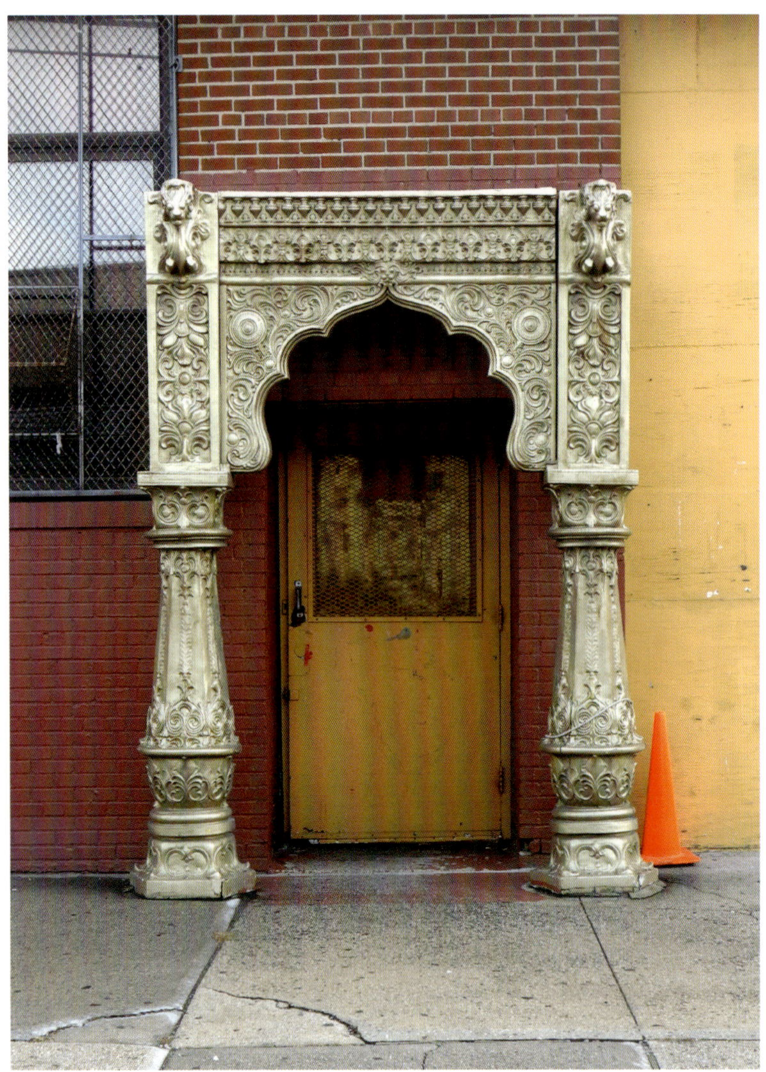

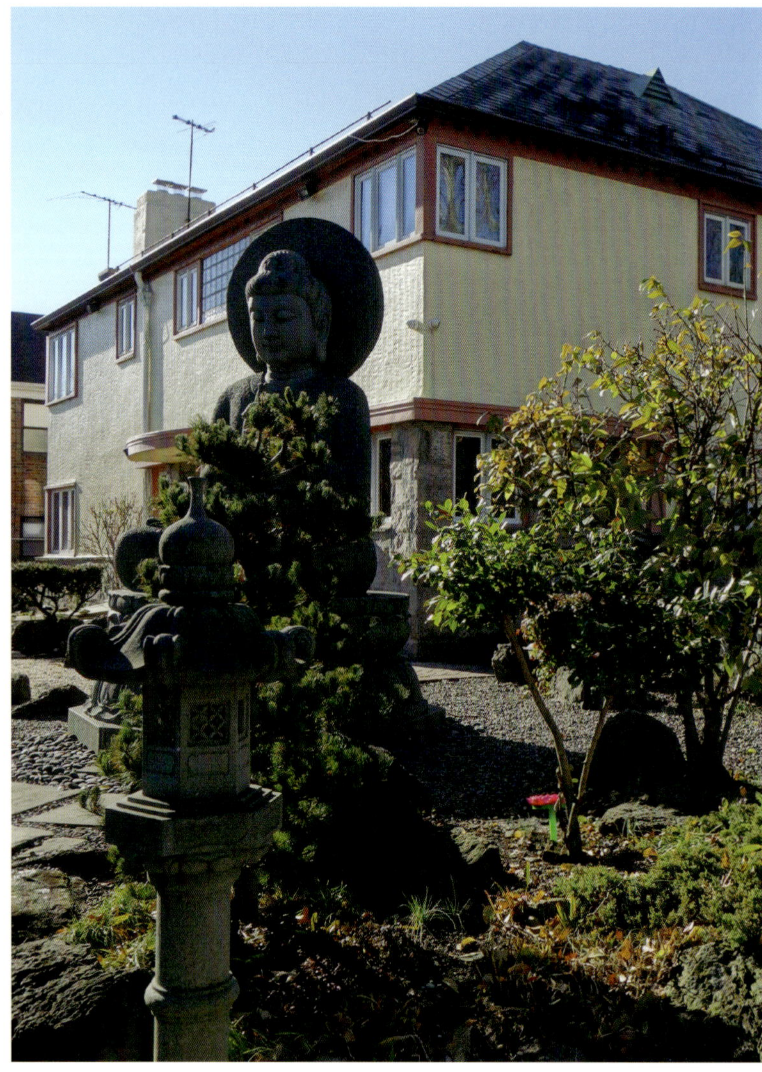

Adapting space for the sacred

Figures 127a–127h. One of the keys to the great diversity of Queens is its highly flexible built environment. This gives people multiple options for establishing homes, businesses, and civic and religious institutions. The latter is particularly important, as newcomers often lack the resources to erect large purpose-built structures for worship. Thus, one of the ways that new immigrant communities assert themselves in the urban landscape is to adapt existing buildings for religious life. It is a practice pioneered since the early twentieth century by Black communities, which often established new spaces of worship in storefronts and houses, or by occupying churches and synagogues vacated by older congregations.

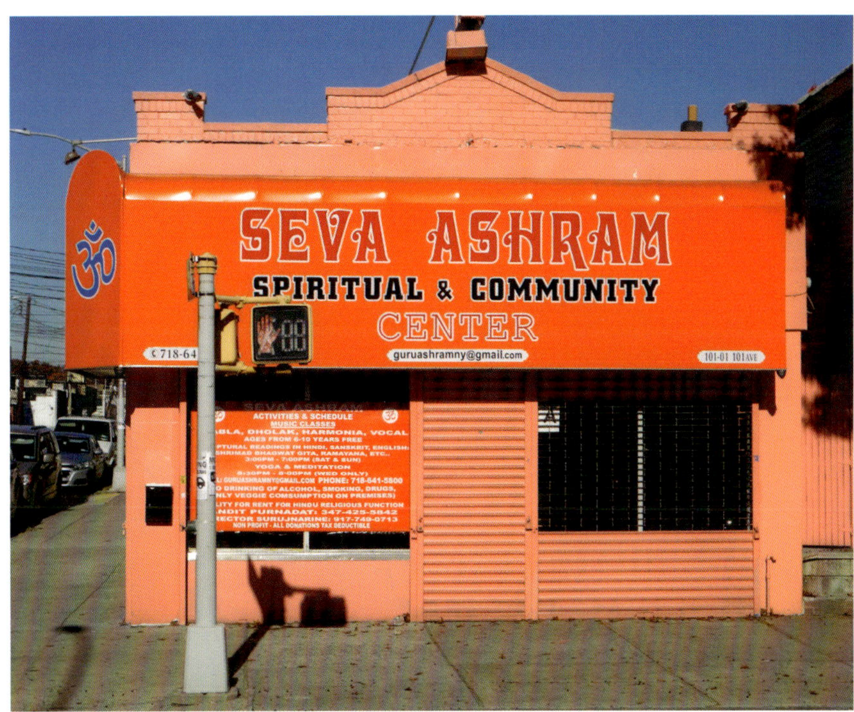

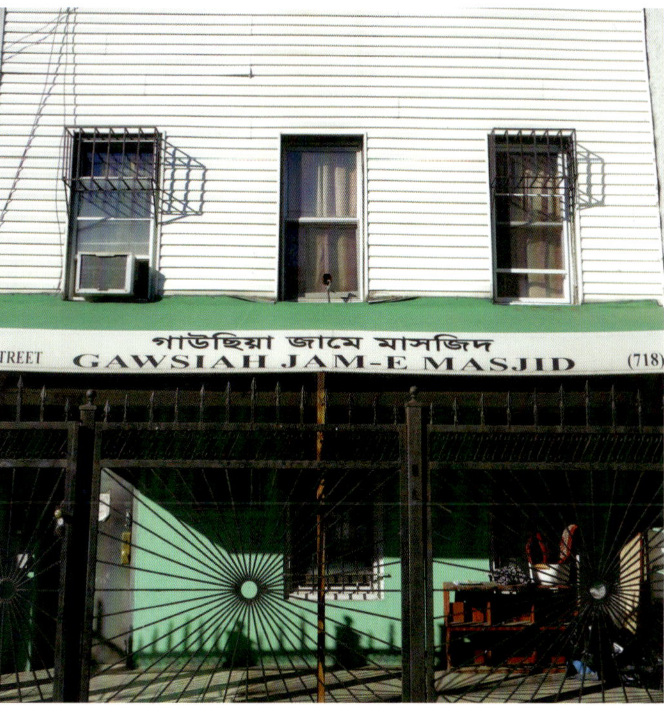

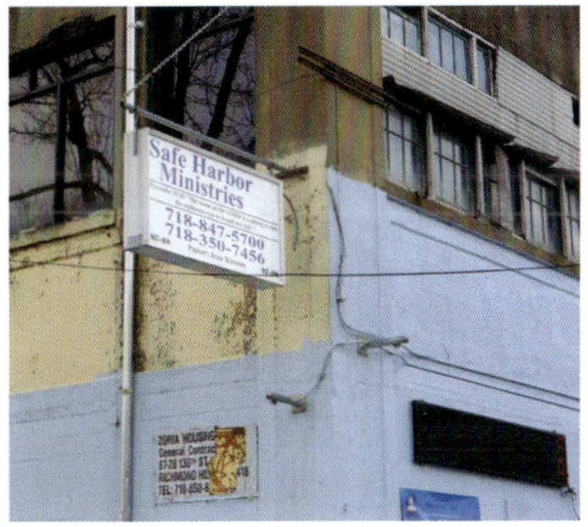

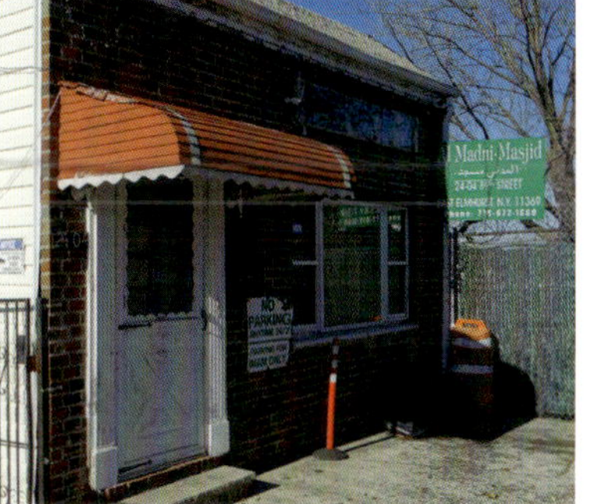

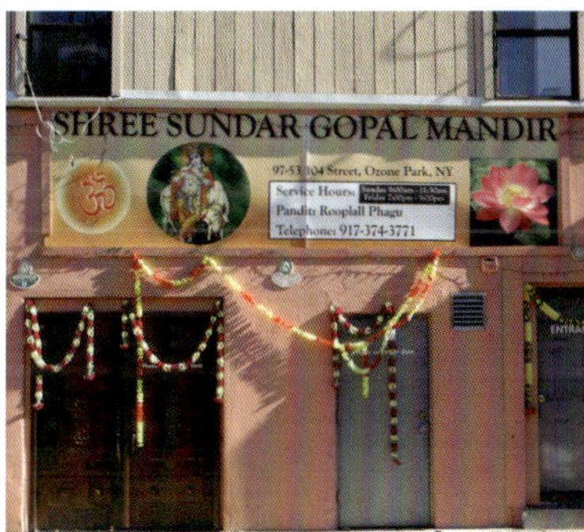

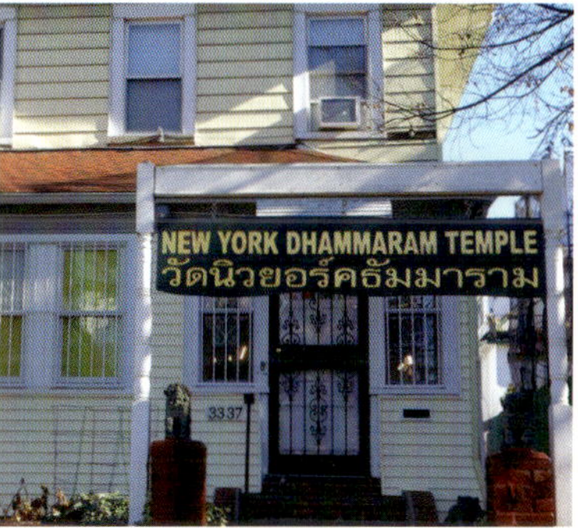

Opposite page, left: Hindu worshippers set up this mandir, or temple, in an old warehouse in Woodside. The elaborately carved entrance canopy is the only marker of the building's new function. Opposite page, right: The Western Buddhist Association established the Fan Yin Monastery and Cultural Center in this ordinary suburban house in Flushing. This page, top row (l. to r.): Hindu ashram in a small commercial building, Ozone Park; storefront mosque, Astoria. Bottom row (l. to r.):; Safe Harbor Ministry, a Pentecostal church located above a garage in Richmond Hill; mosque in a small house by La Guardia Airport; mandir in a converted shop, Ozone Park; Thai Buddhist temple in a town house, East Elmhurst.

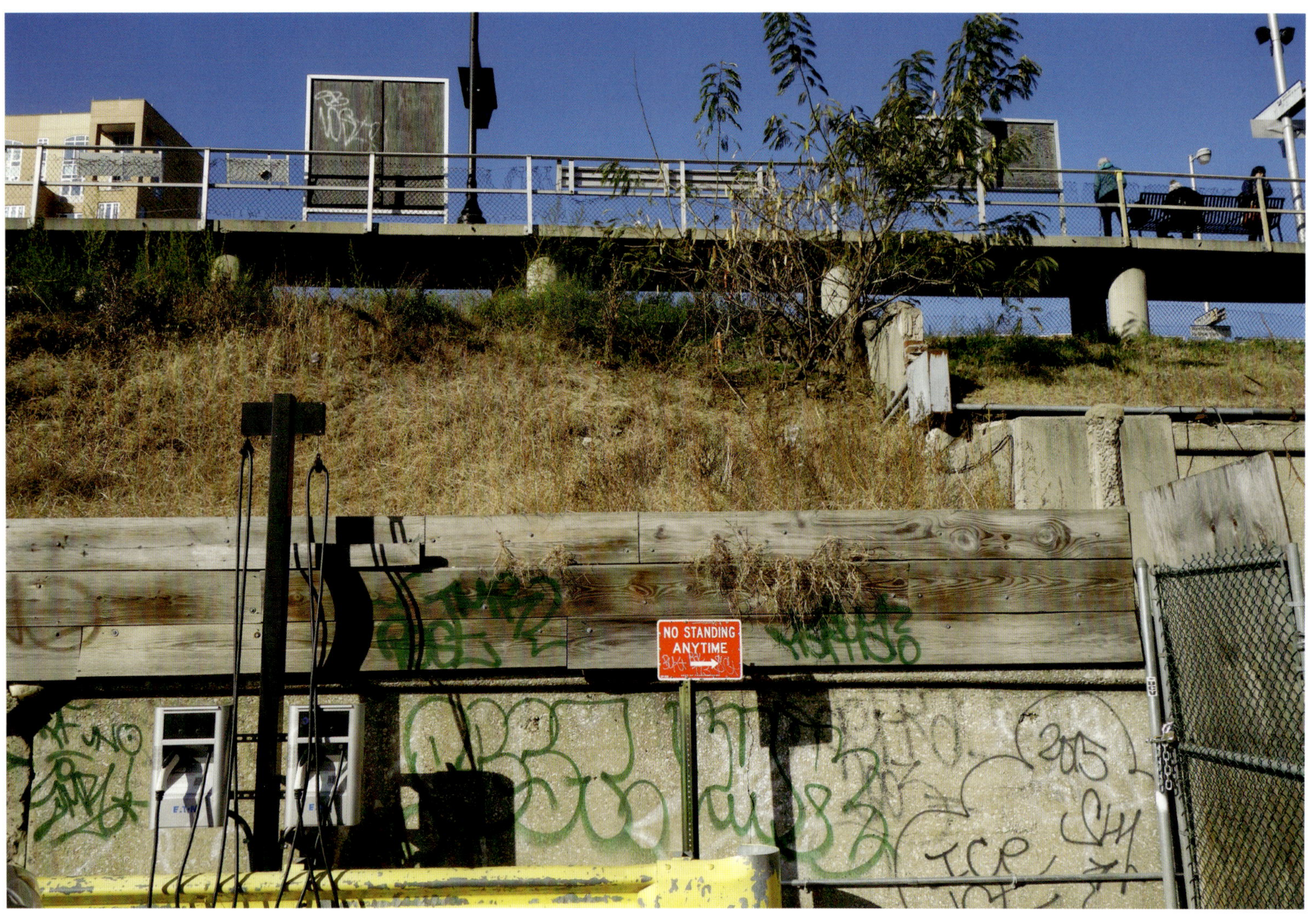

Long Island Railroad, Flushing station

At the top of this berm in downtown Flushing stretches the eastbound platform of the Long Island Railroad's Port Washington line. The line was established as the Flushing Railroad in 1854 and extended in stages until it was incorporated into the LIRR system in 1902. Today the system carries some 80 million passengers yearly on eleven lines stopping at 124 stations. The location of tracks and stations has played a crucial role in the growth of Queens and the spreading of the densely crowded Manhattan population to the counties of Long Island. It has been especially significant for Chinese and Korean families who have moved further out but maintain businesses around downtown Flushing.

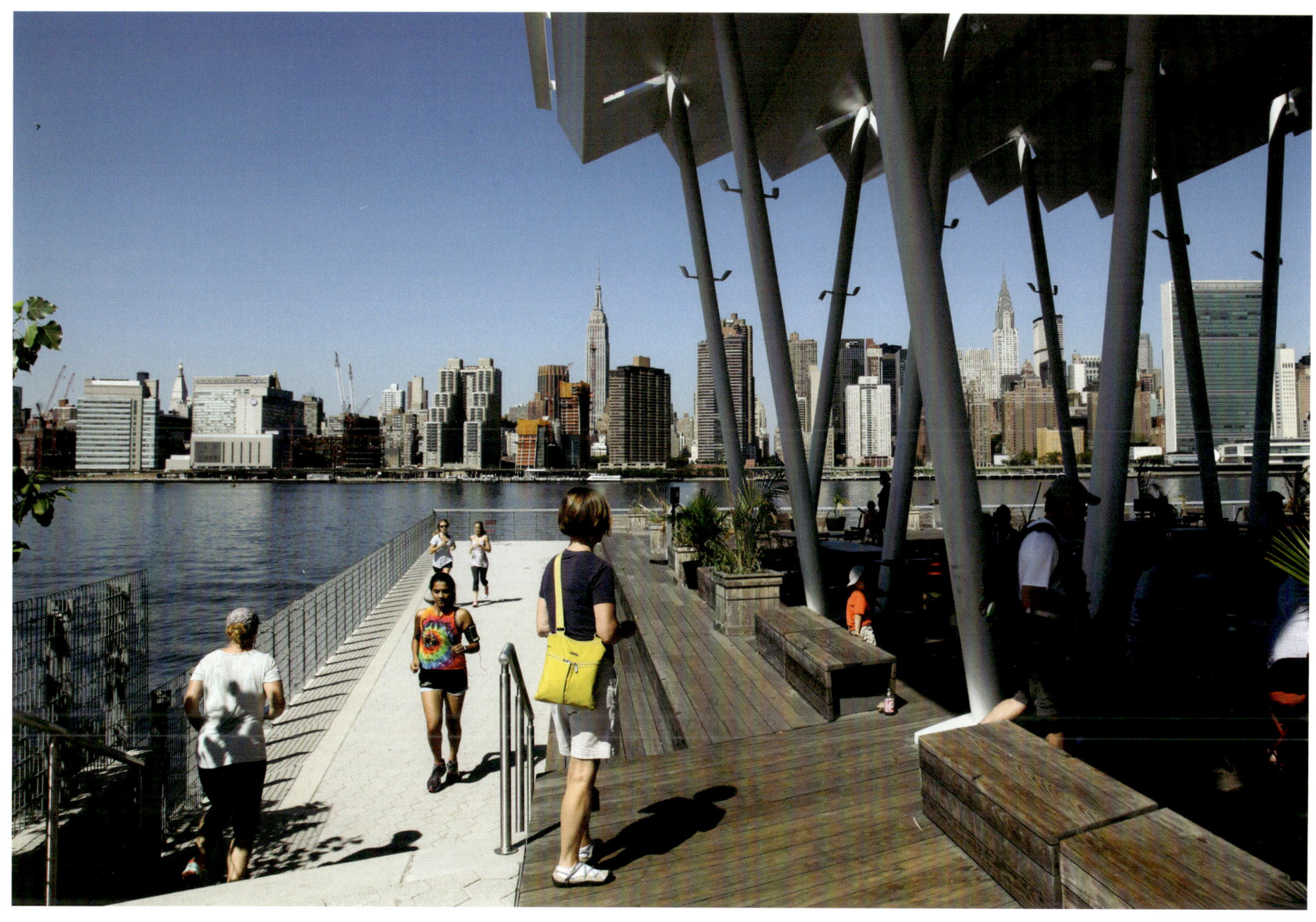

Ferry Terminal Pavilion, Hunters Point South

Completed in 2014, the new pavilion at Hunters Point South serves the East River Ferry. From there, commuters can travel downriver to Greenpoint, Williamsburg, and DUMBO in Brooklyn or to 34th Street and Pier 11 in Manhattan. It also connects passengers to the broader ferry network, which includes six routes, five transfer points, and a summer shuttle to Governors Island. With one transfer, you can travel as far north as Throgs Neck in the Bronx or south to Rockaway. The pavilion includes a concession stand and multiple tables and benches for hanging out and taking in the sweeping views of Manhattan. It is part of a grand transformation of Long Island City's waterfront.

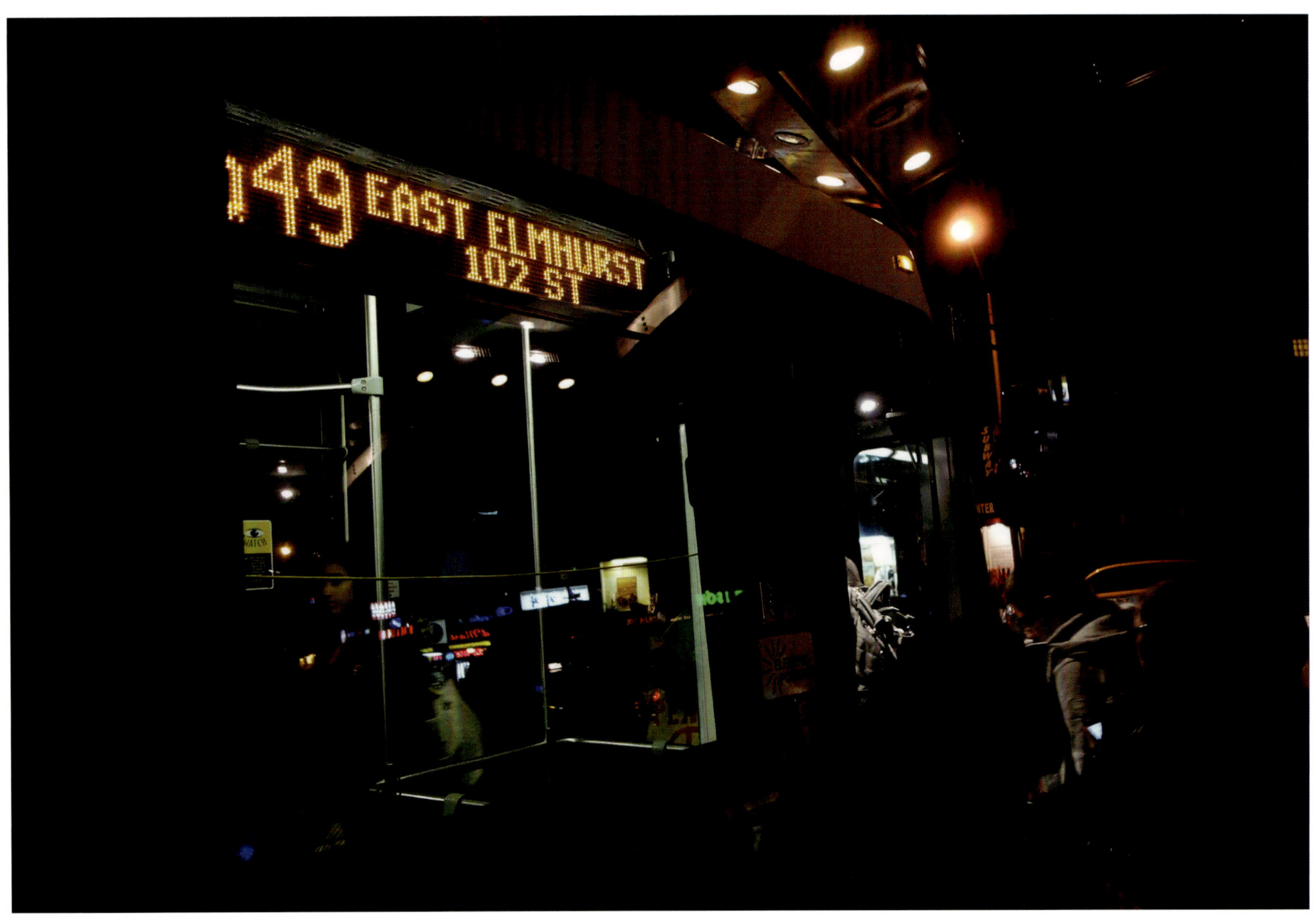

Nighthawks at the bus stop

Passengers board the Q49 bus on Roosevelt Avenue for a journey into the night. The Q49 lumbers slowly through the congested streets of Jackson Heights into East Elmhurst, serving a large immigrant and working-class population. It is often packed during morning and evening rush hours as commuters jostle for space in the standing-room-only aisles. Delays are frequent from double-parked vehicles, blocked intersections, and road construction. The MTA operates eighty-seven bus routes through Queens, a much-relied-upon service for a borough with large expanses of terrain unconnected to the train system. And while Queens is famously the borough of the automobile, more than half of all residents rely on public transportation.

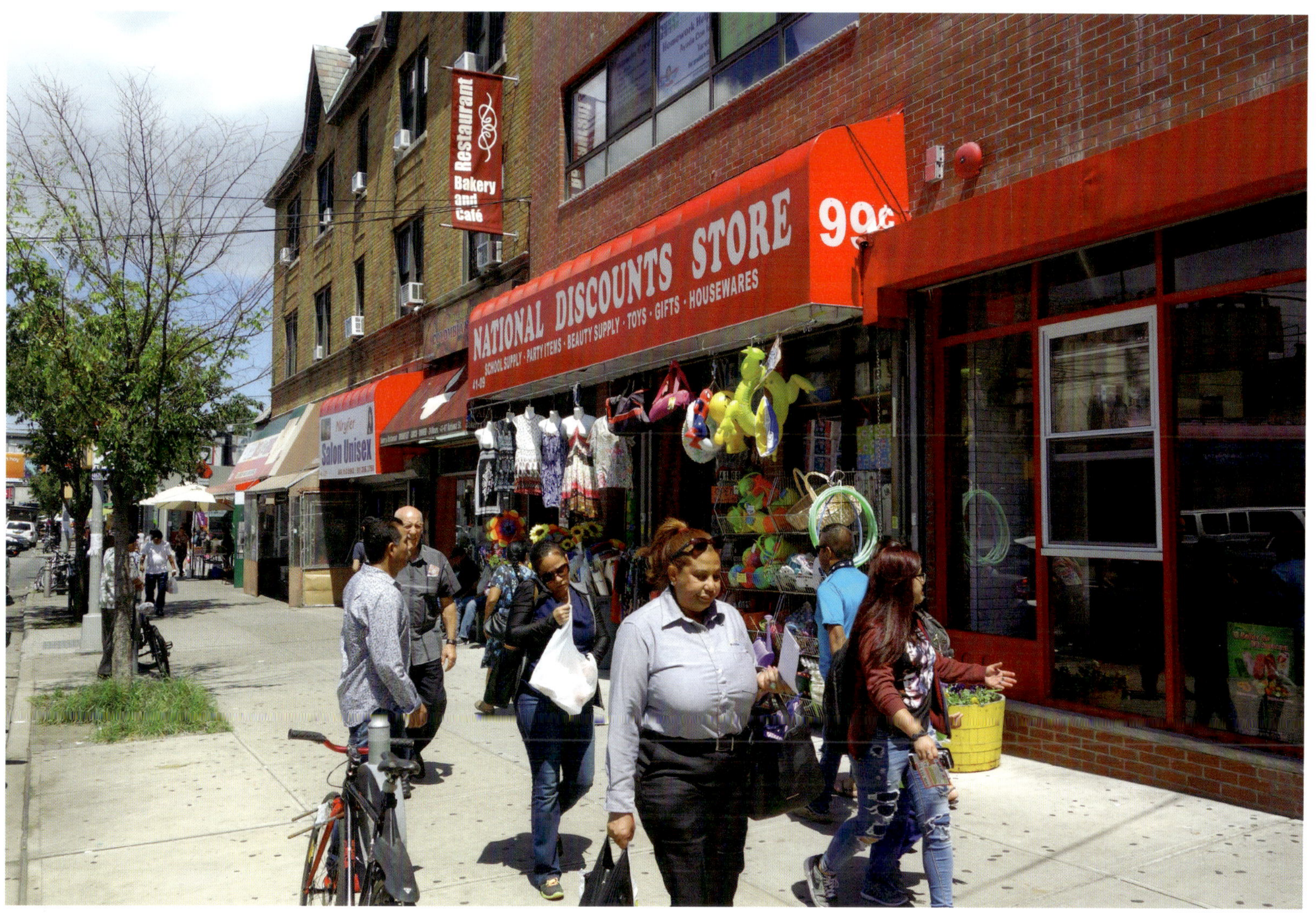

Sidewalks of Corona

Pedestrians stroll along National Street between 41st and 42nd Avenues in Corona. The block reveals a mix of small businesses typical of commercial corridors in this part of Queens. At the top of the block, under the red, white, and green awning, a *tienda* sells groceries and operates an open-air window for selling tacos, tortas, and other lunch items. Next in line is a small florist, a unisex hair salon, a Colombian bakery, a Chinese-owned 99-cent store. At the far right is a tortilleria, one of many established in Corona with the influx of Mexican families. Air conditioners in the upper floor apartments are a reminder that few older residential buildings in Queens have central air.

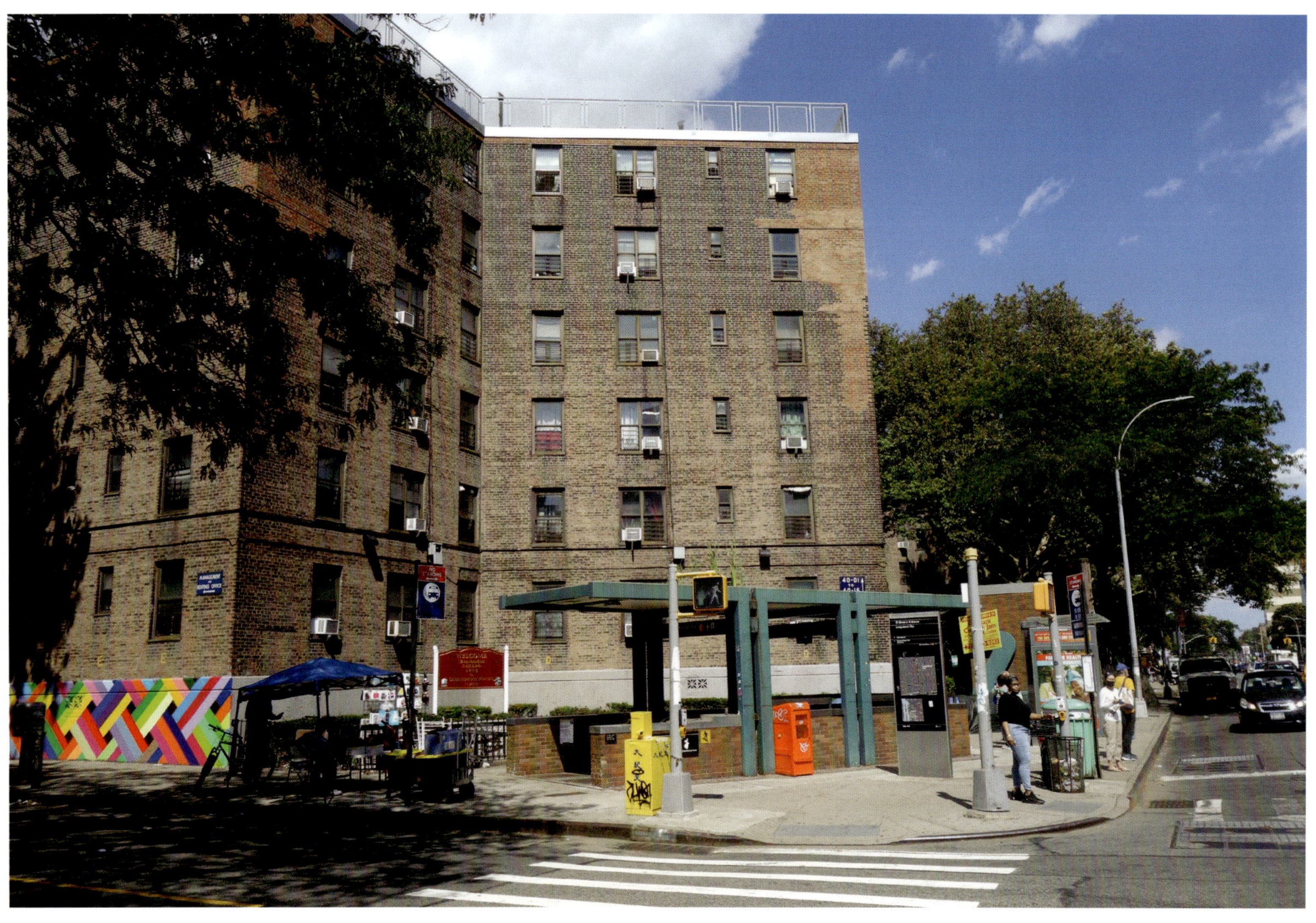

F train station at Queensbridge Houses, Long Island City

Completed in 1939, Queensbridge is the largest public housing complex in the United States. It has 3,150 apartments in 96 Y-shaped buildings spread out over a park-like ground with dozens of large mature trees. It is home to a diverse community of African American, Afro-Caribbean, Latino, and South Asian people. Hip-hop pioneers Roxanne Shanté and Marley Marl grew up here, as did Nas, MC Shan, Ron Artest, and filmmaker Julie Dash. The seven thousand residents are well served by the F train, shown here, on the corner of 21st Street and 41st Avenue. Queensbridge faces many of the same maintenance issues as most NYCHA properties, but an active tenant association keeps the pressure on.

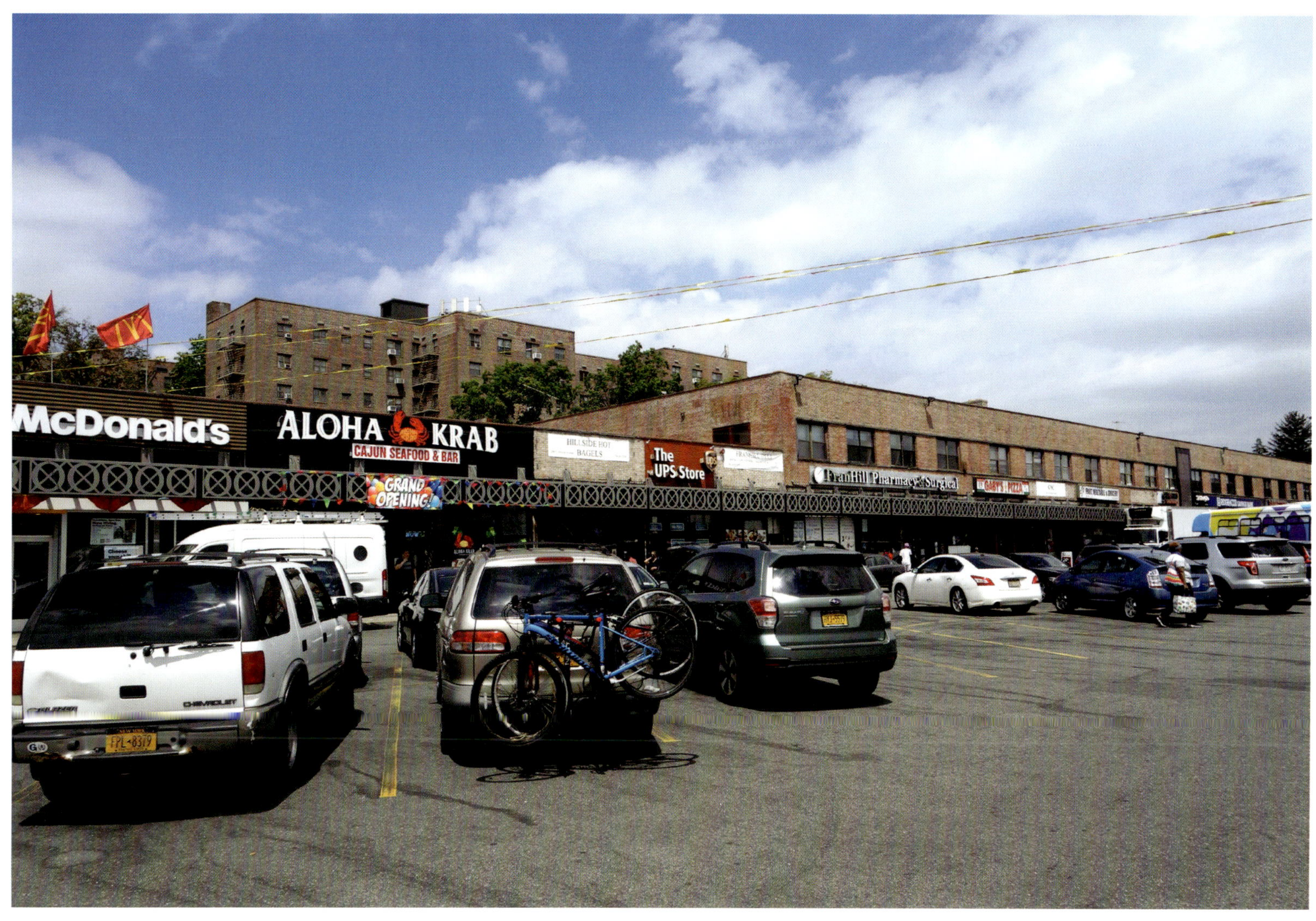

Franhill Plaza, Holliswood

As early as the 1920s, Queens developers were already exploring new land uses oriented toward the automobile. While most commercial streets featured buildings constructed along the lot line, many began to offer dedicated parking in front of the buildings, especially in the rapidly burgeoning eastern sections of the borough. Franhill Plaza, shown here, exemplifies this trend. Situated along Hillside Avenue, the two-story section was completed in 1954, and the one-story extension in 1969; shoppers can take advantage of 165 off-street parking spaces. Behind the plaza, the Hilltop Village cooperative, a nine-story middle-class apartment complex, features underground parking garages for residents.

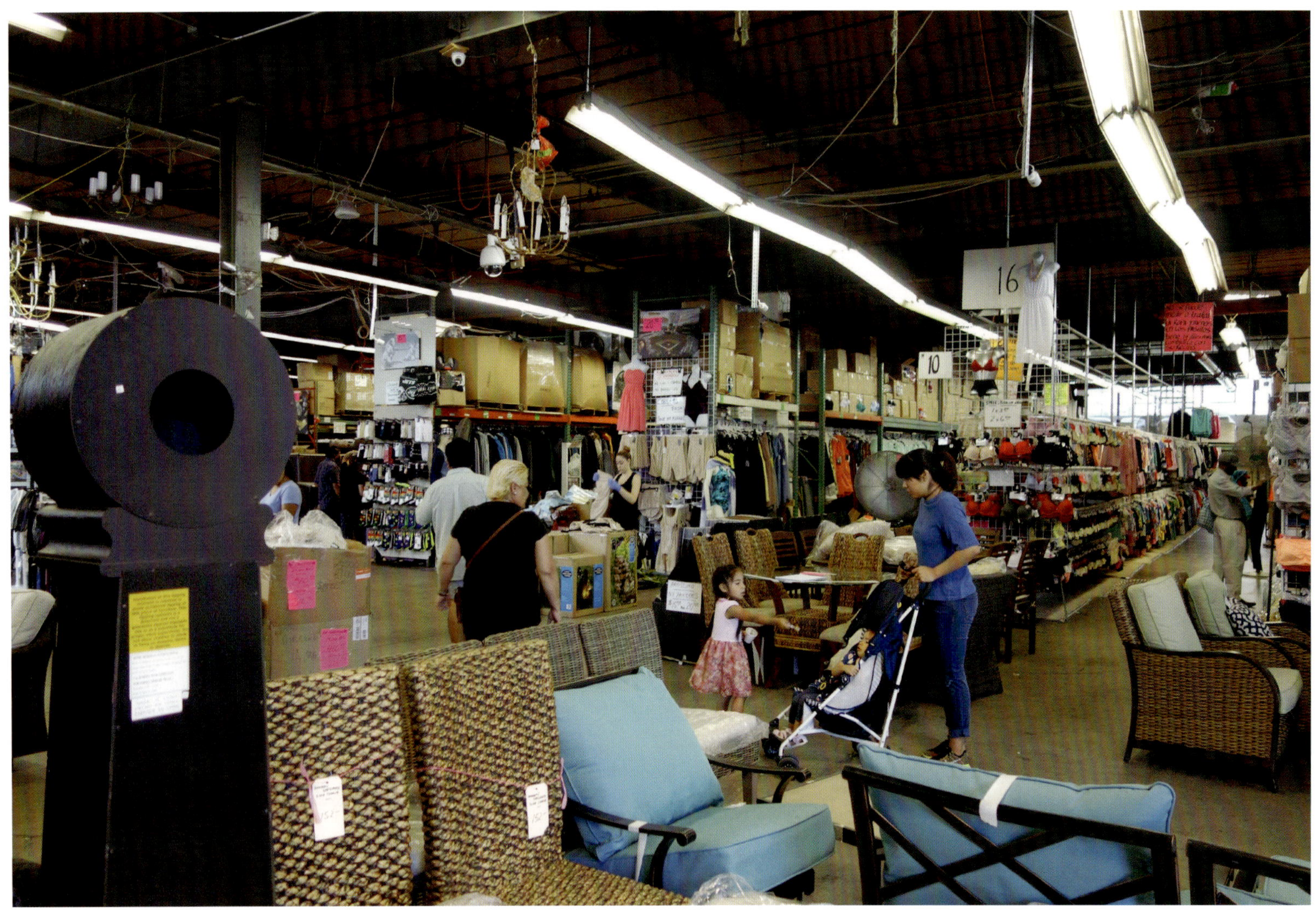

Discount emporium, Elmhurst

Large discount consolidators and outlets are common in Queens, where residents prize low-cost bargains to save hard-earned cash. The borough has an extensive portfolio of underused and highly adaptable buildings, such as the warehouse shown here, with plenty of room to spread out. These stores constitute a shadow world of retail between big box chains and second-hand shops. They generally sell goods sourced through damaged stock, returns and discontinuations, bulk purchases, and "fell off the truck" sales. Thus, they do not sell established "product lines" like Target, Kohl's, or other department stores. Instead, the mix of items on the floor tends to be ad hoc, changing continually.

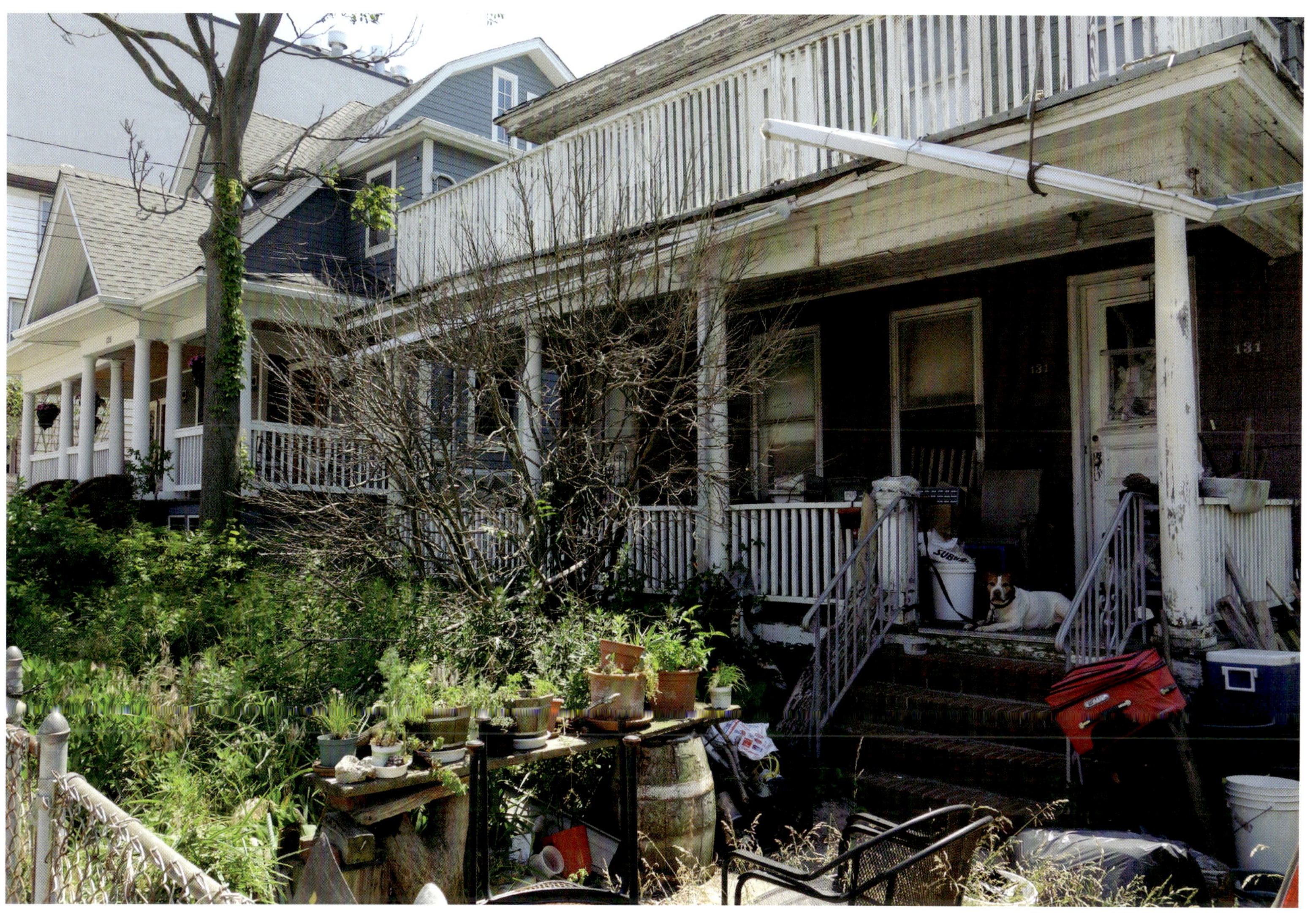

Dog on porch, Beach 91st Street

Rockaway has long been renowned for the relaxed atmosphere and the weather-beaten feel that so often comes with old beach communities. The neighborhood was established in 1897 with the merger of the villages of Holland and Hammels, and in 1900, train service connected the peninsula to Manhattan. Robert Moses opened things up to rapid development in 1939 with the completion of the Marine Parkway Bridge and the Cross Bay Bridge. His goal, largely realized, was to shift Rockaway from a playground for the wealthy to a recreational space accessible to working-class and middle-class people. And the pup on the porch reminds us that we live in a multispecies metropolis.

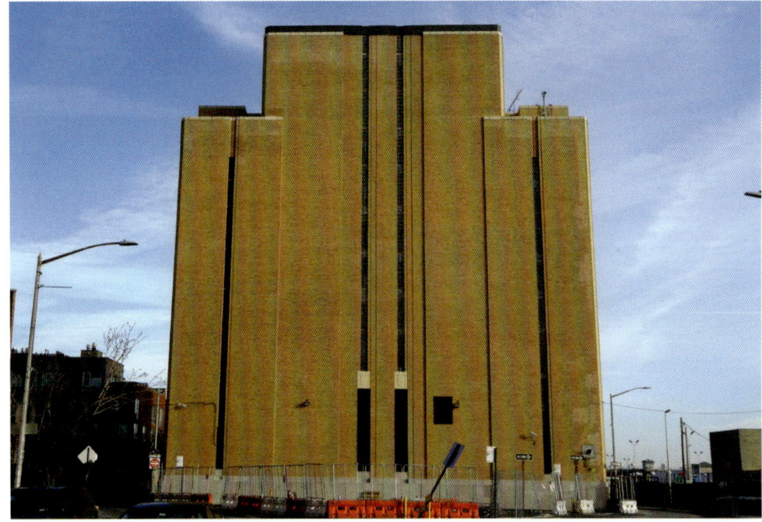

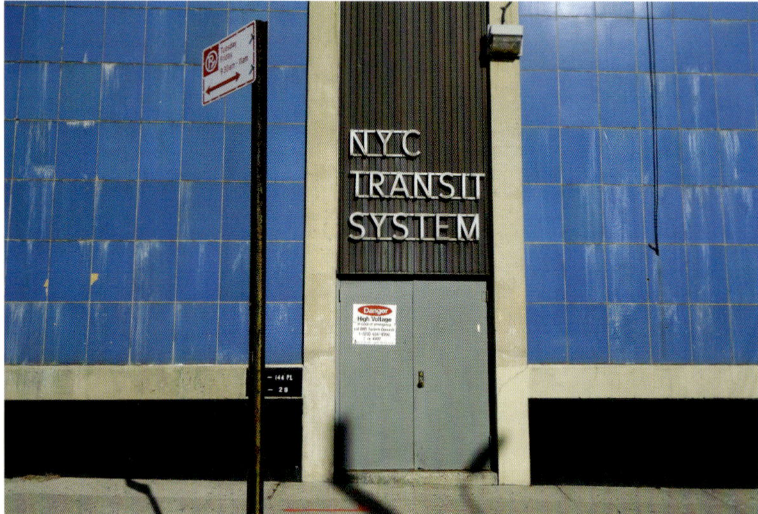

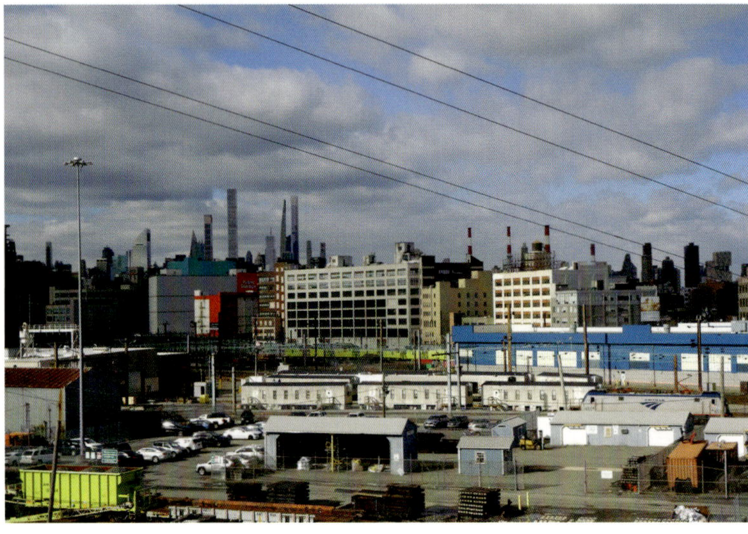

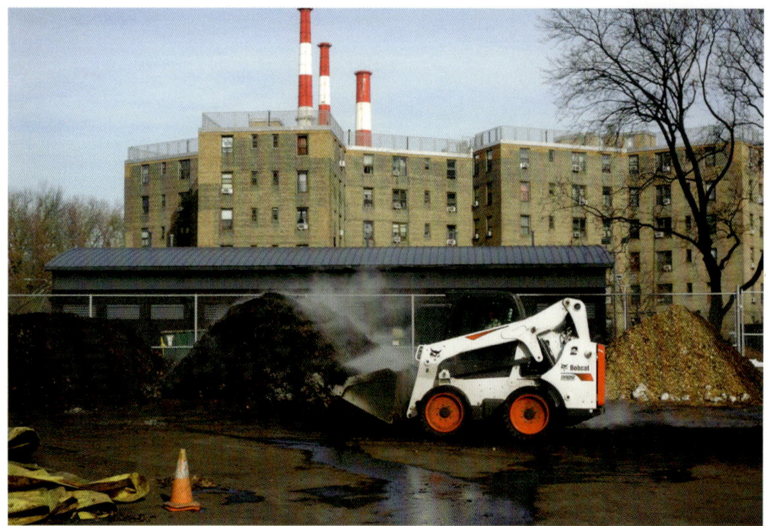

Facilitating the metropolis

Figures 136a–136h. Throughout Queens, hundreds of buildings, structures, campuses, stations, and other kit keep the borough humming from day to day. These facilities are important not only because of their functions, but also because they have been key sources of employment for generations of new immigrants seeking relatively well-paying jobs. Many of these facilities are publicly owned by the city, the borough, or state-chartered agencies such as the MTA. Others are privately owned, whether by for-profit companies or nonprofit organizations. Like bridges, trains, highways, and airports, these municipal facilities provide crucial "backstage" functions to support everyday life in Queens.

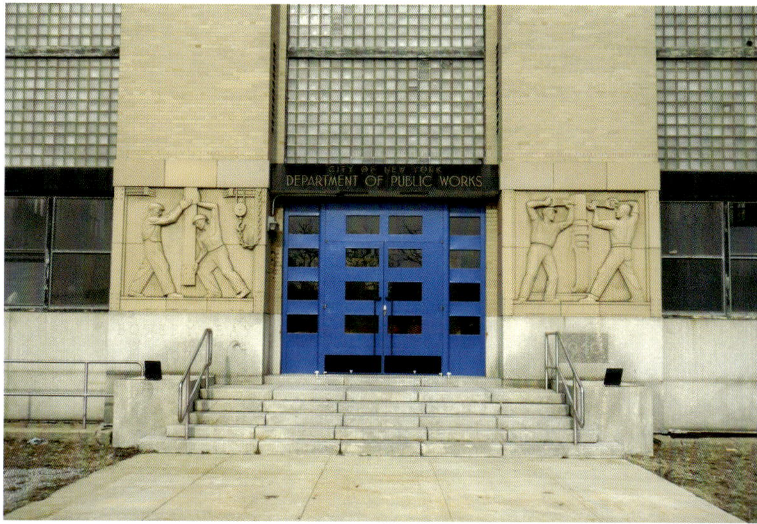

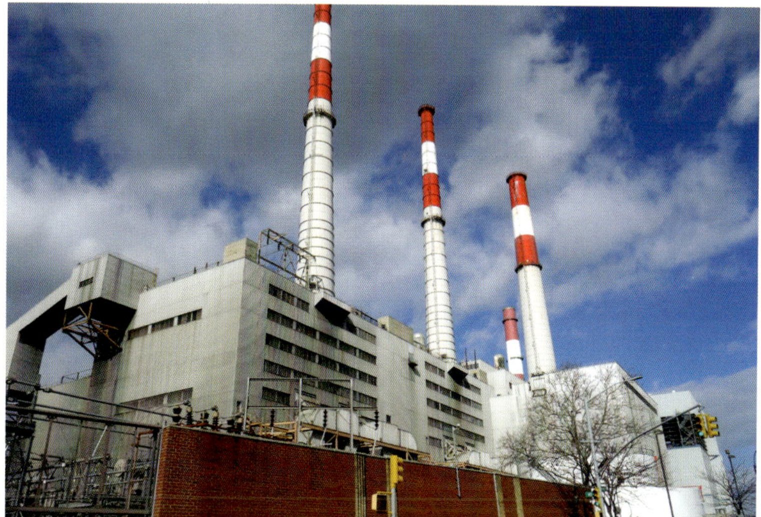

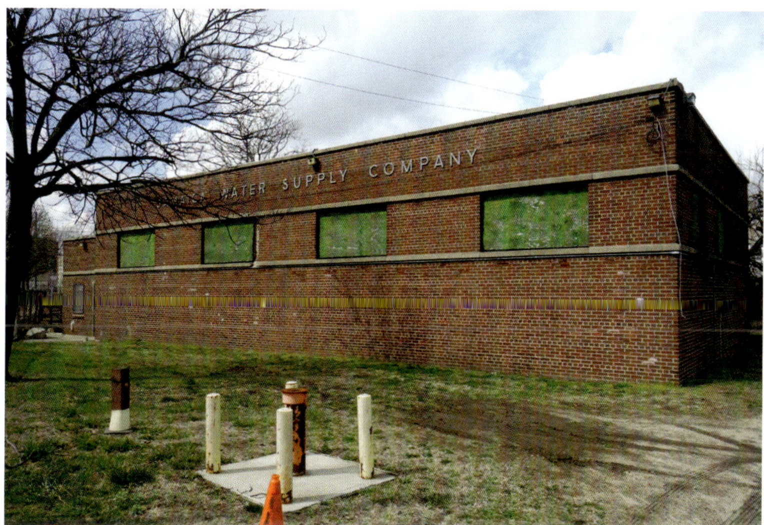

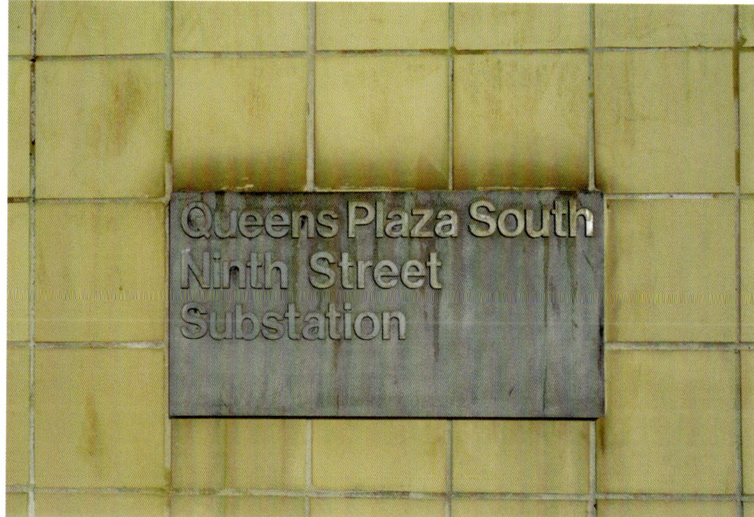

Opposite page, top left: Art Deco ventilation tower for the Midtown Tunnel in Long Island City. Top right: A pre-MTA "NYC Transit System" building, housing repair equipment. Bottom left: Sunnyside Yards, one of the major rail storage, switching, and dispatch facilities in New York. Bottom right: Industrial-scale compost site at Queensbridge. This page, top left: New York Department of Public Works building, designed and constructed during the New Deal by the WPA. Top right: The massive Ravenswood power plant in Astoria. Bottom left: Jamaica Water Supply Company well pump station, decommissioned when the city bought the company. Bottom right: MTA substation sign at Queens Plaza.

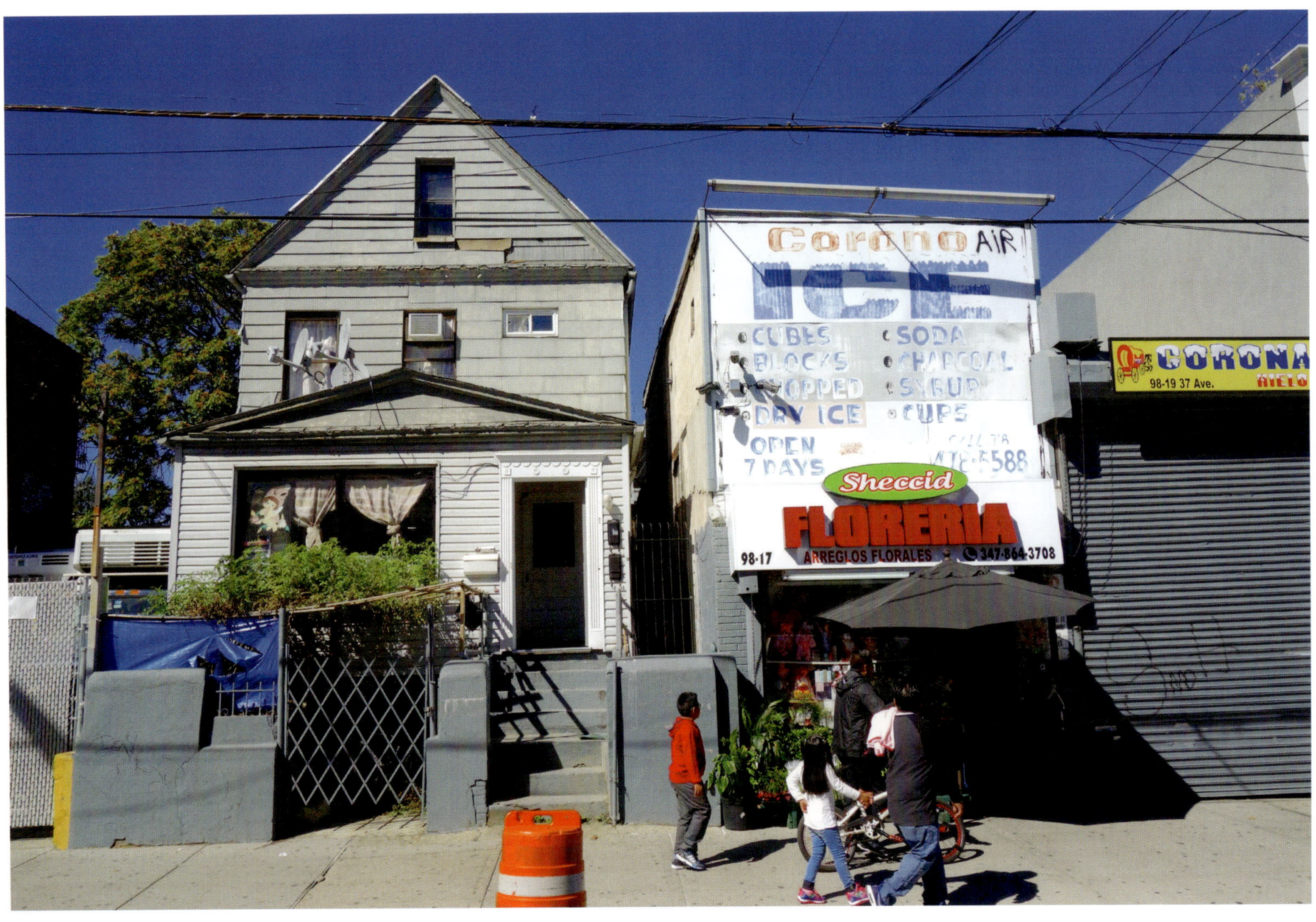

Homes and shops on 37th Avenue, Corona

To get a good sense of the mixed urban landscape of Queens, take a stroll along 37th Avenue between Junction Boulevard and 108th Street in Corona. Here, the avenue narrows to one lane in each direction for a twelve-block stretch, with a complex jumble of wood frame houses and brick commercial structures built right up to the lot line during the early days of the neighborhood. Some of the old houses have been converted into offices and businesses, with many changes of tenants, functions, and décor over the years. While a few have been torn down to build new apartments and commercial buildings, 37th Avenue retains something of an elder Queens streetscape.

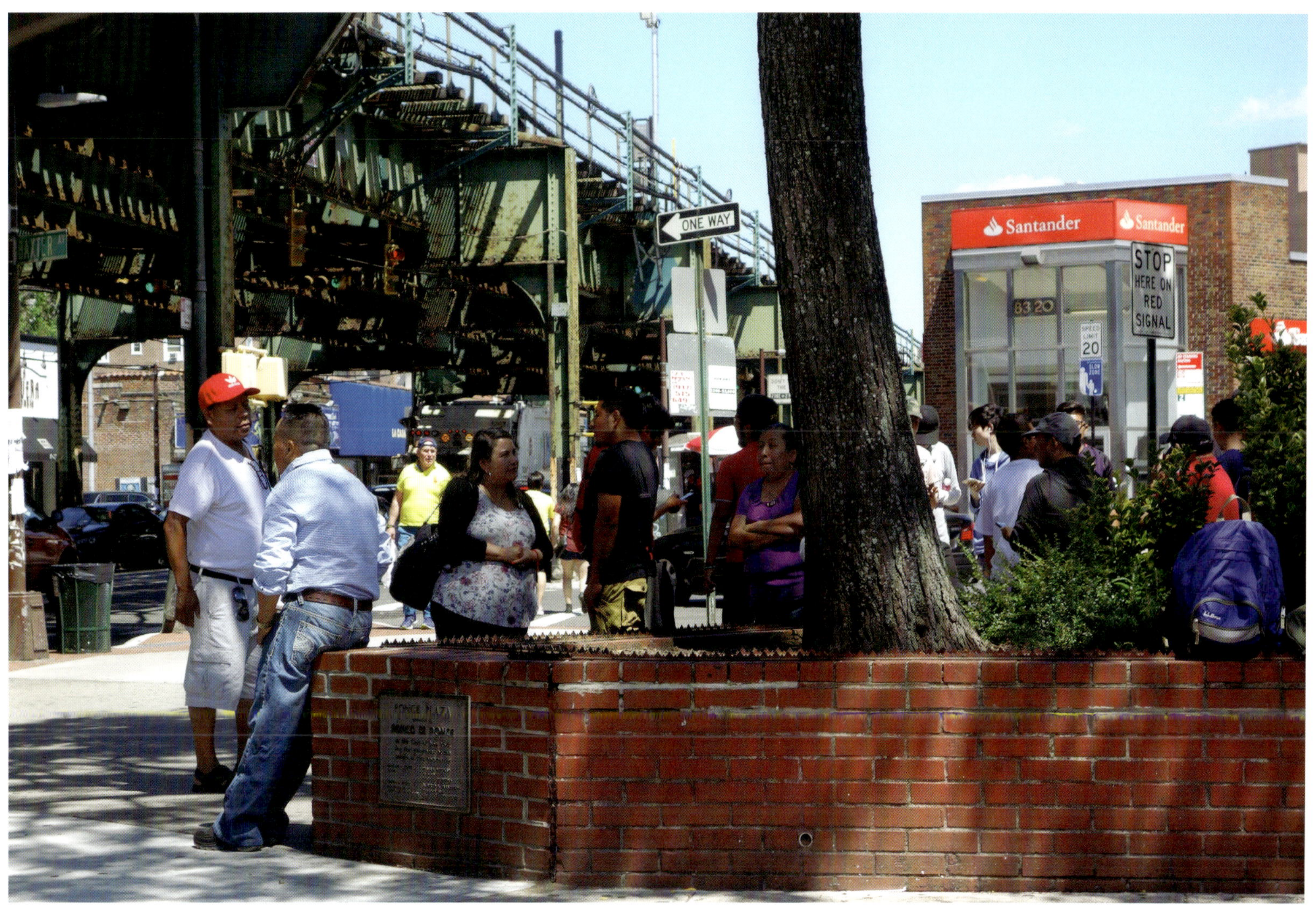

Neighbors catching up at Manuel de Dios Unanue Plaza, Elmhurst

A sociable scene in a small plaza at Baxter and Roosevelt on the border of Jackson Heights and Elmhurst. Today's peaceful scene belies the history of violence that rocked the neighborhood in the 1980s as Colombian gangs fought pitched battles for control over the drug trade. The plaza was long known as Ponce Plaza, after the Puerto Rican bank located here for many years (now Santander Bank, seen in the background). In 1995, it was rededicated to Cuban journalist Manuel de Dios Unanue, who was slain by the Cari cartel at a restaurant across the street for his coverage of drug trafficking. By the early twenty-first century, many of the gang members were aging out, and the neighborhood became much more peaceful.

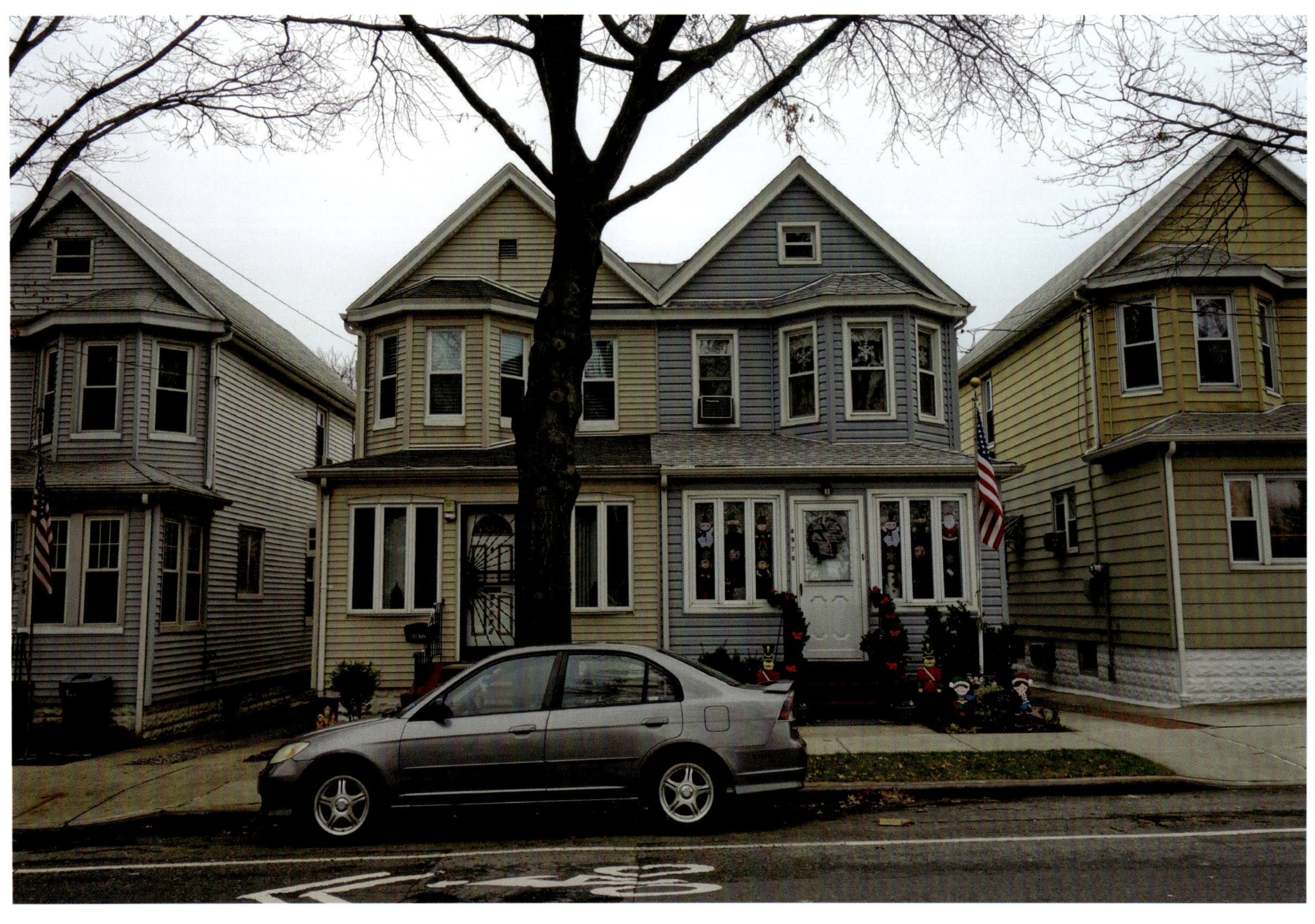

All in the Family, Glendale

The nondescript duplex house on the right was featured in the opening sequence of the popular sitcom *All in the Family*. First aired in 1971, the show starred Carroll O'Connor as Archie Bunker and Jean Stapleton as his long-suffering wife, Edith. From their small house in Queens, they confronted a rapidly changing society beset by the civil rights movement, student protests, inner-city turmoil, and the counterculture. Famously, the Jeffersons, a prosperous Black family, moved into the house next door, forcing Archie Bunker to navigate issues of race, identity, and neighborhood change. Queens was the go-to borough for Manhattan-based television producers and writers who sought to depict workaday American life.

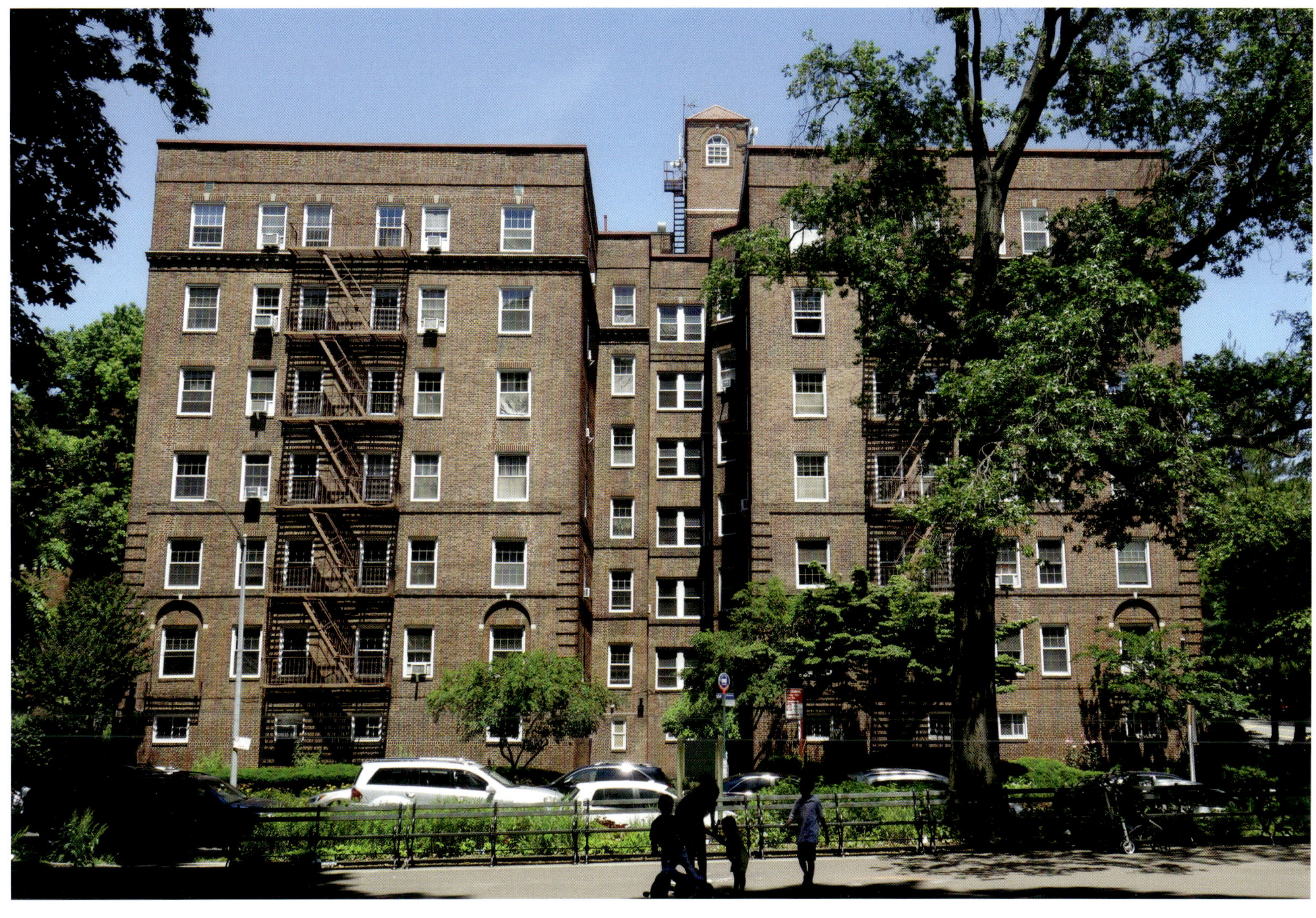

Wallenberg Square, Kew Gardens

Wallenberg Square sits at the northwest corner of Forest Park in Kew Gardens. Built up in the 1920s around Metropolitan Avenue and the Long Island Railroad, the neighborhood expanded rapidly into the 1940s with the extension of the IND subway. Today, Kew Gardens offers a mix of single-family homes, rental apartments, cooperatives, and condominiums. The neighborhood has a large Jewish population comprising older Ashkenazi families from Germany and Poland, many of whom arrived as Holocaust survivors and, more recently, Iranian and Bukharan Jewish immigrants. In this photograph, the Hampton Court co-op, completed in 1936, rises seven stories above the park.

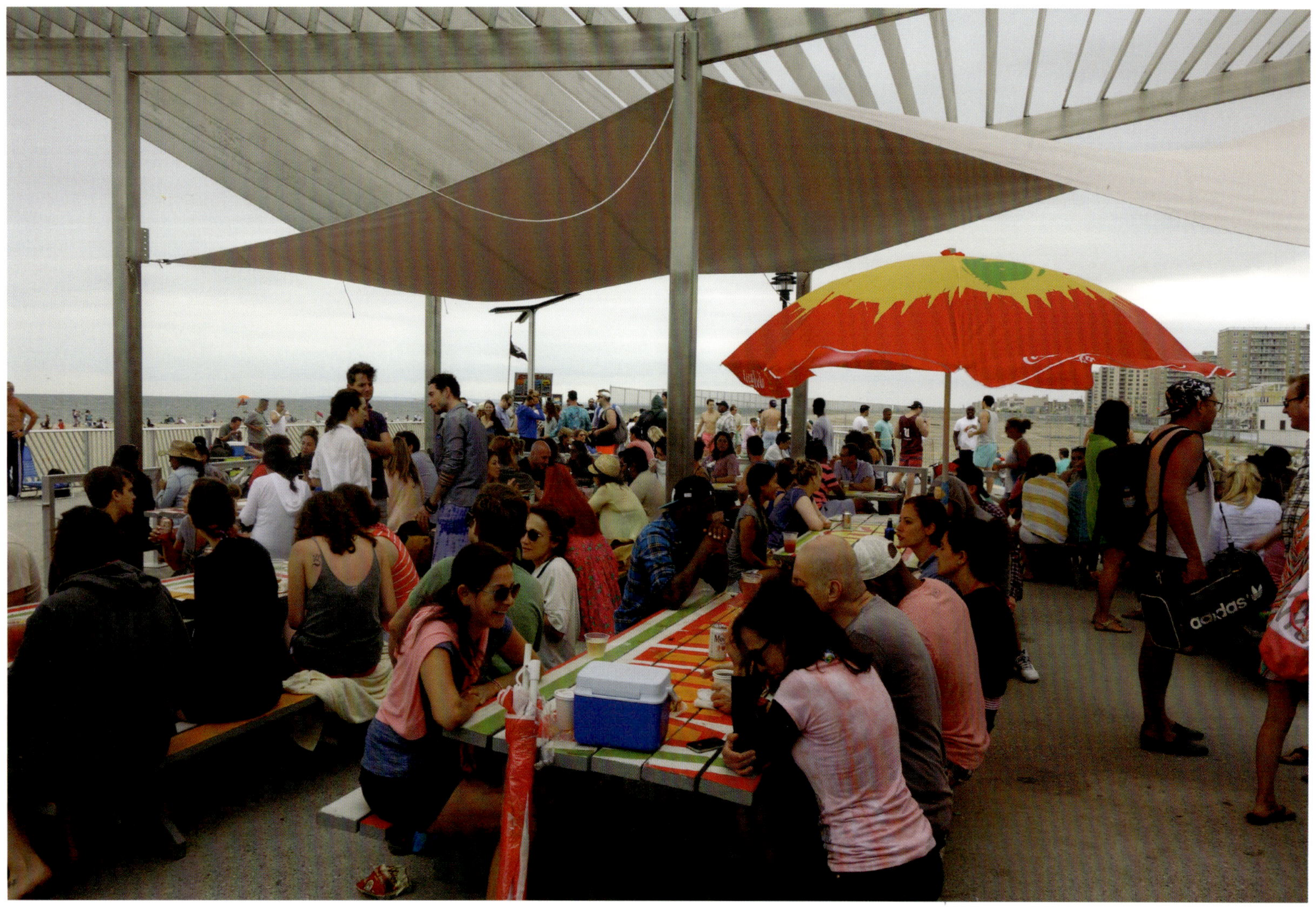

Lunch time at Rockaway Beach

From May to September, Queens residents flock to the beaches along the Rockaway peninsula. Here, a crowd gathers for food and drink under the canopy of the Beach 97th Street pavilion. Some people bring their own food, while others take advantage of food and drink at the concession stands. Several large pavilions are set up at intervals along the five-mile-long boardwalk, interspersed with medical aid stations, surfing schools, playgrounds, skate ramps, and park offices. The beach is served by the A train and the Q53 bus, which travels through Jackson Heights, Elmhurst, Rego Park, Middle Village, Woodhaven, Ozone Park, Howard Beach, and Broad Channel before arriving at Rockaway.

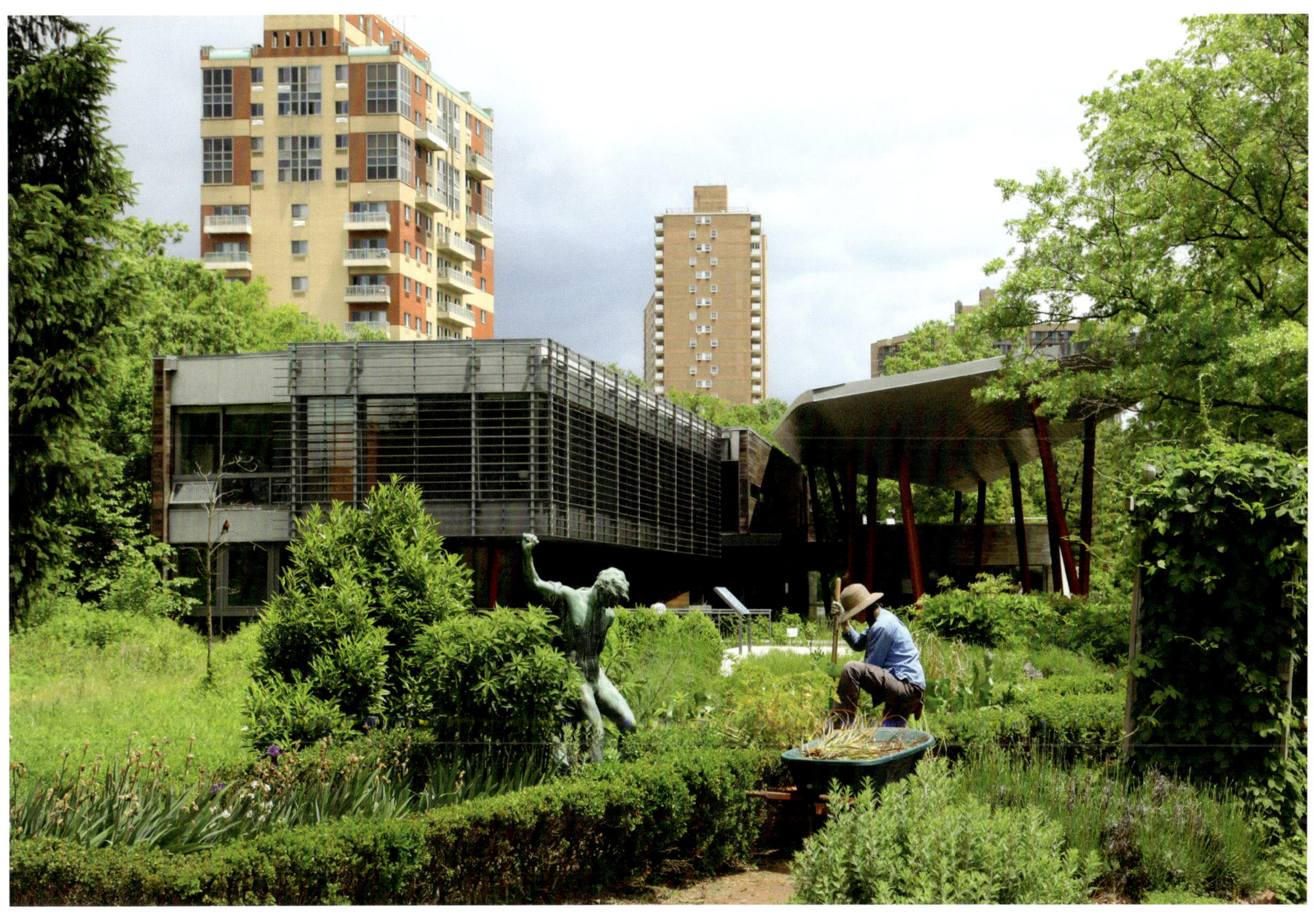

Late spring day at the Queens Botanical Garden, Flushing

A gardener pulls plants from a bed at the Queens Botanical Garden (QBG). The garden was established as a horticultural exhibit for the 1939 World's Fair and moved to its current location to make way for the 1964 World's Fair. In both locations, it sat atop what had once been the city's largest garbage dump. Today, the garden spreads across 40 acres on the southern edge of downtown Flushing. The garden's mission is education for plant and people diversity, and today it serves as one of the key green spaces in the area with 300,000 visitors per year. It is especially well used by the Chinese communities of Flushing, who come here for morning tai chi, walking, floral shows, and other events.

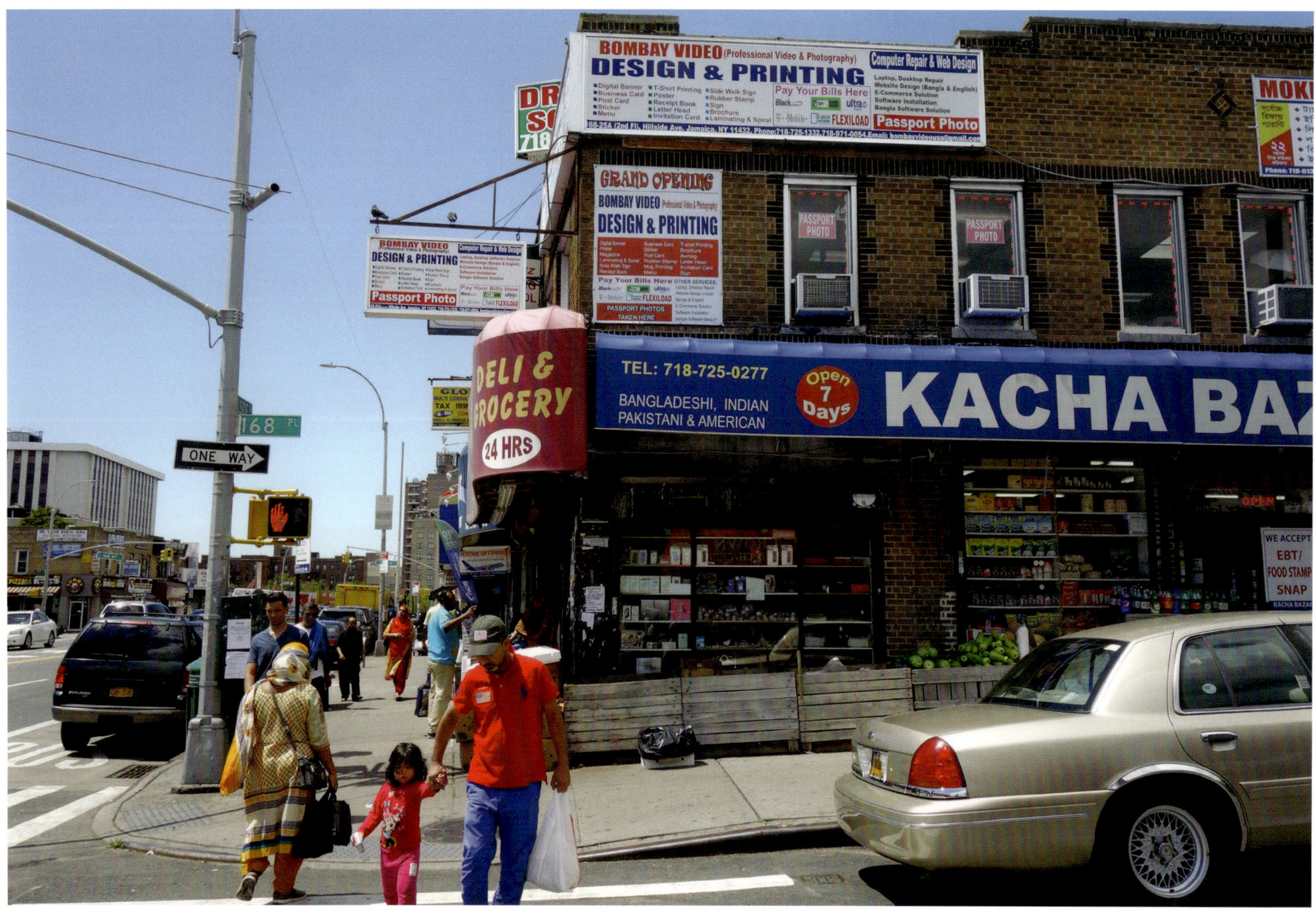

Hillside Avenue

Hillside Avenue is a major commercial thoroughfare serving the largest concentration of South Asian immigrants in the United States. The street stretches twelve miles through the eastern half of Queens and into Long Island's Nassau County. Hillside begins at Myrtle Avenue in Richmond Hill, takes over the Highway 25 designation from Queens Boulevard in Briarwood, and passes through Kew Gardens, Jamaica Hills, Holliswood, and Queens Village. From there, it crosses into Nassau County, where it eventually merges into Jericho Turnpike in Westbury. In the section shown here, the street is lined with South Asian groceries, restaurants, jewelers, sari shops, and other businesses that serve the community.

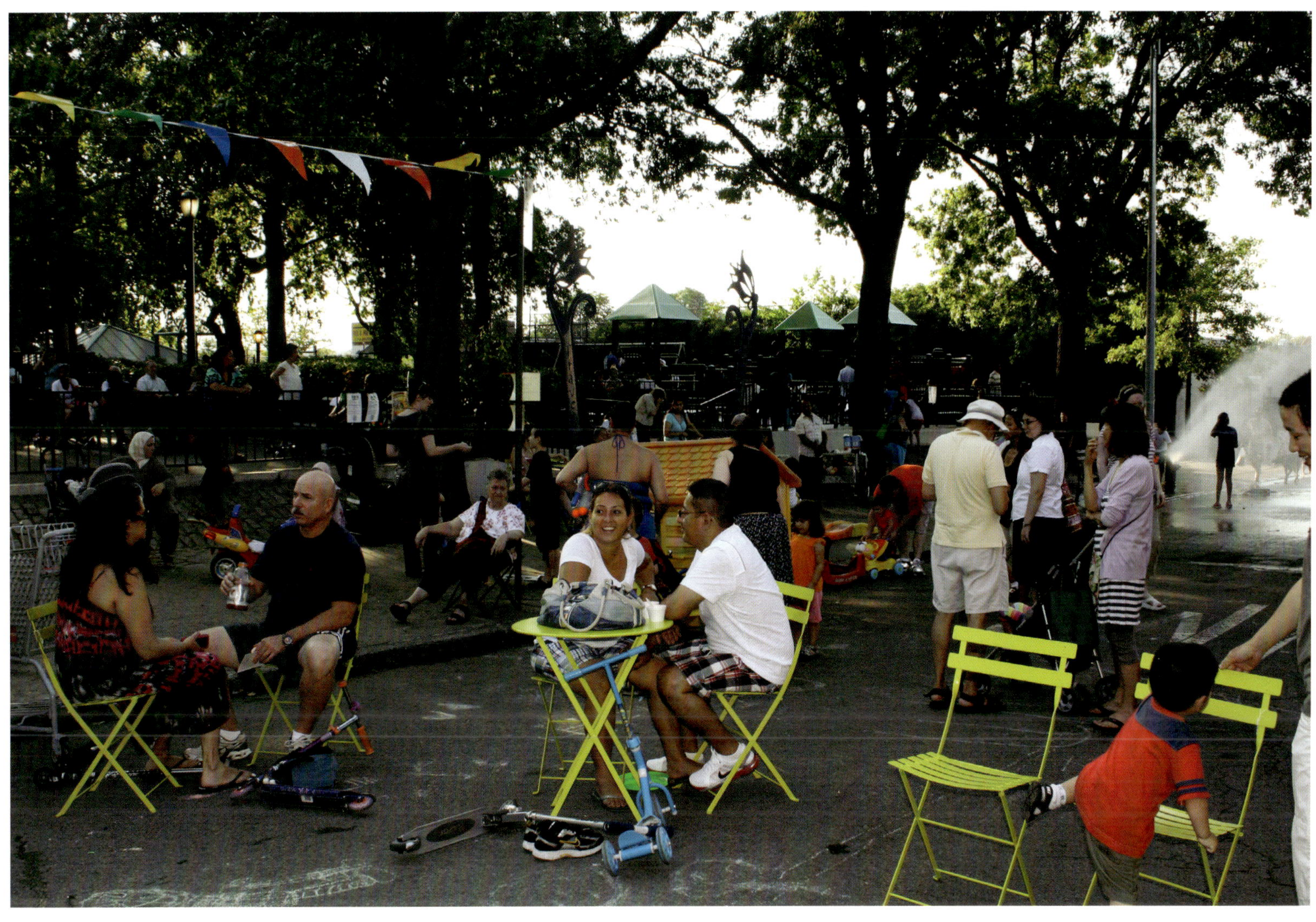

Travers Park, Jackson Heights

Residents of Jackson Heights enjoy tables and chairs set up next to Travers Park along 78th Street, which has been closed off for the summer. In the background, kids play in the water from an open fire hydrant, a quintessential hot weather activity in New York. The city established Travers Park in 1948 to provide much-needed green space for the rapidly increasing population. By the 1980s, however, much of the park had been covered in asphalt to reduce maintenance costs. In 2011, the Department of Transportation began closing off the block of 78th Street, shown here, to expand the park. Finally, the city launched a five-year renovation of the park in 2015, which included permanent closure of 78th Street.

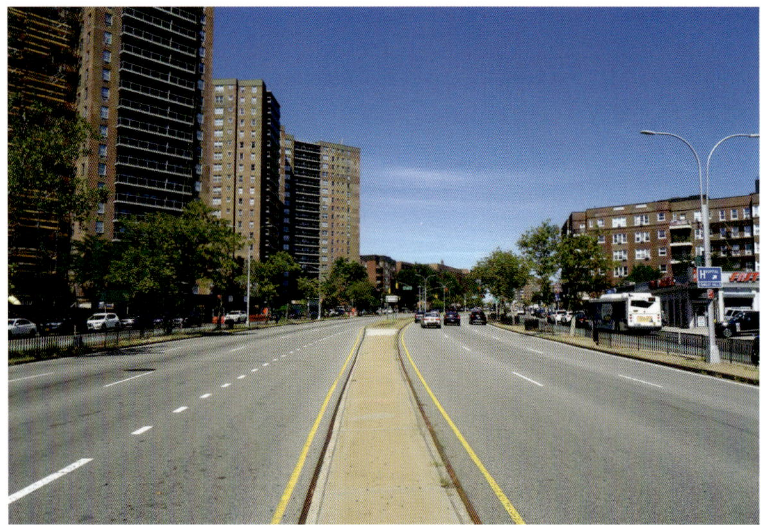

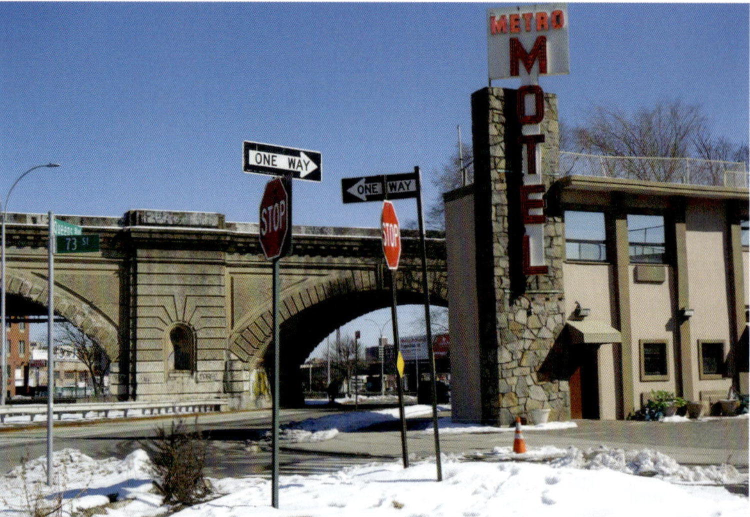

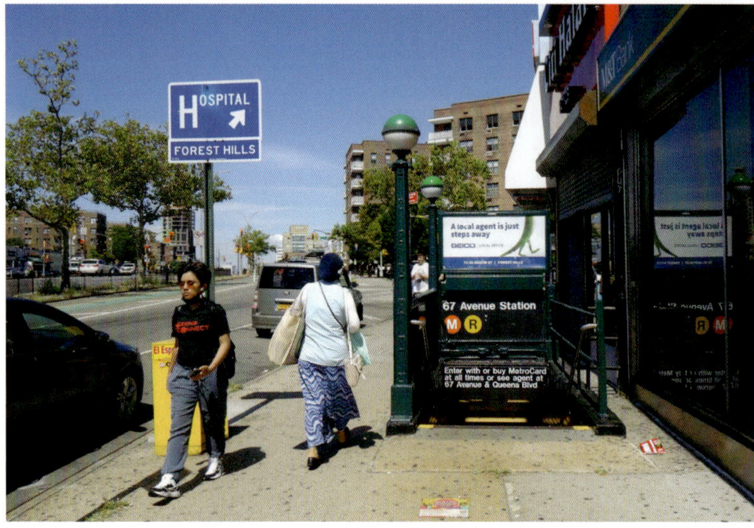

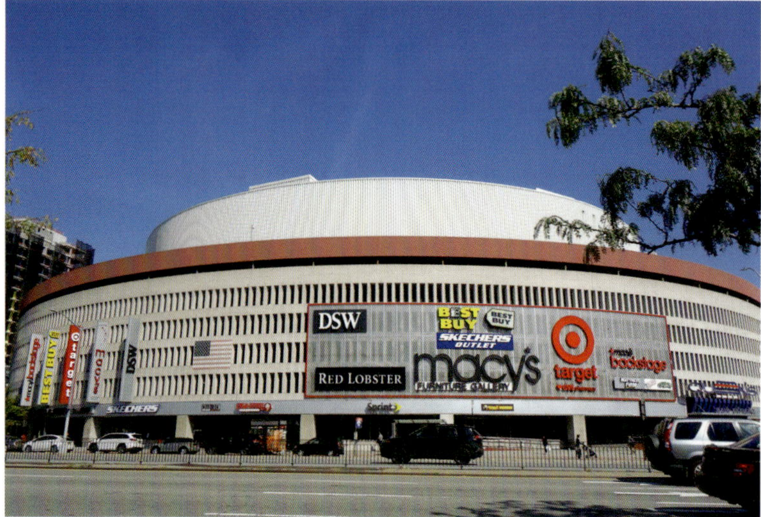

The many moods of Queens Boulevard

Figures 145a–145h. Mighty Queens Boulevard cuts a 200-foot-wide diagonal swath for more than seven miles through the western half of the borough. With its multiple connector streets and grade separations, this corridor functions as a world of its own, with many moods. The boulevard took its current form in the 1920s and 1930s, when a series of roads were connected and expanded with a subway underneath to replace the trolleys. Given its high volume of traffic and legendary hostility toward pedestrians, it is often called the "Boulevard of Death." Still, a wide range of immigrant communities are tied to the boulevard either by residing in nearby towers or operating one of the many hundreds of businesses along its length.

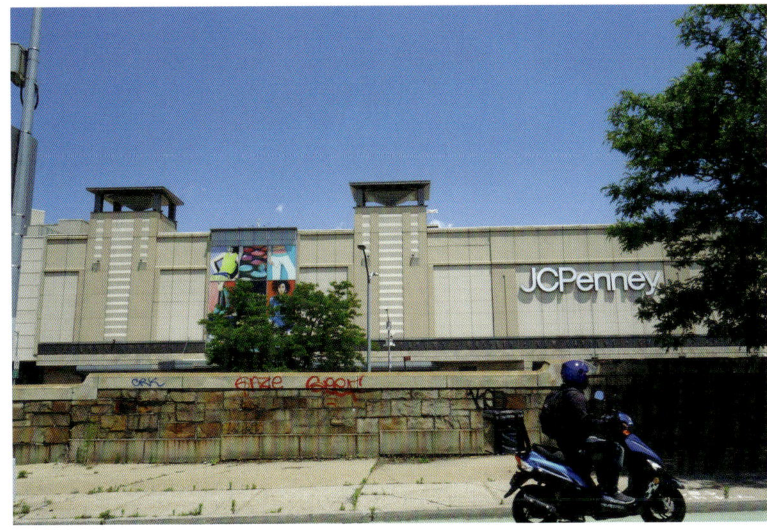

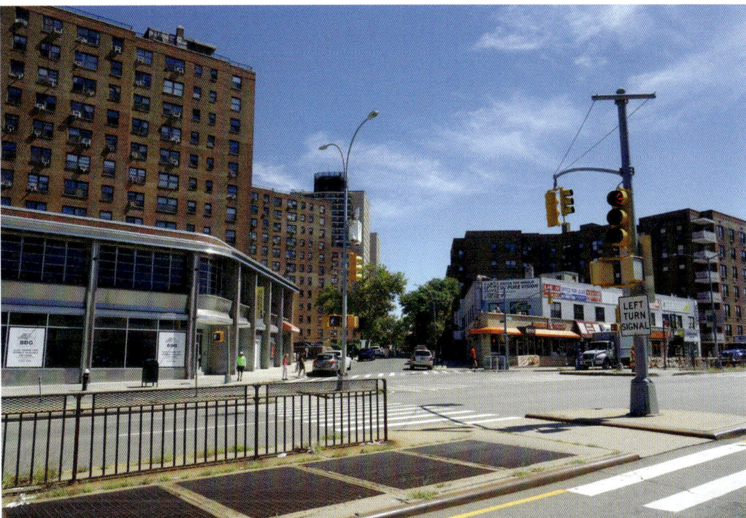

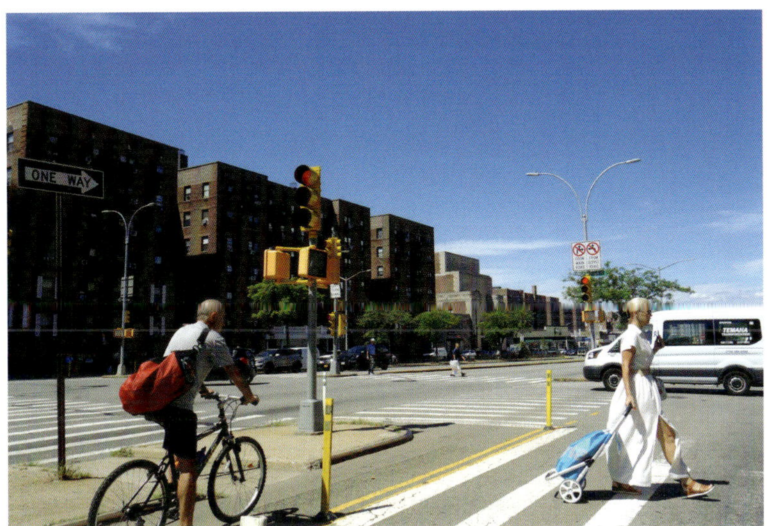

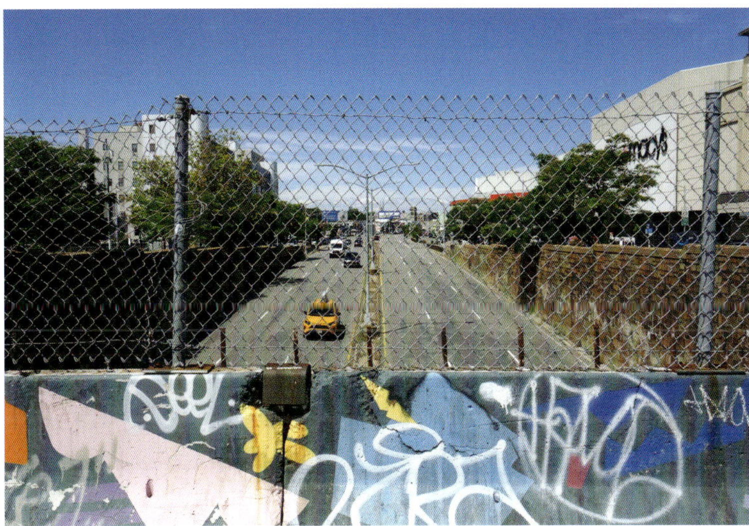

Opposite page, top left: Wide expanse of Queens Boulevard looking west from 69th Road. Top right: Freight rail viaduct and Metro Motel, with rooms by the hour. Bottom left: The 67th Avenue subway station entrance. Bottom right: The immense rotunda of Queens Place Mall, designed by SOM (Skidmore, Owings & Merrill) and completed in 1965 for Macy's, now with several large corporate chain stores. This page, top left: JCPenney, as seen from the Queens Boulevard side access road. Top right: Queens Boulevard at 67th Avenue amid the many high-rise towers of Forest Hills. Bottom left: Pedestrian and cyclist take their chances on the boulevard in Rego Park; bike lanes are only a recent addition. Bottom right: View of Queens Boulevard from the overpass as it dips under Woodhaven Boulevard.

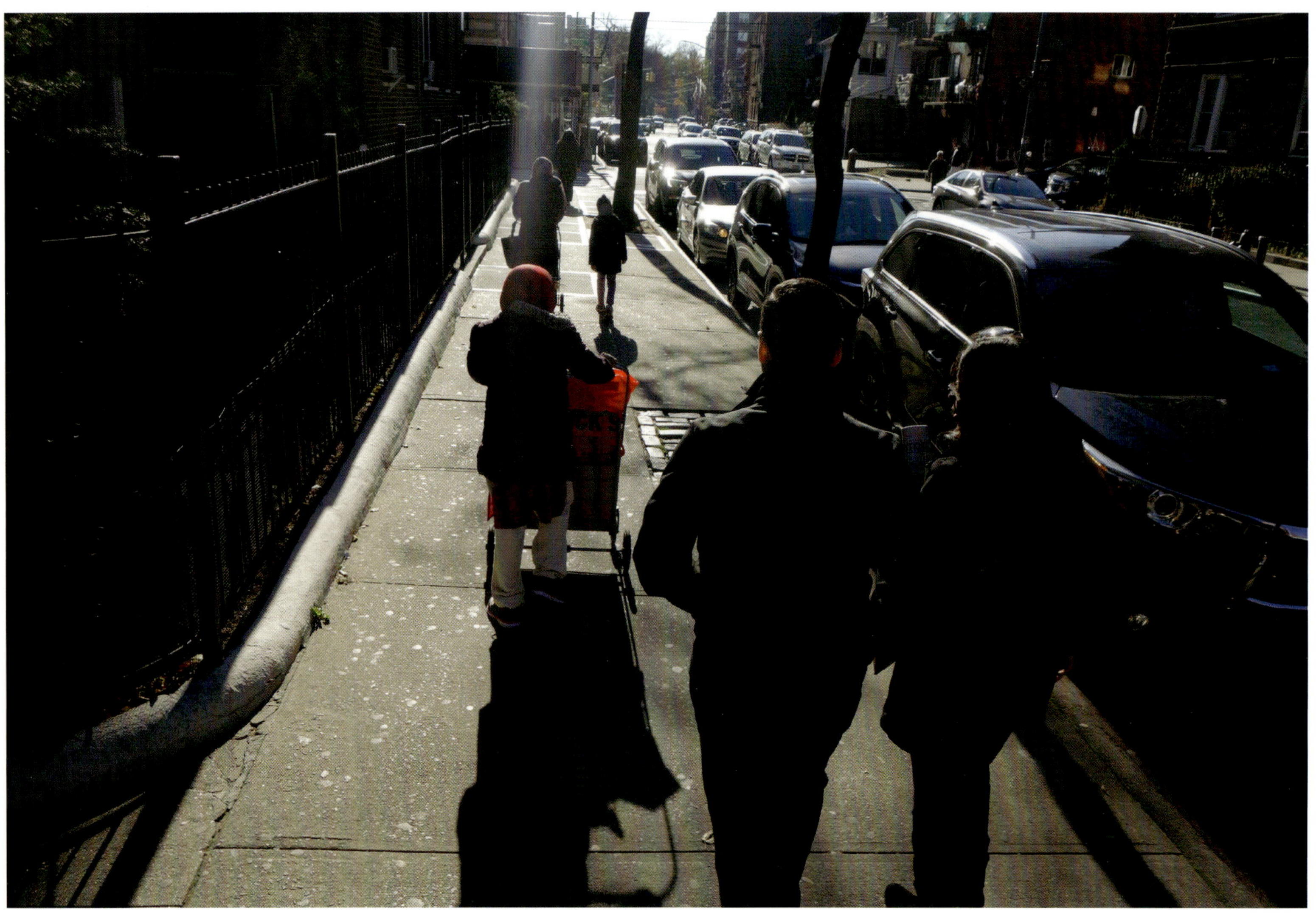

Strolling in Elmhurst

Families walk around Elmhurst on the day after Thanksgiving. Immigrant communities have long embraced Thanksgiving and the Fourth of July as holidays in which they could participate in the nation's rituals of belonging. Elmhurst and Corona, in particular, have large proportions of families with young children living in multigenerational households, so residents can keep their feet in old and new worlds, celebrating U.S. holidays and those from their countries of origin. And for many New Yorkers, escaping small apartments and houses for a post-Thanksgiving dinner walk to the playground or around the neighborhood is a time-honored tradition.

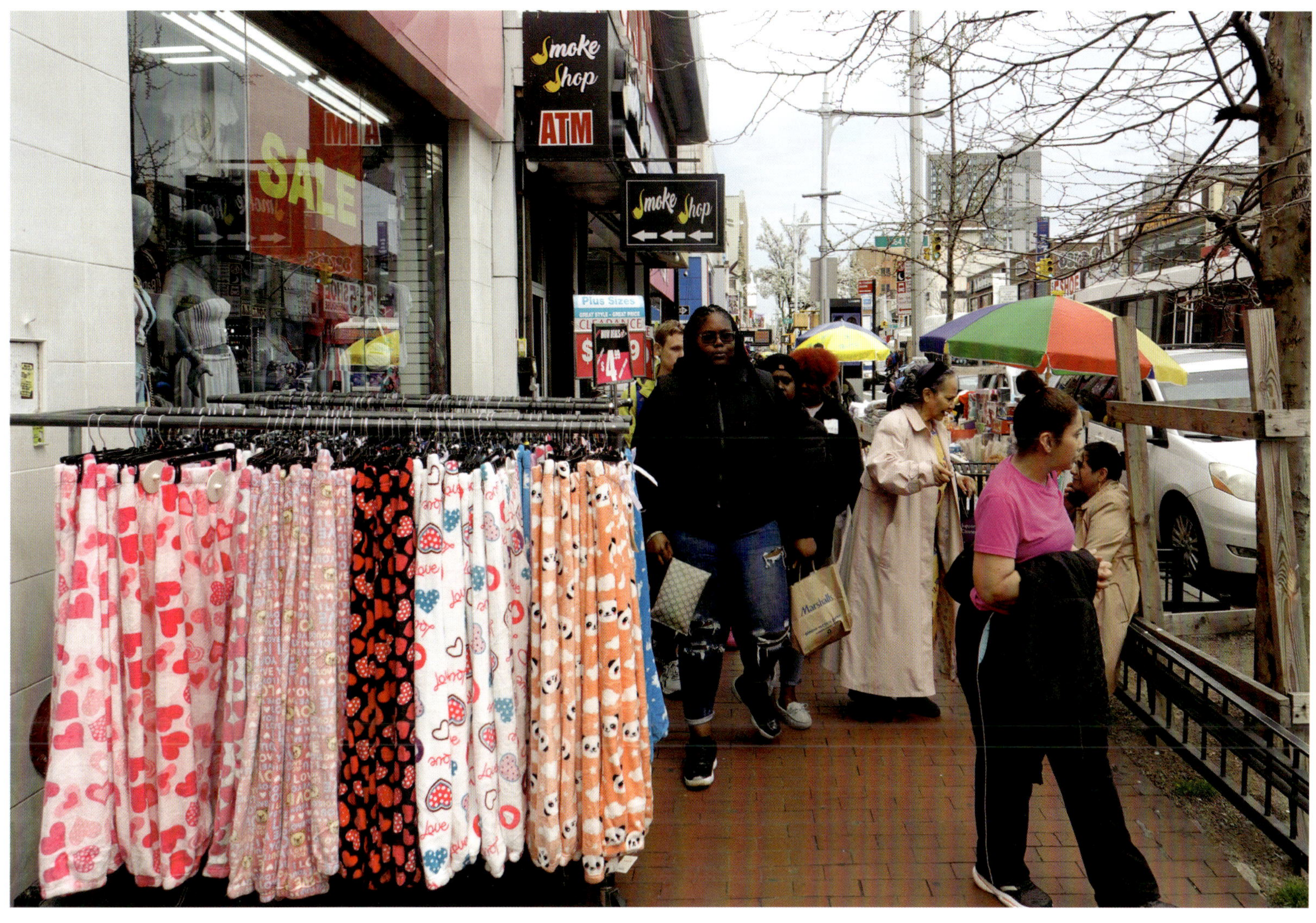

Shops along Jamaica Avenue

While there are hundreds of commercial clusters in Queens, five major hubs are large enough to serve as functional downtowns: Long Island City along Jackson Avenue; Forest Hills along Queens Boulevard and Austin Streets; Steinway Street in Astoria; Main Street in Flushing; and Jamaica Avenue, shown here. The latter has long served as a kind of regional hub of activity for Southeastern Queens. The greatest concentration of shops can be found between Rufus King Park and 170th Streets, a twenty-block collection of clothing stores, restaurants, banks, and electronic shops. Downtown Jamaica also features important civic institutions such as the Supreme Court of Queens County and the Social Security Administration.

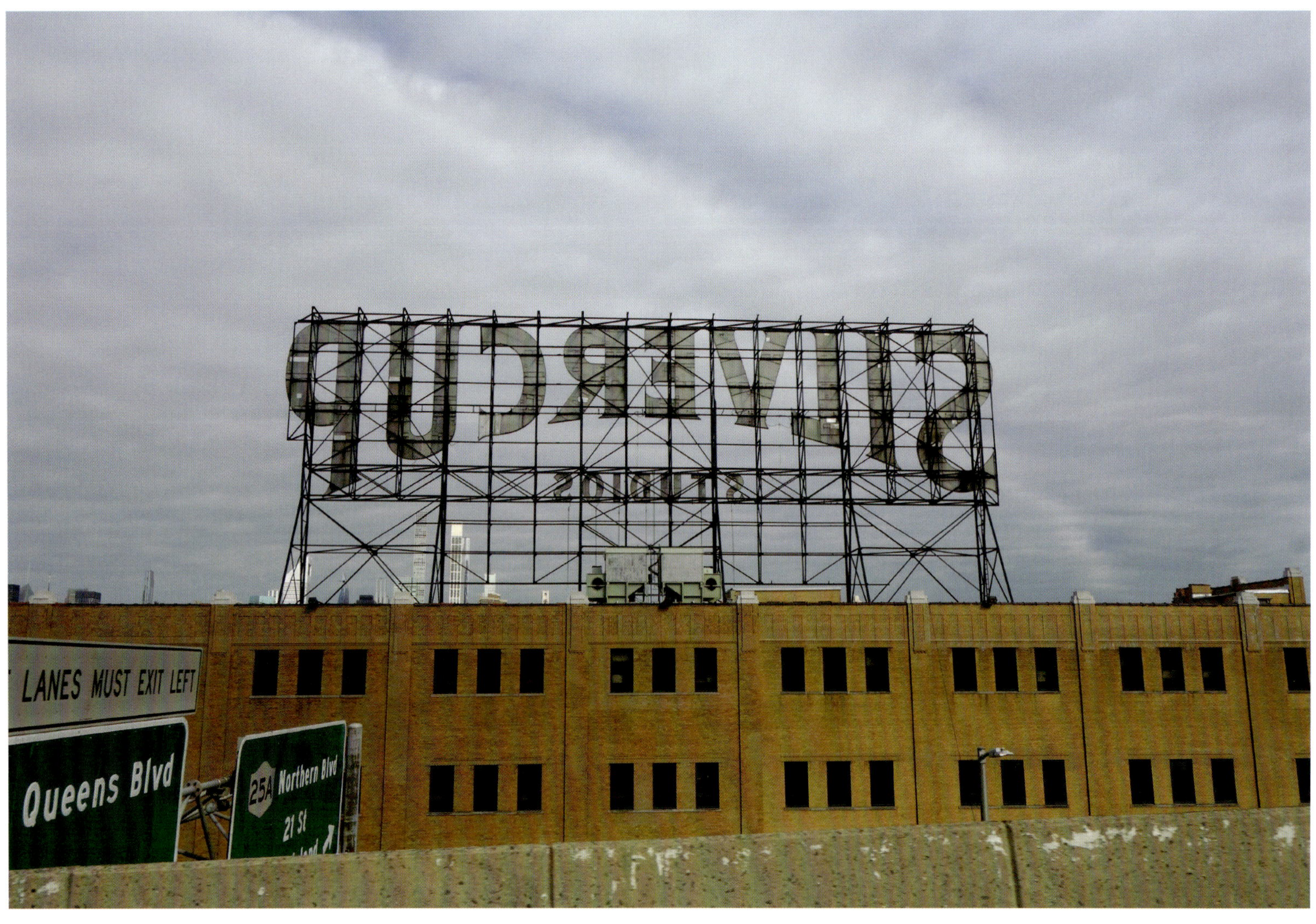

Queens dreaming

Before Hollywood, Queens was the nation's dream factory. In 1920, Adolph Zukor established Astoria Studios to serve his company, Paramount Pictures, with other studios following close behind. Many early silent films, and later "talkies" and television shows, were shot on sound stages in Long Island City and Astoria. Silvercup Studios, founded in 1983, is a relative latecomer, taking its name from the former bakery where it is located. With twenty-three production stages and associated offices, it has provided space for series such as *30 Rock*, *The Sopranos*, *Mad Men*, and *Sex in the City*, as well as films such as *Gangs of New York*, *Krush Groove*, *Meet the Parents*, and *The Devil Wears Prada*.

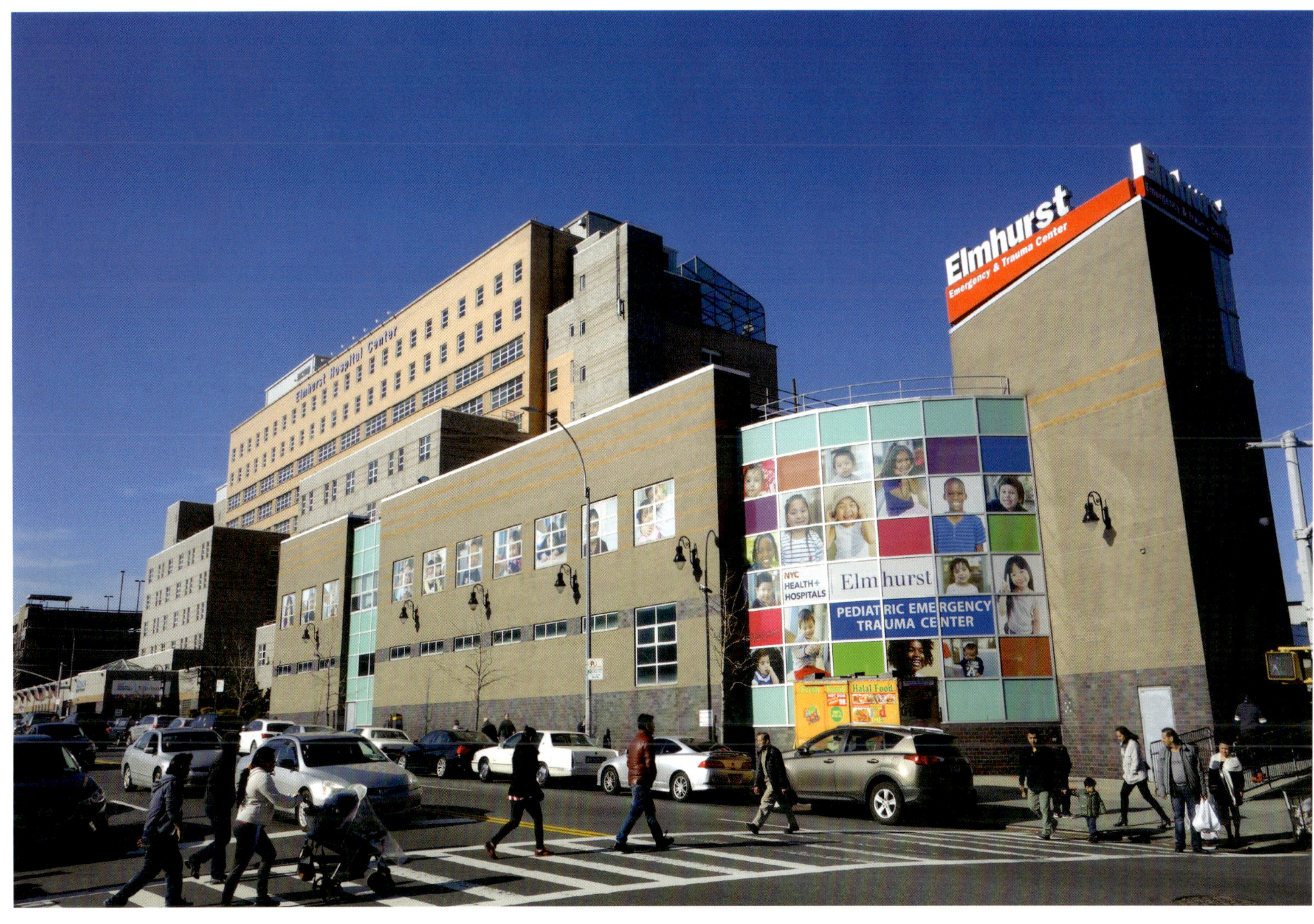

Elmhurst Hospital, Broadway and Baxter Avenue

Elmhurst Hospital is a leading public anchor institution and major employer in Northwestern Queens. Established in 1957 and extensively renovated in the 1990s, the hospital has more than five hundred beds and employs around four thousand staff. In the 1970s, the hospital became nationally noted for creating a "language bank" of interpreters speaking some two dozen languages to care for the rapidly diversifying population. The hospital estimates that residents in the catchment area speak more than one hundred languages, and bring a wide range of cultural practices regarding health and healing. For many weeks in 2020, Elmhurst Hospital was the global epicenter of the COVID-19 pandemic.

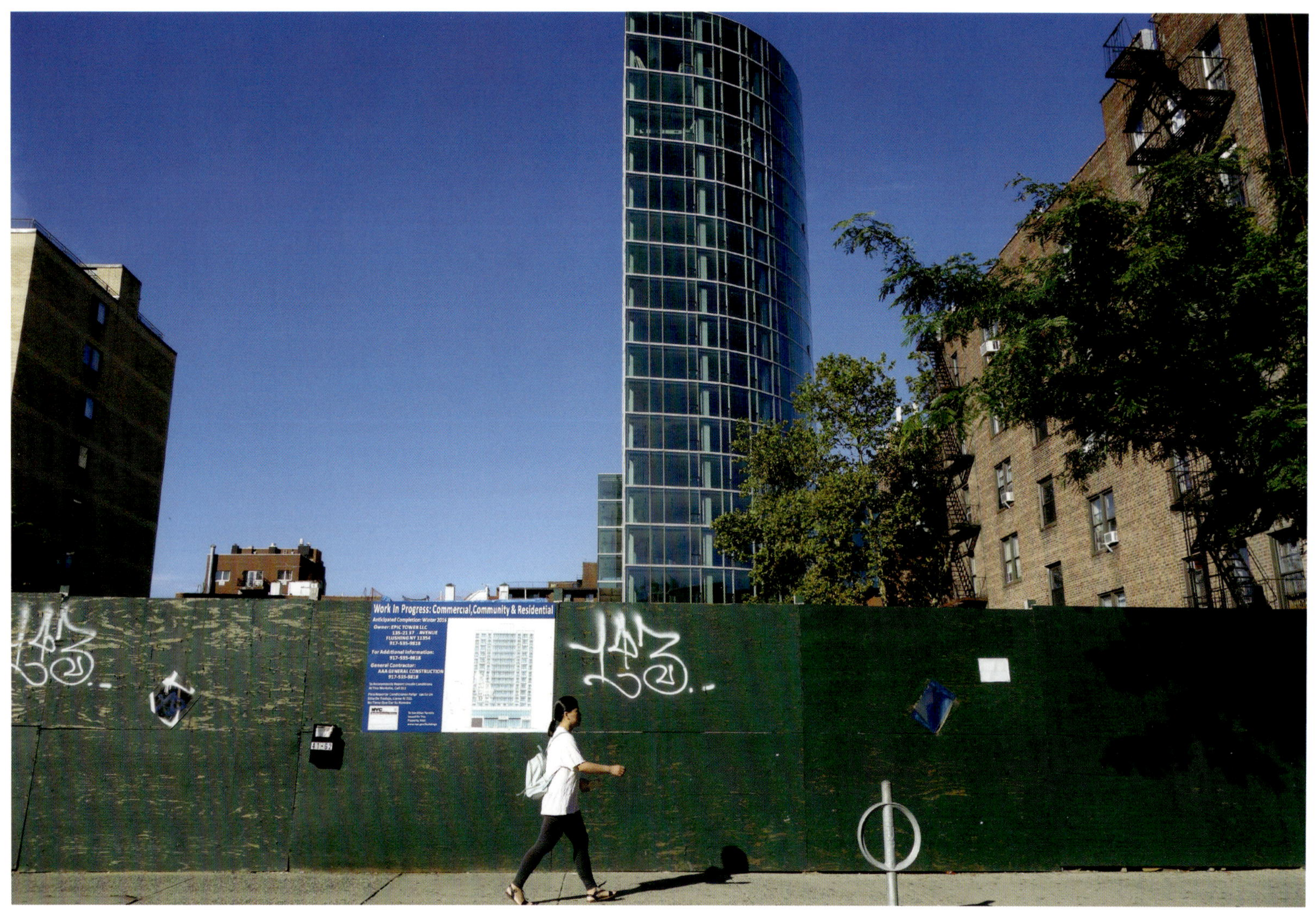

Transforming the borough

Gentrification is a big concern among residents of Queens. Not only do they fear rising rents and property taxes, they also worry about how higher costs and new land uses will transform the borough's character. With immense amounts of cash crashing around the global economy, developers have launched a spate of large building projects, many of which function as investments rather than primary residences for the owners. The luxury tower shown here is just one of dozens currently under construction in Flushing, Long Island City, Astoria, and along Queens Boulevard. Families worry that their children will no longer be able to afford to live in the borough or in New York City, period.

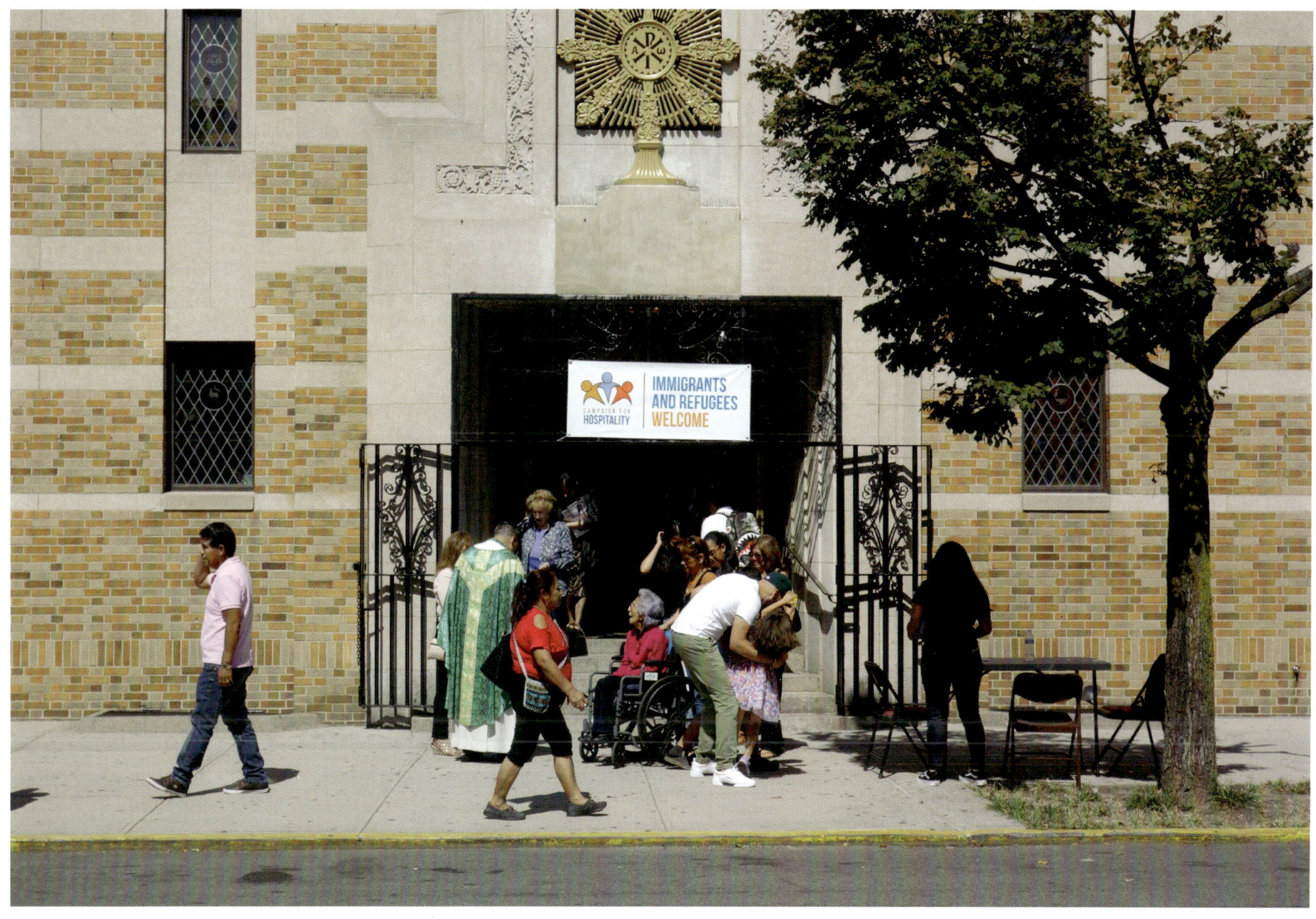

Immigrants and refugees welcome, Jackson Heights

The sign above the entrance to the Blessed Sacrament Church extends hospitality to newcomers, regardless of their place of origin or citizenship status. As families continue to move to Queens from all around the world, civic and religious institutions, neighborhood groups, and nonprofit services work to accommodate them in their new and unfamiliar surroundings. Political and religious leaders have been outspoken in their support of immigrants and opposition to deportation and other harsh federal policies. This sphere of care for vulnerable people, who often arrive in precarious situations, is a central feature of the borough's character and essential to its future as a lodestar for a plural world.

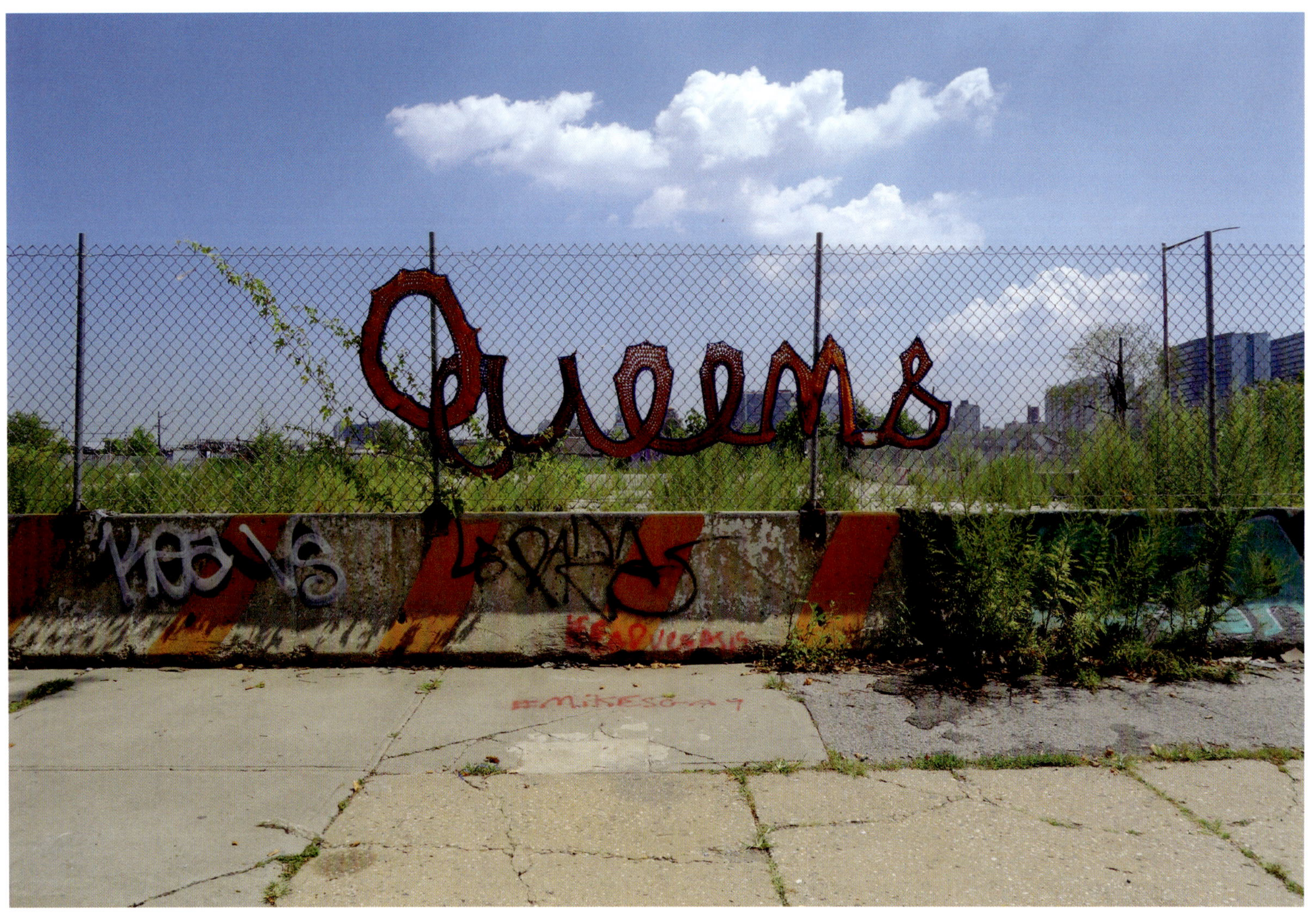

Fence installation, artist unknown, Willets Point

Someone, probably a mechanic from one of the nearby chop shops or a street crew worker, fabricated this sign from orange mesh construction fencing and mounted it to the chain link. The fence surrounds Willets Point, a district of automobile body and engine repair shops demolished and cleared by the city in 2020 to make room for new housing development. The sign could be read in two ways: as a celebration of Queens as a place or as a harbinger of things to come, as working-class landscapes cede to luxury development. In any case, this work of everyday art, making do with materials close at hand, is wonderfully indicative of the creativity and dreams brought to Queens by people from across the world.

Acknowledgments

I could never have undertaken a project of this scope without the support of friends, family, and colleagues. My mother, Jackie Heathcott, instilled in me the determination required for this undertaking, and my father, David Heathcott, was my first photography teacher. Tom and Sharyn Cruce, my parents-in-law, have been generous and encouraging in all things. But I have Ashley Cruce to thank, more than anyone, for making this project what it is. She has been a constant collaborator and sounding board, frequently accompanying me on long jags around the borough's many neighborhoods. I cannot count the number of times I have relied on her superior navigational skills and her thorough knowledge of the tangled map of Queens—the optimal routes, the shortcuts, the back ways, the times of day to avoid this or that thoroughfare. Her background in anthropology and social work makes her as curious about our chosen home as I am, and her work as an environmental educator takes her to schools, nursing homes, gardens, and community centers across the borough. I have learned more about Queens from her than from any other source.

The project also benefited from a network of friends, neighbors, and colleagues who share my fascination with Queens. Some were born and raised here but live elsewhere today, some live here now but were born elsewhere, and some never left. Whether through long conversations, casual exchanges, or even short social media posts, I have gained a great deal of insight from Noah Allison, Edwin Berrios, Casey Blake, Nick Bloom, Carole De Santis, Jeff Donnelly, Jenny Dubnau, Krystyna Grzelak, Rafael Herrin-Ferri, Esneider Huasipungo, Jeff Hou, Hitomi Iwasaki, Veronica Lawlor, Steve Moga, Judy Newland, Angel Nieves, Prerana Reddy, Quilian Riano, Brian Rosa, Arturo Sánchez, Joy Seaton, Sarah Steen, McKenzie Wark, Neil Weisenfeld, and Mia White.

I have been fortunate to have had scholarly and institutional support along the way. The project received a generous publication grant from the Zolberg Institute on Migration and Mobility at The New School, and a David R. Coffin Publication Grant from the Center for Landscape Studies at the University of Virginia. Research assistants Daniel Chu, Veronica Olivotto, and Molly Simpson provided help at critical points along the way, organizing material, chasing down sources, and checking facts. My friend and colleague Miodrag Mitrasinovic conducted a series of public space studios in Corona that have been most instructive, and I have learned substantially from the work of Alex Aleinikoff, Ruby Danta, Tarry Hum, Philip Kasinitz, Janet Lieberman, Richard Lieberman,

John Mollenkopf, and Milagros Ricourt. And, of course, this book would not have been possible without the commitment of Fred Nachbaur at Fordham University Press, who has been a wonderful editor and collaborator.

Above all, it is to the people of Queens that I owe the greatest debt. I am immensely grateful to everyone who shared their thoughts, insights, and experiences with me over the years, usually while standing on a sidewalk or waiting for a bus, sitting on a park bench, or hanging out at a diner. And I am especially grateful to the first responders and essential workers who kept us going through the worst months of the pandemic. The trajectory of COVID-19 through Queens exposed the inequality, precarity, and injustice experienced by many immigrant families, undocumented workers, and communities of color. I dearly hope that this book will show the world what an extraordinary place these communities have made here.

Notes

1 For a detailed study of Queens vernacular architecture, see Rafael Herrin-Ferri's superb book, *All the Queens Houses: An Architectural Portrait of New York's Largest and Most Diverse Borough* (Berlin: Jovis, 2021). Portions of this introduction appear in my introduction to Herrin-Ferri's book.

2 Citizenship is only one dimension of human belonging, but a highly salient one for immigrant families struggling to secure homes and livelihoods in a mobile world. See Partha Chatterjee, *The Politics of the Governed: Reflections on Popular Politics in Most of the World* (New York: Columbia University Press, 2004); Patrick Le Galés, *European Cities: Social Conflicts and Governance* (New York: Oxford University Press, 2002); James Holston, ed., *Cities and Citizenship* (Durham, NC: Duke University Press, 1998); Jonathan Darling and Harald Bauder, eds., *Sanctuary Cities and Urban Struggles: Rescaling Migration, Citizenship, and Rights* (Manchester: Manchester University Press, 2019).

3 I am indebted to many scholars of cities and everyday life, especially John Chase, Margaret Crawford, and John Kaliski, *Everyday Urbanism* (New York: Monacelli Press, 2008); Tim Cresswell, *Place: An Introduction* (Chichester, UK: Wiley-Blackwell, 2014); Michel de Certeau, *The Practice of Everyday Life* (Berkeley: University of California Press, 2011); Paul Groth and Todd W. Bressi, eds., *Understanding Ordinary Landscapes* (New Haven, CT: Yale University Press, 1997); Suzanne Hall, *City, Street, and Citizen: The Measure of the Ordinary* (London: Routledge, 2012).

4 Rebecca Solnit and Joshua Jelly-Schapiro, *Nonstop Metropolis: A New York City Atlas* (Oakland, CA: University of California Press, 2016).

5 Ross Perlin et al., "Mapping Urban Linguistic Diversity in New York City: Motives, Methods, Tools, and Outcomes," *Language Documentation and Conservation* 15 (October 2021): 458–490.

6 Fred J. Gitner and Stuart A. Rosenthal, "Reaching Immigrant Populations: Serving the Culturally and Linguistically Diverse, the Queens Library Model," *BiD: Textos Universitaris de Biblioteconomia i Documentació* 21 (2008).

7 *Coming to America*, directed by John Landis, Paramount Pictures, 1988, 00:24:45, https://www.netflix.com/ls/title/391018.

8 "Street Numbering System in Queens, NY," *The American City* 39 (December 1928): 191.

9 Richard Weir, "Neighborhood Reports: Queens Up Close," *New York Times*, August 23, 1998, Section 14, p. 9.

10 Daniel C. Kramer and Richard M. Flanagan, *Staten Island: Conservative Bastion in a Liberal City* (Lanham, MD: University Press of America, 2012).

11 John A. Strong, *The Algonquian Peoples of Long Island from Earliest Times to 1700* (Interlaken: Heart of the Lakes, 1997).

12 Peter Ross, *A History of Long Island: From Its Earliest Settlement to the Present Time* (Lewis Publishing Company, 1902), 522–523.

13 Joyce Goodfriend, *Before the Melting Pot: Society and Culture in Colonial New York, 1664–1730* (Princeton, NJ: Princeton University Press, 1992); John Strong, "The Thirteen Tribes of Long Island: The History of a Myth," *The Hudson Valley Regional Review* 9, no. 2 (1992).

14 On the use of enslaved Black labor in Queens County, see Ross, *History of Long Island*, 120–138; Richard Shannon Moss, *Slavery on Long Island: A Study in Local Institutional and Early African-American Communal Life* (New York: Garland, 1993).

15 R. Scott Hanson and Martin E. Marty, *City of Gods: Religious Freedom, Immigration, and Pluralism in Flushing, Queens* (New York: Empire State Editions, 2016).

16 Roderic Blackburn, "Transforming Old World Dutch Culture in a New World Environment: Processes of Material Adaptation," in *New World Dutch Studies: Dutch Arts and Culture in Colonial America, 1609–1776* (Albany: State University of New York Press, 1987), 95–98.

17 Platting details gleaned from F. W. Beers, *Newtown, Queens Co. L.I.* (New York: Beers, Comstock and Cline, 1873).

18 Chamber of Commerce of Queens, *Queens Borough, New York City, 1910–1920* (New York: L. I. Star Pub. Co., 1920), 119.

19 Owen Gutfreund, "Rebuilding New York in the Auto Age: Robert Moses and His Highways," in Hilary Ballon and Kenneth Jackson, eds., *Robert Moses and the Modern City: The Transformation of New York* (New York: Wiley, 2007).

20 Jeffrey A. Kroessler, *Building Queens: The Urbanization of New York's Largest Borough* (New York: City University of New York, 1991). See also Jon A. Peterson, ed., *A Research Guide to the History of the Borough of Queens and Its Neighborhoods* (New York: Dept. of History, Queens College, The City University of New York, 1983).

21 Chamber of Commerce, p. 134.

22 Adam Tanaka, "Fiduciary Landlords: Life Insurers and Large-Scale Housing in New York City," Joint Center for Housing Studies, Working Paper, Cambridge, MA: Harvard University (April 2017), 9–17.

23 Richard Plunz, *A History of Housing in New York City* (New York: Columbia University Press, 1990), 130–131, 167–170.

24 Plunz, *History of Housing*, 131.

25 Chamber of Commerce, 124, 126.

26 David Gebhard, "The American Colonial Revival in the 1930s," *Winterthur Portfolio* 22, no. 2–3 (1987); Jan Jennings, "Cheap and Tasteful Dwellings in Popular Architecture," *Perspectives in Vernacular Architecture, Vol. 5, Gender, Class, and Shelter* (1995).

27 Jesse Kling, "Solid Brick Homes: The Continuing Row House Tradition of Postwar Brooklyn and Queens," (M.A. Thesis, Columbia University, 2022).

28 Steven Gregory, *Black Corona: Race and the Politics of Place in an Urban Community* (Princeton, NJ: Princeton University Press, 1998), 22–26.

29 Janet Lieberman and Richard K. Lieberman, *City Limits: A Social History of Queens* (Dubuque, Iowa: Kendall Hunt, 1983).

30 John P. Dean, "Only Caucasian: A Study of Race Covenants," *The Journal of Land and Public Utility Economics* 23, no. 4 (1949): 429–431.

31 Miyares, 481–482.

32 Joseph Lelyveld, "School Busing Put to Queens Test," *New York Times*, September 11, 1970; Thomas J. Sugrue, *Sweet Land of Liberty: The Forgotten Struggle for Civil Rights in the North* (New York: Random House, 2009), 313–315; Bill Moyers, *Rosedale: The Way It Is*, New York: Public Broadcasting Service, 58 minutes, 1976; Alphonso Pinkney, *Lest We Forget, White Hate Crimes: Howard Beach and Other Racial Atrocities* (New York: Third World Press, 1994).

33 Sylvie Murray, *The Progressive Housewife: Community Activism in Suburban Queens, 1945–1965* (Philadelphia: University of Pennsylvania Press, 2003), 21–27, 38–45.

34 Sam Roberts, "Black Income Surpasses White in Queens," *New York Times*, October 1, 2006.

35 Richard Alba and Steven Romaleski, *The End of Segregation? Hardly* (New York: Center for Urban Research, CUNY, 2012); John Logan, *Ethnic Diversity Grows, Neighborhood Integration Lags Behind* (Lewis Mumford Center, University at Albany, 2001), 7–10.

36 Keyi Xu, "Asian Ethnic Entrepreneurship in New York: A Case Study of Chinese and Korean Small Businesses in Flushing, Queens," (M.A. Thesis, Department of Geography, State University of New York at Binghamton, 2011).

37 Philip Kasinitz, Mohamad Bazzi, and Randal Doane, "Chapter 8: Jackson Heights, New York," *Cityscape* 4, no. 2 (1998): 165.

38 Peter Lobo, "The Impact of Immigration on New York City," Center for Migration Studies Special Issues 22, no. 1 (2009): 79–81.

39 Milagros Ricourt and Ruby Danta, *Hispanas de Queens: Latino Panethnicity in a New York City Neighborhood* (Ithaca, NY: Cornell University Press, 2002).

40 Evan Joseph Rapport, "The Musical Repertoire of Bukharian Jews in Queens, New York," (Ph.D. diss., City University of New York, 2006); Lawrence Cappello, "Gentrification in Northern Queens? Demographic and Socioeconomic Transformations in Jackson Heights and Corona, 1990–2016," (Center for Latin American, Caribbean and Latino Studies at the CUNY Graduate Center, June 1, 2018).

41 Brendan McGovern and John W. Frazier, "Evolving Ethnic Settlements in Queens: Historical and Current Forces Reshaping Human Geography," *Focus on Geography* 58, no. 1 (2015).

42 Nancy Foner and Rita James Simon, "Benefits and Burdens: Immigrant Women and Work in New York City," in *Immigrant Women* (New York: Routledge, 2001); Shaolu Yu, "'I Am Like a Deaf, Dumb, and Blind Person': Mobility and Immobility of Chinese (Im)Migrants in Flushing, Queens, New York City," *Journal of Transport Geography* 54 (June 1, 2016): 10–21; Yuval Elmelech, "Housing Inequality in New York City: Racial and Ethnic Disparities in Homeownership and Shelter-Cost Burden," *Housing, Theory and Society* 21, no. 4 (December 1, 2004): 163–175; Lynn McCormick, "The Restructuring of Manufacturing in Queens and Its Impact on Immigrant Workers," in *Immigrant Crossroads: Globalization, Incorporation, and Placemaking in Queens, New York*, ed. Tarry Hum et al. (Philadelphia: Temple University Press, 2021).

43 These figures culled from Astrid Rodríguez, "Demographic, Economic, and Social Transformations in Queens Community District 3: East Elmhurst, Jackson Heights, and North Corona, 1990–2006," (Center for Latin American, Caribbean and Latino Studies at the CUNY Graduate Center, 2008), 8–10.

44 Richard Cimino and Hans Tokke, "Super-Diversity Inside and Outside of Congregations in Elmhurst, Queens," in *The Routledge Handbook of Religion and Cities* (New York: Routledge, 2020).

45 Thea Michailides, "Performing Panethnicity: South Asian Women's Community Leadership in Jackson Heights," (M.A., Sarah Lawrence College, 2011).

46 Madhulika S. Khandelwal, "Indian Immigrants in Queens, New York City: Patterns of Spatial Concentration and Distribution, 1965–1990," in *Nation and Migration: The Politics of Space in the South Asian Diaspora* (Philadelphia: University of Pennsylvania Press, 2016), 178–180.

47 I have many debts when it comes to the development of my work as a scholar and practitioner of photography. A short list would include Peter Bacon Hales, *Silver Cities: Photographing American Urbanization, 1839–1939,* Revised and Expanded Edition (Albuquerque: University of New Mexico Press, 2006); Allan Sekula, *Photography Against the Grain* (London: Mack Books, 2016); Shawn Michelle Smith, *Photography on the Color Line: W. E. B. Du Bois, Race,*

and Visual Culture (Durham, NC: Duke University Press Books, 2004); Camilo Jose Vergara, *The New American Ghetto* (New Brunswick, NJ: Rutgers University Press, 1995); Ine Gevers et al., *Documentary Now! Contemporary Strategies in Photography, Film, and the Visual Arts* (New York: NAi Publishers, 2005); Richard Bolton, *Contest of Meaning: Critical Histories of Photography* (Cambridge, MA: MIT Press, 1989).

48 See important work on the White, Male Gaze by Savannah Dodd and Andrew Jackson, "The Impact of the White, Male Gaze," *Trigger* (blog), June 3, 2020, https://www.fomu.be/trigger/articles/the-impact-of-the-white-male-gaze; Viê.t Lê and Michelle Dizon, *White Gaze* (Chicago: Candor Arts, 2018).

Joseph Heathcott is a writer, photographer, and educator based in New York, where he teaches at The New School. His work has appeared in a wide range of venues, including books, academic journals, magazines, exhibits, and juried art shows. His most recent books include *Urban Infrastructure: Historical and Social Dimensions of an Interconnected World*; *The Routledge Handbook on Infrastructure Designs: Global Views from Architectural History*; and *Capturing the City: Photographs from the Streets of St. Louis, 1900–1930.*

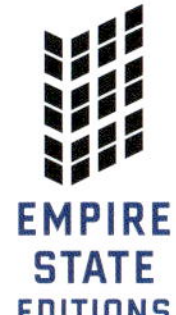

Select titles from Empire State Editions

Daniel Campo, *The Accidental Playground: Brooklyn Waterfront Narratives of the Undesigned and Unplanned*

John Waldman, *Heartbeats in the Muck: The History, Sea Life, and Environment of New York Harbor, Revised Edition*

John Waldman (ed.), *Still the Same Hawk: Reflections on Nature and New York*

Joseph B. Raskin, *The Routes Not Taken: A Trip Through New York City's Unbuilt Subway System*

Phillip Deery, *Red Apple: Communism and McCarthyism in Cold War New York*

North Brother Island: The Last Unknown Place in New York City. Photographs by Christopher Payne, A History by Randall Mason, Essay by Robert Sullivan

Stephen Miller, *Walking New York: Reflections of American Writers from Walt Whitman to Teju Cole*

Tom Glynn, *Reading Publics: New York City's Public Libraries, 1754–1911*

R. Scott Hanson, *City of Gods: Religious Freedom, Immigration, and Pluralism in Flushing, Queens*. Foreword by Martin E. Marty

Dorothy Day and the Catholic Worker: The Miracle of Our Continuance. Edited, with an Introduction and Additional Text by Kate Hennessy, Photographs by Vivian Cherry, Text by Dorothy Day

Mark Naison and Bob Gumbs, *Before the Fires: An Oral History of African American Life in the Bronx from the 1930s to the 1960s*

Robert Weldon Whalen, *Murder, Inc., and the Moral Life: Gangsters and Gangbusters in La Guardia's New York*

Joanne Witty and Henrik Krogius, *Brooklyn Bridge Park: A Dying Waterfront Transformed*

Sharon Egretta Sutton, *When Ivory Towers Were Black: A Story about Race in America's Cities and Universities*

Pamela Hanlon, *A Wordly Affair: New York, the United Nations, and the Story Behind Their Unlikely Bond*

Britt Haas, *Fighting Authoritarianism: American Youth Activism in the 1930s*

David J. Goodwin, *Left Bank of the Hudson: Jersey City and the Artists of 111 1st Street*. Foreword by DW Gibson

Nandini Bagchee, *Counter Institution: Activist Estates of the Lower East Side*

Susan Celia Greenfield (ed.), *Sacred Shelter: Thirteen Journeys of Homelessness and Healing*

Elizabeth Macaulay-Lewis and Matthew M. McGowan (eds.), *Classical New York: Discovering Greece and Rome in Gotham*

Susan Opotow and Zachary Baron Shemtob (eds.), *New York after 9/11*

Andrew Feffer, *Bad Faith: Teachers, Liberalism, and the Origins of McCarthyism*

Colin Davey with Thomas A. Lesser, *The American Museum of Natural History and How It Got That Way*. Forewords by Neil deGrasse Tyson and Kermit Roosevelt III

Wendy Jean Katz, *Humbug: The Politics of Art Criticism in New York City's Penny Press*

Lolita Buckner Inniss, *The Princeton Fugitive Slave: The Trials of James Collins Johnson*

Mike Jaccarino, *America's Last Great Newspaper War: The Death of Print in a Two-Tabloid Town*

Angel Garcia, *The Kingdom Began in Puerto Rico: Neil Connolly's Priesthood in the South Bronx*

Jim Mackin, *Notable New Yorkers of Manhattan's Upper West Side: Bloomingdale–Morningside Heights*

Matthew Spady, *The Neighborhood Manhattan Forgot: Audubon Park and the Families Who Shaped It*

Marilyn S. Greenwald and Yun Li, *Eunice Hunton Carter: A Lifelong Fight for Social Justice*

Jeffrey A. Kroessler, *Sunnyside Gardens: Planning and Preservation in a Historic Garden Suburb*

Elizabeth Macaulay-Lewis, *Antiquity in Gotham: The Ancient Architecture of New York City*

Ron Howell, *King Al: How Sharpton Took the Throne*

Jean Arrington with Cynthia S. LaValle, *From Factories to Palaces: Architect Charles B. J. Snyder and the New York City Public Schools*. Foreword by Peg Breen

Boukary Sawadogo, *Africans in Harlem: An Untold New York Story*

Alvin Eng, *Our Laundry, Our Town: My Chinese American Life from Flushing to the Downtown Stage and Beyond*

Stephanie Azzarone, *Heaven on the Hudson: Mansions, Monuments, and Marvels of Riverside Park*

Ron Goldberg, *Boy with the Bullhorn: A Memoir and History of ACT UP New York*. Foreword by Dan Barry

Peter Quinn, *Cross Bronx: A Writing Life*

Mark Bulik, *Ambush at Central Park: When the IRA Came to New York*

Matt Dallos, *In the Adirondacks: Dispatches from the Largest Park in the Lower 48*

Brandon Dean Lamson, *Caged: A Teacher's Journey Through Rikers, or How I Beheaded the Minotaur*

Raj Tawney, *Colorful Palate: Savored Stories from a Mixed Life*

Edward Cahill, *Disorderly Men*

Francis R. Kowsky with Lucille Gordon, *Hell on Color, Sweet on Song: Jacob Wrey Mould and the Artful Beauty of Central Park*

Jill Jonnes, *South Bronx Rising: The Rise, Fall, and Resurrection of an American City, Third Edition*

Barbara G. Mensch, *A Falling-Off Place: The Transformation of Lower Manhattan*

David J. Goodwin, *Midnight Rambles: H. P. Lovecraft in Gotham*

Felipe Luciano, *Flesh and Spirit: Confessions of a Young Lord*

Maximo G. Martinez, *Sojourners in the Capital of the World: Garifuna Immigrants*

For a complete list, visit www.fordhampress.com/empire-state-editions.